Freedom of the Press
from Zenger to Jefferson

EARLY AMERICAN LIBERTARIAN THEORIES

THE AMERICAN HERITAGE SERIES

THE

American Heritage

Series

UNDER THE GENERAL EDITORSHIP OF

LEONARD W. LEVY AND ALFRED YOUNG

Freedom of the Press
from Zenger to Jefferson

EARLY AMERICAN LIBERTARIAN THEORIES

EDITED BY

LEONARD W. LEVY

Brandeis University

THE BOBBS-MERRILL COMPANY, INC.

A Subsidiary of Howard W. Sams & Co., Inc.

PUBLISHERS • INDIANAPOLIS • NEW YORK • KANSAS CITY

To my mother

RAE LEVY FRIEDENBERG

with love

Foreword

A priceless legacy from early American history, Leonard Levy writes, is "the idea that there is an indispensable condition for the development of free men in a free society: the state must be bitted and bridled by a bill of rights which is to be construed in the most generous terms and whose protections are not to be the playthings of momentary majorities." This legacy, however, as Professor Levy has forcefully argued in *Legacy of Suppression. Freedom of Speech and Press in Early American History* (Cambridge, Mass.: Harvard University Press, 1960), and as he reargues with additional evidence and with his usual incisiveness in the Introduction to this volume, was not the gift of the Founding Fathers who drafted the first amendment to the Constitution. Rather it was bequeathed by the Jeffersonians who cast off the earlier constrained Blackstonian concept of freedom of the press in response to the repressive alien and sedition laws of 1798–1800, forging the first broad absolutist interpretation of the first amendment.

This anthology is valuable on two levels. On the one it is the first compendium of the classic American statements on freedom of the press from Andrew Hamilton's defense in the Zenger case (1735) to Alexander Hamilton's defense in the Croswell case (1804), including the full texts of oft-quoted opinions of Benjamin Franklin, James Madison, and Thomas Jefferson. On the second level, Professor Levy offers a documentary defense of his provocative thesis. Thus here are assembled a representative selection of the only substantial writings that enable us to weigh the intent of the drafters of the first amendment—James Wilson, Richard Henry Lee, William Cushing, and John Adams. Here occupying a major section of the collection are the statements of "The New Libertarianism" of 1799–1800 which hitherto have been available only in rare book depositories: the tracts of George Hay and John Thomson, Madison's *Virginia Report,* Albert Gallatin's speech in Congress and generous excerpts from Tunis Wortman's *A Treatise Concerning Political Enquiry,* a philosophic treatise which rightly deserves a place in the library of libertarianism alongside of Milton's *Areopagitica* and John Stuart Mill's *On Liberty.* Finally, here are some two dozen lengthy selections from the letters and state papers of Thomas Jefferson that will enable readers to draw their own conclusions as to whether Professor Levy's negative verdict in *Jefferson and Civil Liberties: The Darker Side* (Cambridge, Mass: Harvard University Press, 1963) is warranted.

An indispensable "primer" on freedom of the press in America, this volume at the same time is another forceful jolt from an accomplished scholar reminding us that the defenses of liberty rest most solidly not on wishful thinking but on firm historic evidence.

This volume fits in, as it were, between two other volumes in the American Heritage Series that deal with the same theme, between *The English Libertarian Heritage: From the Writings of John Trenchard and Thomas Gordon in the Independent Whig and Cato's Letters,* edited by David Jacobson, and *Freedom of the Press from Hamilton to the Warren Court,* edited by Harold L. Nelson. Nelson's book is a companion to the present work. Starting with the writings of Alexander Hamilton, it picks up the thread of history on freedom of the press and carries it through to the period of the Warren court.

This book is one of a series the aim of which is to provide the essential primary sources of the American experience, especially of American thought. The series, when completed, will constitute a documentary library of American history, filling a need long felt among scholars, students, librarians, and general readers for authoritative collections of original materials. Some volumes will illuminate the thought of significant individuals, such as James Madison or Louis Brandeis; some will deal with movements, organized around special themes, such as Puritan political thought, or American Catholic thought on social questions. Many volumes will take up the large number of subjects traditionally studied in American history for which, surprisingly, there are no documentary anthologies; others will pioneer in introducing subjects of increasing importance to scholars and to the contemporary world. The series aspires to maintain the high standards demanded of contemporary editing, providing authentic texts, intelligently and unobtrusively edited. It will also have the distinction of presenting pieces of substantial length that give the full character and flavor of the original. The series will be the most comprehensive and authoritative of its kind.

Alfred Young

Acknowledgments

Professor Alfred Young of Northern Illinois University, who shares with me the general editorship of the series in which this volume appears, suggested an anthology of original documents that would make available to scholars and students a selection of sources illuminating the development of libertarian theory in early America. I am grateful to him for his encouragement and editorial supervision, and now that the task is complete I can also appreciate his bullying demands, bold suggestions, and meticulous criticism. No one could have had a better editor or a more impatient and severe one. Mr. André Martinsons, a graduate student in the History of Ideas program at Brandeis University, helpfully supervised the photography of the primary sources. Mrs. Dorothy Roach, who good-naturedly put up with my exacting requirements, provided excellent typing assistance. A research grant from Brandeis University aided the production of this anthology. Above all I wish to acknowledge the handsome courtesy extended by the Harvard University Press in permitting me to draw freely on my earlier book, *Legacy of Suppression,* from which the introduction to this volume is substantially derived. For an extended discussion of the materials presented in this documentary anthology, readers are urged to refer to *Legacy of Suppression,* published by the Belknap Press of Harvard University Press, copyright 1960 by the President and Fellows of Harvard College. I have also been given permission by the *American Historical Review* to incorporate in the Introduction an article I published in their pages in October 1962 under the title, "Liberty and the First Amendment: 1790 to 1800."

LEONARD W. LEVY

Brandeis University

Contents

Part One   The Formative Period: "Cato" and Zenger

Part Two   The Revolutionary Period: Patriots and
Blackstonians

Part Three The Constitutional Period:
Neo-Blackstonians

Part Four   The New Libertarianism

Part Five   The Special Case of Thomas Jefferson

Part Six Epilogue: Zenger Redivivus

Introduction

I

Freedom of the press, in the words of the Continental Congress of 1774, is essential to "the advancement of truth, science, morality and arts in general" and to the maintenance of "honorable and just modes" of conducting public affairs.[1] Central to the concept of a free press is freedom of political opinion, and at the core of that freedom lies the right to criticize the government. The acquittal of John Peter Zenger in 1735, in a prosecution for seditious libel, is celebrated, deservedly or not, because it "marked a milestone in the fight for the right to criticize the government."[2]

That right is indispensable to personal liberty and is inseparable from self-government. When any avenues of political expression are closed, government by consent of the governed may be foreclosed. If any information or opinion is denied expression, the formation of public policy has not been founded on a consideration of all points of view; as a result, the will of the majority cannot really be known. Accordingly, libertarian theory, such as that advanced by Zenger's counsel, presents a fairly systematic argument that defines and defends both freedom of the press and the right to criticize the government.

A broad libertarian theory emerged toward the close of the eighteenth century, first in England and then in America. It advocated the utmost freedom of political opinion by repudiat-

---

[1] "To the Inhabitants of the Province of Quebec," October 24, 1774, in *Journals of the Continental Congress, 1774–1789*, eds., Worthington Chauncey Ford, *et al.* (Washington, D.C.: Government Printing Office, 1904–1937), I, 108.

[2] William O. Douglas, *The Right of the People* (Garden City, N. Y.: Doubleday & Company, Inc., 1958), p. 38.

ing the concept that the government can be criminally assaulted—that is, seditiously libeled—simply by the expression of critical views that have a tendency (alleged to be bad) to diminish the public's esteem for the government. The new theory also advocated the same freedom for everyone, even those whose opinions were thought to be detestable, mocking, or pernicious; this included the village atheist and the local extremist, whether radical or reactionary.

II

Seventeenth-century libertarians had advanced a drastically different theory. They did not remotely question the propriety of punishing seditious libels, even though criminal prosecutions for criticism of the government were one of the principal means of muzzling political and religious dissent. Another such means was official censorship, enforced by a licensing system of "prior" or "previous" restraints. Anything published without a license was criminal. All manuscripts had to be submitted to crown officials empowered to expunge objectionable passages or to deny a license altogether. Milton's *"Areopagitica"* derives its fame from its author's incisive and eloquent arguments against censorship, the foremost target of seventeenth-century libertarianism. "Give me liberty," cried Milton, "to know, to utter, and to argue freely according to conscience, above all liberties"[3]—but his use of the personal pronoun is significant.

Milton's well-advertised tolerance did not extend to the thought that he hated. It extended only, as he specified, to "neighboring differences, or rather indifferences," which in 1644 meant Protestantism in its various forms. He explicitly excluded from his spectrum of neighboring opinions "Popery, and open superstition," which he thought "should be extirpat,"

---

[3] *"Areopagitica,"* ed. William Haller, in *The Works of John Milton*, gen. ed. Frank A. Patterson (New York: Columbia University Press, 1931–1938), IV, 346.

and he banned also the "impious or evil" which "no law can possibly permit. . . ." He deplored royalist writings as "libell against the Parliament" and thought they should be censored; he himself later served as one of Cromwell's official censors. In the concluding section of his *Areopagitica* —a section seldom read or quoted today—Milton, after advocating a system of unlicensed printing, endorsed the sanctions of the criminal law for any abuse or licentiousness of the press: "Those which otherwise come forth (unregistered, although unlicensed), if they be found mischievous and libellous, the fire and the executioner will be the timeliest and the most effectual remedy that mans prevention can use."[4]

Roger Williams, a second great libertarian champion of the seventeenth century, in his imperishable defense of toleration, "The Bloudy Tenent, of Persecution, for cause of Conscience," exempted from the civil magistrate's jurisdiction all matters of conscience, even "scandalous" doctrines against the establishment. But he broke into his argument to note parenthetically, "I speak not of scandal against the civil state, which the civil magistrate ought to punish. . . ."[5]

John Locke, the third in the trinity of seventeenth-century libertarians, believed that "no opinions contrary to human society, or to those moral rules which are necessary to the preservation of civil society, are to be tolerated by the magistrate." Advocating that the intolerant should not be tolerated, he proposed punishment of any who "will not own and teach the duty of tolerating all men in matters of mere religion."[6] In both his "Letter concerning Toleration" and his "Fundamental Con-

---

[4] *Ibid.*, IV, 320–321, 349. For Milton as a censor, see William C. Clyde, *The Struggle for the Freedom of the Press from Caxton to Cromwell* (London: Oxford University Press, 1934), pp. 79–80, 172–173.

[5] "The Bloudy Tenent, of Persecution, for cause of Conscience," in *The Writings of Roger Williams*, ed. Samuel L. Caldwell (Providence, R. I.: Narragansett Club, 1866–1874), III, 136.

[6] "A Letter concerning Toleration," in *The Works of John Locke* (11th ed.; London: W. Otridge and Son, 1812), VI, 45, 46.

stitutions of Carolina" he supported an extraordinary latitude for freedom of religion, yet took care to specify that no person should speak anything "irreverently or seditiously of the government or governors, or of state matters."[7] And he regarded the opinions of atheists and the political implications of Catholic doctrine as seditious. Like Milton, Locke opposed the licensing system, though with far greater success. The system, Locke contended, injured the printing trade, was administratively cumbersome, and was unnecessary because the common law gave adequate protection against licentiousness. In 1694 Locke drafted for the House of Commons a statement of eighteen reasons for terminating government censorship.[8] Not a single one of the eighteen, however, was a principled defense of freedom of the press or a philosophical argument for the free mind. The "prior restraint" licensing system finally died in England, but it died on grounds of expediency.

The common law's definition of criminal libels meant that the press was free from censorship in advance of publication, but was subject to subsequent punishment for bad or wrong sentiments about the government. As Chief Justice Holt stated in Tuchin's case in 1704, a "reflection on the government"— such as saying that corrupt officers administered its affairs— must be punished because it tended "to beget an ill opinion" of the government. "If people should not be called to account for possessing the people with an ill opinion of the government, no government can subsist, for it is very necessary for all governments that the people should have a good opinion of it."[9]

---

[7] *Ibid.*, VI, 51–52; and "Fundamental Constitutions of Carolina," Section 103, in *The Federal and State Constitutions, Colonial Charters, and Other Organic Laws,* ed. Francis Newton Thorpe (Washington, D.C.: Government Printing Office, 1909), V, 2784.

[8] For the eighteen reasons, see Lord Peter King, *The Life and Letters of John Locke* (London: Bell and Daldy, 1858), pp. 202–209.

[9] *Rex* v. *Tuchin* (1704), in *A Complete Collection of State Trials to 1783,* comp. Thomas Bayly Howell (London: Printed by T. Hansard for Longman, Hurst, Kees, Orme, and Brown, 1816–1828), XIV, 1128.

No libertarian theorist challenged this proposition or progressed beyond the no-prior-restraints concept of freedom of the press until "Cato" burst upon the scene.

III

"Cato" was the joint pseudonym of the Whig political journalists, John Trenchard and Thomas Gordon. Their essays, first published in London newspapers beginning in 1720, were collected in four volumes that went through six editions between 1733 and 1755.[10] "No one," writes a historian familiar with the sources, "can spend any time in the newspapers, library inventories, and pamphlets of colonial America without realizing that *Cato's Letters* rather than Locke's *Civil Government* was the most popular, quotable, esteemed source of political ideas in the colonial period."[11] "*Cato's Letters* was quoted in every colonial newspaper from Boston to Savannah,"[12] and "the most famous"[13] of his letters was "Of Freedom of Speech: That the same is inseparable from Public Liberty."[14] Another letter of immense popularity was "Reflections upon Libelling," one of three essays on libel law and freedom of the press.[15]

---

[10] "Cato" (John Trenchard and Thomas Gordon), *Cato's Letters: Or, Essays on Liberty, Civil and Religious* (4 vols.; London: Printed for T. Woodward, J. Walthoe and others, 1733–1755). A judicious abridgment of *Cato's Letters*, ably edited and introduced by David L. Jacobson, has recently been published in the American Heritage Series under the title, *The English Libertarian Heritage: From the Writings of John Trenchard and Thomas Gordon* (Indianapolis, Ind.: The Bobbs-Merrill Company, Inc., 1965).

[11] Clinton Rossiter, *Seedtime of the Republic* (New York: Harcourt, Brace and Company, 1953), p. 141.

[12] Elizabeth Cristine Cook, *Literary Influences in Colonial Newspapers* (New York: Columbia University Press, 1912), p. 81.

[13] Rossiter, *Seedtime of the Republic*, p. 299.

[14] No. 15, February 4, 1720, in *Cato's Letters* (6th ed.; London: 1755), I, 96–103.

[15] "Reflections upon Libelling," No. 32, June 10, 1721, in *Cato's Letters*, I; "Discourse upon Libels," No. 100, October 27, 1722, in *Cato's*

Cato brought to his wide audience a bold, systematic theory of intellectual and political liberty. At the core of this theory stood the concept of freedom of expression. Free speech, Cato insisted, was "the Right of every Man, as far as by it he does not hurt and controul the Right of another; and this is the only Check which it ought to suffer, the only Bounds which it ought to know." He explained the relationship between free government and freedom of the press, arguing that they prospered together or died together. Government officials, he declared, were merely trustees of the people's interests, and it was the people "for whose Sake alone all publick Matters are, or ought to be, transacted. . . ." Accordingly, good and honest officials should welcome having their deeds openly examined. "Only the wicked Governors of Men dread what is said of them," and it was only they who complained about the licentiousness of the press and sought to restrain it. If the press misrepresented public measures, the wisest remedy was to represent the measures correctly, rather than to punish the mistake.[16] Libels rarely provoked causeless discontent against the government. The benefits from what the law called libels, by checking the conduct of officials, outweighed their mischiefs. Libels, thought Cato, were the inevitable result of a free press, "an Evil arising out of a much greater Good,"[17] bringing advantages to society in the fields of liberty, property,

---

Letters, III; and "Second Discourse upon Libels," No. 101, November 3, 1722, in *Cato's Letters*, III. A sampling of the Boston press shows that No. 15 was reprinted in *The New England Courant*, July 9, 1722; in the *Boston Gazette*, April 21, 1755, April 26, 1756, November 9, 1767, May 6, 1771, and August 14, 1780; in the *Massachusetts Spy*, March 7 and March 28, 1771. No. 32 was reprinted in *The New England Courant*, Sept. 11, 1721; in the *Boston Gazette*, April 26, 1756, and May 6, 1771; and the *Boston Post-Boy*, September 27, 1773. For citations to Zenger's *New-York Weekly Journal*, see notes 27 and 28, below.

[16] "Of Freedom of Speech," No. 15, in *Cato's Letters*, I, 96–103. See this volume, Document 2.

[17] "Reflections upon Libelling," No. 32, in *Cato's Letters*, I, 252. See this volume, Document 3.

government, religion, science, the arts, and general knowledge. He conceded that there was a risk in allowing freedom of expression; let men talk as they wished about government, philosophy, or religion, and they might reason seditiously, wrongly, or irreligiously. But restrain their opinions, and the results would be worse—injustice, tyranny, and ignorance.[18]

Cato did not wish to be misunderstood as arguing for the uncontrolled liberty of men to calumniate each other or the government. Libels against the government were "always base and unlawful,"[19] especially when untrue, and should be punished as an abuse of liberty as long as England's good laws were prudently and honestly enforced.[20] Notwithstanding this genuflection by Cato toward the law, keeping him on its safe side, he made it abundantly clear in his essays that he thought the law of criminal libel was neither good nor prudently enforced; indeed, that it was quite dangerous to public liberty and to good government. He approved of libel prosecutions only in extreme cases, and even then only under a law which did not penalize criticism that could be proved to be true. On the grounds that the public had an interest in knowing the truth about public measures and men, Cato contended that truth should be admitted as a defense against a criminal-libel charge—in other words, a defendant who could prove the accuracy of his allegedly seditious utterance should be acquitted.[21]

The law, however, did not regard truth as a defense. On the contrary, the theory of the law was, the greater the truth, the greater the scandal against the government. Judges in libel cases reserved exclusively to themselves, as a matter of law, decision of the crucial question whether the defendant's re-

---

[18] "Discourse upon Libels," No. 100, in *Cato's Letters*, III, 295–297. See this volume, Document 4.

[19] "Reflections upon Libelling," No. 32, in *Cato's Letters*, I, 252.

[20] "Discourse upon Libels," No. 100, in *Cato's Letters*, III, 299.

[21] "Reflections upon Libelling," No. 32, in *Cato's Letters*, I, 247.

marks were libelous. Cato condemned the courts' practice of implying a criminal or seditious intention on the part of defendants by stretching the defendants' words to find in them a danger to the government. The best way to treat undeserved libels, said Cato, was to "laugh at them, and despise them," rather than to prosecute them.[22] Such prosecutions, he thought, represented far too great a threat to liberty. "I must own, that I would rather many Libels should escape, than the Liberty of the Press should be infringed. . . ."[23]

Cato's Letters was the high-water mark of libertarian theory until the close of the eighteenth century. In the American colonies, Cato was adored, quoted, and plagiarized. In fact, American libertarian theory, neither original nor independent, was at its best little more than an imitation of Cato. Ben Franklin, the towering figure among American printers and theorists, illustrates the point. His own writings on freedom of the press were trite, brief, vague, and philosophically on a par with his "Poor Richard" pieces.[24]

But Franklin, in 1721 and 1722, was the first American to reprint Cato's "Of Freedom of Speech" and "Reflections upon Libelling" essays.[25] He also published a four-part essay on the same topics by Cato's greatest American pupil, James Alexander.[26] Alexander was the lawyer-editor who contributed articles on freedom of the press to Zenger's *New-York Weekly Journal,* masterminded Zenger's legal defense, and edited the

---

[22] "Discourse upon Libels," No. 100, in *Cato's Letters,* III, 297–298.

[23] "Reflections upon Libelling," No. 32, in *Cato's Letters,* I, 252–253.

[24] See, for example, "An Apology for Printers," in *The Writings of Benjamin Franklin,* ed. Albert Henry Smyth (New York: The Macmillan Company, 1905–1907), II, 172–179, reprinted in this volume, Document 1; and "An Account of the Supremest Court of Judicature of the State of Pennsylvania, Viz, The Court of the Press," 1789, *ibid.,* X, 36–40, reprinted in this volume, Document 24.

[25] *The New England Courant,* September 11, 1721, and July 9, 1722.

[26] *The Pennsylvania Gazette* (Philadelphia), November 10–December 8, 1737, Nos. 466–469. Reprinted in Zenger's *New-York Weekly Journal,* December 19, 1737–January 9, 1738. See this volume, Document 10.

narrative of the trial. With the possible exception of *Cato's Letters*, this narrative was the most widely known source of libertarian thought in the English-speaking world during the eighteenth century. Alexander used to copy extensive selections from Cato for his private instruction, as well as reprinting them for the readers of the *New-York Weekly Journal*, which he edited. The paper in its early years carried frequent excerpts, references, and paraphrases from the "almost divine" Cato. The "Of Freedom of Speech" essay was republished, for the second time, in the issue immediately following the public burning of "seditious" copies of the paper at the order of the Governor's Council.[27] Shortly afterward, the leader of the Zenger party against Governor Cosby, Lewis Morris, read Cato's "Discourse upon Libels" to the General Assembly and Alexander ran it in the *Weekly Journal*.[28]

Even the defense of Zenger, as planned by James Alexander and presented by Andrew Hamilton, was substantially derived from Cato, who was the first to popularize the idea that truth should be admitted as a defense against a charge of criminal libel.[29] Moreover, Cato also provided the basis of the argument that "while men keep within the bounds of truth, I hope they may with safety both speak and write their sentiments of the conduct of men in power."[30] The only essential of Zenger's

---

[27] *New-York Weekly Journal*, February 18 and November 11, 1734.

[28] *Ibid.*, December 9, 1734.

[29] The origin of the principle that truth should be a defense is sometimes attributed to the Zenger defense, but the idea can be found earlier in *The Thoughts of a Tory Author, concerning the Press*, attributed to Joseph Addison (London: 1712), pp. 25–26.

[30] James Alexander, *A Brief Narrative of the Case and Trial of John Peter Zenger, Printer of the New-York Weekly Journal*, ed. Stanley Nider Katz (Cambridge, Mass.: The Belknap Press of Harvard University Press, 1963), p. 87. A literal reprint of the first edition of the trial narrative, as published by the Zenger press in New York in 1736, appears in Livingston Rutherfurd, *John Peter Zenger, His Press, His Trial, and a Bibliography of Zenger Imprints* (New York: Dodd, Mead & Company,

defense that could not be traced to Cato was Hamilton's appeal to the jury to decide for themselves, rather than be bound by the court's instructions, whether the defendant's words were libelous.[31] If freedom of the press was the palladium of public liberty, as the colonists were so fond of reiterating, *Cato's Letters* was its intellectual source and provided virtually the entire content of its philosophy as well.

IV

Although eighteenth-century American libertarian theory was extraordinarily inventive in many areas—producing, for example, the ideas for a written fundamental law, bills of rights, a federal system, and constitutional conventions—American thought on freedom of the press remained stationary after the 1730's. Indeed, in some respects it stagnated and even regressed. From the time of the Zenger defense until the response to the Sedition Act, there were certainly no innovations in libertarian theory on freedom of the press. And practice, of course, lagged behind theory. In the 1720's, when Trenchard

---

1904). An abridgment of the literal reprint is included in this volume, Document 9. The Katz edition, which presents a modernized version, is cited in this Introduction because it is easily available to readers, is superbly annotated, has an excellent introduction, and includes many valuable related documents.

[31] The first voicing of the principle that the jury should decide the law as well as the facts in a case of seditious libel is sometimes attributed to the Zenger defense, but the principle was explicitly stated in 1692 by William Bradford during his trial for seditious libel in Philadelphia. See *New-England's Spirit of Persecution Transmitted to Pennsilvania . . . in the Tryal of Peter Boss, George Keith, Thomas Budd, and William Bradford . . . 1692* (Philadelphia: William Bradford, 1693), pp. 33–34. Thomas Maule, who was tried for seditious libel in Boston in 1696, also claimed that the jury should decide the law as well as the facts. See Theo. Philanthes (Thomas Maule), *New-England Persecutors Mauld with Their Own Weapons . . . Together with a Brief Account of the Imprisonment and Tryal of Thomas Maule of Salem, for Publishing a Book . . .* (New York: William Bradford, 1697), pp. 61–62.

and Gordon wrote *Cato's Letters,* Samuel Mulford was summarily expelled from the New York Assembly for having suggested that the people ought to clean out some of the members of that body;[32] Benjamin Franklin's brother was jailed in Boston for insinuating in his newspaper that the provincial government was not taking effective action against coastal pirates;[33] the Reverend John Checkley was convicted in Massachusetts for distributing a book critical of Calvinist doctrines;[34] two Philadelphians were pilloried for daring to "speak evil of dignitaries";[35] and, also in the City of Brotherly Love, the printer Andrew Bradford was imprisoned for publishing a letter allegedly reflecting on the government of Great Britain.[36]

The persistent image of colonial America as a society that cherished freedom of expression is a sentimental hallucination that ignores history. The evidence provides little support for the notion that the colonies hospitably received advocates of obnoxious or detestable ideas on matters that counted. Nor is there reason to believe that rambunctious unorthodoxies suffered only from Puritan bigots and tyrannous royal judges. The American people and their representatives simply did not understand that freedom of thought and expression means equal freedom for the other fellow, particularly the fellow with the hated ideas.

To be sure, the utmost freedom often existed on the frontier.

---

[32] *Journal of the Votes and Proceedings of the General Assembly of the Colony of New-York, 1691–1765* (New York: 1764–1766), I, 443.

[33] Isaiah Thomas, *The History of Printing in America* (Worcester, Mass.: Isaiah Thomas, Jr., 1810), II, 217; and Clyde Augustus Duniway, *The Development of Freedom of the Press in Massachusetts* (New York: Longmans, Green & Co., 1906), pp. 98–99.

[34] Edmund F. Slafter, *John Checkley: or the Evolution of Religious Tolerance in Massachusetts Bay* (Boston: The Prince Society, 1897), I, 56–66.

[35] David Paul Brown, *The Forum: Or, Forty Years Full Practice at the Philadelphia Bar* (Philadelphia: R. H. Small, 1856), I, 262–265.

[36] *Ibid.,* I, 285–286; and *Minutes of the Provincial Council of Pennsylvania* (Harrisburg, Pa.: Theophilus Fenn, 1838–1840), III, 392.

The test of free speech, however, is not the right of a man to soliloquize, or to shout his outrageous opinions from the top of a lonely mountain; it is, rather, his right to speak openly and with impunity among his neighbors. Colonial America may have been the scene of the most extraordinary diversity of opinion on religion, politics, and other vital subjects, but each community, especially outside the few "cities," tended to be a tight little island clutching its own orthodoxy and willing to banish unwelcome dissidence or punish it extralegally. As John P. Roche says so strikingly, "Colonial America was an open society dotted with closed enclaves, and one could generally settle in with his co-believers in safety and comfort and exercise the right of oppression."[37]

When vigorously expressed nonconformist opinions were suffered to exist by the community, they were likely to run afoul of the law. In colonial America, as in England, the common law of seditious libel was strung out like a chicken wire of constraint making the open discussion of public issues hazardous except when public opinion opposed administration policy. The judiciary, however, was not the agency in eighteenth-century America that menaced those who would disturb an acquiescent public opinion. It is traditional, of course, although inaccurate, to state that "Colonial times were rife with a continuing struggle between the royal judges and American writers and printers, who demanded freedom to criticize" the government.[38] The trial of Zenger is usually presented in the context of such a struggle, and Zenger's acquittal is construed as a great victory for freedom of the press against the judges and the common law. No such struggle really existed, and though Zenger's acquittal was a victory it had little if any appreciable

[37] John P. Roche, "American Liberty: An Examination of the 'Tradition' of Freedom," in *Shadow and Substance: Essays on the Theory and Structure of Politics* (New York: The Macmillan Company, 1964), p. 11.

[38] John Kelly "Criminal Libel and Free Speech," *Kansas Law Review*, VI (1958), 306.

effect upon the freedom of the press in New York or elsewhere in the colonies.

The jury in the Zenger case, swayed by the magnificent forensics of a great lawyer, collectively turned a deaf ear to the law as explained by the prosecutor and the presiding judge. The prosecutor and the judge ably stated the precedents, such as Tuchin's case, and the law as summarized in such leading treatises as Sergeant William Hawkins' *Pleas of the Crown.* They accurately informed the jury that seditious libel consisted of scandalizing the government, by reflecting on those who were entrusted with the administration of public affairs, by publishing material tending to breed in the people a dislike of their governors, or by alienating the affections of the people from the government in any way. But Hamilton's reply had the greater popular appeal. The law, he argued, was intended to protect the King, not his despotic provincial governors. If the people could not remonstrate against the oppressions of a bad governor (confining themselves always to truthful accusations), they would in no time lose their liberty and property and become "slaves." Because Governor William Cosby was heartily disliked, Hamilton's argument was tactically sound; the jury's acquittal of Zenger was its way of safely striking at Cosby.

But the jury's verdict of "not guilty" left the common law unaltered. Moreover, Hamilton never conducted a frontal assault on the concept of seditious libel. He never argued that publications tending to damage the reputation of the government in the minds of the people should be free from prosecution. He defended criticism of a "bad administration" or an "arbitrary government" (with Cosby in mind, of course), but he did not justify criticism of any government that he might think to be good or just.

Hamilton's conduct as a member of the Governor's Council of Pennsylvania suggests that he believed in salutary limitations on the freedom of political discourse. When Andrew

Bradford printed a pamphlet on the "dying Credit of the Province," the Council censured him for aspersive innuendoes against the government and ordered him never again to publish "anything relating to or concerning the Affairs of this Government . . . without the permission of the Governour."[39] A few years later, in 1729, the Council jailed Bradford for publishing "a wicked & seditious Libell." Hamilton, the Recorder of the Council, was one of those who conducted the examination of Bradford and committed him to prison.[40]

Hamilton was not likely, in his defense of Zenger, to advocate an unrestricted freedom of the press. His argument was that although some publications were seditious libels, Zenger's, being "true," were not. If a defendant could prove the truth of his criticism, the jury should acquit him; in other words, truth should be a defense against a charge of seditious libel.[41] When the court rejected this proposition, Hamilton retreated to the argument that the jury should not return a special verdict on the question whether the defendant had, as a matter of fact, published the statement charged. (By returning such a special verdict, the jury would be leaving to the court, as a matter of law, a ruling on the main question whether the words were criminal per se.) He urged instead that the jury should return a general verdict, deciding the law as well as the facts.[42]

Hamilton did not appreciate that truth is a mischievous, often an illusory, standard that often defies knowledge or understanding and cannot always be established by the rules of evidence. He did not appreciate that one man's truth is another's falsehood or that political opinions, which notoriously differ, may not even be susceptible of proof. Nor did he appreciate that a jury in a case of seditious libel is a court of public opinion (often synonymous with public prejudice), and is hardly adequate as an instrument for measuring the truth of

---

[39] *Minutes of the Provincial Council of Pennsylvania*, I, 143.
[40] *Ibid.*, III, 392.
[41] Alexander, *A Brief Narrative* . . . ed. Katz, pp. 62, 68, and 69–74.
[42] *Ibid.*, pp. 75, 78, 91–93, and 99.

an accusation that the government, or its policies, or its officials, may be unjust, tyrannical, or repugnant to the public interest.

When judges were dependent tools of the state, a jury of one's peers and neighbors seemed a promising bulwark against the tyrannous prosecution of seditious libel by the Administration and its judges. But later events proved that juries with the power of ruling on the guilt or innocence of alleged libels could be as influenced by prevailing passions as were judges, when deciding the fate of defendants who had expressed unpopular sentiments. In England, where the power of juries in libel cases was secured by Fox's Libel Act of 1792, the most repressive prosecutions were, with very few exceptions, successful.[43] In America only one verdict of "not guilty" was returned in the numerous prosecutions under the Sedition Act which entrusted criminality to the jury and admitted truth as a defense.[44]

Embattled libertarians of the eighteenth century belatedly discovered that they had mistaken a prop of straw for one of brick when they accepted Hamilton's position instead of repudiating the concept of seditious libel. His argument, which hinged on the fact that public opinion was opposed to the Administration, had its limitations as a libertarian defense of the press and, despite the jury's verdict, left the law unchanged. Indeed, judging from its impact on the bench, Hamilton's argument was like the stagecoach ticket inscribed: "Good for this day only." As late as 1804 Chief Justice Morgan Lewis of

[43] More trials for seditious utterances were reported in Howell's *State Trials* for the two years following Fox's Libel Act than had been reported for the whole of the eighteenth century before that time. Within a year of the statute the attorney general declared that he had on file 200 informations for seditious libel. Thomas Erskine May, *The Constitutional History of England Since the Accession of George III, 1760–1860* (New York: A. C. Armstrong and Son, 1880), II, pp. 142–150.

[44] The American Sedition Act cases are too familiar to require review. For an excellent treatment, see James Morton Smith, *Freedom's Fetters: The Alien and Sedition Laws and American Civil Liberties* (Ithaca, N.Y.: Cornell University Press, 1956). Smith reports the single acquittal on p. 185.

New York—a Jeffersonian, no less—was of the opinion that truth does not constitute a defense against a charge of criminal libel.[45]

Alexander's report of the Zenger trial saved Hamilton's argument for posterity. The account was reprinted in America, as well as in England, at politically strategic moments. It was reprinted in 1770 in New York, for example, when Alexander McDougall was prosecuted for seditious libel; and it appeared in 1799 in Boston, during the Sedition Act controversy.[46] The Zenger case became famous partly because it was so well publicized and partly because it was so isolated a phenomenon. Except for an obscure trial of a New Yorker in 1745 for "singing in praise of the Pretender,"[47] and another insignificant prosecution in Virginia at about the same time,[48] Zenger's case was the last of its kind under the "royal judges." Altogether, there were probably not more than half a dozen prosecutions for seditious libel in the whole of the American colonial period.[49] Indeed, the maligned judges were virtually angels of self-restraint when compared with the intolerant public—or

---

[45] *People* v. *Croswell,* 3 Johnson (N.Y.), 336 (·1804). Lewis' opinion is reported *ibid.,* pp. 394–411. See this volume, Document 59.

[46] For a bibliography of eighteenth-century reprints, see Rutherfurd, *John Peter Zenger,* pp. 249–253.

[47] MS Minutes, New York Court of Quarter Sessions, 1732–62, p. 181, cited in Julius Goebel, Jr., and T. Raymond Naughton, *Law Enforcement in Colonial New York, a Study in Criminal Procedure (1664–1776)* (New York: The Commonwealth Fund, 1944), p. 99*n.*

[48] Thomas, *The History of Printing in America,* II, 143–144. The Virginia case ended in an acquittal. In the McDougall case of 1770, discussed below, the common-law prosecution, which was never brought to trial, was instigated by the legislature.

[49] There were probably more prosecutions for oral utterances of a seditious nature than there were for seditious libels or publications, but there is no way of estimating the number of the former, because most of them were tried before inferior courts whose records are, with few exceptions, unpublished. Goebel and Naughton, however, systematically examined the manuscript records of the inferior courts of New York, and reported that there were only "occasional exceptional" prosecutions for seditious oral utterances during the whole of the colonial period up to 1776. See their *Law Enforcement in Colonial New York,* pp. 98–99.

when compared with the oppressive governors who, acting in a quasi-judicial capacity with their councils, were more dreaded and active instruments of suppression than the common-law courts.

The most suppressive body by far, however, was that acclaimed bastion of the people's liberties, the popularly elected assembly. That the law bore down harshly on verbal crimes in colonial America was the result of the inquisitorial propensities of the governors and legislatures, which vied with each other in ferreting out slights upon the government. The law of seditious libel was enforced in America primarily by the provincial assemblies, exercising their power to punish alleged "breaches of parliamentary privilege." Needing no grand jury to indict and no petty jury to convict, the assemblies zealously sought to establish the prerogative of being as immune to criticism as the House of Commons they all emulated. An assembly might summon, interrogate, and fix criminal penalties against anyone who had supposedly libeled its members, its proceedings, or the government generally. Any words, spoken or printed, that were imagined to have a tendency to impeach an assembly's behavior, question its authority, derogate from its honor, affront its dignity, or defame its members individually or collectively, were regarded as seditious and punishable as a breach of parliamentary privilege.[50]

---

[50] Between 1706 and 1720 there were four such cases in New York. In one case nine citizens, and in another seventeen grand jurors, were arrested for seditious reflections on the Assembly. In each of the other two cases the victim of the Assembly's wrath was one of its own members— Lewis Morris in 1710, and Samuel Mulford in 1720. See *Journal of the Votes and Proceedings of the General Assembly of the Colony of New-York,* I, 211 (1706), 283 (1710), 411 (1717), 443 (1720). Mary Patterson Clarke makes this guarded understatement: "Literally scores of persons, probably hundreds, throughout the colonies were tracked down by the various messengers and sergeants and brought into the house to make inglorious submission for words spoken in the heat of anger or for writing which intentionally or otherwise had given offense." See her *Parliamentary Privilege in the American Colonies* (New Haven, Conn.: Yale University Press, 1943), p. 117.

Had John Peter Zenger attacked the New York General Assembly instead of Governor Cosby, he would have been summarily convicted at the bar of the house and then jailed, and in all likelihood he would have remained unknown to posterity. Happily, he was tried before a jury. Hamilton's argument was especially appealing because his defendant symbolized the popular cause. It should be remembered that the grand jury, despite the Administration's urgings, refused to indict Zenger, and that the Assembly refused to cooperate with the Governor's Council at every step of the prosecution. When, for example, the Council requested the Assembly's concurrence in its order that four issues of the *New-York Weekly Journal* "be burnt by the hands of the Common Hangman," and that their printer be prosecuted, the Assembly ordered "that the said . . . request lie on the table."[51] Moreover, the Court of Quarter Sessions, the lower house of the city's legislature, formally protested the actions of the Governor's Council. The Court, which comprised the mayor and aldermen of the city, argued that it was duty bound to protect liberty of the press, and it noted: ". . . an Assembly of the Province and several Grand Juries have refused to meddle with the papers when applied to by the Council. . . ."[52]

The Zenger case at best gave the press the freedom to print the "truth"—if the truth were not directed against the legislature. The power of the legislature to punish nonmembers as well as members for alleged breach of privilege—criticism of the assembly—enabled it to control the press. Indeed, long after the right to publish without first obtaining government approval or license had been won, the provincial legislatures continued to regard the unlicensed publication of their votes and proceedings as a breach of privilege. This information, of the most vital interest to the public, could be printed only

---

[51] Alexander, *A Brief Narrative* . . . , ed. Katz, pp. 43–44.
[52] *Ibid.*, pp. 44–46.

after first being submitted to the speaker of the house for his examination and signature.

V

That the Zenger case did not emancipate the press in colonial New York is suggested by subsequent events. The contrast between the Assembly's behavior in 1747 and its behavior in 1753 is especially illuminating. In 1747 Governor George Clinton ordered James Parker, the colony's official printer, not to publish the Assembly's angry remonstrance against his policies. Unanimously, the legislators voted that it was "the undoubted Right of the People of this Colony, to know the Proceedings of their Representatives." The Assembly commanded Parker to print its remonstrance in order that the people might be apprised of their representatives' "firm Resolution to preserve the Liberty of the Press."[53] The legislature's professed commitment to the principle of a free press was abandoned a few years later, in 1753, when a printer, Hugh Gaine, believing the royal instructions to the new governor and the latter's speech to the Assembly to be matters of public interest, published them in his *New York Mercury*. The Assembly, upon learning that Gaine had "presumed" to print part of its proceedings without license, summoned him to its bar and demanded to know by what authority he had dared to breach its privileges. Gaine, intimidated, most abjectly humbled himself. He had done wrong, he claimed, only out of ignorance; profusely sorry for having given offense, he "humbly asked their pardon." Mollified by this proper display of contrition, the Assembly magnanimously released Gaine after formal censure, a warning, and exaction of the costs of the case.[54]

---

[53] *Journal of the Votes and Proceedings of the General Assembly of the Colony of New-York*, II, 173, 192, 193, and 198.

[54] *Ibid.*, II, 358–359.

In 1756 James Parker became the next victim of parliamentary privilege. He had published in his *New York Gazette* an article on the distressed condition of the people in Orange and Ulster counties, and the house saw the article as "greatly reflecting" upon it and calculated "to irritate the People of this Colony against their Representatives. . . ." Parker and his associate, William Weyman, were voted to be guilty of a "high misdemeanour" and contempt of authority. Taken into custody by the sergeant at arms of the house, they were interrogated before the bar. Parker, a most cooperative witness, revealed that the offensive article had been written by the Reverend Hezekiah Watkins of Newburg. The publishers confessed their fault for printing the article, denied any intention of giving affront, and humbly begged the pardon of the honorable house. The honorable house kept its prisoners in jail for a week before discharging them. The Reverend Mr. Watkins, who was promptly arrested, confessed his authorship but pleaded that he had acted out of a mistaken zeal for the welfare of the people rather than from disrespect for the house. He was heartily sorry, he declared, and pleaded to be forgiven. He was jailed anyway. The next day he was officially reprimanded, forced to pay the costs, and then discharged.[55]

In 1758 the speaker of the house received a letter from one Samuel Townsend, a justice of the peace in Queen's County, asking legislative relief for certain refugees quartered on Long Island. The speaker, presenting the letter to the house, termed it "insolent," whereupon that body commanded Townsend's appearance. When he daringly failed to show up, he was cited for contempt and a warrant was issued for his arrest. He was hauled before the bar and examined in the usual intimidating fashion, but he showed no signs of repentance. The Assembly then voted that, because his letter reflected on its "Honour, Justice and Authority," he was guilty of a "high Misdemeanour

---

[55] *Ibid.*, II, 487–489.

and a most daring Insult." The gloomy prison in which Townsend found himself provoked him to reconsider his position. He sent a petition expressing his deep sorrow for having written the letter that had inadvertently cast reflection on the house. He also promised faithfully to avoid committing such misdeeds in the future, and he concluded by asking for the house's "Compassion." Moved by this respectful submission from a judge, the Assembly released him from jail and discharged him, with an official reprimand from the speaker.[56]

As New York approached the revolutionary controversy, its press was only as free as its legislature permitted. In practice, all political comment was tolerated as long as criticism did not anger the people's representatives. The courts were merely a formal threat against unfettered discussion, as the Zenger case demonstrated. It was the legislature, with unlimited discretion to punish supposed breaches of parliamentary privilege, that actively exercised repressive power. The frequency of the cases and the incidence of punishment hardly suggest tyranny, but the house's arbitrary use of its prerogative did have a smothering effect on the free expression of opinion relating to legislative matters and measures. Libertarian theorists had argued that freedom of speech and press would have the salutary effect of checking evil or incompetent rulers and stimulating responsible government. But in New York the legislature never permitted this libertarian theory to be practiced. The royal governor, his policies, and his administration were almost always fair game for popular disapprobation; the Zenger case proved that, but little more. In the struggle of the Assembly for independence from the governor, most anti-administration criticism played into the hands of the Assembly and the "popular" party. "Freedom of the press," in other words, was a useful instrument for the expansion of legislative prerogative, but in any clash between parliamentary privilege and liberty of dis-

---

[56] *Ibid.*, II, 551–555.

cussion the victory went to parliamentary privilege, which was deemed the superior right.

The limited experience of colonial New York with broad freedom of the press matched the limited thinking of libertarian theorists on the scope of permissible expression. No one even dared to criticize the Assembly's restraints on the press. No one suggested that the press's freedom ought not to be fixed by the extent to which a jury's emotions might be swayed. And even Andrew Hamilton himself, in his defense of Zenger, had admitted that a "false" charge against the government merited punishment. "For as it is truth alone which can excuse or justify any man for complaining of a bad administration," Hamilton declared, "I as frankly agree that nothing ought to excuse a man who raises a false charge or accusation, even against a private person, and that no manner of allowance ought to be made to him who does so against a public magistrate."[57] Similarly, James Alexander acknowledged in the columns of Zenger's paper, before the trial, "That Abuses that disolve Society, and sap the Foundations of Government, are not to be sheltered under the Umbrage of the Liberty of the Press."[58] In 1737, in the midst of an essay on freedom of the press, Alexander confessed that "to infuse into the minds of the people an ill opinion of a just administration, is a crime that deserves no mercy. . . ."[59]

The colonial understanding of the scope of free expression was further revealed in 1753 by an editorial in *The Independent Reflector*, a New York magazine that was the voice of libertarian thought of mid-century America. When an opposition journal refused to publish an essay composed by one of *The Independent Reflector*'s regular contributors, the editor, William Livingston, published this credo on liberty of the press: "A Printer ought not to publish every Thing that is of-

---

57 Alexander, *A Brief Narrative* . . . , ed. Katz, p. 84. See also p. 77.
58 *New-York Weekly Journal*, November 4, 1734.
59 *The Pennsylvania Gazette*, December 1, 1737.

fered to him; but what is conducive of general Utility, he
should not refuse, be the Author a Christian, Jew, Turk or
Infidel. Such Refusal is an immediate Abridgement of the
Freedom of the Press. When on the other Hand, he prostitutes
his Art by the Publication of any Thing injurious to his Country, it is criminal,—It is high Treason against the State. The
usual Alarm rung in such Cases, the common Cry of an Attack upon the LIBERTY OF THE PRESS, is groundless and trifling.
The Press neither has, nor can have such a Liberty, and whenever it is assumed, the Printer should be punished."[60]

The most willing tool of the crown could hardly have disagreed with this definition of a free press by the republican
patriots from the colony identified with Zenger. On the other
hand, there could be no greater danger to the right of the open
political debate than the vague crime of constructive treason,
especially if it could be committed by mere words. Even a
crown lawyer knew that the law ruled out treason in any case
where words against the government were unconnected with
some treasonous project for carrying them out; such words
were criminally punishable only as a seditious libel. The
severity of the remarks by New York's Whig lawyer-editor is
revealed by the fact that seditious libel was a misdemeanor,
treason a capital crime.

A few years after the publication of this credo on the liberty
of the press, James Parker, who had been *The Independent
Reflector*'s printer and editor, wrote a broadside opposing a
stamp tax on newspapers that was being proposed by the
New York Assembly (1759). Parker announced that in countries "where Liberty truly reigns, every one hath a Privilege
of declaring his Sentiments upon all Topicks with the utmost

---

[60] "Of the Use, Abuse, and LIBERTY OF THE PRESS," in *The Inde-
pendent Reflector*, August 30, 1753. See this volume, Document 11; and
William Livingston and Others, *The Independent Reflector or Weekly
Essays on Sundry Important Subjects*, ed. Milton M. Klein (Cambridge,
Mass.: The Belknap Press of Harvard University Press, 1963).

Freedom, provided he does it with proper Decency and a just Regard to the Laws."[61] Yet "the Laws" provided for the punishment of words that tended, however remotely, to disturb the peace, to lower the government in the esteem of the public, or to breach parliamentary privilege. Parker's statement was a neat way of saying that all opinions short of illegal ones were free—an epitome of the American view of the matter.

The New York General Assembly, which had intimidated a printer and his journeyman in 1766 for inadvertently publishing an address of the house with two typographical errors,[62] proved that it was capable of dealing effectively even with a radical of the patriot party. In December 1769, the Assembly had voted to supply provisions for the King's troops in New York City in return for Governor Cadwallader Colden's signature on an act authorizing needed bills of credit. Three days later a handbill, addressed "To the Betrayed Inhabitants of New-York" and signed by a "Son of Liberty," was broadcast throughout the city. The author condemned the Assembly for abandoning the liberties of the people by passing the provisions bill, and called upon the public to rise against unjust measures. The Assembly retaliated by declaring the handbill to be "a false seditious and infamous Libel," and by calling upon the Governor to offer rewards for information leading to the discovery of the author or authors. The provisions bill had passed the Assembly by a bare majority, but the resolves against the seditious writer passed unanimously. Governor Colden gladly complied with the Assembly's request and issued proclamations offering a reward of £150.[63]

Dazzled by so much money, a journeyman printer in the shop of James Parker betrayed his employer, declaring him the

---

[61] November 1759, quoted in "James Parker versus New York Province," ed. Beverly McAnear, *New York History*, XXXII (1941), 322.

[62] Thomas, *The History of Printing in America*, II, 302–303.

[63] *The Documentary History of the State of New York*, ed. Edmund B. O'Callaghan (Albany, N.Y.: Weed Parsons and Co., 1849–1851), III, 528–536.

printer of "To the Betrayed." Parker, who in 1756 had been jailed for a week by the Assembly for printing a reflection, was now charged with having published a seditious libel. He was arrested and brought before the Governor and Council. His apprentices and journeymen were taken into custody for questioning at the same time. Their testimony substantiated that of the informer, and also revealed that one Alexander McDougall had corrected the proofs at the printing office. Parker himself balked at naming the author, but he could not withstand the threats of imprisonment and dismissal from his post as comptroller of the post office. He made a deal with the Council. He received immunity from prosecution and a guarantee against loss of his post, in return for identifying the author and pledging to appear against him as a government witness.[64]

The man identified by Parker was Alexander McDougall, a local merchant who was one of the commanders of the Sons of Liberty. Later McDougall would serve in both the First and Second Continental Congresses and as a major general during the Revolution. He died in 1786 a pillar of conservatism, the first president of the Bank of New York and founder and head of the New York Society of Cincinnati. In February 1770, however, he was arrested on a charge of seditious libel against the Assembly. With Parker as a witness of McDougall's authorship, the legislature had a sure-fire case and turned the prisoner over to the common-law courts. McDougall, on examination before Chief Justice Daniel Horsmanden, remained silent except to demand a trial by jury. Bail was set at the

---

[64] *New-York Gazette; or The Weekly Post-Boy*, February 12, February 26, December 24, 1770; *The New York Journal; or, the General Advertiser*, February 15, 1770. On McDougall's case, see Thomas Jones, *History of New York during the Revolutionary War*, ed. E. F. de Lancey (New York: New York Historical Society, 1879), I, 24–33, 426–435; Isaac Q. Leake, *Memoir of the Life and Times of General John Lamb* (Albany, N.Y.: J. Munsell, 1850), pp. 60–73; *Historical Memoirs from 16 March 1763 to 9 July 1776 of William Smith*, ed. William H. W. Sabine (New York: Colburn and Tegg, 1956), pp. 71–81; Dorothy Rita Dillon, *The New York Triumvirate* (New York: Columbia University Press, 1949), pp. 106–123.

inordinately high sum of £500, which McDougall refused to pay. He preferred a martyr's prison while awaiting the action of the grand jury.

McDougall remained in jail for two and a half months. His imprisonment did more to publicize the cause of liberty of the press than any event since Zenger's trial. Alexander's account of that trial was republished for the first time in New York since 1736, and Parker's paper and John Holt's *New York Journal* courageously plumped for McDougall and for freedom of discussion. The editor and the prisoner against whom he was to testify each wrote hortatory articles urging all the colonies to enact statutes abolishing the "tyrannical Tenets" of the common law of seditious libel—which was invariably associated with the infamous Star Chamber. Yet the concept of seditious libel, the idea that political criticism could be a crime, was never attacked. Beneath the epithetical rhetoric was only the proposition that truth be accepted as a defense.[65]

The New York Mercury, however, defended the common law and backed the Assembly against McDougall.[66] The editor of conservatism's voice was Hugh Gaine, who in 1753 had been forced by the Assembly to humble himself in order to avoid prosecution for having printed its proceedings without prior license. Notwithstanding Gaine's policy, the McDougall case as managed by the Sons of Liberty became America's equivalent of the Wilkes case in England.[67] Indeed, McDougall himself consciously posed as the American Wilkes, and turned his imprisonment into a theatrical triumph, while his supporters used the issue of the free press as an anti-adminis-

---

[65] *The Weekly Post-Boy,* February 12, 19, and 26, March 19 and April 9, 1770; *The New York Journal,* March 1 and 15, 1770, and January 26, 1771. See this volume, Documents 16 and 17.

[66] See, for example, the "Dougliad" articles, in the *New York Gazette; and the Weekly Mercury,* April 9–June 25, 1770.

[67] See George Nobbe, *The North Briton: A Study in Political Propaganda* (New York: Columbia University Press, 1939); George Rudé, *Wilkes and Liberty* (New York: Oxford University Press, 1962); and Robert R. Rea, *The English Press in Politics, 1760–1774* (Lincoln, Neb.: University of Nebraska Press, 1963).

tration weapon. Forty-five, the number of the *North Briton* which had earned Wilkes his conviction for seditious libel, became the talismanic symbol of libertarianism and of the American cause against England. On the forty-fifth day of the year, for example, forty-five Liberty Boys dined in honor of McDougall on forty-five pounds of beef from a forty-five-month-old bull, drank forty-five toasts to liberty of the press and its defenders, and after dinner marched to the city jail to salute McDougall with forty-five cheers. On one particularly festive liberty day, forty-five songs were sung to him by forty-five virgins (every one of whom, reported a damned Tory, was forty-five years old).[68]

At the end of April, McDougall, attended by a mob of his partisans on the way from prison to court, was finally brought before the grand jury, which indicted him as the author of a seditious libel against the Assembly. It was the only indictment of its kind against a popular leader during the Revolutionary controversy, and the first of its kind in twenty-five years. Yet the unique fact that the prosecution was supported by every branch of the government, particularly the Assembly, makes the indictment understandable. So does the fact that the grand jurors were carefully picked from the "most . . . opulent & substantial gentlemen of the city." The trial was set for the next session of the court, in July. McDougall, this time paying the huge bail assessed against him, was released from prison. On July 2, just before the trial, James Parker, the star witness of the prosecution and the only one who could testify from personal knowledge that McDougall had written the seditious broadside, suddenly died. With his death the case against the defendant vanished. The trial was postponed till October and then again indefinitely. But if McDougall gloated over the turn of events that promised him a discharge from the indictment, he failed to consider the power of a revengeful Assembly.

---

[68] *The New York Weekly Post-Boy*, February 19, 1770; *The New York Journal*, March 22, 26, and 29, 1770.

With the collapse of the common-law prosecution, the Assembly resolved to punish McDougall on its own authority. Late in 1770, he was arrested on a warrant from the speaker by order of the house. After a week in jail, he was brought before the bar by the sergeant at arms. Speaker John Cruger then informed him that he was charged with having libeled the house and asked whether he was guilty or not. McDougall refused to plead to the charge until, he declared, he was informed of the identity of his accusers and the evidence against him. Cruger interrupted to threaten that he would be held in contempt for addressing the house without its prior leave, but Assemblyman George Clinton interceded on the prisoner's behalf, with the result that McDougall was permitted to give his reasons for not pleading. He explained that he had no counsel, that the case was still pending in the courts, and that the Assembly itself had already declared the broadside to be a seditious libel and its author guilty—in other words, he feared incriminating himself. Moreover, he added, the Assembly, having initiated the prosecution against him, was now acting as his judge and jury. This it had no power to do, particularly when it would be placing him under double jeopardy because he was still answerable at common law. For these reasons, McDougall declared, he would not answer the question. Representative John de Noyelles interjected that the house had the power to extort his answer and threatened infliction of *peine forte et dure,* a form of torture, recognized in English law, to force a suspect to plead one way or the other just so the trial might then proceed. McDougall braved de Noyelles' barbaric threat and obstinately refused to plead to the charge, thereby stymieing the proceedings.

The members fell to arguing among themselves whether they might coerce a prisoner to answer an incriminating question or even take jurisdiction of a case still pending in the courts. George Clinton, though he originally had voted for the resolution to prosecute McDougall's seditious libel, now supported him on technical grounds. (Clinton observed, however, that

if the Assembly were not a party to the common-law indictment it would have full power over McDougall and, if necessary to make him plead, might even throw him out of the
window.) The Assembly finally agreed to investigate the extent of its own powers in the case. McDougall was then ordered to state in writing his objections against entering a plea.
He did so, and his statement provoked Speaker Cruger to announce that McDougall had reflected on the honor and dignity of the house. The members then voted that McDougall's
fresh libels were in contempt of their parliamentary privilege
and demanded that he beg for pardon. His refusal prompted
another vote sentencing him to an indeterminate period in
prison. Only five members of the Assembly, including Clinton,
opposed the sentence. McDougall obtained a writ of habeas
corpus, but to no avail; the sheriff—who was ordered not to
honor such a writ—notified the court that the matter was not
within its jurisdiction, because the prisoner had been committed for breach of privilege. The court deferred to the legislature and McDougall remained in jail. Meanwhile the Assembly accepted a committee report, based on precedents of
the House of Commons, supporting the lawfulness of its authority and actions in the case. Thus once more an American
legislature endorsed the principle that it possessed an unbounded prerogative when personal liberty and freedom of
expression were involved. McDougall finally was released
when the legislative session ended. He had served nearly three
months in jail. The common-law charge against him was dis-
missed, and America's Wilkes won his freedom.[69]

---

[69] Microfilm copy of the *Journal of the Votes and Proceedings of the
General Assembly of the Colony of New-York,* 1769–1771, Public Records Office, London, Document #953, C.O. 5/1219. Extracts of the Assembly's *Journal* for December 13, 1770, when McDougall was interrogated, appeared in *The New York Weekly Post-Boy,* December 24,
1770, and *The New York Mercury,* December 24, 1770. See also the
Post-Boy for March 11 and 25, 1771, and *The New York Journal,* January
29 and February 21, 1771.

VI

No cause was more honored by rhetorical declamation and more dishonored in practice than the cause of freedom of expression during the Revolutionary period, from the 1760's through the War for Independence. The irony of the period might best be portrayed by a cartoon depicting the tarring and feathering of a Tory speaker or printer under a banner run up by the patriots inscribed, "In Liberty's Cause." Yankee Doodle's Liberty Boys vociferously claimed for themselves the right to freedom of expression which they denied their opponents, revealing an extraordinarily narrow understanding of the liberty of the press. But there was nothing in their heritage or experience which fitted them for a broader understanding. It is not surprising, even if ironical, that when the New York Sons of Liberty rode out to smash Tory presses they were led by Alexander McDougall, who in 1770 had been jailed for criticizing the provincial assembly. Nor is it surprising that the Continental Congress, in its Quebec Declaration in 1774, advertised as one of the virtues of freedom of the press that it made possible the "diffusion of liberal sentiments on the administration of government. . . ."[70] Illiberal—that is, loyalist—sentiments were simply suppressed during the Revolution. It was not, regrettably, an object of the Revolution "to get rid of the English common law on liberty of speech and of the press."[71]

Indeed, the Revolution wrought no change whatever in the common law, nor did it effect any breakthroughs in the field of

---

[70] *Journals of the Continental Congress, 1774–1789,* I, 108.

[71] Henry Schofield, "Freedom of the Press in the United States," in his *Essays on Constitutional Law and Equity* (Boston: Chipman Law Publishing Co., 1921), II, 521–522. Schofield has been quoted with approval by Zechariah Chafee, Jr., in *Free Speech in the United States* (Cambridge, Mass.: Harvard University Press, 1948), p. 20; quoted by the Supreme Court, in *Bridges* v. *California,* 314 U.S. 252, 264 (1941); and endorsed by many scholars.

libertarian thought on freedom of political opinion. Republican forms of government had been established; the first written constitutions had been framed; the first bills of rights, having the force of fundamental law, had been adopted; even the first constitutional guarantees of freedom of speech and press had been specified. But law and theory remained the same. They were epitomized best in a statement by Sir William Blackstone: "The liberty of the press is indeed essential to the nature of a free state; but this consists in laying no previous restraints upon publications, and not in freedom from censure for criminal matter when published. Every freeman has an undoubted right to lay what sentiments he pleases before the public; to forbid this is to destroy the freedom of the press; but if he publishes what is improper, mischievous, or illegal, he must take the consequences of his own temerity."[72]

To be sure, the principle of a free press, like flag, home, and mother, had no enemies in America after the Revolution. Only seditious libels, licentious opinions, and malicious falsehoods were condemned. The question, therefore, is not whether freedom of the press was favored, but what it meant and whether its advocates would extend it to a political opponent whose criticism cut to the bone on issues that really mattered. Jefferson once remarked that he did not care whether his neighbor said that there are twenty gods or no God, because "It neither picks my pocket nor breaks my leg."[73] But in drafting a constitution for Virginia in 1776 he considered proposing that freedom of religion "shall not be held to justify any seditious preaching or conversation against the authority of the civil

---

[72] Sir William Blackstone, *Commentaries on the Laws of England* (Oxford: Clarendon Press, 1765–1769), IV, 151–152. See this volume, Document 15.

[73] Query XVII, "Religion," in *Notes on the State of Virginia*, ed. William Peden (Chapel Hill, N.C.: University of North Carolina Press, 1955), p. 159.

government."[74] And in the same year he helped frame a statute on treasonous crimes, punishing anyone who "by any word" or deed defended the cause of Great Britain.[75] Apparently political opinions could break his leg or pick his pocket. What, then, did Jefferson mean by freedom of the press? He and his contemporaries supported an unrestricted public discussion of issues, but "unrestricted" meant merely the absence of censorship in advance of publication; although no one needed a government license to express himself, everyone was accountable under the criminal law for abuse of the right to speak or publish freely. Significantly, neither Jefferson himself nor anyone else in the United States, prior to 1798, extended his "overt acts" test to freedom of political opinion.

Jefferson had devised that test when seeking a way to insure the free exercise of religion. In one of his most enduring and noble achievements, the Act for Establishing Religious Freedom, which became law in Virginia in 1786, he declared that

---

[74] "A Bill for new modelling the form of government and for establishing the Fundamental principles of our future Constitution," dated by Boyd as "before 13 June 1776," in *The Papers of Thomas Jefferson*, ed. Julian P. Boyd (Princeton, N.J.: Princeton University Press, 1950), I, 353. Jefferson copied this provision from a similar one in an earlier draft, then bracketed it out, and omitted it from a third draft. *Ibid.*, p. 347.

[75] "That the mere utterance of a political opinion is being penalized in these cases becomes even clearer in a statute such as that in Virginia, which declared the utterance of the opinion, or action upon it, to be equally offensive, providing a fine not exceeding £20,000 and imprisonment not exceeding five years 'if any person residing or being within this commonwealth shall . . . by any word, open deed, or act, advisedly and willingly maintain and defend the authority, jurisdiction, or power, of the king or parliament of Great Britain, heretofore claimed and exercised within this colony, or shall attribute any such authority, jurisdiction, or power, to the king or parliament of Great Britain.'" Willard Hurst, "Treason in the United States," *Harvard Law Review*, LVIII (1944), 267, quoting *The Statutes at Large Being a Collection of All The Laws of Virginia (1619–1792)*, ed. William W. Hening (J. & G. Cochran, 1821), IX, 170. For Jefferson's role, see Hurst, 251; and *The Papers of Thomas Jefferson*, ed. Boyd, I, 598.

"to suffer the civil magistrate to intrude his powers into the field of opinion, and to restrain the profession or propagation of principles, on supposition of their ill tendency, is a dangerous fallacy, which at once destroys all religious liberty, because he being of course judge of that tendency, will make his opinions the rule of judgment, and approve or condemn the sentiments of others only as they shall square with or differ from his own; that it is time enough for the rightful purposes of civil government for its officers to interfere when principles break out into overt acts against peace and good order. . . ."[76] The overt-acts test applied in Jefferson's words, only to "opinions in matters of religion," although its principle should have been as relevant in cases of political opinion, and had been specifically extended to such cases by many English theorists.

Before 1798, the *avant garde* among American libertarians staked everything on the principles of the Zenger case, which they thought beyond improvement. They believed that no greater liberty could be conceived than the right to publish without restriction, if only the defendant could plead truth as a defense in a criminal prosecution for libel, and if the criminality of his words might be determined by a jury of his peers rather than by a judge. The substantive law of criminal libels was unquestioned. But libertarians who accepted Zengerian principles painted themselves into a corner. If a jury returned a verdict of "guilty" despite a defense of truth, due process had been accorded and protests were groundless, because the substance of the law that made the trial possible had not been challenged.

American acquiescence in the common-law definition of a free press was so widespread that even the frail Zengerian principles seemed daring, novel, and had few adherents. It was not until 1790 that the first state, Pennsylvania, took the then

---

[76] *The Papers of Thomas Jefferson,* ed. Boyd, II, 545–553.

radical step of adopting the Zengerian principles,[77] which still left the common law of seditious libel intact. The Pennsylvania provision was drafted by James Wilson who, in the state convention that ratified the Constitution, declared without challenge by any of the ardent proponents of a bill of rights that "what is meant by the liberty of the press is that there should be no antecedent restraint upon it; but that every author is responsible when he attacks the security or welfare of the government. . . ." The mode of proceeding, Wilson added, should be by prosecution.[78] The state constitutional provision of 1790 reflected this proposition, as did state trials before and after 1790.[79]

Delaware and Kentucky followed Pennsylvania's lead in 1792,[80] but elsewhere the status quo prevailed. In 1789 William Cushing and John Adams worried about whether the guarantee of a free press in Massachusetts ought to mean that truth

---

[77] "That the printing-presses shall be free to every person who undertakes to examine the proceedings of the legislature, or any branch of government, and no law shall ever be made to restrain the right thereof. The free communication of thoughts and opinions is one of the invaluable rights of man; and every citizen may freely speak, write, and print on any subject, *being responsible for the abuse of that liberty.* In *prosecutions* for the publication of papers investigating the official conduct of officers or men in a public capacity, or where the matter published is proper for public information, the truth thereof may be given in evidence; and in all indictments for libels the jury shall have a right to determine the law and the facts, under the direction of the court, as in other cases." "Pennsylvania Constitution of 1790," Article IX, Section 7, in *The Federal and State Constitutions,* ed. Thorpe, V, 3100. Italics added.

[78] *Pennsylvania and the Federal Constitution, 1787–1788,* ed. John Bach McMaster and Frederick D. Stone (Philadelphia: Historical Society of Pennsylvania, 1888), pp. 308–309. See this volume, Document 19.

[79] *Respublica* v. *Oswald,* 1 Dallas (Penn.) Reports 319 (1788); "Trial of William Cobbett," November 1797, in *State Trials of the United States during the Administrations of Washington and Adams,* ed. Francis Wharton (Philadelphia: 1849), pp. 323–324; *Respublica* v. *Dennie,* 4 Yeates' (Penn.) Reports 267 (1805).

[80] "Delaware Constitution of 1792," Article I, Section 5, in *The Federal and State Constitutions,* ed. Thorpe, I, 569; and "Kentucky Constitution of 1792," Article XII, Sections 7–8, *ibid.,* III, 1274.

was a good defense to a charge of criminal libel, but they agreed that false publications against the government were punishable.[81] In 1791, when a Massachusetts editor was prosecuted for a criminal libel against a state official, the Supreme Judicial Court divided on the question of truth as a defense, but agreed, like the Pennsylvania judges,[82] that the state constitutional guarantee of a free press was merely declaratory of the common law in simply prohibiting a licensing system.[83]

The opinions of Jefferson, the acknowledged libertarian leader in America, and of Madison, the father of the Bill of Rights, are especially significant. In 1783, when proposing a new constitution for Virginia, Jefferson exempted the press from prior restraints but carefully provided for prosecution—a state trial—in cases of false publication.[84] In 1788, when urging Madison to support a bill of rights to the new federal Constitution, Jefferson made the same recommendation.[85]

---

[81] "Hitherto Unpublished Correspondence Between Chief Justice Cushing and John Adams in 1789," ed. Frank W. Grinnell, *Massachusetts Law Quarterly*, XXVII (1942), 12–16. See this volume, Document 23. Adams, of course, signed the Sedition Act into law and urged its enforcement; and Cushing, as a Supreme Court judge, presided over some of the Sedition Act trials and charged juries on the Act's constitutionality. See Smith, *Freedom's Fetters*, pp. 97–98, 152, 242, 267, 268, 271, 284, 311, 363, and 371.

[82] See cases cited above at note 79. The judges in Oswald's case were Thomas McKean, then a Federalist but subsequently a Republican, and George Bryan, an Anti-Federalist and libertarian advocate of a national bill of rights.

[83] *Commonwealth* v. *Freeman*, reported in the *Independent Chronicle* (Boston), February 24 and March 3, 10, 17, 24, 1791.

[84] "Draught of a Fundamental Constitution for the Commonwealth of Virginia," in *The Papers of Thomas Jefferson*, ed. Boyd, VI, 304: "PRINTING PRESS shall be subject to no other restraint than liableness to legal prosecution for false facts printed and published." Boyd dates this document between May 15 and June 17, 1783.

[85] "A declaration that the federal government will never restrain the press from printing any thing they please, will not take away the liability of the printers for false facts printed." Jefferson to Madison, July 31, 1788, in *The Papers of Thomas Jefferson*, ed. Boyd, XIII, 442.

liv *Introduction*

Madison construed it in its most favorable light, observing: "The Exemption of the press from liability in every case for *true facts* is . . . an innovation and as such ought to be well considered."[86] But, on consideration, he did not add the truth-as-a-defense principle to the amendment on the press which he offered when proposing a bill of rights to Congress.[87] Yet Madison's phrasing appeared too broad for Jefferson, who stated that he would be pleased if the press provision were altered to exclude freedom to publish "false facts . . . affecting the peace of the confederacy with foreign nations"[88]—a clause whose suppressive possibilities can be imagined in the context of a foreign-policy controversy like the one on Jay's Treaty.

Madison fortunately ignored Jefferson's proposal, but there is no warrant for the belief that he dissented from the universal American acceptance of the Blackstonian definition of a free press. In 1788, at the Virginia ratifying convention, Madison remained silent when George Nicholas, one of his closest supporters, declared that the liberty of the press was secure because there was no power to license the press;[89] Madison was silent, too, when John Marshall rose to say that Congress would never make a law punishing men of different political opinions "unless it be such a case as must satisfy the

---

[86] "Madison's Observations on Jefferson's Draft of a Constitution for Virginia," October 1788, *ibid.*, VI, 316.

[87] Madison's original proposal, June 8, 1789, was: "The people shall not be deprived or abridged of their right to speak, to write, or to publish their sentiments; and the freedom of the press, as one of the great bulwarks of liberty, shall be inviolable." *The Debates and Proceedings in the Congress of the United States* (Washington, D.C.: 1834), I, 451, 1st Cong., 1st Sess. Cited hereafter as *Annals of Congress*, the bookbinder's title.

[88] Jefferson to Madison, August 28, 1789, in *The Papers of Thomas Jefferson*, ed. Boyd, XV, 367.

[89] "The liberty of the press is secured. . . . In the time of King William, there passed an act for licensing the press. That was repealed. Since that time it has been looked upon as safe." *The Debates in the Several State Conventions on the Adoption of the Federal Constitution*, ed. Jonathan Elliot (2nd ed., rev.; Philadelphia: J. B. Lippincott Co. 1941), III, 247.

people at large."[90] In October of 1788, when replying to Jefferson's argument[91] that powers of the national government should be restricted by a bill of rights, Madison declared that "absolute restrictions in cases that are doubtful, or where emergencies may overrule them, ought to be avoided."[92] When Madison proposed an amendment in Congress guaranteeing freedom of the press, he did not employ the emphatic language of the Virginia ratifying convention's recommendation that freedom of the press should not be subject to abridgment "by any authority of the United States."[93] As Madison introduced the amendment, it omitted the important clause, "by any authority of the United States,"[94] which would have covered the executive and judiciary as well as Congress; the omitted clause, in other words, would have prohibited the federal courts from exercising any common-law jurisdiction over criminal libels. As ratified, the First Amendment declared only that Congress should make no law abridging the freedom of speech or press.

What did the amendment mean at the time of its adoption? First of all (if the amendment is analyzed by focusing on the phrase, "the freedom of the press"), it was merely an assurance that Congress was powerless to authorize restraints in advance of publication. On this point the evidence for the period from 1787 to 1791 is uniform and nonpartisan. For example, Hugh Williamson of North Carolina, a Federalist signatory of the Constitution, used freedom of the press in Blackstonian or common-law terms,[95] as did Melancthon Smith of New

---

[90] *Ibid.*, III, 560.

[91] Jefferson to Madison, July 31, 1788, in *The Papers of Thomas Jefferson*, ed. Boyd, XIII, 422–423.

[92] Madison to Jefferson, October 17, 1788, *ibid.*, XIV, 20.

[93] *The Debates in the Several State Conventions*, ed. Elliott, III, 656.

[94] See note 87, above.

[95] "There was a time in England when neither book, pamphlet, nor paper could be published without a license from government. That restraint was finally removed in the year 1694; and, by such removal, the press became perfectly free, for it is not under the restraint of any

York, an anti-Federalist. Demanding a free-press guarantee in the new federal Constitution, despite the fact that New York's constitution lacked that guarantee, Smith argued that freedom of the press was "fully defined and secured" in New York by "the common and statute law of England," making a state constitutional provision unnecessary.[96] No other definition of freedom of the press by anyone anywhere in America before 1798 has been discovered. There was no dissent from the proposition that the punishment of a seditious libeler did not abridge the proper or lawful freedom of the press.[97]

Nevertheless, the injunction of the First Amendment was not intended to imply that a sedition act might be enacted without abridging "the freedom of the press." A sedition act would not be an abridgment, but that was not the point of the amendment. To understand its framers' intentions, the amendment should not be read with the focus on the meaning of "the freedom of the press." It should not, in other words, be read merely to mean that Congress could impose no prior restraints. It should be read, rather, with the stress on the opening clause, "Congress shall make no law . . ." The injunction, that is, was intended to prohibit any Congressional regulation of the press, whether by means of a licensing act, a tax act, or a sedition act. The framers meant Congress to be

license. Certainly the new government can have no power to impose restraints." Hugh Williamson, "Remarks in the New Plan of Government," in *Essays on the Constitution of the United States*, ed. Paul Leicester Ford (Brooklyn, N.Y.: Historical Printing Club, 1892), p. 394.

[96] Melancthon Smith, "An Address to the People of the State of New York," 1788, in *Pamphlets on the Constitution of the United States*, ed. Paul Leicester Ford (Brooklyn, N.Y.: 1888), p. 114.

[97] The brief and vague statement by Oswald in 1788 may be regarded by some as an exception to this proposition. Oswald, having been indicted for a criminal libel on a private party, published an address to the public in which he stated: "The doctrine of libel being a doctrine incompatible with law and liberty, and at once destructive of the privileges of a free country, in the communication of our thoughts, has not hitherto gained any footing in *Pennsylvania*. . . ." Quoted in *Respublica* v. *Oswald*, 1 Dallas 319, at p. 320 (1788). See this volume, Document 20.

totally without power to enact legislation respecting the press. They intended a federal system in which the national government could exercise only such powers as were specifically enumerated, or were necessary and proper to carry out those enumerated. Thus James Wilson declared that, because the national government had "no power whatsoever" concerning the press, "no law . . . can possibly be enacted" against it; thus Alexander Hamilton, referring to the demand for a free-press guarantee, asked, ". . . why declare that things shall not be done which there is no power to do?"[98] The illustrations may be multiplied fiftyfold. In other words, no matter what was meant or understood by freedom of speech and press, the national government, *even in the absence of the First Amendment,* could not make speech or press a legitimate subject of restrictive legislation. The amendment itself was superfluous. To quiet public apprehension it offered an added security that Congress would be limited to the exercise of its delegated powers. The phrasing was intended to prohibit the possibility that those powers might be used to abridge speech and press. From this view of the matter, the Sedition Act of 1798 was unconstitutional.

That act was also unnecessary as a matter of law, however necessary it was as a matter of Federalist Party policy. It was unnecessary because the federal courts exercised jurisdiction over nonstatutory or common-law crimes against the United States. At the Pennsylvania ratifying convention, James Wilson had declared that, whereas Congress could enact no law against the press, a libel against the United States might be prosecuted in the state where the offense was committed—under Article III, Section two, of the Constitution, which refers to the judicial power of the United States. A variety of common-law crimes against the United States were in fact tried in the

---

[98] Wilson's statement at the Pennsylvania ratifying convention, quoted in *Pennsylvania and the Federal Constitution,* ed. McMaster and Stone, p. 308; Hamilton in *The Federalist,* No. 84. See this volume, Documents 19 and 22.

federal courts during the first decade of the courts' existence.[99] There were even a couple of common-law indictments in the federal courts for the crime of seditious libel.[100] All the early Supreme Court judges, including several who had been influential in the Philadelphia Convention, or in the state ratifying conventions, or in the Congress that passed the Judiciary Act of 1789, assumed the existence of a federal common law of crimes.[101] Ironically, it was a case originating as a federal prosecution of Connecticut editors for seditious libels against President Jefferson that finally resulted in a ruling by a divided Supreme Court, in 1812, that there was no federal common law of crimes.[102]

---

[99] "Trial of Joseph Ravara" (1792), in *State Trials . . .* , ed. Wharton, pp. 90–92; "Trial of Gideon Henfield" (1793), *ibid.*, pp. 49–92; *United States* v. *Worrall*, 2 Dallas 384 (1798), *ibid.*, pp. 188–199; "Trial of the Northhampton Insurgents" (1799), *ibid.*, p. 476; "Trial of Isaac Williams" (1799), *ibid.*, pp. 652–654. See also *U.S.* v. *Smith* (1797), MS Final Record of the United States Circuit Courts of Massachusetts, 1790–1799, I, 242, 244 (Federal Records Center, Boston). Smith's case is reported in *Federal Cases* #16323, where the date is erroneously given as 1792. In Worrall's case, mentioned above, Justice Chase disagreed with his associate, Judge Peters, who supported the jurisdiction of the federal courts in cases of common-law crime. Chase, however, changed his opinion in *U.S.* v. *Sylvester* (1799), MS Final Record, I, 303, an unreported case.

[100] A federal grand jury in Richmond presented Congressman Samuel J. Cabell for seditious libel in 1797. Prosecutions for seditious libel were also begun against Benjamin F. Bache of the Philadelphia *Aurora* and John Daly Burk of the New York *Time Piece*, in 1798, shortly before the enactment of the Sedition Act. See Smith, *Freedom's Fetters*, pp. 95, 183–184, and 188–220.

[101] Supreme Court Justices known to have accepted jurisdiction in cases of common-law crimes included Wilson, Ellsworth, Paterson, Jay, Iredell, and Chase. See cases mentioned in note 99, above.

[102] *U.S.* v. *Hudson and Goodwin*, 7 Cranch 32, at p. 34 (1812). Justice Johnson, speaking for the "majority," gave an unreasoned opinion. The case had been decided without arguments of counsel. W. W. Crosskey, *Politics and the Constitution* (Chicago: University of Chicago Press, 1953), II, 782, claims that Chief Justice Marshall and Justices Story and Washington dissented from Johnson's opinion without noting the fact of their dissent on the record.

There was unquestionably a federal common law of crimes at the time of the Sedition Act. Why, then, was the Act passed if it was not legally needed? Because even in England, where the criminal courts exercised an unquestioned jurisdiction over seditious libels, it was politically advisable in the 1790's to declare public policy in unmistakable terms by the enactment of sedition statutes.[103] Legislation helped ensure effective enforcement of the law, stirred public opinion against the law's intended victims, and in every way served Federalist Party objectives. The Federalists, hoping to control public opinion and elections, emulated the British model. A federal statute was expedient also because the Republicans insisted that libels against the United States might be tried only by the *state* courts, which were not so trustworthy in some states as the Federal courts.

This suggests another original purpose of the First Amendment. We have noted that a constitutional guarantee of a free press did not per se preclude a sedition act, but the prohibition on Congress did, although it left the federal courts free to try cases of seditious libel. It now appears that the prohibition on Congress was motivated far less by a desire to give immunity to political expression than by a solicitude for states' rights and the federal principle. The primary purpose of the First Amendment was to reserve to the states an exclusive authority, as far as legislation was concerned, in the field of speech and press.

---

[103] On the English legislation of the 1790's, see May, *The Constitutional History of England* . . . , II, 161–174. The Parliamentary debates and the texts of the Treasonable Practices Act and of the Sedition Act of 1795, known together as "The Two Acts," were published in London in 1796 under the title, *The History of the Two Acts,* and were imported into the United States and advertised under the title, *History of the Treason and Sedition Bills lately passed in Great Britain.* For the influence of the English experience and legislation on Federalist thought, see Manning J. Dauer, *The Adams Federalists* (Baltimore: Johns Hopkins University Press, 1953), pp. 157–159.

This is clear enough from the countless states' rights arguments advanced by the anti-Federalists during the ratification controversy; it is explicitly clear from the Republican arguments during the Sedition Act controversy. In the House debates on the bill, Albert Gallatin, Edward Livingston, John Nicholas, and Nathaniel Macon all agreed (to quote Macon on the subject of liberty of the press) that "The States have complete power on the subject. . . ."[104] Jefferson's Kentucky Resolutions of 1798 expressed the same proposition,[105] and so did Madison's "Address of the General Assembly to the People of the Commonwealth of Virginia" in 1799.[106]

It is possible that the opponents of the Sedition Act did not want or believe in state prosecutions, but argued for an exclusive state power over political libels because such an argument was tactically useful as a means of denying national jurisdiction, judicial or legislative. If so, how shall we explain the Republican prosecution in New York in 1803 against Croswell, a Federalist editor, for a seditious libel against President Jefferson?[107] How shall we explain the Blackstonian opinions of the Republican judges in that case?[108] How shall we explain Jefferson's letter to the governor of Pennsylvania in the same year? The President, enclosing a newspaper piece

---

[104] *Annals of Congress,* 5th Cong., 2nd Sess., p. 2152; see also, *ibid.,* Macon at p. 2106, Gallatin at p. 2163, Nicholas at p. 2142, and Livingston at p. 2153.

[105] *The Debates in the Several State Conventions,* ed. Elliot, IV, 540–541.

[106] *The Writings of James Madison,* ed. Gaillard Hunt (New York: G. P. Putnam's Sons, 1900–1910), VI, 333–334.

[107] *People* v. *Croswell,* 3 Johnson's (N.Y.) Cases 336 (1804).

[108] Chief Justice Morgan Lewis, joined by Judge Brockholst Livingston, whom Jefferson appointed to the United States Supreme Court in 1806, explicitly defined freedom of the press in common-law terms. In 1805 the state legislature enacted a bill allowing truth as a defense if published "with good motives and for justifiable end," and allowing the jury to decide the whole issue. The statute is reported at 3 Johnson's Cases 411–413, following the arguments of counsel and the judicial opinions. See this volume, Document 32.

that attacked him unmercifully, urged a "few prosecutions" because they "would have a wholesome effect in restoring the integrity of the presses."[109] How shall we explain Jefferson's letter to Abigail Adams in 1804 in which he said: "While we deny that Congress have a right to controul the freedom of the press, we have ever asserted the right of the states, and their exclusive right to do so."[110] And if exclusive state power was advanced not as a principle but as a tactic for denying federal jurisdiction, how shall we explain what Jefferson's opponents called his "reign of terror":[111] the common-law indictments in 1806 in the United States Circuit Court in Connecticut against six men charged with seditious libel of the President?[112] How shall we explain his letter of 1807 in which he said of the "prosecutions in the Court of the U.S." that they could "not lessen the useful freedom of the press," if truth were admitted as a defense?[113]

VII

British libertarian theory provides an instructive contrast. English lawyers, pamphleteers, and ministers had progressed

---

[109] Jefferson to Governor Thomas McKean, February 19, 1803, in *The Writings of Thomas Jefferson*, ed. Paul Leicester Ford (New York: G. P. Putnam's Sons, 1892–1899), IX, 451–452. See this volume, Document 50.

[110] Jefferson to Abigail Adams, September 4, 1804, *ibid.*, X, 90. In the eloquent First Inaugural Address, Jefferson declared, in a deservedly much-quoted passage: "If there be any among us who would wish to dissolve this Union or to change its republican form, let them stand undisturbed as monuments of the safety with which error of opinion may be tolerated where reason is left free to combat it." But in the Second Inaugural Address he spoke quite differently. See the present volume Document 52.

[111] "Hampden," *A Letter to the President of the United States, touching the Prosecutions under his Patronage, before the Circuit Court in the District of Connecticut* (New Haven, Conn.: 1808), p. 28.

[112] *Ibid.*, pp. 8–12.

[113] Jefferson to Thomas Seymour, February 11, 1807, in *The Writings of Thomas Jefferson*, ed. Ford, IX, 90.

beyond Cato and Zengerian principles. Abandoning the concept of verbal political crimes, they embraced the overt-acts
test as a measurement of the scope of permissible freedom of
expression, and they cleaved the air with impassioned yet
elaborate analyses of freedom of the press and the right to
criticize the government. The most notable English statement
was Robert Hall's *An Apology for the Freedom of the Press
and for General Liberty*,[114] published in 1793, when men were
being jailed in wholesale batches for political opinions that
were condemned as false, dangerous, and subversive. Hall's
position was that all men should have an absolute liberty to
discuss "every subject which can fall within the compass of
the human mind," and he meant what he said without any ifs
or buts. He flatly denied the power of the government to punish the mere expression of political opinions. Distinguishing
words, sentiment, and opinions from "conduct" or "behavior,"
Hall demanded that only the latter be regarded as criminal.[115]

---

[114] First issued as a tract (London: 1793). The reprint cited here is
from *The Miscellaneous Works and Remains of the Reverend Robert
Hall,* ed. John Foster (London: H. G. Bohn, 1846), pp. 159–233. For
other British precursors of the new American libertarianism, see "Father
of Candor," *A Letter Concerning Libels, Warrants, the Seizure of Papers,
and Sureties for the Peace of Behaviour* (7th ed., London: John Almon,
1771), pp. 20, 34, 71, and 161; Ebenezer Ratcliffe, *Two Letters Addressed to the Right Rev. Prelates* (London: J. Johnson, 1773), p. 100;
Andrew Kippis, *A Vindication of the Protestant Dissenting Ministers*
(London: G. Robinson, 1773), pp. 98–99; Francis Maseres, *An Enquiry
Into the Extent of the Power of Juries* (1776) (Dublin: 1792), pp. 6,
13, 18, 22, 24, and 28; Jeremy Bentham, *A Fragment on Government*
(London: T. Payne, 1776), p. 154; Capel Lofft, *An Essay on the Law of
Libels* (London: C. Dilly, 1785), pp. 60–61; James Adair, *Discussions
of the Law of Libels As at Present Received* (London: T. Cadell,
1785), pp. 27–28; Manasseh Dawes, *The Deformity of the Doctrine of
Libels, and Informations Ex-Officio* (London: T. Cadell, 1785), pp. 11–
24, 28; and the celebrated argument of Thomas Erskine in defense of
Tom Paine, in a trial for seditious libel, 1792, published as a contempo-
rary tract and available in *Speeches of Thomas Lord Erskine,* ed. Edward
Walford (London: Reeves & Turner, 1870), I, 309, 313.

[115] *An Apology for the Freedom of the Press* . . . , in *The Miscellaneous Works* . . . , ed. Foster, p. 172.

He sought to make the crime of sedition, like that of treason, depend upon nonverbal, overt acts. He made an otherwise commonplace point—that freedom of expression is to be cherished as a step to the truth—by noting that opinions possessing a social value were frequently mixed with error and falsehoods. Publications, he wrote, "like every thing else that is human, are of a mixed nature, where truth is often blended with falsehood, and important hints suggested in the midst of much impertinent or pernicious matter; nor is there any way of separating the precious from the vile, but by tolerating the whole."[116] This observation was original and cogent when such leading American libertarians as John Adams and Thomas Jefferson believed, even in time of calm, that falsehoods published against the government were criminal. Hall's courage and the libertarian character of his thought must be measured in the context of the repressive prosecutions that were sweeping England when he wrote:

[Government] being an institution purely human, one would imagine it were the proper province for freedom of discussion in its utmost extent. It is surely just that every one should have a right to examine those measures by which the happiness of all may be affected. . . . Under pretence of its being seditious to express any disapprobation of the *form* of our government, the most alarming attempts are made to wrest the liberty of the press out of our hands. . . . An inquiry respecting the comparative excellence of civil constitutions can be forbidden on no other pretence than that of its tending to sedition and anarchy. This plea, however, will have little weight with those who reflect to how many ill purposes it has already applied; and that when the example has been introduced of suppressing opinions on account of their imagined ill tendency, it has seldom been confined within any safe or reasonable bounds. . . . The law hath amply provided against overt acts of sedition and disorder, and to suppress mere opinions by any other method than reason and argument, is the height of tyranny. Freedom of thought

---

[116] *Ibid.*

being intimately connected with the happiness and dignity of man in every stage of his being, is of so much more importance than the preservation of any constitution, that to infringe the former, under pretence of supporting the latter, is to sacrifice the means to the end.[117]

The closest American approximation to British libertarianism before 1798 was reflected, somewhat uncertainly, in a Congressional debate of 1794. President Washington, having in mind the Democratic societies of western Pennsylvania, referred critically, in a Congressional message, to "certain self-created societies" that had urged resistance against the whiskey excise.[118] The Senate, in a formal response to the President, declared that the activities of these societies had injured the government and helped foment the insurrection. A motion by Senator Aaron Burr to expunge this passage in the Senate's response was defeated.[119] In the House, however, the Republicans, after a four-day debate, managed to expunge the reference to "self-created societies." The House simply expressed its great concern that any misrepresentations of the government so serious as to foment the insurrection should have been made by anyone.[120] A Virginia trio, Representatives William B. Giles, John Nicholas, and James Madison, in conducting their successful fight to water down the statement, expressed the libertarian position.

Giles, who spoke first, declared that the motion to express the House's "reprobation of the self-created societies" was intended "to censure the Democratic societies." Defending the right of free association, whether for religious, political, philosophical, or other purposes, he stated that Congress was not constitutionally empowered "to attempt checking or restrain-

---

[117] *Ibid.*, pp. 174, 176–177, and 179.
[118] *Annals of Congress*, 3rd Cong., 2nd Sess., p. 792, November 19, 1794.
[119] *Ibid.*, p. 794, November 21, 1794.
[120] *Ibid.*, pp. 946–947, November 28, 1794.

ing public opinion." If any societies had acted illegally, they were punishable under the law. But the House simply had no "business to pass random votes of censure."[121] The response by William Smith, a South Carolina Federalist, sharpened the controversy and made the debate a precursor of the elaborate controversy on the floor of the House four years later when the Sedition Act was at issue. Smith, alleging that he was a friend to freedom of the press, believed that "the dissemination of improper sentiments . . . subversive of good order" was a suitable object of the House's reprobation. The matter in question was not the legality of the self-created societies, but the mischievous consequences of their calumnies against the government.[122]

Nicholas, in reply, repeated Giles's point that censure was beyond the powers of the House. In a statement marked by confusion, he declared: "It was wrong to condemn societies for particular acts. . . . I cannot agree to persecution for the sake of opinion."[123] It was a poor libertarian argument that could not distinguish acts from opinions, particularly when the societies stood accused of having provoked an actual insurrection. Later, Nicholas arose to answer a contention that the existence of libel prosecutions proved that calumnious attacks on government were just objects of reprehension. He failed wholly to assault libel prosecutions, thereby revealing how impoverished or stunted was his libertarian thought in comparison to the arguments he was to make only four years later. In 1794 he merely contended that it was not fair to compare the censure of a society with the prosecution of a libel, because in the latter case the accused party had an opportunity to defend himself. The Democratic societies had no such opportunity. They were accused, said Nicholas, of never having once said a good word about government policies. "If

---

[121] *Ibid.*, pp. 900–901, November 24, 1794.
[122] *Ibid.*, pp. 901–902, November 24, 1794.
[123] *Ibid.*, p. 905, November 24, 1794.

these societies had censured every proceeding of Government, there would have been," he remarked, "the greatest reason for taking some measures." But they had taken no notice whatever of many acts of the government.[124] Aside from its unintended sinister implication, Nicholas' argument was confused and fatuous.

Giles, in a rambling speech, passingly reflected a genuine libertarian position. "Many people who condemn the proceedings of the Democratic societies, yet will not choose to see them divested of the inalienable privilege of thinking, of speaking, of writing, and of printing. Persons may condemn the abuse in exercising a right, and yet feel the strongest sympathy with the right itself. Are not Muir and Palmer, and the other martyrs of Scotch despotism, toasted from one end of the Continent to the other? And why is it so? These men asserted the right of thinking, of speaking, of writing, and of printing."[125] The significance of this statement lies in Giles's condemnation of the convictions of Thomas Muir and the Reverend T. Fyshe Palmer for the crime of seditious libel. Their notoriously unfair, even brutal, trials in Scotland in 1793 were the result of their outspoken campaign for annual parliaments and universal suffrage.[126] Given the facts of these cases, and the severe sentences, Giles's statement should not be stretched from an obvious censure of the two trials to a repudiation of all trials for seditious libel. Moreover, he never took the trouble of explaining what he meant by freedom of speech and press. Indeed, Fischer Ames observed in reply that Giles "had been occupied in refuting what nobody had asserted, and in proving what nobody had denied." Ames himself spoke warmly of freedom of speech and press, attacking only, he said, its abuses.[127]

---

[124] *Ibid.*, p. 911, November 25, 1794.
[125] *Ibid.*, p. 918, November 26, 1794.
[126] May, *The Constitutional History of England . . .* , II, 145–149.
[127] *Annals of Congress,* 3rd Cong., 2nd Sess., pp. 921, 924, November 26, 1794.

Madison responded that the people, in forming the Constitution, had retained all rights not delegated, making Congress powerless to legislate on certain subjects. "Opinions," he stated, "are not the objects of legislation. You animadvert on the abuse of reserved rights: how far will this go? It may extend to the liberty of speech, and of the press. . . . If we advert to the nature of Republican Government, we shall find that the censorial power is in the people over the Government, and not in the Government over the people."[128] That proposition, a few years later, served as the basis for a powerful libertarian argument against the concept of seditious libel. In 1794, however, Madison merely proceeded to restate the seventeenth-century argument that truth would prevail over error, making it unnecessary to proceed against the publications of the societies in question.

The Republicans rewrote the offensive passage in the House's response to President Washington, but it should be remembered that at no point had the Federalists proposed action against the publications or opinions of the "self-created societies." Publications and opinions were not the subject of repressive legislation until 1798. Only then did the new libertarian theories emerge.

Before then, a clear opportunity presented itself for the development of the libertarian argument. In 1796 New York had a new "McDougall case." The victim was William Keteltas, a Republican lawyer and member of the local Democratic Society. Keteltas had been present at the unfair and juryless trial of two Irish ferrymen who were convicted for allegedly insulting an alderman by refusing to ferry him off-schedule. Outraged by the proceedings in the Court of General Sessions, Keteltas published a newspaper article denouncing the tyranny of the trial magistrates—the mayor and five aldermen. He demanded a grand-jury investigation and impeachment of the guilty officials by the State Assembly. When the grand jury

---

[128] *Ibid.*, p. 934, November 27, 1794.

went fishing and the Assembly took up whitewashing, Keteltas aimed his blistering newspaper comments against the Assembly itself. That august body, smarting from his censure, which it took to be a seditious insult, summoned him to appear before its bar. Keteltas had to answer for his articles, which were condemned as "highly injurious to the honor and dignity" of the Assembly and as "calculated to create distrust and destroy the confidence" of the people in their representatives.[129]

Before the bar of the house, Keteltas admitted authorship of the offensive articles. The Assembly promptly and without debate found him guilty of "a misdemeanor and contempt of the authority of this House." When Keteltas refused to humble himself by admitting his wrong and asking pardon, the house immediately ordered him jailed.[130]

The case presented a perfect opportunity for a libertarian argument in defense of Keteltas. The issue was raised in precisely the right terms by Representative John Bird, a Republican member of the Assembly, who demanded: "Shall we attempt to prevent citizens from thinking? from giving their opinion on acts of the legislature? Shall we stop freedom of the press?"[131] Bird's questions were not only asked in vain; they were virtually unique, almost eccentric, certainly ignored or forgotten, and unsupported by any argument in development of the theme. Keteltas became a popular hero among the Jeffersonian faithful in New York, and his case became a *cause célèbre*. Yet freedom of the press and the right of the citizen to criticize his government played no part in the ex-

---

[129] I am indebted to Professor Alfred Young for bringing the Keteltas case to my attention, and for permitting me to read his unpublished dissertation, "The Democratic-Republican Movement in New York State, 1788–1797" (1958), which discusses the case at pp. 713–751. See also *Journal of the Votes and Proceedings of the General Assembly of New York*, 19th Sess., March 8, 1796, and *Greenleaf's New York Journal and Patriotic Register*, March 11, 1796.

[130] *Ibid.*

[131] *Greenleaf's New York Journal*, March 11, 1796.

tensive argument in Keteltas' behalf. Not even Keteltas himself, an experienced politician and lawyer, spoke to the issue, although while in prison he published five articles protesting the "unconstitutional, tyrannical, and illegal" proceedings of the Assembly.[132]

In the last article he discoursed at length on "freedom of speech," but did so exclusively in the context of a discussion of parliamentary privilege. That is, he spoke only of the right of the legislator's freedom of debate. Not once did he allude to his own right, or that of the people, to debate public matters—let alone have the same scope of freedom of political expression as members of the house. His defense was based on the narrow argument that he had not breached any of the privileges of the house and that the house could not lawfully deprive any citizen of his liberty without benefit of grand-jury proceedings and trial by jury. An anonymous supporter, signing himself "Camillus Junius" after a hero of the ancient Roman Republic, trenchantly put forth the same argument in the press.[133] The assault on the power of the Assembly to punish citizens for alleged breaches of privilege was surely a significant libertarian action. But equally revealing was the total absence of discussion of Representative Bird's questions about the right of the citizen to criticize his government.

Keteltas, who was freed on a writ of habeas corpus as soon as the legislature ended its session, later brought an unsuccessful suit for false imprisonment against the speaker of the house. The Assembly supported its speaker by a vote of 88 to 1, and the court ruled against Keteltas. A "Spectator" concluded his report of the trial by remarking: ". . . the freedom of the press is taken away, and personal liberty is no longer secure in the state of New York."[134] Other than Bird's, this was

---

[132] *The Argus, or Greenleaf's New Daily Advertiser,* April 4, 5, 7, 8, and 12, 1796.

[133] *Ibid.,* March 15 and April 6, 1796. See this volume, Document 25.

[134] *The Time Piece* (New York), December 22, 1797.

the only reference to freedom of the press that emerged from the case.

Thus, as late as 1794 and 1796, as the Congressional debates on self-created societies and the Keteltas case reveal, American libertarian theory was in a state of arrested development on the crucial question of the right of the citizen to criticize his government without being accused of a verbal political crime. "Freedom of the press" was invoked, to be sure, but the phrase was not self-defining, its meaning was neither self-evident nor static, and its mere utterance *ex vi termini* was neither a sovereign remedy nor adequate to support a libertarian theory. Pithy slogans and glittering generalities reflected sentiment and perhaps a principle, but not a theory. Bird's sloganeering, Keteltas' evasions, Nicholas' inconsistency, and Madison's ultimate reliance on the federal principle together with Milton's truth-shall-prevail-over-error, can scarcely be compared, for libertarian qualities, freshness, or boldness, to the arguments of Cato or Alexander, let alone Robert Hall.

VIII

Then, in 1798, there was a sudden breakthrough in American libertarian thought on freedom of political expression. The change was abrupt, radical, and transforming, like that caused by an underwater volcano erupting its lava upwards from the ocean floor to form a new island. The Sedition Act, which was a thrust in the direction of a single-party press and a monolithic party-system, triggered the libertarian surge among the Republicans. The result was the emergence of a new peak of libertarian thought, jutting out of a stagnant Blackstonian sea.

The Federalists in 1798 believed that true freedom of the press would benefit if truth—*their* truth—were the measure of freedom. Their infamous Sedition Act was, in the words of Gilbert and Sullivan, the true embodiment of everything excellent. It was, that is, the very epitome of libertarian thought since the time of Zenger's case—indicating that American libertarianism went from Zengerian principles to the Sedition Act in a single degeneration. Everything that the libertarians had ever demanded was incorporated in the Sedition Act: a requirement that criminal intent be shown; the power of the jury to decide whether the accused's statement was libelous as a matter of law as well as of fact; and truth as a defense, which was an innovation not accepted in England until 1843.[135] By every standard the Sedition Act was a great victory for libertarian principles of freedom of the press—except that libertarian standards abruptly changed, because the Republicans immediately recognized a Pyrrhic victory.

The Sedition Act provoked them to develop a new libertarian theory. It began to emerge when Congressmen Gallatin, John Nicholas, Nathaniel Macon, and Edward Livingston argued against the enactment of the Sedition bill.[136] It was further developed by defense counsel, most notably George Blake, in Sedition Act prosecutions.[137] It reached its most reflective and systematic expression in tracts and books that are now unfortunately rare and little known, even by historians. The main body of original Republican thought on the scope, meaning, and rationale of the First Amendment is to be found in George Hay's tract, *An Essay on the Liberty of the Press;*[138] in Madi-

---

[135] Sir James Fitzjames Stephen, *A History of the Criminal Law of England* (London: Macmillan and Co., 1883), II, 383; and Frank Thayer, *Legal Control of the Press* (Brooklyn, N.Y.: Foundation Press, 1950), pp. 17, 25, and 178.

[136] *Annals of Congress,* 5th Cong., 2nd Sess., pp. 2102–2111, 2139–2143, 2153–2154, and 2160–2166.

[137] *Independent Chronicle* (Boston), issues of March 4–7, April 8–11, April 11–15, and April 29–May 2, 1799, reporting the trial of Abijah Adams, editor of the *Chronicle,* for seditious libel against the state legislature of Massachusetts.

[138] "Hortensius," *An Essay on the Liberty of the Press. Respectfully Inscribed to the Republican Printers Throughout the United States* (Philadelphia: 1799), 51 pp. Reprinted in Richmond, Va., in 1803 by

son's *Report* on the Virginia Resolutions for the Virginia House of Delegates;[139] in the book, *A Treatise Concerning Political Enquiry, and the Liberty of the Press,* by Tunis Wortman of New York;[140] in John Thomson's book, *An Enquiry, Concerning the Liberty, and Licentiousness of the Press;*[141] and in St. George Tucker's appendix to his edition of Blackstone's *Commentaries,*[142] a most significant place for the repudiation of Blackstone on the liberty of the press. Of these works, Wortman's philosophical book is pre-eminent; it is an American masterpiece, the only equivalent on this side of the Atlantic to Milton and Mill.

Samuel Pleasants, Jr., but set in small type, in an edition of 30 pages. The latter edition is cited here. Hay also published, in 1803, a different tract with a similar title, *An Essay on the Liberty of the Press, Shewing, That the Requisition of Security for Good Behaviour from Libellers, is Perfectly Compatible with the Constitution and Laws of Virginia* (Richmond, Va.: Samuel Pleasants, Jr., 1803), 48 pp. See this volume, Document 27.

139 The *Report* originally appeared as a tract of over 80 pages. The copy in the Langdell Treasure Room, Harvard Law Library, is bound together with the 1799 issue of Hay's *Essay.* Madison wrote the *Report* at the close of 1799; it was adopted on January 11, 1800, by the Virginia legislature, which immediately published it. It is reproduced in *The Debates in the Several State Conventions,* ed. Elliot, IV, 546–580, under the title, "Madison's Report on the Virginia Resolutions. . . . Report of the Committee to whom were referred the Communications of various States, relative to the Resolutions of the last General Assembly of this State, concerning the Alien and Sedition Laws." The *Report* is also available in *The Writings of James Madison,* ed. Hunt, VI, 341–406. The edition cited here is *The Virginia Report of 1799–1800, Touching the Alien and Sedition Laws; together with the Virginia Resolutions of December 21, 1798, The Debates and Proceedings thereon, in the House of Delegates in Virginia* (Richmond, Va.: J. W. Randolph, 1850); see pp. 189–237. This is a book of great value for its inclusion of the Virginia debates on the Sedition Act, at pp. 22–161. While those debates added little to the debates of the House of Representatives, the remarks of Republican speakers constitute another example of the new libertarianism. See this volume, Document 28.

140 (New York: 1800), 296 pp. See this volume, Document 29.

141 (New York: 1801), 84 pp. See this volume, Document 30.

142 (5 vols.; Philadelphia: 1803), Vol. I, Part II, Note G, pp. 11–30 of Appendix. See this volume, Document 31.

The new libertarians abandoned the strait-jacketing doctrines of Blackstone and the common law, including the recent concept of a federal common law of crimes. They scornfully denounced the no-prior-restraints definition. Said Madison: ". . . this idea of the freedom of the press can never be admitted to be the American idea of it," because a law inflicting penalties would have the same effect as a law authorizing a prior restraint. "It would seem a mockery to say that no laws shall be passed preventing publications from being made, but that laws might be passed for punishing them in case they should be made."[143] As Hay put it, the "British definition" meant that a man might be jailed or even put to death for what he published, provided that no notice was taken of him before he published.[144]

The old yardstick for measuring the scope of freedom was also rejected by the new libertarians. "Liberty" of the press, for example, had always been differentiated from its "licentiousness," which was the object of the criminal law's sanctions. "Truth" and "facts" had always divided the realm of lawfulness from "falsehoods," and a similar distinction had been made between "good motives" and "criminal intent." All such distinctions were now discarded, on the ground that they did not distinguish and therefore were not meaningful standards that might guide a jury or a court in judging an alleged verbal crime. The term "licentiousness," wrote Thomson, "is destitute of any meaning"; it was used, according to him, by those who wished "nobody to enjoy the Liberty of the Press but such as were of their own opinion."[145] The term "malice," in Wortman's view, was invariably confused with mistaken zeal or

---

[143] *The Virginia Report of 1799–1800*, p. 220.

[144] *An Essay on the Liberty of the Press* (1803 ed. of 1799 tract), p. 29; and *An Essay on the Liberty of the Press, Shewing . . .* (1803), p. 32. See note 138, above.

[145] *An Enquiry, Concerning the Liberty, and Licentiousness of the Press*, pp. 6–7.

prejudice.[146] It was merely an inference drawn from the supposed evil tendency of the publication itself, and just a further means of punishing the excitement of unfavorable sentiments against the government even when the people's contempt of the government was richly deserved. The punishment of "malice," or intent to defame the government, concluded Madison, necessarily struck at the right of free discussion, because critics intended to excite unfavorable sentiments.[147] Finding criminality in the tendency of words was merely an attempt to erect public "tranquility . . . upon the ruins of Civil Liberty," wrote Wortman.[148]

The wholesale abandonment of the common law's limitations on the press was accompanied by a withering onslaught against the constrictions and subjectivity of Zengerian principles. The Sedition Act, Hay charged, "appears to be directed against falsehood and malice only; in fact . . . there are many truths, important to society, which are not susceptible of that full, direct, and positive evidence, which alone can be exhibited before a court and a jury."[149] If, argued Gallatin, the Administration prosecuted a citizen for his opinion that the Sedition Act itself was unconstitutional, would not a jury, composed of the friends of that Administration, find the opinion "ungrounded, or, in other words, false and scandalous, and its publication malicious? And by what kind of argument or evidence, in the present temper of parties, could the accused convince them that his opinions were true?"[150] The truth of opinions, the new libertarians concluded, could not be proved. Allowing "truth" as a defense and thinking it to be a protection for freedom, Thomson declared, made as much sense as letting

---

[146] *A Treatise Concerning Political Enquiry*, p. 173.

[147] *The Virginia Report of 1799–1800*, pp. 226–227.

[148] *A Treatise Concerning Political Enquiry*, p. 253.

[149] *An Essay on the Liberty of the Press* (1803 ed. of 1799 tract), p. 28.

[150] *Annals of Congress*, 5th Cong., 2nd Sess., p. 2162.

a jury decide which was "the most palatable food, agreeable drink, or beautiful color."[151] A jury, he asserted, could not give an impartial verdict in political trials. Madison agreed, commenting that the "baleful tendency" of prosecutions for seditious libel was "little diminished by the privilege of giving in evidence the truth of the matter contained in political writings."[152]

The renunciation of traditional concepts reached its climax in the assault on the idea that there was such a thing as a crime of seditious libel. That crime, Wortman concluded, could "never be reconciled to the genius and constitution of a Representative Commonwealth."[153] He and the others constructed a new libertarianism, genuinely radical because it broke sharply with the past and advocated an absolute freedom of political expression. One of the major tenets of this new libertarianism was that a free government cannot be criminally attacked by the opinions of its citizens. Hay, for example, insisted that freedom of the press, like chastity, was either "absolute"[154] or did not exist. Abhorring the very concept of verbal political crimes, he declared that a citizen should have a right to "say everything which his passions suggest; he may employ all his time, and all his talents, if he is wicked enough to do so, in speaking against the government matters that are false, scandalous and malicious,"[155] and yet he should be "safe within the sanctuary of the press" even if he "condemns the principle of republican institutions . . . censures the measures of our government, and every department and officer thereof, and ascribes the measures of the former, however salutary, and the conduct of the latter,

---

[151] *An Enquiry, Concerning the Liberty, and Licentiousness of the Press,* p. 68.

[152] *The Virginia Report of 1799–1800,* p. 226.

[153] *A Treatise Concerning Political Enquiry,* p. 262.

[154] *An Essay on the Liberty of the Press* (1803 ed. of 1799 tract), pp. 23–24.

[155] *Ibid.,* p. 25.

however upright, to the basest motives; even if he ascribes to them measures and acts, which never had existence; thus violating at once, every principle of decency and truth."[156]

In brief, the new libertarians advocated that only "injurious conduct," as manifested by "overt acts" or deeds, rather than words, should be criminally redressable.[157] They did not refine this proposition except to recognize that the law of libel should continue to protect private reputations against malicious falsehoods. They did not even recognize that under certain circumstances words may immediately and directly incite criminal acts.

This absolutist interpretation of the First Amendment was based on the now familiar, but then novel and democratic, theory that free government depends for its very existence and security on freedom of political discourse. The scope of the amendment, according to this theory, is determined by the nature of the government and its relationship to the people. Because the government is the people's servant, exists by their consent and for their benefit, and is constitutionally limited, responsible, and elective, it cannot, said Thomson, tell the citizen: "You shall not think this, or that upon certain subjects; or if you do, it is at your peril."[158] The concept of seditiousness can exist only in a relationship based on inferiority, when people are subjects rather than sovereigns and their criticism implies contempt of their master. "In the United States," Madison declared, "the case is altogether different."[159] Coercion or abridgment of unlimited political opinion, Wortman explained,

---

[156] *An Essay on the Liberty of the Press, Shewing* . . . (1803 tract), p. 29.

[157] Wortman, *A Treatise Concerning Political Enquiry,* pp. 140, 253; Thomson, *An Enquiry, Concerning the Liberty, and Licentiousness of the Press,* p. 79.

[158] *An Enquiry, Concerning the Liberty, and the Licentiousness of the Press,* p. 22.

[159] *The Virginia Report of 1799–1800,* p. 222.

would violate the very "principles of the social state"—by which he meant a government of the people.[160] Because such a government depended upon popular elections, all the new libertarians agreed that the widest possible latitude must be maintained to keep the electorate free, informed, and capable of making intelligent choices. The citizen's freedom of political expression had the same scope as the legislator's, and had the same reasons behind it.[161] That freedom might be dangerously abused, but the people, if exposed to every opinion, would decide men and measures wisely.

This brief summary of the new libertarianism barely does justice to its complexity and sophistication, but should at least suggest its boldness, originality, and democratic character. The new libertarianism developed, to be sure, as an expediency of self-defense on the part of a besieged political minority that was struggling to maintain its existence and its right to function unfettered. But the new libertarians established, virtually all at once and in nearly perfect form, a theory justifying the rights of individual expression and of opposition parties. That the Jeffersonians in power did not always adhere to their new principles does not diminish the enduring nobility and rightness of those principles. It proves only that the Jeffersonians set the highest standards of freedom for themselves and posterity. Their legacy was the idea that there is an indispensable condition for the development of free men in a free society: the state must be bitted and bridled by a bill of rights that is to be construed in the most generous terms and whose protections are not to be the playthings of momentary majorities. That legacy deepened and enriched American libertarian theory, but it did not surmount the resistance of the law. Ultimate vic-

---

[160] *A Treatise Concerning Political Enquiry*, p. 29.

[161] Thomson, *An Enquiry, Concerning the Liberty, and Licentiousness of the Press*, pp. 20, 22; Hay, *An Essay on the Liberty of the Press* (1803 ed. of 1799 tract), p. 26.

tory in the courts and statutes belonged to Alexander Hamilton's restatement of Zengerian principles.[162]

Hamilton, a supporter of the Sedition Act and of prosecutions for criminal libel, believed that the law of libel should be governed by the principles of the Zenger case, in order to protect the legitimate freedom of the press. In 1804 he was permitted by his Jeffersonian opponents in New York, who were then in power, to make political capital and legal history by advocating these old principles. The state indicted Harry Croswell, an obscure Federalist editor, for the common-law crime of seditious libel against President Jefferson. Croswell's crime was his publishing of the accusation that Jefferson had paid to have Washington denounced as a traitor and Adams as an incendiary. Chief Justice Morgan Lewis, a Jeffersonian, refused Croswell the opportunity of introducing evidence to prove the truth of his statements. In instructing the jury, Lewis told the jurors that their only duty was to determine whether the defendant had in fact published the statements as charged; that they must leave to the court, as a matter of law, the determination of the statements' libelous character. Lewis, in other words, charged the jury that the law of New York was the law as laid down by Chief Justice DeLancey in the Zenger case.

On the appeal of Croswell's conviction, before the highest court of the state, Alexander Hamilton played the role of Andrew Hamilton, eloquently championing the cause of freedom of the press. That freedom, he said (in words that were even more restrictive than those of his precursor or of the Sedition Act), "consists in the right to publish, with impunity, truth, with good motives, for justifiable ends, though reflecting on government, magistracy, or individuals." The Sedition Act itself did not require proof of "good motives, for justifiable ends," but Alexander Hamilton's position, of course, seemed a

---

162 See *People* v. *Croswell*, 3 Johnson's (N.Y.) Cases 336 (1804), reprinted in this volume, Document 59.

shining standard of libertarianism when compared with the reactionary views of Chief Justice Lewis—or of the prosecutor, Attorney General Ambrose Spencer, another Jeffersonian. Spencer argued from Blackstone (not Tucker's version), and declared that a libel, even if true, was punishable because of its dangerous tendency. The former prosecutor became a member of the Supreme Court of Judicature by the time it decided the case. Had Spencer not been ineligible to participate in the decision, the repressive opinion re-expressed by Chief Justice Lewis would have commanded a majority. Instead, the court divided evenly, two against two. The opinion of Judge James Kent expressed Hamilton's position.

In the following year, 1805, the state legislature enacted a bill allowing the jury to decide the criminality of an alleged libel and permitting truth as a defense, if published "with good motives and for justifiable ends." It is this standard that has prevailed in the United States.

Selected Bibliography

BOORSTIN, DANIEL J. *The Americans: the Colonial Experience.* New York: Random House, 1958. Part Twelve, "A Conservative Press," is the best short treatment of the subject.

CHAFEE, ZECHARIAH, JR. *Free Speech in the United States.* Cambridge, Mass.: Harvard University Press, 1948. An eloquent analysis of enduring value by a great libertarian lawyer; the foremost modern account.

CHENERY, WILLIAM L. *Freedom of the Press.* New York: Harcourt, Brace and Co., 1955. An outstanding discussion of contemporary concepts and problems, with historical background.

CLARKE, MARY PATTERSON. *Parliamentary Privilege in the American Colonies.* New Haven, Conn.: Yale University Press, 1943. The only history of the subject.

DE ARMOND, ANNA JANNEY. *Andrew Bradford, Colonial Journalist.* Newark, Del.: University of Delaware Press, 1949. A readable biography of the best colonial printer.

DUNIWAY, CLYDE AUGUSTUS. *The Development of Freedom of the Press in Massachusetts.* New York: Longmans, Green & Co., 1906. A model scholarly monograph.

HOCKING, WILLIAM ERNEST. *Freedom of the Press: A Framework of Principle.* Chicago: The University of Chicago Press, 1947. A judicious and reflective analysis by an eminent philosopher.

HUDON, EDWARD G. *Freedom of Speech and Press in America.* Washington, D.C.: Public Affairs Press, 1963. A legalistic discussion from a liberal viewpoint by a distinguished law librarian.

JACOBSON, DAVID L., ed. *The English Libertarian Heritage: From the Writings of John Trenchard and Thomas Gordon in The Independent Whig and Cato's Letters.* Indianapolis,

Ind.: The Bobbs-Merrill Company, Inc., 1965. The first re-printing of *Cato's Letters* since the eighteenth century, ably edited, with an excellent introduction.

KATZ, STANLEY NIDER, ed. James Alexander. *A Brief Narrative of the Case and Trial of John Peter Zenger, Printer of the New-York Weekly Journal.* Cambridge, Mass.: The Belknap Press of Harvard University Press, 1963. The most recent edition of the trial, in modernized English, superbly an-notated, with many other related documents and a first-rate introduction.

KONVITZ, MILTON R. *Fundamental Liberties of a Free People: Religion, Speech, Press, Assembly.* Ithaca, N.Y.: Cornell Uni-versity Press, 1957. An analysis of the contemporary constitu-tional law on the subject; the best work since Chafee.

LEVY, LEONARD W. *Legacy of Suppression: Freedom of Speech and Press in Early American History.* Cambridge, Mass.: The Belknap Press of Harvard University Press, 1960. Re-printed in 1963, with a new introduction, by Harper Torch-books.

————. *Jefferson and Civil Liberties: the Darker Side.* Cam-bridge, Mass.: The Belknap Press of Harvard University Press, 1963.

MEIKLEJOHN, ALEXANDER. *Free Speech and Its Relation to Self Government.* New York: Harper & Brothers, 1948. An un-sophisticated but already classic statement in the tradition of Milton, Wortman, Thomson, and Mill.

MILLER, JOHN C. *Crisis in Freedom: The Alien and Sedition Acts.* Boston: Little, Brown and Company, 1952. A brief and popularly written but penetrating study.

MOTT, FRANK LUTHER. *American Journalism: A History of Newspapers in the United States, 1690–1940.* New York: The Macmillan Company, 1941. A useful, encyclopedic account.

NELSON, HAROLD L., ed., *Freedom of the Press from Hamilton to the Warren Court.* Indianapolis, Ind.: The Bobbs-Merrill Company, Inc., 1966. An anthology, following the present one in chronological coverage, that is a work of creative scholarship. An original collection of the utmost value for a study of the subject.

RUTHERFURD, LIVINGSTON. *John Peter Zenger, His Press, His Trial, and a Bibliography of Zenger Imprints. Also a Reprint of the First Edition of the Trial.* New York: Dodd, Mead & Company, 1904. Includes the definitive text of the trial, with a sound and still quite useful introduction.

SCHLESINGER, ARTHUR M. *Prelude to Independence: The Newspaper War on Britain, 1764–1776.* New York: Alfred A. Knopf, 1958. The best account of the press, its propaganda activities, and its exercise of freedom, by one of the nation's leading historians.

SCHOFIELD, HENRY. "Freedom of the Press in the United States," in Schofield's *Essays on Constitutional Law and Equity.* 2 vols. Boston: Chipman Law Publishing Co., 1921. Vol. II, pp. 510–571. An influential account by a legal scholar.

SCHUYLER, LIVINGSTON ROWE. *The Liberty of the Press in the American Colonies before the Revolutionary War.* New York: T. Whittaker, 1905. A brief and superficial account.

SIEBERT, FREDERICK S. *Freedom of the Press in England, 1476–1776.* Urbana, Ill.: University of Illinois Press, 1952. Easily the best book on the subject.

SMITH, JAMES MORTON. *Freedom's Fetters: The Alien and Sedition Laws and American Civil Liberties.* Ithaca, N.Y.: Cornell University Press, 1956. The definitive work.

THOMAS, ISAIAH. *The History of Printing in America.* 2 vols. Worcester, Mass.: Isaiah Thomas, Jr., 1810. A very useful, if antiquated, account by one of the outstanding Revolutionary printers.

Freedom of the Press
from Zenger to Jefferson

EARLY AMERICAN LIBERTARIAN THEORIES

PART ONE

The Formative Period:
"Cato" and Zenger

Ben Franklin's Credo for Colonial Printers

Benjamin Franklin, a giant among American colonial printers and thinkers, was not quite the champion of a free press that he is reputed to have been. Nor did he contribute anything to libertarian theory. His few essays on freedom of the press offer a platitude in every literary longitude. His essays were derivative, flaccid, and unanalytical, almost anti-intellectual. Yet Franklin was an admirer of *Cato's Letters* and first introduced American readers to the splendid essay on "Freedom of Speech." In 1731 Franklin's "most influential statement on freedom of the press" appeared in his *Pennsylvania Gazette*. In the view of Clinton Rossiter, the statement is "worth quoting at length, for it is an accurate representation of the principles of a free press which governed popular thinking in eighteenth-century America." Yet Franklin simply contended that the press should express all opinions, that truth would best error, and that vice and immorality ought not to be countenanced. That Franklin practiced freedom of the press is undoubted, but his celebrated "Apology for Printers," reprinted here, hardly presented a definition of a philosophy of a free press. He wrote as if oblivious to the problem of prosecutions for seditious libel or breach of parliamentary privilege, or any of the other problems connected with freedom of the press. His own paper habitually presented diverse views on many subjects, but reported the activities of the Pennsylvania Assembly with discretion. Franklin, after all, was the official printer of the province; dependent upon the legislature's support, he was its clerk for many years. It is not surprising, then, that his *Gazette* sided with the Assembly when it prosecuted its critics for seditious libel in 1758; Franklin himself, as the Assembly's London agent, defended its actions before the Privy Council. As postmaster in Philadelphia, Franklin was not averse to delivering his own newspaper at public expense while denying the mails to his competitor. If his "Apology for Printers" was as influential and representative as reputed, it simply shows how superficial was American thinking on this subject.

1. AN APOLOGY FOR PRINTERS

Being frequently censur'd and condemn'd by different Persons for printing Things which they say ought not to be printed, I have sometimes thought it might be necessary to make a standing Apology for my self, and publish it once a Year, to be read upon all Occasions of that Nature. Much Business has hitherto hindered the execution of this Design; but having very lately given extraordinary Offence by printing an Advertisement with a certain N.B. at the End of it, I find an Apology more particularly requisite at this Juncture, tho' it happens when I have not yet Leisure to write such a Thing in the proper Form, and can only in a loose manner throw those Considerations together which should have been the Substance of it.

I request all who are angry with me on the Account of printing things they don't like, calmly to consider these following Particulars.

"An Apology for Printers," *The Pennsylvania Gazette* (Philadelphia), June 10, 1731, reprinted in *The Writings of Benjamin Franklin*, ed. Albert Henry Smyth (10 vols.; New York: The Macmillan Company, 1905–1907), II, 172–179.

1. That the Opinions of Men are almost as various as their Faces; an Observation general enough to become a common Proverb, *So many Men so many Minds.*

2. That the Business of Printing has chiefly to do with Mens Opinions; most things that are printed tending to promote some, or oppose others.

3. That hence arises the peculiar Unhappiness of that Business, which other Callings are no way liable to; they who follow Printing being scarce able to do any thing in their way of getting a Living, which shall not probably give Offence to some, and perhaps to many; whereas the Smith, the Shoemaker, the Carpenter, or the Man of any other Trade, may work indifferently for People of all Persuasions, without offending any of them: and the Merchant may buy and sell with Jews, Turks, Hereticks and Infidels of all sorts, and get Money by every one of them, without giving Offence to the most orthodox, of any sort; or suffering the least Censure or Ill will on the Account from any Man whatever.

4. That it is as unreasonable in any one Man or Set of Men to expect to be pleas'd with every thing that is printed, as to think that nobody ought to be pleas'd but themselves.

5. Printers are educated in the Belief, that when Men differ in Opinion, both Sides ought equally to have the Advantage of being heard by the Publick; and that when Truth and Error have fair Play, the former is always an overmatch for the latter: Hence they chearfully serve all contending Writers that pay them well, without regarding on which side they are of the Question in Dispute.

6. Being thus continually employ'd in serving both Parties, Printers naturally acquire a vast Unconcernedness as to the right or wrong Opinions contain'd in what they print; regarding it only as the Matter of their daily labour: They print things full of Spleen and Animosity, with the utmost Calmness and Indifference, and without the least Ill-will to the Persons reflected on; who nevertheless unjustly think the Printer as

much their Enemy as the Author, and join both together in their Resentment.

7. That it is unreasonable to imagine Printers approve of every thing they print, and to censure them on any particular thing accordingly; since in the way of their Business they print such great variety of things opposite and contradictory. It is likewise as unreasonable what some assert, "That Printers ought not to print any Thing but what they approve;" since if all of that Business should make such a Resolution, and abide by it, an End would thereby be put to Free Writing, and the World would afterwards have nothing to read but what happen'd to be the Opinions of Printers.

8. That if all Printers were determin'd not to print any thing till they were sure it would offend no body, there would be very little printed.

9. That if they sometimes print vicious or silly things not worth reading, it may not be because they approve such things themselves, but because the People are so viciously and corruptly educated that good things are not encouraged. I have known a very numerous Impression of Robin Hood's Songs go off in this Province at 2s. per Book, in less than a Twelve-month; when a small Quantity of David's Psalms (an excellent Version) have lain upon my Hands above twice the Time.

10. That notwithstanding what might be urg'd in behalf of a Man's being allow'd to do in the Way of his Business whatever he is paid for, yet Printers do continually discourage the Printing of great Numbers of bad things, and stifle them in the Birth. I my self have constantly refused to print anything that might countenance Vice, or promote Immorality; tho' by complying in such Cases with the corrupt Taste of the Majority I might have got much Money. I have also always refus'd to print such things as might do real Injury to any Person, how much soever I have been solicited, and tempted with Offers of Great Pay; and how much soever I have by refusing got the Ill-will of those who would have employ'd me. I have hitherto

fallen under the Resentment of large Bodies of Men, for refusing absolutely to print any of their Party or Personal Reflections. In this Manner I have made my self many Enemies,
and the constant Fatigue of denying is almost insupportable.
But the Publick being unacquainted with all this, whenever
the poor Printer happens either through Ignorance or much
Persuasion, to do any thing that is generally thought worthy
of Blame, he meets with no more Friendship or Favour on the
above Account, than if there were no Merit in't at all. Thus, as
Waller says,

> Poets lose half the Praise they would have got
> Were it but known what they discretely blot;

Yet are censur'd for every bad Line found in their Works with
the utmost Severity.

I come now to the Particular Case of the N.B. above
mention'd, about which there has been more Clamour against
me, than ever before on any other Account. —In the Hurry of
other Business an Advertisement was brought to me to be
printed; it signified that such a Ship lying at such a Wharff,
would sail for Barbadoes in such a Time, and that Freighters
and Passengers might agree with the Captain at such a Place;
so far is what's common: But at the Bottom this odd Thing
was added, "N.B. No Sea Hens nor Black Gowns will be admitted on any Terms." I printed it, and receiv'd my Money;
and the Advertisement was stuck up round the Town as usual.
I had not so much Curiosity at that time as to enquire the
Meaning of it, nor did I in the least imagine it would give so
much Offence. Several good Men are very angry with me on
this Occasion; they are pleas'd to say I have too much Sense
to do such things ignorantly; that if they were Printers they
would not have done such a thing on any Consideration; that
it could proceed from nothing but my abundant Malice
against Religion and the Clergy. They therefore declare they
will not take any more of my Papers, nor have any farther

Dealings with me; but will hinder me of all the Custom they can. All this is very hard!

I believe it had been better if I had refused to print the said Advertisement. However, 'tis done, and cannot be revok'd. I have only the following few Particulars to offer, some of them in my behalf, by way of Mitigation, and some not much to the Purpose; but I desire none of them may be read when the Reader is not in a very good Humour.

1. That I really did it without the least Malice, and imagin'd the N.B. was plac'd there only to make the Advertisement star'd at, and more generally read.

2. That I never saw the Word Sea-Hens before in my Life; nor have I yet ask'd the meaning of it; and tho' I had certainly known that Black Gowns in that place signified the Clergy of the Church of England, yet I have that confidence in the generous good Temper of such of them as I know, as to be well satisfied such a trifling mention of their Habit gives them no Disturbance.

3. That most of the Clergy in this and the neighbouring Provinces, are my Customers, and some of them my very good Friends; and I must be very malicious indeed, or very stupid, to print this thing for a small Profit, if I had thought it would have given them just Cause of Offence.

4. That if I had much Malice against the Clergy, and withal much Sense; 'tis strange I never write or talk against the Clergy myself. Some have observed that 'tis a fruitful Topic, and the easiest to be witty upon of all others; yet I appeal to the Publick that I am never guilty this way, and to all my Acquaintances as to my Conversation.

5. That if a Man of Sense had Malice enough to desire to injure the Clergy, this is the foolishest Thing he could possibly contrive for that Purpose.

6. That I got Five Shillings by it.

7. That none who are angry with me would have given me so much to let it alone.

8. That if all the People of different Opinions in this Province would engage to give me as much for not printing things they don't like, as I can get by printing them, I should probably live a very easy Life; and if all Printers were everywhere so dealt by, there would be very little printed.

9. That I am oblig'd to all who take my Paper, and am willing to think they do it out of meer Friendship. I only desire they would think the same when I deal with them. I thank those who leave off, that they have taken it so long. But I beg they would not endeavour to dissuade others, for that will look like Malice.

10. That 'tis impossible any Man should know what he would do if he was a Printer.

11. That notwithstanding the Rashness and Inexperience of Youth, which is most likely to be prevail'd with to do things that ought not to be done; yet I have avoided printing such Things as usually give Offence either to Church or State, more than any Printer that has followed the Business in this Province before.

12. And lastly, That I have printed above a Thousand Advertisements which made not the least mention of *Sea-Hens* or *Black Gowns;* and this being the first Offence, I have the more Reason to expect Forgiveness.

I take leave to conclude with an old Fable, which some of my Readers have heard before, and some have not.

"A certain well-meaning Man and his Son, were travelling towards a Market Town, with an Ass which they had to sell. The Road was bad; and the old Man therefore rid, but the Son went a-foot. The first Passenger they met, asked the Father if he was not ashamed to ride by himself, and suffer the poor Lad to wade along thro' the Mire; this induced him to take up his Son behind him: He had not travelled far, when he met others, who said, they are two unmerciful Lubbers to get both on the Back of that poor Ass, in such a deep Road. Upon this the old Man gets off, and let his Son ride alone. The next they met called the Lad a graceless, rascally young Jackanapes, to ride in that Manner thro' the Dirt, while his aged Father trudged along on Foot; and they said the old Man was a Fool, for suffering it. He then bid his Son come down, and walk with him, and they travell'd on leading the Ass by the Halter; 'till they met another Company, who called them a Couple of senseless Blockheads, for going both on Foot in such a dirty Way, when they had an empty Ass with them, which they might ride upon. The old Man could bear no longer; My Son, said he, it grieves me much that we cannot please all these People. Let me throw the Ass over the next Bridge, and be no further troubled with him."

Had the old Man been seen acting this last Resolution, he would probably have been called a Fool for troubling himself about the different Opinions of all that were pleas'd to find Fault with him: Therefore, tho' I have a Temper almost as complying as his, I intend not to imitate him in this last Particular. I consider the Variety of Humors among Men, and despair of pleasing every Body; yet I shall not therefore leave off Printing. I shall continue my Business. I shall not burn my Press and melt my Letters.

Zenger's Journal *Presents "Cato"*

The immense popularity of *Cato's Letters* in America has been noted. The one hundred and thirty-eight essays by Trenchard and Gordon, originally published in London newspapers, were collected in four volumes that went through several editions, were imported by colonial booksellers, and were republished piecemeal in American newspapers. Stanch defenders of constitutional government and the rights of Englishmen, Trenchard and Gordon addressed themselves to such subjects as "The destructive Spirit of Arbitrary Power," "The Right and Capacity of the People to Judge Government," "Liberty proved to be the unalienable Right of all Mankind," "Civil Liberty produces all Civil Blessings," "Of the Restraints which ought to be laid upon publick Rulers," and "All Government proved to be instituted by Men, and only to intend the general Good of Men." In an age when newspapers were composed as much with the scissors and pastepot as with the pen, "Cato" was conscripted to serve a variety of American causes. "Cato's Letters," declared the *Massachusetts Spy* in 1771, as the situation with Britain worsened, "are now busily parceling out in almost every essay with which of late we are pretty plentifully served up." The process began half a century earlier, when Franklin reprinted "Of Freedom of Speech" after the Massachusetts legislature imprisoned his critical brother. Here is an abridgment of that same essay, followed by Cato's "Reflections upon Libelling" and "Discourse upon Libels," as reprinted by Zenger's *New-York Weekly Journal* when its editor was under attack by Governor Cosby's Administration.

2. OF FREEDOM OF SPEECH:

That the same is inseparable from Public Liberty

MR. ZENGER;

I beg you will give the following Sentiments of CATO, a Place in your weekly *Journal,* and you'll oblige one of your Subscribers.

Without Freedom of Thought, there can be no such Thing as Wisdom, and no such Thing as public Liberty, without Freedom of Speech, which is the Right of every Man, as far as by it he does not hurt or controul the Right of another: And this is the only Check it ought to suffer, and the only Bounds it ought to know.

This sacred Priviledge is so essential to free Governments, that the Security of Property, and the Freedom of Speech

---

Cato's Letters: Or, Essays on Liberty, Civil and Religious, No. 15, as reprinted in the *New-York Weekly Journal,* February 18, 1734.

always go together; and in those wretched Countries where a Man cannot call his Tongue his own he can scarce call any Thing else his own. Whoever would overthrow the Liberty of a Nation must begin by subduing the Freeness of Speech; a Thing terrible to publick Traytors.

This secret was so well known, to the Court of King *Charles* the First, that his wicked Ministry procured a Proclamation to forbid the People to talk of Parliaments, which those Traytors had laid aside.

To assert the undoubted Right of the Subject, and defend his Majesty's legal Prerogative, was called Disaffection and punished as Sedition.

That Men ought to speak well of their Governours, is true, while their Governours deserve to be well Spoken of, but to do publick Mischief without Hearing of it is only the Prerogative and Felicity of Tyranny [and] a free People will be shewing that they are so, by their Freedom of Speech.

The Administration of Government, is nothing else but the Attendance of the Trustees of the People upon the Interest, and Affairs of the People. And it is the Part and Business of the People, for whose sake alone all publick Matters are or ought to be transacted, to see whether they be well or ill transacted; so it is the Interest, and ought to be the Ambition of all honest Magistrates, to have their Deeds openly examined and publickly scanned.

Freedom of Speech is ever the Symptom as well as the Effect of good Government. In old *Rome* all was left to the Judgment and Pleasure of the People, who examined the public Proceedings with such Discretion, and censured those who administered them with such Equity and Mildness, that in the Space of three Hundred Years, not five public Ministers suffered unjustly. Indeed whenever the Commons proceeded to Violence, the great ones had been the Aggressors.

Guilt only dreads Liberty of Speech, which drags it out of its Lurking Holes and exposes its Deformity and horror to Day light; the best Princes have ever incouraged and promoted freedom of Speech [because] they know that upright Measures would defend themselves and that all upright Men would defend them. Tacitus speaking of the Reign of good Princes says with extasy, *A blessed Time, when you might think what you would, and Speak what you Thought.*

I doubt not but old *Spencer* and his Son who were the chief Ministers and Betrayers of *Edward* the Second would have been glad to have stopt the Mouths of all the honest Men in England. They dreaded to be called Traytors because they were Traytors. And I dare say Queen *Elizabeths Walsingham,* who deserved no Reproaches feared none. Misrepresentation, of publick Measures is easily over thrown by representing publick Measures truly; when they are honest they ought to be publickly known that they may be publickly commended; but if they are Knavish or Pernicious they ought to be publickly exposed in order to be publickly detested.

That King *James* was a Papist and a Tyrant, was only so far hurtfull to him, as it was true of him; and if the Earl of Strafford had not deserved to be Impeached he need not have feared a Bill of Attainder.

Freedom of Speech is the great Bulwark of Liberty; they prosper and Die together: And it is the Terror of Traytors and Oppressors and a Barrier against them [and] it produces excellent Writers and encourages Men of fine Genius.

All Ministers therefore who were Oppressors, or intended to be Oppressors, have been loud in their Complaints against Freedom of Speech and the Lycence of the Press; and always restrained or endeavour to restrain both [; and] in consequence of this they have browbeaten Writers and punished them violently, and against Law, and Burnt their Works; by all which they shewed how much Truth allarmed them and how much they were at Enmity with Truth.

Freedom of Speech therefore being of such infinite importance to the Preservation of Liberty; every one who loves

Liberty ought to encourage Freedom of Speech. The Defence of Liberty, is a noble and heavenly Office which can only be performed where Liberty is.

3. REFLECTIONS UPON LIBELLING

Mr. Zenger;

As Libeling seems at Present the Topick that is canvassed both at Court and among the People, I must beg you will insert in your weekly Journal, *the following Sentiment of* CATO, *upon that Subject, and you'll oblige*

Your Humble Servant, &c,

A Lible is not the less a Libel for being true, this may seem a Contradiction; but it is neither one in Law, or in common Sense. There are some Truths not fit to be told; where, for Example, the Discovery of a finall Fault may do mischief; or where the Discovery of a great Fault can do no good, there ought to be no discovery at all, and to make Faults where there are none is still worse.

But this Doctrine only holds true as to private and personal failings; and it is quite otherwise when the Crimes of Men come to Affect the Publick. Nothing ought to be so dear to us as our Country, and nothing ought to come in Competition with its Interests. Every crime against the publick, is a great crime, tho' there be some greater then others. Ignorance and Folly may be pleaded in Alleviation of private Offences; but when they come to be publick Offences, they loose all Benefit of such a Plea; we are then no longer to consider, to what Causes they are owing, but what Evils they may produce, and

---

Cato's Letters, No. 32, as reprinted in the *New-York Weekly Journal,* February 25 and March 4, 1734.

here we shall readily find, that Folly has overturned States, and private Interest been the parent of publick Confusion.

The exposing therefore of publick Wickedness, as it is a Duty which every Man owes to Truth and his Country, can never be a Libel in the Nature of Things; and they who call it so, make themselves no Complement; he who is affronted at the reading of the Ten Commandments would make the Decalogue a Libel, if he durst, but he Tempts us at the same Time to form a Judgment of his Life and Morals, not at all to his Advantage: Whoever calls publick and necessary Truths Libels, does apprise us of his own Character, and Arms us with Caution against his Designs.

I have long thought, that the World are very much mistaken in their Idea and Distinction of Libels, it has been hitherto generally understood, that there was no other Libels but those against Magistrates and those against private Men. Now to me there seems to be a Third sort of Libels, full as Destructive as any of the former can probably be, I mean Libels against the People. It was otherwise at Athens and Rome, where the particular Men, and even great Men, were often treated with much Freedom and Severity, when they deserved it; yet the People, the body of the People, were spoken of with the utmost Regard and Reverence. *The Sacred Priviledge of the People, the Inviolable Majesty of the People, the awful Authority of the People, and the unappealable Judgment of the People*, were phrases Common in these wise, great and free Cities.

Some will tell us, this is setting up the Mob for Statesmen, and for the censurers of States. The word Mob does not at all move me, on this Occasion, nor weaken the Ground I go upon, it is certain that the whole People, who are the publick, are the best Judges, whether Things go ill or well, with the publick. It is true they can't all of them see distant Dangers, nor watch the Motions nor guess the designs of neighbouring States: But every Cobler can Judge as well as a Statesman, whether he can fit peaceably in his Stall; whether he is paid for his Work; whether the Market where he buys his Victuals is well provided; and whether a Dragoon, or a parish Officer comes to him for his Taxes, if he pays any.

In short the People often Judge better than their Superiors, and have not so many Biasses to Judge wrong, and Politicians often rail at the People, chiefly because they have given the People occasion to rail: Those Ministers who cannot make the People their Friends, it is to be shrewdly suspected, do not deserve their Friendship.

I have indeed often wondered that the Inveighing against the Interest of the People, and calling their Liberty in Question, as has been and is commonly done amongst us, by old Knaves, and young Fools, has never been made an Express Crime.

I must own, I know not what Reason is if sapping and betraying the Liberties of a People be not Treason, in the Eternal and Original Nature of Things: Let it be remembered for whose sake Government is, or could be appointed, and then let it be considered, who are more to be regarded, the Governours, or the governed. They indeed owe one another mutual Duties; but if there are any·Transgressions committed, the Side that is most obliged ought Doubtless to bear the Most; and yet it is so far otherwise, that almost all over the Earth, the People for one Injury they do their Governors, receive Ten Thousand from them. Nay, in some Countries it is made Death and Damnation, not to bear all the Oppressions and Cruelties, which Men made Wanton by Power inflict upon those that gave it them.

The Truth is, if the People are suffered to keep their own, it is the most they Desire: But even this is a Happiness which in few Places falls to their Lot; they are frequently robbed by those whom they pay to protect them. I know it is a general Charge against the People, that they are *Turbulent, Restless, Fickle,* and *Unruly,* than which there can be nothing more untrue; for they are only so when they are made so, as for their being Turbulent, it is false, since there is scarce an Example in a 100 Years of any Peoples giving Governours any Uneasiness, till their Governours had made them uneasy: Nay, for the most Part, they bear many Evils without returning one, and seldom throw off their Burthens so long as they can stand under them.

Continuation of the Sentiments of CATO *begun in our last, and promised to be continued.*

But I'll return more directly to the Business of Lybels; as to Libels against Government, like all others, they are Base and Unlawful and often Mischievous; especially when Governments are impudently charged with Actions and Designs of which they are not guilty, it is certain, that we ought not to Enter into the private Vices or Weaknesses of Governours, any farther than their private Vices Enter into their publick Administration; and when they do, it will be impossible to stop Peoples Mouths. They will be provoked and shew that they are so, in spight of Art or Threat, if they suffer Hardships and Woe from the private Gratifications of their Superiors, from whom they have a Right to expect Ease and Happiness, and if they are disappointed, they will be apt to deal very freely with their Characters.

The Praise of well doing is the highest Reward that worthy and disinterested Men aim at, and it is villainous and ungrateful to rob them of it; and those that do it are Libellers and Slanderers, on the other Hand while Censure and Infamy attend evil Doers, it will be some restraint if not upon them, yet upon others, from following their Example: But if Men are ever suffered to do what they please without hearing of it, or being accountable for it, Liberty and Law will be lost, tho' their Names may remain. And whether acting wickedly with impunity, or speaking falsely with impunity, are likely to do most Hurt to humane Society and the peace of the World, I leave all the World to judge; common Equity says they both ought to be punished, tho' not both alike.

As long as there is such Things as Printing and Writing, there will be Libels: It is an evil Ariseing out of a much greater good, and as for those who are for locking up the Press, because it produces Monsters, they ought to consider, that so do the Sun and the Nile; and that it is something better for the World to bear some particular ill Conveniences arising from General Blessings, then to be wholly deprived of Fire and Water.

I must own, I would rather many Libels should Escape, than the liberty of the Press should be Infringed; yet no Man in England thinks worse of Libels than I do; especially such as bid open Defiance to the present Protestant Establishment.

It is commonly said, that no Nation in the World would suffer such Papers to come abroad as England suffers; which is only saying, that no Nation in the World enjoys the Liberty which England Enjoys. In Countries where there is no Liberty, there can be no ill Effects of it, no Body is punished at Constantinople for Lybelling; nor is there any Distinction there between the Liberty of the Press and the Licentiousness of the Press; a Distinction ever to be observed by Honest Men and Freemen.

4. DISCOURSE UPON LIBELS

Mr. Zenger;

As Naration seems at present what you Aim at, I send you one of Cato's *Letters, which was read in the House by* Lewis Morris, junr. *in the Course of his Argument upon a Motion being*

Cato's Letters, No. 100, as reprinted in the *New-York Weekly Journal*, December 9, 1734.

made, that the Request of the Council should be comply'd with, which Request appears in your Journal, No. LV. I beg you will insert it, and you'll oblige your humble Servant.

Sir.

I Intend in this, and my next Letter, to write a Dissertation upon Libels, which are Liberties assumed by private Men, to Judge of, and censure the Actions of their Superiors, or such as have Possession of Power and Dignities. When Persons of no superior Merit to the rest of their fellow Subjects, came to be possessed of Advantages, by means which for the most part, they condemned in another Situation of Fortune, they often have grown upon a sudden, to think themselves different Species of Mankind, [and] they took it into their Heads to call themselves the Government, and thought others had nothing to do but to sit still, Act as they bid them, and follow their Motions; [they] were unwilling to be interrupted in the Progress of their Ambition and of making their private Fortunes by such ways as they could best and soonest make them; and consequently have call'd every Opposition to their wild and ravenous Schemes and every attempt to preserve the Peoples right, by the odious Names of Sedition and Faction, and charged them with principles and Practices inconsistent with the safety of all Government.

This Liberty has been approved or condemned by all Men, and all parties, in Proportion as they were advantaged, or annoy'd by it: When they were in power, they were unwilling to have their Actions scann'd and censur'd, and cry'd out, that such Licence ought not to be borne and tolerated in any well constituted commonwealth; And when they suffer'd under the weight of Power, they thought it very hard not to have been allowed the Liberty to utter their Groans, and to alleviate their pain, by venting some Part of it in Complaints; and it is certain, there are Benefits and Mischiefs on both sides the Question.

What are usually called Libels, undoubtedly keep great Men

in Awe, and are some check upon their Behaviour by shewing them the Deformity of their Actions, as well as warning other People to be upon their Guard against Oppression; and if there was no further harm in them, then in personally attacking those who too often deserve it, I think the Advantages such Persons receive, will fully attone for the mischiefs they suffer. But I confess that Libels may some Times, though very rarely foment popular and perhaps causeless Discontents, blast and obstruct the best Measures, and now and then promote Insurections and Rebellions; but these latter mischiefs are much seldomer produced than the former Benefits; for power has so many advantages, so many gifts and allurements to bribe those who bow to it, besides the constant Reverence and Superstition ever paid to greatness, [splendid] Equipage, and the shew of Wisdom, as well as the natural desire all or most Men have to live in quiet, and the dread they have of publick disturbances, that I think I may safely affirm, much more is to be feared from flattering great Men, than detracting from them.

However, 'tis to be wished that both could be prevented; but since that is not in the Nature of Things, whilst Men have desires or Resentments, we are next to consider how to prevent the great abuse of it, and, as far as human prudence can direct, preserve the Advantages of Liberty of Speech, and Liberty of Writing, (which preserves all other Liberties,) without giving more indulgence to Detraction than is necessary to secure the other; for 'tis certainly of much less consequence to Mankind, that an innocent Man should be now and then aspersed, than that all Men should be enslaved.

Many Methods have been tried to Remedy this evil: In Turky, and the Eastern Monarchies, all Printing is forbid; which does it with a Witness; for if there can be no Printing at all, there can be no Libels Printed; and by the same Reason there ought to be no Talking, lest People should talk Treason, Blasphemy or Nonsense; and for a stronger Reason yet, no Preaching ought to be allowed, because the Orator has an Opportunity of Haranguing often to a larger Auditory than he can perswade to read his Lucubrations; but I desire it may be remembered, that there is neither Liberty, Property, true Religion, Arts, Sciences, Learning or Knowledge in these Countries.

But another Method has been thought on in these western Parts of the World, much less effectual, and yet more mischievous than the former, namely, to put the Press under the Direction of the prevailing Party, and authorise Libels on one side only, and deny the other side the Oportunity of Defending themselves. Whilst all Opinions are equally indulged, and all parties equally allowed to speak their Minds, the Truth will come out; and even, if they are all restrained, common Sense will often get the better; but to give one side Liberty to say what they will, and not suffer the other to say any Thing, even in their own Defence, is Comprehensive of all the Evils that any nation can groan under, and must soon extinguish every Seed of Religion, Liberty, Virtue, or Knowledge.

It is rediculous to argue from the Abuse of a Thing, to the Destruction of it. Great mischiefs have happen'd to Nations from their Kings, and their Magistrates; ought therefore all Kings and Magistrates to be extinguish'd? A Thousand enthusiastick sects have pretended to deduce themselves from the Scripture, ought therefore the Holy Writings to be Destroy'd? Are Mens hands to be cut off, because they may, and some times do, steal and murder with them? Or their Tongues to be pulled out, because they may tell lyes, swear, or talk Sedition?

There is scarce a Virtue but borders upon a Vice, and carried beyond a certain Degree, becomes one: Courage soon grows into rashness; Generosity into extravagance; Frugality into avarice; Justice into Severity; Religion into Superstition; Zeal into Biggotry and Censoriousness; and the Desire of Esteem, into vain Glory; nor is there a Convenience, or Advantage to be proposed in human Affairs, but has some inconvenience attending it. The most flaming State of Health is nearest to a Phlethory: There can be no Protection, without hazarding Oppression; no going to Sea, without some danger of being drown'd; no engageing in the most necessary Battle, without venturing the Loss of it, or being killed; no purchasing an Estate, going to Law, or taking Physick, without hazarding ill Titles, spending your Money, and perhaps loosing your Suit, or being poison'd, [and] if [we are] not always accompanied by some evil, and cannot be separated from it, we are to consider which does predominate, and accordingly determine our choice by taking both or leaving both.

To apply this to Libels: If Men are suffer'd to preach, or Reason publickly and freely upon certain Subjects, as for Instance, upon Philosophy, Religion or Government, they may Reason wrongly, irreligiously, or seditiously, and some Times will do so; and by such means may possibly now and then pervert and mislead an ignorent and unwary Person; and if they are suffered to write their Thoughts, the mischief may be still more diffusive, but if they are not permitted by any, or all these ways, to communicate their Opinions and Improvements to one another, the World must soon be overrun with Barbarism, Superstition, Injustice, Tyrany, and the most stupid Ignorance. They will know nothing of the Nature of Government beyond a servile Submission to Power, nor of Religion, more than a blind adherence to unintelligible Speculations, and a furious and implacable animosity to all whose Mouths are not form'd to the same Sounds; nor will they have the Liberty or means to search Nature and investigate her Works; which Employment may break in upon received and gainfull Opinions, and discover hidden and darling secrets. Particular Societies shall be establish'd and endowed to teach them backwards, and to share in their Plunder: Which Societies by degrees from the want of Opposition, shall grow as ignorent as themselves: Arm'd Bands shall Rivet their Chains, and their haughty Governors assume to be Gods, and be treated as such in Proportion, as they cease to have humane Compassion, Knowledge, and Virtue. In short, their Capacities will not be beyond the beasts of the Field, and their Condition worse; which is universally true in those Governments where they ly under those restraints.

On the other side, what mischief is done by Libels to Ballance all the evils? They seldom or never annoy an innocent Man, or promote any considerable Error. Wise and Honest Men laugh at them, and despise them, and such Arrows always fly over their Heads, or fall at their Feet. If *James* had acted according to his Coronation Oath and kept to the Law, LILLY-BURLERO might have been tun'd long enough before he had been Sung out of his Kingdoms. And if there had been no south Sea Scheme, or if it had been justly executed, there had been no Libles upon that head, or very Harmeless ones. Most of the World take part with a virtuous Man, and punish calumny by their Detestation of it. The best Way to prevent Libels, is not to deserve them, and then they always lose their force; for certain Experience shews us that the more Notice is taken of them, the more they are published. Guilty Men alone fear them, or are hurt by them, whose Actions will not bear Examination, and therefore must not be examin'd. 'Tis Fact alone which annoys them; for if you will tell no truth, I dare say you may have their leave to tell as many lyes as you please.

The same is true in Speculative Opinions. You may write nonsense and folly as long as you think fit, and no one complains of it, but the Bookseller; but if a bold, honest, and wise Book sallies forth, and attacks those who think themselves secure in their Trenches, then their Camp is in danger, and they call out all Hands to Armes, and their Enemy is to be destroy'd by Fire, Sword or Fraud. But 'tis senseless to think that any Truth can suffer by being throughly search'd, or examin'd into; or that the Discovery of it can Prejudice right Religion, equal Government or the Happiness of Society in any Respect: She has so many Advantages above error that she wants only to be shewn to gain Admiration and Esteem; and we see that every Day she breaks the Bonds of Tyrany and Fraud, and shines thro' the mists of Superstition and ignorance: And what then would we do, if these Barriers were removed, and her fetters taken off?

Notwithstanding, I would not be understood by what I have said, to argue that Men should have an uncontroll'd Liberty to calumniate their superiors, or one another; decency, and good Manners, and the Peace of Society, forbid it: But I would not destroy this Liberty by Methods which will inevitably destroy all Liberty. We have very good Laws to punish any abuses of this Kind all ready, and I will approve them, whilst they are prudently and honestly executed, which I really believe they have for the most part been since the Revolution: But as it cannot be deny'd, that they have been formerly made the Stales of Ambition and Tyrany, to oppress any Man who durst assert the Laws, of his Country, or the true Christian Religion; so I hope the Gentlemen skill'd in the Profession of the Law will forgive me, If I entrench a little upon their province, and endeavour to fixe stated Bounds for the Interpretation, and Execution of them. . . .

Zenger's Journal *Theorizes on Freedom of the Press*

The *New-York Weekly Journal*, printed by John Peter Zenger, originated as a propaganda vehicle for a political faction, led by Lewis Morris, which lost power when William Cosby became governor of New York. The "publick printer" of the province was William Bradford, whose *New York Gazette* supported the Administration. Zenger himself, a poorly educated man, was neither editor nor writer of his paper. Its principal contributors were Lewis Morris, William Smith, Cadwallader Colden, and James Alexander, who was in effect the managing editor and chief editorial writer. Existing to maintain the viewpoint of a political opposition, the *Weekly Journal* scalded Administration measures and officials. As the first politically independent and truly "free" press in America, engaging weekly in the dangerous practice of opposing the Administration, the *Weekly Journal* needed a theory to legitimate its editorial policies. Its reading public as well as the crown officers had to be educated. The first edition of *Cato's Letters,* freshly imported from England, served the *Journal's* needs; also helpful was *The Doctrine of Innuendo's Discuss'd; Or The Liberty of the Press Maintain'd,* an English tract anonymously published in 1731. It was a product of the indictment for seditious libel against Richard Francklin, publisher of the *Craftsman,* who had protested against the prosecution of Tory opinions as seditious libels.

The *Journal* essays reprinted here are original compositions, almost certainly by James Alexander, reflecting the influence of both *Cato's Letters* and the *Craftsman.* The first essay (see Document 5), under the pseudonym of "Cato," appeared in the second and third issues of the *Journal,* indicating how quickly the *Journal* turned to a libertarian philosophy of freedom of the press to justify its practice of that freedom. Taken as a group, and including the four by Alexander in 1737 (see Document 10), these essays constitute the finest and broadest libertarian statements published in America until after the Sedition Act of 1798. Indeed, until that late date no American composition can be remotely compared with these.

It is noteworthy that Alexander, though advocating a wide latitude for freedom of political opinion, always stopped short of repudiating the concept of seditious libel and never took the position that all opinion should be free. When the Administration's organ, William Bradford's *Gazette,* warned that there was a distinction between liberty and licentiousness, and that abuses of liberty were punishable, the *Journal* did not deny the general propositions; it denied only that its publications were licentious abuses. Nevertheless, the *Journal's* essays persuasively—for the first time in America—argued for the right to criticize the government without being subject to the penalties of the law.

Several of the essays presented here are responses to the *Gazette's* arguments in defense of the laws against seditious libel. Document 6 rather acidly makes the point that the concept of libel defies definition. Document 7 is a comment on an essay, quite libertarian in character, that was published in Andrew Bradford's *American Weekly Mercury* of Philadelphia (and is reprinted in the present volume as Document 8). There is no essential disagreement between the *Journal* and the Mercury on the question of principles.

Yet Andrew Bradford, who was William's son, believed that it was a crime to pass the bounds of "decency" and "moderation" by assaulting the government with "fury" and "scurrility." Alexander read an implication which he sought to turn to the *Journal's* advantage. One of his most effective points, despite its self-extenuating character, was made in the oft-reiterated argument that the butt of criticism regards as libelous the opinions that others, especially in succeeding generations, regard as harmless or even as a blow for liberty.

James Alexander is a greatly neglected colonial figure. His name has been obscured by the attention lavished upon his famed printer and client, John Peter Zenger, and upon his fellow attorney, Andrew Hamilton. A man of versatile talents, Alexander was an engineer, mathematician, lawyer, journalist, and politician. He was a founder, with Benjamin Franklin, of the American Philosophical Society, surveyor general of both New Jersey and New York, a member of the New York General Assembly, a legal reformer, attorney general of New Jersey, and a member of the Governor's Council of both New Jersey and New York. (Cosby, on becoming governor, excluded him from the New York Council.) Alexander was the first American to develop a philosophy of freedom of the press.

5. AN AMERICAN "CATO" DEFENDS CRITICISM OF THE GOVERNMENT

Mr. Zenger.

Incert the following in your next, and you'll oblige your Friend,

CATO.

The Liberty of the Press is a Subject of the greatest Importance, and in which every Individual is as much concern'd as

---

New-York Weekly Journal, November 12 and 19, 1733.

he is in any other Part of Liberty: Therefore it will not be improper to communicate to the publick the Sentiments of a late excellent Writer upon this Point. Such is the Elegance and Perspicuity of his Writings, such the inimitable Force of his Reasoning, that it will be difficult to say any Thing new that he has not said, or not to say that much worse which he has said.

There are two Sorts of Monarchies, an absolute and a limited one. In the first, the Liberty of the Press can never be maintained, it is inconsistent with it; for what absolute Monarch would suffer any Subject to animadvert on his Actions when it is in his Power to declare the Crime and to nominate the Punishment? This would make it very dangerous to exercise such a Liberty. Besides the Object against which those Pens must be directed is their Sovereign, the sole Supream Magistrate; for there being no Law in those Monarchies but the Will of the Prince, it makes it necessary for his Ministers to consult his Pleasure before any Thing can be undertaken: He is therefore properly chargeable with the Grievances of his Subjects, and what the Minister there acts being in Obedience to the Prince, he ought not to incur the Hatred of the People; for it would be hard to impute that to him for a Crime which is the Fruit of his Allegiance, and for refusing which he might incur the Penalties of Treason. Besides, in an absolute Monarchy, the Will of the Prince being the Law, a Liberty of the Press to complain of Grievances would be complaining against the Law and the Constitution, to which they have submitted or have been obliged to submit; and therefore, in one Sense, may be said to deserve Punishment; so that under an absolute Monarchy, I say, such a Liberty is inconsistent with the Constitution, having no proper Subject to Politics on which it might be exercis'd, and if exercis'd would incur a certain Penalty.

But in a limited Monarchy, as *England* is, our Laws are known, fixed, and established. They are the streight Rule and sure Guide to direct the King, the Ministers, and other his

Subjects: And therefore an Offense against the Laws is such an Offense against the Constitution as ought to receive a proper adequate Punishment; the several Constituents of the Government, the Ministry, and all subordinate Magistrates, having their certain, known, and limited Sphere in which they move; one part may certainly err, misbehave, and become criminal, without involving the rest or any of them in the Crime or Punishment.

But some of these may be criminal, yet above Punishment, which surely cannot be denied, since most Reigns have furnished us with too many instances of powerful and wicked Ministers, some of whom by their Power have absolutely escaped Punishment, and the Rest, who met their Fate, are likewise Instances of this Power as much to the Purpose; for it was manifest in them that their Power had long protected them, their Crimes having often long preceded their much desired and deserved Punishment and Reward.

That *Might over comes Right,* or which is the same Thing, that Might preserves and defends Men from Punishment, is a Proverb established and confirmed by Time and Experience, the surest Discoverers of Truth and Certainty. It is this therefore which makes the Liberty of the Press in a limited Monarchy and in all its Colonies and Plantations proper, convenient, and necessary, or indeed it is rather incorporated and interwoven with our very Constitution; for if such an over grown Criminal, or an impudent Monster in Iniquity, cannot immediately be come at by ordinary Justice, let him yet receive the Lash of satyr, let the glaring Truths of his ill Administration, if possible, awaken his Conscience, and if he has no Conscience, rouse his Fear by Shewing him his Deserts, sting him with the Dread of Punishment, cover him with Shame, and render his Actions odious to all honest Minds. These Methods may in Time, and by watching and exposing his Actions, make him at least more Cautious, and perhaps at last bring down the great haughty and secure Criminal within the Reach and Grasp of ordinary Justice. This Advantage therefore of Exposing the exorbitant Crimes of wicked Ministers under a limited Monarchy makes the Liberty of the Press not only consistent with, but a necessary Part of, the Constitution itself.

It is indeed urged, that the Liberty of the Press ought to be restrained, because not only the Actions of evil Ministers may be exposed, but the Character of good ones traduced. Admit it in the strongest Light that Calumny and Lyes would prevail, and blast the Character of a great and good Minister; yet that is a less Evil than the Advantages we reap from the Liberty of the Press, as it is a Curb, a Bridle, a Terror, a Shame, and Restraint to evil Ministers; and it may be the only punishment, especially for a Time. But when did Calumnies and Lyes ever destroy the Character of one good Minister? Their benign Influences are known, tasted, and felt by every body: Or if their Characters have been clouded for a Time, yet they have generally shined forth in greater Luster: Truth will always prevail over Falsehood.

The Facts exposed are not to be believed, because said or published; but it draws People's Attention, directs their View, and fixes the Eye in a proper Position that everyone may judge for himself whether those Facts are true or not. People will recollect, enquire and search, before they condemn; and therefore very few good Ministers can be hurt by Falsehood, but many wicked Ones by seasonable Truth: But however the Mischief that a few may possibly, but improbably, suffer by the Freedom of the Press is not to be put in Competition with the Danger which the KING and the *people* may suffer by a shameful, cowardly Silence under the Tyranny of an insolent, rapacious, infamous Minister.

The Remainder of the Letter, concerning the Liberty of the Press, begun in our last.

Inconveniences are rather to be endured than that we should suffer an entire and total Destruction. Who would not lose a

Leg to save his Neck? And who would not endanger his Hand to Guard his heart? The Loss of Liberty in general would soon follow the Suppression of the Liberty of the Press; for as it is an essential Branch of Liberty, so perhaps it is the best Preservation of the whole. Even a Restraint of the Press would have a fatal Influence. No Nation Antient or Modern ever lost the Liberty of freely Speaking, Writing, or Publishing their Sentiments, but forthwith lost their Liberty in general and became Slaves. LIBERTY and SLAVERY! how amiable is one! how odious and abominable the other! Liberty is universal Redemption, Joy, and Happiness; but Servitude is absolute Reprobation and everlasting Perdition in Politics.

All the venal Supporters of wicked Ministers are aware of the great use of the Liberty of the Press in a limited free Monarchy: They know how vain it would be to attack it openly, and therefore endeavor to puzzle the Case with Words, Inconsistencies, and Nonsense; but if the Opinion of the most numerous, unprejudiced and impartial Part of Mankind is an Argument of Truth, the Liberty of the Press has that as well as Reason on its Side. I believe every honest *Britton* of whatever Denomination, who loves his Country, if left to his own free and unbyassed Judgment, is a Friend to the Liberty of the Press, and an Enemy to any Restraint upon it. Surely all the independent Whiggs, to a man, are of this Opinion. By an *Independent Whigg* I mean one whose principles lead him to be firmly attached to the present happy Establishment, both in Church and State, and whose Fidelity to the Royal Family is so staunch and rivetted as not to be called in Question, tho' his Mind is not overswayed, or rather necessitated, by the extraordinary Weight of lucrative Posts or Pensions. The Dread of Infamy hath certainly been of great Use to the Cause of Virtue, and is a stronger Curb upon the Passions and Appetites of some Men, than any other Consideration Moral or Religious. Whenever, therefore, the Talent of Satyr is made use of to restrain Men by the Fear of Shame from immoral Actions,

which either do or do not fall under the Cognizance of the
Law, it is properly, and justly, and commendably applied: On
the contrary, to condemn all Satyr is in Effect the same Thing
as countenancing Vice, by screening it from Reproach and
the just Indignation of Mankind. The Use of Satyr was of
great service to the patriot Whiggs in the reign of King *Charles*
and King *James* the second, as well as in that of Queen *Anne*.
They asserted the Freedom of Writing against wicked Ministers; and tho' they knew it would signify nothing to accuse
them publicly whilst they were in the Zenith of their Power,
they made use of Satyr to prepare the Way and alarm the
People against their Designs. If Men in Power were always
Men of Integrity, we might venture to trust them with the
Direction of the Press, and there would be no Occasion to
plead against the Restraint of it; but as they have Vices like
their Fellows, so it very often happens that the best intended
and the most valuable Writings are the Objects of their Resentment, because opposite to their own Tempers or Designs.
In short, I think, every Man of common Sense will judge that
he is an Enemy to his King and Country who pleads for any
Restraint upon the Press; but by the Press, when Nonsense,
Inconsistencies, or personal Reflections are writ, if despised,
they die of Course; if Truth, solid Arguments, and elegant, just
Sentiments are published, they should meet with Applause
rather than Censure; if Sense and Nonsense are blended, then,
by the free Use of the Press, which is open to all, the Inconsistencies of the Writer may be made apparent; but to grant a
Liberty only for Praise, Flattery, and Panegyric, with a Restraint on every Thing which happens to be offensive and disagreeable to those who are at any Time in Power, is absurd,
servile, and rediculous; upon which, I beg Leave to quote one
Observation of the ingenious Mr. *Gordon,* in his excellent Dis-
courses upon *Tacitus.* "In truth," says he,

where no Liberty is allowed to speak of Governours besides that of
praising them, their praises will be little believed; their Tenderness

and Aversion to have their Conduct examined will be apt to prompt people to think their conduct guilty or weak, to suspect their Management and Designs to be worse perhaps than they are, and to become turbulent and seditious, rather than be forced to be silent.

6. THE *Journal* CLAIMS THAT LIBELS DEFY

DEFINITION

Government is that sacred Institution, the late Chief Justice called it, and the Magistrates and Ministers of it, the Channels thro' which the Blessings intended by it flow to the Society, and the Protectors of them in the Injoyment of them; and to speak irreverently and disrespectfully of Magistrates and Government, considered as such, was and is, always will be, criminal in the Sight of God and Men. —A good Magistrate is one of the greatest temporal blessings, and an ill one is one of the greatest Curses, God can give to Men; and while Magistrates Act suitable to the good Intention of their Institution, they will acquire (as they deserve) a suitable Return of Praise for, and gratefull Acknowledgments of, the good they do: But when a Magistrate acts differently from the Ends of his Institution, and in Stead of Protecting of me uses his Power to oppress me, when he warps the Laws, which were made for the Preservation of the Society, and turns them to their Destruction, and makes Power, and not Right, the Rule and Measure of his Actions, he cannot, nor ought not, to claim any Respect, because he deserves none. —To give such a Magistrate publick or private Respect, is acting against the Ends of Government and common Sense; is joyning with him, in making those miserable, that he was sent to make happy: And to speak well of him,

---

New-York Weekly Journal, February 11 and 18, 1734.

when he is known to do Ill, is right down Lying; which the greatest Advocates for Tyrany, how much so ever they desire it, won't have the Face to own, that any Man is under a natural or moral Obligation to do, but the contrary, I am sure the People of England thought so, in the latter end of the Reign of Charles the 2d, and in the Reign of King James the 2d, when the Liberties of the Nation were given up by the Judges, whose Names and Memory will be infamous, while Liberty and History remain. If they had not thought it lawfull to speak of Men as they deserved, and had not spoke, AND ACTED TOO, against that King and his Ministers (not withstanding their high Stations) we should not now have been sensible of the blessed Effects of A GLORIOUS REVOLUTION, where the Hand of God (as it often has done) as well as Man, appeared on the Side of LIBERTY. . . .

I don't well know what the Observer means by Libels against the Government. Some People have a Knack of calling any Paper they don't like, that treats of Governours or Magistrates, a Libel against the Government; or if an ill Governour or Magistrate is described, or the ill Actions of any such, they (by a Happiness of Invention peculiar to themselves) presently think it is leveled at the Governour and Magistrates for the Time being. Ask them why they think so? They'll immediately reply, that the Thing is very plain: Ask them wherein? But to that they'll make no Reply, but that it is so. . . .

. . . some People think that Paragraph in Zenger's Paper is an aggravated Libel, it may be they do think so: For my Part I don't understand the Term. I have heard of a Difference made, betwixt a *roasted Goose,* and a *Goose roasted;* a roasted Goose can't be had under Half a Crown; but you may have a Goose roasted for Six-pence: So, whether a Libel aggravated, or an aggravated Libel be the same Thing, or something Different, I don't know, but as I take it any thing aggravated is rendered something worse than it was before: And a Libel (bad as it is) by Aggravation is made worse then it was at first; and then he or they that aggravated it, and made it worse, are more in Fault than the first Maker; but who the aggravators were if more than one? I for my Part, do not know: But if they are induced to think so from what is said by Serjeant *Hawkin's,* they must be very few that think so, because there are but few in the Province have that Book: And I have some Reason to know, that all that have that Book do not think that Paragraph in *Zenger's* Paper a Libel, neither do I see, how reading Serjeant *Hawkin's,* can induce any Body to think so. For Serjant *Hawkin's* could tell pretty well what a Libel was, but who is Guilty of it, (with humble Submission to better Judgments) I think twelve good Men and true can only tell. . . .

Every Body knows what has been called Lybeling in one Age has met with different Treatment in another; in King *Jame's* Time the Petition of the seven Bishops was called a Libel: But after the Revolution a Godly and pious Petition.

I am surprised to find the Conduct of those Times which gave rise to the Petition of Right; and to the Act of 16 *Car.* I. for Abolishing the Starr Chamber Court, attempted to be now justified upon the Credit of a noble Historian: (whose Book having passed thro' suspected Hands) at this Time of Day, is much more Admired for the Beauty of the Stile, then believed for the Truth of the Relations, tho' even he says *Prynn* was as good a Lawyer as Books could make him. *Prynn* was far from a despicable Person, he was long a Member (if I mistake not the Name) of the House of Commons after the Restoration; and by King *Charles* the 2d, made Keeper of the Records in the Tower, a Place of no small Trust. And it is hard he should be new branded in America, so long after his Death: It discovers the Principles of the Men, and what is to be expected from them, were their Power equal to their Inclinations, but thank God, we still have, and I hope, always will have Juries.

I agree with the Author that it is the Abuse, and not the Use of the Press, is blameable. But the Difficulty Lies who shall be the Judges of this Abuse. And from whence we shall take the Presidents [*precedents*] to Judge by. In *Spain* and *Portugal* to write against Transubstantiation is an horrible abuse, in *England* as great a one (tho' not so fatal) to write for it. In *England* in the Reign of the *Stewarts,* to write any Thing that savourd of Liberty, or what they called republican Principles, was dangerous. Nay in King *James* the 2d, Time Dr. *Eades* was find 100 Marks for but barely commending a Book. Make our Adversarys the Judges; I don't well know what will not be a Libel; and perhaps, if we be the Judges it will be as Difficult to tell what will. I would have the Readers Judges: But they cant Judge, if nothing is wrote. Those of the side of the Government in any Country, will no doubt write in Favour of it; and every Thing Magnified to the Skyes: But, they are generally so lavish in their Praises, that those who have the Reputation of honest Men among them are Thought by way of Irony to Lybell the Government they Praise. . . .

7. THE *Journal* COMMENTS ON ANDREW BRADFORD'S DEFINITION OF FREEDOM OF THE PRESS

MR. ZENGER;

The Gentleman who made the Liberty of the Press an essential Part of the Constitution, tells us he meant by it, *a Liberty for every Man to communicate his Sentiments freely to the Publick, upon political or religious Points;* that this Liberty has been called by Authors of the first Class, *The Liberty of the Press.* And he instances an Author, who he says is of some

---

New-York Weekly Journal, November 4, 1734.

Repute in the learned World, who calls that Liberty the Liberty of the Press: But he mentions a marginal Note, which shews the learned Auther was justly aware of the same Objection made to Mr. *Bradford's* Writer, and guards against it by letting the World know what he meant by it; and had Mr. *Bradford's* Writer done so, we should not have differed much on that Head; an Altercation about Words (tho' improperly used) when what is meant by them is known being useless. —He insists upon the Terms *Liberty of the Press,* as essential to the Constitution: But then he carries this Constitution no farther back than the Revolution. —I confess that there was a greater Liberty allow'd of Printing then, than had been admitted in the preceeding Reigns: But if by this Liberty of the Press, *essential* to that Constitution, be meant essential to its Preservation, he pays no small Complement to the Writers of that Time against it. —He makes the Satisfaction he *expressed that the Liberty of the Press was carried to such a Height that some Men continued even to abuse it with Impunity.* A great Puzzle to the poor Gentleman's Brains. —I confess that it is still as much a Puzzle to my poor Brains as ever; for I cannot understand how any honest Man see any Thing, especially a Thing essential to the Preservation of the Constitution, or an essential Part of the Constitution, abused, with great Satisfaction. When he tells me how this can be done by a Lover of the Constitution he sees thus abused with great Satisfaction, he will make that intelligible to me which at present is not. —I am glad to see it own'd in Mr. *Bradford's* Paper by one of his Writers, *that every Man ought to have a Liberty to communicate his Sentiments* FREELY *to the Publick, upon political or religious Points.* —I hope by *freely* he means without the Fear or the Danger of being punished. When they can so write, it will then be *Felicitas,* and *rara felicitas temporum.* It is true, That Abuses that disolve Society, and sap the Foundations of Government, are not to be sheltered under the Umbrage of the Liberty of the Press: But if those in Power will term a trifling Song, or any Thing of so minute a Nature, a Disolving of Society, and Sapping of the Foundations of Government; if they will fix determinate Meanings to Sentences and even Blanks, which the Authors have not fixt, and to which other Meanings can with equal Justice be applyed; I would be glad to know wherein this Liberty of Writing consists? If no Endeavours have been left untryed, either with Grand Juries, and even with one of the Branches of the Legislature to treat the Papers with the greatest Ignominy, and to discover the Authors. —Even of Papers (as those of the Continuance of the Middletown Letter) which were purely argumentative upon political Points, without the least Syllable of an indecent Reflection upon any Body, and the Reasons given for this Discovery was, that the Authors might meet with condign Punishment; with what Propriety of Speech can we be said to have the Liberty of freely communicating our Sentiments upon any Points, when so great Endeavours are used to prevent its being done? Have not the Authors all the Reason in the World to fear a Repetition of the Exorbitant Fines and sanguinary Cruelties that stain'd the Reigns preceeding the Revolution? —Is it not a ridiculous Farce and an Affront to the common Sense of Mankind to talk of the Liberty of the Press enjoyed with Impunity in this Case? —We are unpunish'd, it is true; but whom are we to thank? And how long shall we be so? Glorious Liberty of the Press! We may write what we please, but then we must take Care that what pleases us pleases our Masters too. —We may Write! but if we do not Write as they think fit, they'll make us smart for it! O glorious Liberty! *O rara felicitas temporum!*

Andrew Bradford Distinguishes Liberty from Licentiousness

Andrew Bradford was the son of Zenger's rival, William Bradford, who established the first newspaper in New York. The younger Bradford was Franklin's rival in Philadelphia. The founder of the first newspaper in Pennsylvania, *The American Weekly Mercury,* Andrew Bradford was twice censured by the Governor's Council and once imprisoned. Yet he became a city councilman and, until displaced by Franklin, city postmaster. His later enmity to Zenger's cause is attributable chiefly to his hatred of Andrew Hamilton, whom he held responsible for his imprisonment. Bradford subsequently assaulted Hamilton's reputation as a champion of freedom of the press.

Andrew Bradford's own claim as a libertarian has been overlooked because he was on the "wrong" side of a popular cause and he was the journalistic opponent of the revered Franklin. The essay printed here is one of the very few well-reasoned statements on press liberty made by any American of the colonial period. Although he contended for a liberty "within the Bounds of Law," thereby acknowledging the validity of the common law's restraints, Bradford said nothing that Franklin did not endorse, and he said it far more effectively.

8. "SENTIMENTS ON THE LIBERTY OF THE PRESS"

MR. BRADFORD,

IN *a former Paper; I promised you my Sentiments on the Liberty of the Press. . . .*

IN this as in all other Cases where the Subject of Liberty, is treated, we must carefully distinguish, between *Liberty* and *Licentiousness.* I have perused many virulent Declamations against the *Liberty of the Press,* that have proceeded on Maxims evidently false: Not so much for want of Skill in the Compilers, as want of *Shame* and even common *Honesty.* They have supposed things which no good Man acquainted with the Nature of civil Government, would have supposed, and from

---

The American Weekly Mercury (Philadelphia), April 25, 1734.

those Principles weak and base, they have deduced Consequences equally weak and destructive of the Happiness of Societies. For, 'tis undoubtedly true, that there is a certain *Legerdemain* in Argument, by which, if you may suppose what you please; you may conclude what you will.

The Caprice and Fury of a Mobb undisciplined and under no Restraints from Law, may be as pernicious as the uncontroulable Edicts of an absolute Tyrant, —The Extreams that seperate Liberty from License, are closer than most Men imagine; they ought therefore to be carefully distinguish'd.

By the *Liberty of the Press* then, I am far from understanding, (as I hope every *Englishman* is) a treasonable *Licence*, of calling into Question his most Sacred Majesty's undoubted Title, to the Realm of *Great-Britain,* or any his Dominions thereunto belonging. Nor do I think that his Conduct in private or public Life ought to be arraign'd. That *the King can do no wrong,* is a Maxim (a just Maxim too) in the *English* Law. His Ministers indeed are accountable to the Public for their Male Administration, and have frequently felt the Resentment of a good natured but an injur'd People.

Nor, by the *Liberty of the Press,* do I mean that unwarrantable License, which some People of much Fire, but little judgment have taken of endeavouring to subvert the Fundamental Points of *Religion* or *Morality.* Religion ought to be treated with Veneration, and without Morality whose Doctrines true Religion always recommends and strengthens, Societies could not subsist. I have been astonish'd to hear some Men, who make high Pretences to Wit and Learning advance these and the like *Stupidities;* that Virtue and Vice are meer Words: That in the Nature of things there is no Distinction between the one and the other, that all Mankind are Villains; That what we call beautiful and generous in Life proceeds only from the sordid Motives of Pride or Self Interest; that Patriotism is a Word without a Meaning, and Public Virtue a thing to be laughed at. —I must confess I don't know any Business such unnatural Wretches have in Society, to whom by their own avowed Principles, they publickly disclaim all manner of Relation.

But on the other Hand, to expose the ridiculous Claims of certain Priests, to examine with Freedom and Impartiality the Conduct of some spiritual Councils and Convocations, is a Liberty, I think every free People, is entitled to. Nor was I ever acquainted with a sensible and honest Clergyman, who did not acknowledge this to be true. Since I have mentioned that *Reverend Order of Men,* for some of whom, I entertain the highest Regards, allow me to say further, that the Observations I have made, proceed from no Prejudice. I peruse with Pleasure the Writings of a *Tillotson,* or a *Stillingfleet;* I think they were an Ornament to their Country, and I can never reflect on the brave Stand, the *Bishops* made in Favour of *English* Liberty, without the utmost Degree of Veneration. I think they ought to have their Statues erected in Brass, and I doubt not in the least that their Names will be transmitted with Honour to Ages yet to come. The Petulance of Tongue and the vile Scurrility with which the Gentlemen of that Robe have sometimes been treated provokes my Indignation, that they have their Foibles, is as true, as that they are Men: But, why the whole Order should be condemned in Gross, for the Whims or Vices of a few, is what I could never comprehend.

Nor, by the *Liberty of the Press,* do I understand a *License,* of traducing the Conduct, of those Gentlemen who are appointed our Lawful Governors: When they behave themselves well, they ought to be treated with all the Respect and Gratitude, that's due from an obliged People; should they behave themselves ill, their Measures are to be remonstrated against in Terms of *Decency,* and Moderation not of Fury or Scurrility.

Thanks to the indulgent Stars, that shed their kindly influence on *Pennsylvania,* a Country where the Goddess *Liberty,* hath chosen her particular Abode, we have nothing from that Quarter to dread. We are blest with Proprietors, who we have just Reason to hope, will imitate the Virtues of their renowned Father; a *Name,* a *Character* never to be forgotten! And, we have a *Governour,* who hath deservedly gained the Hearts of the People under his Care; to whom he hath been always willing to Grant any Favours, proper for them to ask.

But, should it please God, as a Punishment for our Sins, to visit us with a *Governor,* so far intoxicated with *Pride and Ambition,* as to endeavour to set himself above the *Laws,* and affect an independent Sway: Should he remove from Places of the highest Trust, those Persons, who had discharged them, with unquestioned Abilities and Integrity, in Order to promote the immediate *Creatures* of his own Will; should he presume to erect *Arbitrary Courts,* unknown to an English Constitution, and to Stop or Poison the streams of *Justice.* In such a Case, I doubt not in the least, but there would be found Men of *Spirit,* and *Honesty* enough, to let that Governor know that ————— *Such a Conduct did not become him.*

Nor, under the Colour of this *Liberty,* ought such Doctrines to be publish'd, as tend to lessen or take away, that sacred Veneration, which is due to the upright Dispensers of the *Laws.* Nor, should the *Press* be made use of as an Engine, to insult *Personal Deformities, Frailties* or *Misfortunes* much less to expose the secrets of Families. This is mean, and unbecoming a Writer. And indeed all such irregular Sallies are sufficiently provided against by the Laws in being.

But, by the *Freedom of the Press,* I mean a Liberty, within the Bounds of Law, for any Man to communicate to the Public, his Sentiments on the Important Points of *Religion* and *Government;* of proposing any Laws, which he apprehends may be for the Good of his Countrey, and of applying for the Repeal of such, as he Judges pernicious. I mean a *Liberty* of detecting the wicked and destructive Measures of *certain Politicians;* of dragging Villany out of it's obscure lurking Holes, and exposing it in it's full Deformity to open Day; of attacking Wickedness in high Places, of disintangling the intricate

Folds of a wicked and corrupt Administration, and pleading freely for a Redress of *Grievances:* I mean a *Liberty* of examining the great Articles of our Faith, by the Lights of *Scripture and Reason,* a Privilege derived to us in it's fullest Latitude, from our most excellent *Charter.*

This is the *Liberty of the Press,* the great *Palladium* of all our other *Liberties,* which I hope the good People of this Province, will forever enjoy; and that every *Pennsylvanian,* will resent with *Scorn and Indignation,* the least Attempt to weaken or subvert it. For, it may be demonstrated from numerous Instances in History, that whenever this inestimable Jewel was lost, Slavery, Desolation and Ruine ensued.

This Doctrine of the *Liberty of the Press* can never be too much inculcated, tho' it hath been almost exhausted by Authors of signal Renown. I shall conclude this Paper with a Quotation from an excellent Pamphlet publish'd in the Reign of the late King *William.*

"All Sorts of Men, whose Interest it is, not to have their Actions exposed to the Publick, (which I am afraid) are no small Number, will be for *restraining the Press;* but, this is not the worst that may happen; because the *Press* may be so managed as to become the powerful Engine to overturn and subvert the Constitution it self: For, should a *Magistrate* arise with arbitrary Designs in his Head, no Papers that plead the *Rights and Privileges* of the People, could be publish'd with Security. The *Press* would be employ'd only to extol the Promoters of *arbitrary Power,* as the chief *Patriots* of their Country; and to traduce those that were really so, which would not only be the greatest Discouragement, to all brave and virtuous Actions; but be apt to make the People mistake their *Friends,* when they had not the *Liberty* to publish a Vindication of their *Principles* or *Actions* of their *Enemies,* in a Word, if the *Pulpits* and *Westminster-Hall,* should chime in with an *arbitrary Court,* what can warn the People of their Danger, except the *Press?* But, if that too be wholy against them, they may easily be so blinded as not to see the Chains that are preparing for them, till they are fettered beyond all Power of Redemption."

As therefore you love your *Liberties*, (my dear Countreymen) support and defend the *Liberty of the Press.*

Andrew Hamilton Defends Zenger

Zenger's original attorneys were James Alexander and William Smith, ardent supporters of the leader of the anti-Administration party, Lewis Morris. Governor Cosby had summarily removed Morris from the chief justiceship in 1733 and appointed James De-Lancey in his place. When Alexander and Smith sought to turn the defense of Zenger into an assault on the Cosby Administration by formally questioning the legitimacy of DeLancey's credentials, the new chief justice refused to hear their petition and summarily disbarred them, leaving Zenger without counsel. James Alexander then engaged the services of an old friend, Andrew Hamilton of Philadelphia, to defend his client.

Hamilton, who had the reputation of being the best advocate in the colonies, had been attorney general of Pennsylvania and at the time of the Zenger trial was speaker of the Pennsylvania Assembly. His case was ready made for him, for Alexander had prepared a masterful brief. Alexander was a poor speaker, but Andrew Hamilton was an eloquent and lively one, quick on his feet and attractive to jurymen. He opened the defense with Alexander's daring gambit of admitting Zenger's responsibility for the allegedly seditious articles, and then pleaded that truthful criticism of the government warranted an acquittal. When DeLancey ruled against him on points of law, Hamilton brilliantly appealed to the jury over De-Lancey's head. His argument, which was peppered with grossly distorted precedents—most of which have been eliminated in the following extract from the trial—made good sense to the jury. On the fictitious grounds that the rights he claimed for his client and the jury had long existed, he concocted an argument that was destined to survive first in public opinion, then in the law itself.

9. THE ZENGER TRIAL

. . . *Mr. Hamilton.* May it Please your Honour; I am concerned in this Cause on the Part of Mr. Zenger the Defendant. . . . I cannot think it proper for me (without doing Violence to my own Principles) to deny the Publication of a Complaint, which I think is the Right of every free-born Subject to make, when the Matters so published can be supported with Truth; and therefore I'll save Mr. Attorney the Trouble of examining his Witnesses to that Point; and I do (for my Client) confess, that he both printed and published the two News Papers set forth in the Information, and I hope in so doing he has committed no Crime.

Mr. Attorney. Then if Your Honour pleases, since Mr. *Hamilton* has confessed the Fact, I think our Witnesses may be discharged; we have no further Occasion for them.

Mr. Hamilton. If you brought them here, only to prove the Printing and Publishing of these News Papers, we have acknowledged that, and shall abide by it. . . .

Mr. Chief Justice. *Well Mr. Attorney, will you proceed?*

Mr. Attorney. Indeed, Sir, as Mr. *Hamilton* has confessed the Printing and Publishing these Libels, I think the Jury must find a Verdict for the King; for supposing they were true, the Law says that they are not the less libellous for that; nay indeed the Law says, their being true is an Aggravation of the Crime.

Mr. Hamilton. Not so neither, Mr. Attorney, there are two Words to that Bargain. I hope it is not our bare Printing and

---

A brief Narrative of the Case and Tryal of John Peter Zenger, *Printer of the* New-York Weekly Journal (New York: Printed and sold by John Peter Zenger, 1736, from a Literal Reprint of the first edition of the trial), reprinted in Livingston Rutherfurd, *John Peter Zenger, His Press, His Trial, and a Bibliography of Zenger Imprints* (New York: Dodd, Mead & Company, 1904), pp. 198–241, *passim.*

Publishing a Paper, that will make it a Libel: You will have something more to do, before you make my Client a Libeller; for the Words themselves must be libellous, that is, *false, scandalous, and seditious,* or else we are not guilty. . . .

May it please Your Honour; I agree with Mr. Attorney, that Government is a sacred Thing, but I differ very widely from him when he would insinuate, that the just Complaints of a Number of Men, who suffer under a bad Administration, is libelling that Administration. . . .

I was in Hopes, as that terrible Court, where those dreadful Judgments were given, and that Law established, which Mr. Attorney has produced for Authorities to support this Cause, was long ago laid aside, as the most dangerous Court to the Liberties of the People of *England,* that ever was known in that Kingdom; that Mr. Attorney knowing this, would not have attempted to set up a Star-Chamber here, nor to make their Judgments a Precedent to us: For it is well known, that what would have been judg'd Treason in those Days for a Man to speak, I think, has since not only been practiced as lawful, but the contrary Doctrine has been held to be Law. . . .

Mr. Attorney. . . . The Case before the Court is, whether Mr. *Zenger* is guilty of Libelling His Excellency the Governor of *New-York,* and indeed the whole Administration of the Government? Mr. *Hamilton* has confessed the Printing and Publishing, and I think nothing is plainer, than that the Words in the Information are *scandalous, and tend to sedition, and to disquiet the Minds of the People of this Province.* And if such Papers are not Libels, I think it may be said, there can be no such Thing as a Libel.

Mr. Hamilton. May it please Your Honour; I cannot agree with Mr. Attorney: For tho' I freely acknowledge, that there are such Things as Libels, yet I must insist at the same Time, that what my Client is charged with, is not a Libel; and I observed just now, that Mr. Attorney in defining a Libel, made use of the Words, *scandalous, seditious, and tend to disquiet the People;* but (whether with Design or not I will not say) he omitted the Word *false.*

Mr. Attorney. I think I did not omit the Word *false:* But it has been said already, that it may be a Libel, notwithstanding it may be true.

Mr. Hamilton. In this I must still differ with Mr. Attorney; for I depend upon it, we are to be tried upon this Information now before the Court and Jury, and to which we have pleaded *Not Guilty,* and by it we are charged with Printing and publishing *a certain false, malicious, seditious and scandalous Libel.* This Word *false* must have some Meaning, or else how came it there? I hope Mr. Attorney will not say, he put it there by Chance, and I am of Opinion his Information would not be good without it. But to shew that it is the principal Thing which, in my Opinion, makes a Libel, I put the Case, the Information had been for printing and publishing a certain *true* Libel, would that be the same thing? Or could Mr. Attorney support such an Information by any Precedent in the *English* Law? No, the Falsehood makes the Scandal, and both make the Libel. And to shew the Court that I am in good Earnest, and to save the Court's Time, and Mr. Attorney's Trouble, I will agree, that if he can prove the Facts charged upon us, to be *false,* I'll own them to be *scandalous, seditious,* and *a Libel.* So the Work seems now to be pretty much shortened, and Mr. Attorney has now only to prove the Words *false,* in order to make us Guilty.

Mr. Attorney. We have nothing to prove; you have confessed the Printing and Publishing; but if it was necessary (as I insist it is not) how can we prove a Negative? But I hope some Regard will be had for the Authorities that have been produced, and that supposing all the Words to be true, yet that will not help them, that Chief Justice *Holt* in his Charge to the Jury, in the Case of *Tutchin,* made no Distinction, whether

Tutchin's Papers were *true* or *false;* and as Chief Justice *Holt* has made no Distinction in that Case, so none ought to be made here; nor can it be shewn in all that Case, there was any Question made about their being *false* or *true.*

Mr. Hamilton. I did expect to hear, That a Negative cannot be proved; but every Body knows there are many Exceptions to that general Rule: For if a Man is charged with killing another, or stealing his Neighbour's Horse, if he is innocent in the one Case, he may prove the Man said to be killed, to be really alive; and the Horse said to be stolen, never to have been out of his Master's Stable. &c., and this, I think, is proving a Negative. But we save Mr. Attorney the Trouble of proving a Negative, and take the *Onus probandi* upon ourselves, and prove those very Papers that are called Libels to be *true.*

Mr. Ch. Justice. You cannot be admitted, Mr. *Hamilton,* to give the Truth of a Libel in Evidence. A Libel is not to be justified; for it is nevertheless a Libel that it is true.

Mr. Hamilton. I am sorry the Court has so soon resolved upon that Piece of Law; I expected first to have been heard to that Point. I have not in all my Reading met with an Authority that says, we cannot be admitted to give the Truth in Evidence, upon an information for a Libel.

Mr. Ch. Justice. The Law is clear, That you cannot justify a Libel. . . .

. . . Mr. Attorney, you have heard what Mr. *Hamilton* has said, and the Cases he has cited, for having his Witnesses examined, to prove the Truth of the several Facts contained in the Papers set forth in the Information, what do you say to it?

Mr. Attorney. The Law in my opinion is very clear; they cannot be admitted to justify a Libel; for, by the Authorities I have already read to the Court, it is not the less a Libel because it is true. I think I need not trouble the Court with reading the Cases over again; the Thing seems to be very plain, and I submit it to the Court.

Mr. Ch. Just. Mr. *Hamilton,* the Court is of the Opinion, you ought not to be permitted to prove the Facts in the Papers: these are the Words of the Book. *"It is far from being a Justification of a Libel, that the Contents thereof are true, or that the Person upon whom it is made, had a bad Reputation, since the greater Appearance there is of Truth in any malicious Invective, so much the more provoking it is."*

Mr. Hamilton. These are Star Chamber Cases, and I was in hopes, that Practice had been dead with the Court.

Mr. Ch. Just. Mr. *Hamilton,* the Court have delivered their Opinion, and we expect you will use us with good Manners; you are not to be permitted to argue against the Opinion of the Court.

Mr. Hamilton. With Submission, I have seen the Practice in very great Courts, and never heard it deemed unmannerly to —

Mr. Ch. Just. After the Court have declared their Opinion, it is not good Manners to insist upon a Point, in which you are over-ruled.

Mr. Hamilton. I will say no more at this Time; the Court I see is against us in this Point; and that I hope I may be allowed to say.

Mr. Ch. Just. Use the Court with good Manners, and you shall be allowed all the Liberty you can reasonably desire.

Mr. Hamilton. I thank your Honour. Then, Gentlemen of the Jury, it is to you we must now appeal, for Witness, to the Truth of the Facts we have offered, and are denied the Liberty to prove; and let it not seem strange, that I apply my self to you in this Manner, I am warranted so to do, both by Law and Reason. The Last supposes you to be summoned, *out of the Neighbourhood where the Fact is alleged to be committed;* and the Reason of your being taken out of the Neighbourhood is, *because you are supposed to have the best Knowledge of the fact that is to be tried.* And were you to find a Verdict against my client, you must take upon you to say, the

Papers referred to in the Information, and which we acknowledge we printed and published, are *false, scandalous and seditious:* but of this I can have no Apprehension. You are Citizens of *New-York;* you are really what the Law supposes you to be, *honest and lawful Men;* and, according to my Brief, the Facts which we offer to prove were not committed in a Corner; they are notoriously known to be true; and therefore in your Justice lies our Safety. And as we are denied the Liberty of giving Evidence, to prove the Truth of what we have published, I will beg Leave to lay it down as a standing Rule in such Casess, *That the suppressing of Evidence ought always to be taken for the strongest Evidence;* and I hope it will have that Weight with you. But since we are not admitted to examine our Witnesses, I will endeavor to shorten the Dispute with Mr. Attorney, and to that End, I desire he would favor us with some Standard Definition of a Libel, by which it may be certainly known, whether a Writing be a Libel, yea or not.

Mr. Attorney. The Books, I think, have given a very full definition of a Libel; they say it is *in a strict Sense taken for a malicious Defamation, expressed either in Printing or Writing, and tending either to blacken the Memory of one who is dead, or the Reputation of one who is alive, and to expose him to publick Hatred, Contempt or Ridicule.* . . . *But it is said, That in a larger Sense the Notion of a Libel may be applied to any Defamation whatsoever, expressed either by Signs or Pictures, as by fixing up a Gallows against a Man's Door, or by painting him in a shameful and ignominious Manner.* . . . *And since the chief Cause for which the Law so severely punishes all Offences of this Nature, is the direct Tendency of them to a Breach of Publick Peace, by provoking the Parties injured, their Friends and Families to Acts of Revenge, which it would be impossible to restrain by the severest Laws, were there no Redress from Publick Justice for Injuries of this kind, which of all others are most sensibly felt* . . .

Mr. Hamilton. Ay, Mr. Attorney; but what certain Standard

Rule have the Books laid down, by which we can certainly know, whether the Words or the Signs are malicious? Whether they are defamatory? Whether they tend to the Breach of the Peace, and are a sufficient Ground to provoke a Man, his Family, or Friends to Acts of Revenge, especially those of the ironical sort of Words? And what Rule have you to know when I write ironically? I think it would be hard, when I say, *such a Man is a very worthy honest Gentleman, and of fine Understanding,* that therefore I meant *he was a Knave or a fool.*

Mr. Attorney. I think the Books are very full. . . .

Mr. Hamilton. I agree the Words are very plain and I shall not scruple to allow (when we are agreed that the Words are *false and scandalous, and were spoken in an ironical and scoffing Manner, &c.*) that they are really *libellous;* but here still occurs the Uncertainty, which makes the Difficulty to know, what Words are *scandalous* and what not; for you say, they may be *scandalous, true* or *false;* besides, how shall we know whether the Words were spoke in a *scoffing and ironical Manner,* or seriously? Or how can you know whether the Man did not think as he wrote? For by your Rule, if he did, it is no *Irony,* and consequently no *Libel.* . . .

Mr. Ch. Just. Mr. *Hamilton,* do you think it so hard to know, when Words are ironical, or spoke in a scoffing Manner?

Mr. Hamilton. I own it may be known; but I insist, the only Rule to know is, as I do or can *understand* them; I have no other Rule to go by, but as I *understand* them.

Mr. Ch. Just. That is certain. All Words are libellous, or not, as they are *understood.* Those who are to judge of the Words, must judge whether they *are scandalous or ironical, tend to the Breach of the Peace,* or are *seditious:* There can be no Doubt of it.

Mr. Hamilton. I thank your Honour; I am glad to find the Court of this Opinion. Then it follows that those twelve Men must *understand* the Words in the Information to be *scandalous,* that is to say *false;* for I think it is not pretended they are of the *ironical* Sort; and when they understand the Words to be so, they will say we are guilty of Publishing a *false Libel,* and not otherwise.

Mr. Ch. Just. No, Mr. *Hamilton* the Jury may find that *Zenger* printed and published those Papers, and leave it to the Court to judge whether they are libellous; you know this is very common; it is in the Nature of a special Verdict, where the Jury leave the Matter of Law to the Court.

Mr. Hamilton. I know, may it please Your Honour, the Jury may do so; but I do likewise know, they may do otherwise. I know they have the Right beyond all Dispute, to determine both the Law and the Fact, and where they do not doubt of the Law, they ought to do so. This of leaving it to the Judgment of the Court, *whether the Words are libellous or not,* in Effect renders Juries useless (to say no worse) in many Cases; but this I shall have Occasion to speak to by and by; and I will with the Court's Leave proceed to examine the Inconveniences that must inevitably arise from the Doctrines Mr. Attorney has laid down; and I observe, in support of this Prosecution, he has frequently repeated the Words taken from the Case of *Libel, famosus,* in 5 *Co.* This is indeed the leading case, and to which almost all the other Cases upon the Subject of Libels do refer; and I must insist upon saying, That according as this Case seems to be understood by the [Court] and Mr. Attorney, it is not Law at this Day: For thou' I own it to be base and unworthy to scandalize any Man, yet I think it is even villanous to scandalize a Person of publick Character, and I will go so far into Mr. Attorney's Doctrine as to agree, that if the faults, Mistakes, nay even the Vices of such a Person be private and personal, and don't affect the Peace of the Publick, or the Liberty or Property of our Neighbour, it is unmanly and unmannerly to expose them either by Word or Writing. But when a Ruler of the People brings his personal Failings, but much more his Vices, into his Administration, and the People find themselves affected by them, either in their Liberties or Properties, that will alter the Case mightily, and all the high Things that are said in Favour of Rulers, and of Dignities, and upon the side of Power, will not be able to stop People's Mouths when they feel themselves oppressed, I mean in a free Government. It is true in Times past it was a crime to speak Truth, and in that terrible Court of Star Chamber, many worthy and brave Men suffered for so doing; and yet even in that Court, and in those bad Times, a great and good Man durst say, what I hope will not be taken amiss of me to say in this Place, *to wit, The Practice of informations for Libels is a Sword in the Hands of a wicked King, and an arrant Coward, to cut down and destroy the innocent; the one cannot, because of his high Station, and the other dares not, because of his want of Courage, revenge himself in another Manner.*

Mr. Attorney. Pray Mr. *Hamilton,* have a Care what you say, don't go too far neither, I don't like those Liberties.

Mr. Hamilton. Sure, Mr. Attorney, you won't make any Applications; all Men agree that we are governed by the best of Kings, and I cannot see the Meaning of Mr. Attorney's Caution; my well known Principles, and the Sense I have of the Blessings we enjoy under His present Majesty, makes it impossible for me to err, and I hope, even to be suspected, in that Point of Duty to my King. May it please Your Honour, I was saying, That notwithstanding all the Duty and Reverence claimed by Mr. Attorney to Men in Authority, they are not exempt from observing the Rules of Common Justice, even in their private or public Capacities; the Laws of our Mother Country know no Exemption. It is true, Men in Power are harder to be come at for Wrongs they do, either to a private Person, or to the Publick; especially a Governor in the Plantations, where they insist upon an Exemption from answering Complaints of any Kind in their own Government. We are indeed told, and it is true they are obliged to answer a Suit in the King's Courts at *Westminster,* for a Wrong done to any Person here: But do we not know how impracticable this is to most Men among us, to leave their Families (who depend upon their Labour and Care for their Livelihood) and carry Evidences to *Britain,* and at a great, nay, a far greater Expense than almost any of us are able to bear, only to prosecute a Governour for an Injury done here. But when the Oppression is general, there is no Remedy even that Way, no, our Constitution has (blessed be God) given us an Opportunity, if not to have such Wrongs redressed, yet by our Prudence and Resolution we may in a great Measure prevent the committing of such Wrongs, by making a Governour sensible that it is to his interest to be just to those under his Care; for such is the Sense that Men in General (I mean Freemen) have of common Justice, that when they come to know, that a chief Magistrate abuses the Power with which he is trusted, for the good of the People, and is attempting to turn that very Power against the Innocent, whether of high or low degree, I say, Mankind in general seldom fail to interpose, and as far as they can, prevent the Destruction of their fellow Subjects. And has it not often been seen (and I hope it will always be seen) that when the Representatives of a free People are by just Representations or Remonstrances, made sensible of the Sufferings of their Fellow-Subjects, by the Abuse of Power in the Hands of a Governour, they have declared (and loudly too) that they were not obliged by any Law to support a Governour who goes about to destroy a Province or Colony, or their Priviledges, which by His Majesty he was appointed, and by the Law he is bound to protect and encourage. But I pray it may be considered of what Use is this mighty Priviledge, if every Man that suffers must be silent? And if a Man must be taken up as a Libeller, for telling his Sufferings to his Neighbour? I know it may be answer'd, *Have you not a Legislature? Have you not a House of Representatives, to whom you may complain?* And to this I answer, we have. But what then? Is an Assembly to be troubled with every Injury done by a Governour? Or are they to hear of nothing but what those in the Administration will please to tell them? Or what Sort of a

Tryal must a Man have? And how is he to be remedied; especially if the Case were, as I have known it to happen in *America* in my Time; That a Governour who has Places (I will not [say] Pensions, for I believe they seldom give that to another which they can take to themselves) to bestow, and can or will keep the same Assembly (after he has modeled them so as to get a Majority of the House in his Interest) for near *twice Seven Years* together? I pray, what Redress is to be expected for an honest Man, who makes his Complaint against a Governour to an Assembly who may properly enough be said, to be made by the same Governour against whom the Complaint is made? The Thing answers it self. No, it is natural, it is a Priviledge, I will go farther, it is a Right which all Freemen claim, and are entitled to complain when they are hurt; they have a Right publickly to remonstrate the Abuses of Power, in the strongest Terms, to put their Neighbours upon their Guard, against the Craft or open Violence of Men in Authority, and to assert with Courage the Sense they have of the Blessings of Liberty, the Value they put upon it, and their Resolution at all Hazards to preserve it, as one of the greatest Blessings Heaven can bestow. . . .

. . . I beg Leave to insist, That the Right of complaining or remonstrating is natural; And the Restraint upon this natural Right is the Law only, and that those Restraints can only extend to what is *false;* For as it is Truth alone which can excuse or justify any Man for complaining of a bad Administration, I as frankly agree, that nothing ought to excuse a Man who raises a false Charge or Accusation, even against a private Person, and that no manner of Allowance ought to be made to him who does so against a publick Magistrate. *Truth* ought to govern the whole Affair of Libels, and yet the Party accused runs Risque enough even then; for if he fails of proving every Tittle of what he has wrote, and to the Satisfaction of the Court and Jury too, he may find to his Cost, that when the Prosecution is set on Foot by Men in Power, it seldom wants

Friends to Favour it. And from thence (it is said) has arisen
the great Diversity of Opinions among Judges, about what
words were or were not scandalous or libellous. I believe it
will be granted, that there is not greater Uncertainty in any
Part of the Law than about Words of Scandal; it would be
mispending of the Court's Time to mention the Cases; they
may be said to be numberless; and therefore the uttermost
Care ought to be taken in following Precedents; and the
Times when the Judgments were given, which are quoted for
Authorities in the Case of Libels, are much to be regarded.
I think it will be agreed, That ever since the Time of the Star
Chamber, where the most arbitrary and destructive Judgments
and Opinions were given, that ever an *Englishman* heard of,
at least in his own Country: I say, Prosecutions for Libels since
the Time of that arbitrary Court, and until the glorious Revolution, have generally been set on Foot at the Instance of the
Crown or its Ministers; and it is no small Reproach to the Law,
that these Prosecutions were too often and too much countenanced by the Judges, who held their Places at Pleasure, (a
disagreeable Tenure to any Officer, but a dangerous one in the
Case of a Judge.) To say more to this Point may not be
proper. . . .

. . . If Power has had so great an Influence on Judges; how
cautious ought we to be in determining by their Judgments,
especially in the Plantations, and in the Case of Libels? There
is Heresy in Law, as well as in Religion, and both have
changed very much; and we well know that it is not two Centuries ago that a Man would have been burnt as an Heretick,
for owning such Opinions in Matters of Religion as are publickly wrote and printed at this Day. They were fallible Men, it
seems, and we take the Liberty not only to differ from them
in religious Opinion, but to condemn them and their Opinions
too; and I must presume, that in taking these Freedoms in
thinking and speaking about Matters of Faith and Religion, we
are in the right: For, tho' it is said there are very great Liber-

ties of this Kind taken in *Newe York,* yet I have heard of no Information prefered by Mr. Attorney for any Offences of this Sort. From which I think it is pretty clear, That in *New-York* a Man may make very free with his God, but he must take special Care what he says of his Governour. It is agreed upon by all Men that this is a Reign of Liberty, and while Men keep within the Bounds of Truth, I hope they may with Safety both speak and write their Sentiments of the Conduct of Men in Power, I me[a]n of that Part of their Conduct only, which affects the Liberty or Property of the People under their Administration; were this to be denied, then the next Step may make them Slaves. For what Notions can be entertained of Slavery, beyond that of suffering the greatest Injuries and Oppressions, without the Liberty of complaining; or if they do, to be destroyed, Body and Estate, for so doing?

It is said and insisted upon by Mr. Attorney, *That Government is a sacred Thing; That it is to be supported and reverenced; It is Government that protects our Persons and Estates; That prevents Treasons, Murders, Robberies, Riots, and all the Train of Evils that overturns Kingdoms and States, and ruins particular Persons; and if those in the Administration, especially the Supream Magistrate, must have all their Conduct censured by private Men, Government cannot subsist.* This is called *a Licentiousness not to be tollerated.* It is said, *That it brings the Rulers of the People into Contempt, and their Authority not to be regarded, and so in the End the Laws cannot be put in Execution.* These I say, and such as these, are the general Topicks insisted upon by Men in Power, and their Advocates. But I wish it might be considered at the same Time, How often it has happened, that the Abuse of Power has been the primary Cause of these Evils, and that it was the Injustice and Oppression of these great Men, which has commonly brought them into Contempt with the People. The Craft and Art of such Men is great, and who, that is the least acquainted with History or Law, can be ignorant of the specious Pretences,

which have often been made use of by Men in Power, to introduce arbitrary Rule, and destroy the Liberties of a free People. . . .

. . . This is the second Information for Libelling of a Governour that I have known in *America*. And the first, tho' it may
look like a Romance, yet as it is true, I will beg Leave to mention it. Governor *Nicholson*, who happened to be offended with
one [of] his Clergy, met him one Day upon the Road, and as
was usual with him (under the Protection of his Commission)
used the poor Parson with the worst of Language, threatened
to cut off his Ears, slit his Nose, and at last to shoot him
through the Head. The Parson being a reverend Man, continued all this Time uncovered in the Heat of the Sun, until he
found an Opportunity to fly for it; and coming to a Neighbours
House felt himself very ill of a Fever, and immediately writes
for a doctor; and that his Physician might the better judge of
his Distemper, he acquainted him with the Usage he had received; concluding, that the Governor was certainly mad, for
that no Man in his Senses would have behaved in that manner.
The Doctor unhappily shews the Parson's Letter; the Governour came to hear of it; and so an Information was preferred
against the poor Man for saying *he believed the Governour
was mad;* and it was laid in the Information to be *false, scandalous,* and *wicked, and wrote with Intent to move Sedition
among the People, and bring His Excellency into Contempt.*
But by an Order from the late Queen *Anne,* there was a Stop
put to that Prosecution, with sundry others set on foot by the
same Governour, against Gentlemen of the greatest Worth
and Honour in that Government.

And may not I be allowed, after all this, to say, That by a
little Countenance, almost any Thing which a Man writes,
may, with the Help of that useful Term of Art, called an
Innuendo, be construed to be a Libel, according to Mr. Attorney's Definition of it. . . .

. . . If a Libel is understood in the large and unlimited Sense urged by Mr. Attorney, there is scarce a Writing I know that may not be called a Libel, or scarce any Person safe from being called to an Account as a Libeller. . . .

. . . The Danger is great, in Proportion to the Mischief that may happen, through our too great Credulity. A proper Confidence in a Court is commendable; but as the Verdict (whatever it is) will be yours, you ought to refer no Part of your Duty to the Discretion of other Persons. If you should be of Opinion, that there is no Falsehood in Mr. *Zenger's* Papers, you will, nay (pardon me for the Expression) you ought to say so; because you don't know whether others (I mean the Court) may be of that Opinion. It is your Right to do so, and there is much depending upon your Resolution, as well as upon your Integrity. . . .

. . . I hope to be pardon'd Sir for my Zeal upon this Occasion; it is an old and wise Caution, *That when our Neighbours House is on Fire, we ought to take Care of our own.* For tho' Blessed be God, I live in a Government where Liberty is well understood, and freely enjoy'd; yet Experience has shewn us all (I'm sure it has to me) that a bad Precedent in one Government, is soon set up for an Authority in another; and therefore I cannot but think it mine, and every Honest Man's Duty, that (while we pay all due Obedience to Men in Authority) we ought at the same Time to be upon our Guard against Power, wherever we apprehend that it may affect ourselves or our Fellow-Subjects.

I am truely very unequal to such an Undertaking on many Accounts. And you see I labour under the Weight of many Years, and am born down with great Infirmities of Body; yet Old and Weak as I am, I should think of it my Duty, if required, to go to the utmost Part of the Land, where my Service could be of any Use in assisting to quench the Flame of Prosecutions upon Informations, set on Foot by the Government, to deprive a People of the Right of Remonstrating (and complaining too) of the arbitrary Attempts of Men in Power. Men who injure and oppress the People under the Administration provoke them to cry out and complain; and then make that very Complaint the Foundation for new Oppressions and Prosecutions. I wish I could say there were no Instances of this Kind. But to conclude; the Question before the Court and you, Gentlemen of the Jury, is not of small nor private Concern, it is not the Cause of a poor Printer, nor of *New-York* alone, which you are now trying: No! It may in its Consequence, affect every Freeman that lives under a British Government on the main of *America*. It is the best Cause. It is the Cause of Liberty; and I make no Doubt but your upright Conduct, this Day, will not only entitle you to the Love and Esteem of your Fellow-Citizens; but every Man who prefers Freedom to a Life of Slavery will bless and honour You, as Men who have baffled the Attempt of Tyranny; and by an impartial and uncorrupt Verdict, have laid a noble Foundation for securing to ourselves, our Posterity, and our Neighbours, That, to which Nature and the Laws of our Country have given us a Right— The Liberty—both of exposing and opposing arbitrary Power (in these Parts of the World, at least) by speaking and writing Truth.

(Here Mr. Attorney observ'd, that Mr. Hamilton *had gone very much out of the Way, and had made himself and the People very merry: But that he had been citing Cases, not at all to the Purpose; he said, there was no such Cause as Mr.* Bushel's *or Sir* Edward Hales *before the Court; and he could not find out what the Court or Jury had to do with Dispensations, Riots or unlawful Assemblies: All that the Jury had to consider of was Mrs. (sic)* Zenger's *Printing and Publishing two scandalous Libels, which very highly reflected on his Excellency and the principal Men concern'd in the Administration of this Government, which is confess'd. That is, the Printing and Publishing of the Journals set forth in the Information is confess'd. And concluded that as Mr.* Hamilton *had confess'd the Printing and there could be no doubt but they were scan-*

dalous Papers, highly reflecting upon his Excellency, and the principal Magistrates in the Province. And therefore he made no Doubt but the Jury would find the Defendant Guilty, and would refer to the Court for their Direction.)

Mr. Ch. Just. Gentlemen of the Jury. The great pains Mr. *Hamilton* has taken, to shew how little Regard Juries are to Pay to the Opinion of the Judges; and his insisting so much upon the Conduct of some Judges in Tryals of this kind; is done, no doubt, with a Design that you should take but very little Notice, of what I might say upon this Occasion. I shall therefore only observe to you that, as the Facts or Words in the Information are confessed: The only Thing that can come in Question before you is, whether the Words as set forth in the Information, make a Lybel. And that is a Matter of Law, no Doubt, and which you may leave to the Court. But I shall trouble you no further with any Thing more of my own, but read to you the Words of a learned and upright Judge[1] in a Case of the like Nature.

"To say that corrupt Officers are appointed to administer Affairs, is certainly a Reflection on the Government. If People should not be called to account for possessing the People with an ill Opinion of the Government, no Government can subsist. For it is very necessary for all Governments that the People should have a good Opinion of it. And nothing can be worse to any Government, than to endeavour to procure Animosities; as to the Management of it, this has always been look'd upon as a Crime, and no Government can be safe without it be punished."

Now you are to consider, whether these Words I have read to you, do not tend to beget an ill Opinion of the Administration of the Government? To tell us, that those that are employed know nothing of the Matter, and those that do know

---

[1] Ch. J. *Holt* in *Tutchin's* Case.

are not employed. Men are not adapted to Offices, but Offices, to Men out of a particular Regard to their Interest, and not to their Fitness for the Places; this is the Purport of these Papers.

Mr. *Hamilton.* I humbly beg Your Honours Pardon; I am very much mis-apprehended, if you suppose what I said was so designed.

Sir, you know; I made an Apology for the Freedom I found myself under a Necessity of using on this Occasion. I said, there was Nothing personal designed; it arose from the Nature of our Defence.

(The Jury withdrew and in a small Time returned and being asked by the Clerk whether they were agreed of their Verdict, and whether *John Peter Zenger* was guilty of Printing and Publishing the Libels in the Information mentioned? They answered by *Thomas Hunt,* their Foreman, *Not Guilty,* Upon which there were three Huzzas in the Hall which was crowded with People. . . .

James Alexander Draws a Lesson from History

In 1737 two West Indian lawyers, one of whom was probably Jonathan Blenman, the King's attorney in Barbados, published severe strictures of a technical character against the Zenger defense. They purported to disprove on legal grounds the contention that truth was a defense against a libel charge. The thesis of both "Anglo-Americanus" and "Indus-Britannicus" was that truth not only could be libelous but necessarily exacerbated the libel. An impartial observer must admit that they scored heavily on points of law against Hamilton and Alexander. They also argued that the press was not the proper place in which to remonstrate against an arbitrary or corrupt government. Their essays were republished in Philadelphia by Andrew Bradford, Andrew Hamilton's old enemy.

It was James Alexander who replied, in a four-part essay that was first published in the paper of Bradford's competitor, Franklin's *Pennsylvania Gazette*, and then republished in Zenger's *New-York Weekly Journal*. Alexander failed to confront many of his opponents' technical arguments of law. He admitted believing that in a "popular cause," when the defendant was unjustly prosecuted, counsel should use his "art" to "raise passions," rather than observe "dry rules of strict pleading." In these essays Alexander drew some lessons from history, more freely construed a few precedents, and concluded that constitutional government and freedom of the press could not survive without each other.

10. FREE SPEECH IS A PILLAR OF FREE GOVERNMENT

To the author of the Pennsylvania Gazette.

SIR, THE FREEDOM OF SPEECH is a *principal pillar* in a free Government: when this support is taken away the Constitution is dissolved, and tyranny is erected on its ruins. Republics and limited monarchies derive their strength and vigor from a *popular examination* into the actions of the Magistrates. This privilege in all ages has been and always will be abused. The best of Princes could not escape the censure and envy of the times they lived in. But the evil is not so great as it may appear at first sight. A Magistrate who sincerely aims at the *good* of the society will always have the inclinations of a great majority on his side; and impartial posterity will not fail to render him Justice.

These abuses of the Freedom of Speech are the excrescences of Liberty. They ought to be suppressed; but to whom dare we commit the care of doing it? An evil Magistrate entrusted with a POWER to *punish Words* is armed with a WEAPON the

---

The Pennsylvania Gazette (Philadelphia), November 17–December 8, 1737.

most *destructive* and *terrible*. Under pretense of pruning off the exuberant branches, he frequently destroys the tree.

It is certain that he who robs another of his moral reputation more richly merits a gibbet than if he had plundered him of his purse on the highway. *Augustus Caesar* under the specious pretext of preserving the characters of the Romans from defamation introduced the law whereby libeling was involved in the penalties of *treason* against the State. This established his tyranny, and for one mischief it prevented, ten thousand evils, horrible and tremendous, sprung up in the place. Thenceforward every person's Life and Fortune depended on the vile breath of informers. The construction of words being arbitrary and left to the decision of the judges, no man could write or open his Mouth without being in danger of forfeiting his head. . . .

. . . THOSE of the British kings who aimed at despotic power or the oppression of the subject constantly encouraged prosecutions for Words. . . .

. . . [Charles I's] Ministers, to let the Nation see they were absolutely determined to suppress all Freedom of Speech, caused a prosecution to be carried on by the Attorney General against three of the Commons for words spoken in the House Anno 1628. The Members pleaded to the Information, that Expressions in Parliament ought only to be examined and punished There: This notwithstanding they were all Three condemned as disturbers of the state. . . .

That Englishmen of all ranks might be effectually intimidated from publishing their thoughts on any subject *except on the side of the Court;* His Majesty's ministers caused an information for several libels to be exhibited in the Star Chamber against Mr. Prynn, Burton and Bastwick. They were, each of them, fined £5000, adjudged to lose their ears on the pillory, to be branded on the cheeks with hot irons, and to suffer perpetual imprisonment. Thus these three gentlemen, each of figure and quality in their several professions, *viz., divinity, law* and *physic,* were, for no other offense than writing on controverted Points of Church-Government, exposed on public scaffolds, and stigmatized and mutilated as common signal Rogues, or the most mechanic Malefactors.

Such corporal Punishments, inflicted with all the circumstances of cruelty and infamy, bound down all other Gentlemen under a servile fear of the like treatment; so that, for several Years, no one durst publickly speak or write in defense of the Liberties of the People, which the King's Ministers, his privy Council, and his Judges had trampled under their feet.

The SPIRIT of the administration looked HIDEOUS and DREADFUL. The Hate and Resentment which the People conceived against it for a long time lay smothered in their breasts; where these Passions festered and grew venomous, and at last discharged themselves by an armed and VINDICTIVE hand.

———————

KING CHARLES II aimed at the subversion of the government, but concealed his designs under a deep hypocrisy. A method which his Predecessor, *in the beginning of his reign,* scorned to make use of. The Father, who affected a high and rigid gravity, discountenanced all barefaced immorality. The Son, of a gay luxurious disposition, openly encouraged it. So their inclinations being different, the restraint laid on some Authors and the encouragement given to others were managed after a different manner.

In this reign a Licenser was appointed for the Stage and the Press. No plays were encouraged but what had a tendency to debase the minds of the people. . . .

. . . The doctrine of servitude was chiefly managed by Sir *Roger L'Estrange.* He had great advantages in the argument, being licenser for the press, and might have carried all before him without contradiction if Writings on the other side of the question had not been printed by stealth. The authors were prosecuted as seditious libelers. On all these Occasions the King's counsil, particularly *Sawyer* and *Finch,* appeared most abjectly obsequious to the ends of the Court. . . .

. . . *Sidney,* the sworn foe of Tyranny, was a Gentleman of noble birth, of sublime understanding and exalted courage. The ministry were resolved to remove so great an obstacle out of the way of their Designs. He was prosecuted for High Treason. The overt-fact charged in the indictment was a *Libel* found in his private study. Mr. *Finch,* the King's Solicitor-General, urged with great vehemency *to this effect; That the imagining the death of the King is Treason, even while that imagination remains covert in the mind, though the law cannot punish such secret treasonable thoughts till it arrives to the knowledge of them by some overt fact. That the matter of the Libel composed by Sidney was an imagining how to compass the death of King Charles II and the writing of it was an overt fact of the Treason, for that* scribere est agere. It seems the King's Counsil in this Reign had not received the same direction as Queen *Elizabeth* gave her's. She told them they were to look upon themselves as retained, not so much *pro domina Regina,* as *pro domina veritate.*

Mr. *Sidney* made a strong and legal defense. He insisted that all the words in the book contained no more than general speculations of government, free for any man to write down, especially since the same are written in the Parliament rolls and in the Statute laws.

He argued on the injustice of applying, by *innuendoes,* general assertions concerning government as overt-facts to prove the writer was compassing the death of the King; for then no man could write of things done by our Ancestors in defense of the constitution and freedom of Britain without exposing himself to capital danger.

He denied that *scribere est agere,* but allowed that *scribere et publicare est agere;* and therefore He urged, That as his book was never published or imparted to any person, it could not be an overt fact within the Statute of Treasons, admitting it contained treasonable positions; That on the contrary it was a covert fact locked up in his private study, as much concealed from the knowledge of any man as if it were locked up in the author's mind. This was the substance of Mr. *Sidney's* defense. But not Law, nor Reason, nor Eloquence, nor Innocence ever availed where *Jeffreys* sat as judge. Without troubling himself with any part of the defense, he declared *in furore* that *Sidney's* known principles was a sufficient proof of his intention to compass the death of the King: A packt jury thereupon found him guilty of High-treason. Great appplications were made for his pardon. He was executed as a Traitor. This case is a pregnant instance of the danger that attends a law for punishing words; and of the little security the most valuable men have for their lives in that society where a judge by remote inferences and distant innuendo's may construe the most innocent expressions into capital crimes. . . .

In the two former papers the writer endeavored to prove by historical facts the fatal dangers that necessarily attend a Restraint on freedom of speech and the liberty of the press: Upon which the following Reflection naturally occurs, viz., THAT WHOEVER ATTEMPTS TO SUPPRESS EITHER OF THOSE, *OUR NATURAL RIGHTS*, OUGHT TO BE REGARDED AS AN *ENEMY* TO LIBERTY AND THE CONSTITUTION. *An inconveniency is always to be suffered when it cannot be removed without introducing a worse.*

I proceed in the next place to enquire into the nature of the English Laws in relation to libeling: To acquire a just idea of Them the knowledge of history is necessary, and the genius and disposition of the Prince is to be considered, in whose time They were introduced and put in practice.

To infuse into the minds of the people an ill opinion of a just administration is a crime that deserves no mercy: But to expose the evil designs or weak management of a magistrate is the duty of every member of society. Yet King *James* I thought it an unpardonable presumption in the subject to pry into the *arcana imperii.* He imagined that the people ought to believe the authority of the government infallible, and that their submission should be implicit. It may therefore be reasonably presumed that the judgment of the *Star chamber* concerning libels was influenced by His majesty's notions of government. No law could be better framed to prevent people from publishing their thoughts on the administration than that which makes no distinction whether a libel be true or false. It is not pretended that any such decision is to be found in our books before this reign. That is not at all to be wondered at. King *James* was the first of the british Monarchs that laid claim to a *divine right. . . .*

. . . The punishment for writing Truth is Pillory, loss of ears, branding the face with hot irons, fine and imprisonment at the discretion of the court. Nay, the punishment is to be heightened in proportion to the Truth of the facts contained in the libel. But if this monstrous doctrine could have been swallowed down by that *worthy* Jury who were on the Trial of the seven Bishops prosecuted for a libel in the reign of King *James* II, the liberties of *Britain* in all human probability had been lost, and popery and slavery established in the three kingdoms.

This was a cause of the greatest expectation and importance that ever came before the Judges in Westminster-hall. The bishops had petitioned the King, *That he would be graciously pleased not to insist upon their reading in the churches his Majesty's declaration for liberty of conscience; BECAUSE* IT WAS FOUNDED ON A DISPENSING POWER DECLARED ILLEGAL IN PARLIAMENT. *And They said that they could not, in prudence, honor or conscience, so far make themselves parties to it.* In the information exhibited by the Attorney-General, the Bishops were charged with writing and publishing a false malicious and seditious libel (*under pretense of a petition*) in diminution of the King's prerogative and contempt of his government. . . .

. . . The King's Counsel having produced their evidences as to the publication of the petition, The Question then to be debated was whether it contained Libelous Matter or no.

It was *Argued,* in substance, for the Bishops, That the Matter could not be libelous, because It was true. . . .

It was strongly *Urged* in behalf of the King: That the Only Point to be looked into was, whether the Libel be reflecting or scandalous, and not whether it be true or false. That the Bishops had injured and affronted the King by presuming to prescribe to him their Opinions in matters of Government. That under pretense of delivering a petition, they come and tell his Majesty He has commanded an illegal Thing. That by such a proceeding They threw dirt in the King's face, and so were Libellers with a Witness.

Previous to the opinions of the Judges, it will be necessary to give the Reader a short sketch of their Characters. . . . *Wright* in his Charge called the petition a libel, and declared that anything which disturbs the Government is within the Case de libellis famosis [the Star chamber doctrine]. *Holloway* told the Jury that the end and intention of every action is to be considered, and that as the Bishops had *no ill Intention* in delivering their petition, it could not be deemed MALICIOUS OR LIBELLOUS. *Powell* declared that falsehood and malice are two essential qualities of a Libel, which the Prosecutor is obliged to prove. *Allibone* replied upon *Powell* that we are not to measure things from any Truth they have in themselves, but from the Aspect they have on the Government; for that every tittle of a libel may be true and yet be a libel still.

The compass of this paper would not admit me to quote the opinions of the Judges at length. But I have endeavored, with the strictest regard to Truth, to give the substance and effect of them.

It has been generally said that the Judges in this Trial, were equally divided in their Opinions. But we shall find a Majority on the Bench in favor of the Bishops when we consider that the cause as to *Allibone* was *coram non judice.*

Here then is a *Late* Authority which sets aside, Destroys, and Annuls the Doctrine of the *Star-chamber* reported by Sir *Edward Coke* in his Case *de libellis famosis.* . . .

. . . In civil actions an advocate should never appear but when he is persuaded the merits of the cause lie on the side of his client. In criminal actions it often happens that the defendant in strict justice deserves punishment; yet a Counsel may oppose it when a magistrate cannot come at the offender without making a breach in the barriers of liberty, and opening a floodgate to arbitrary power. But when the defendant is innocent and unjustly prosecuted, his Counsel may, nay ought to take all advantages and use every Stratagem that his skill, art and learning can furnish him with. This last was the case of *Zenger* at *New-York,* as appears by the printed Trial and the VERDICT of the Jury. It was a popular cause. The LIBERTY OF THE PRESS in that Province depended on it. On such occasions the dry Rules of strict pleading are never observed. The Counsel for the Defendant sometimes argues from the known principles of Law, then raises doubts and difficulties to confound his Antagonist, now applies himself to the affections, and chiefly endeavors to raise the passions. *Zenger's* Defense is to be considered in all those different lights. Yet a Gentleman of *Barbadoes* assures us that it was published as a Solemn argument in the Law, and therefore writes a very elaborate confutation of it.

I propose to consider some of his objections as far as they interfere with the *Freedom of Speech* and the *Liberty of the Press* contended for. . . .

Our Author labours to prove that a Libel whether true or false is punishable. The first Authority for his purpose is the *Case of John de Northampton* adjudged in the reign of *Edward* III. *Northampton* had wrote a libelous letter to one of the King's Council, purporting that the Judges no great thing would do at the commandment of the King, etc., said *John* was called and the Court pronounced judgment against him on those grounds that the Letter contained no Truth in it and might incense the King against his Judges. Mr. *Hamilton* says *that by this judgment it appears the libelous words were utterly false, and there the falsehood was the crime and is the ground of the judgment.* The Remarker rejects this explanation, and gives us an ingenious comment of his own. . . .

It requires no great penetration to make this decision in question appear reasonable and intelligible. But it ought first to be observed, that *Edward* III was *One* of the best and wisest, as well as the bravest of our Kings, and that the Law had never a freer course than under his Reign. Where the Letter mentions that the Judges would do no great Things (*i.e.,* illegal Things) by the King's commandment, it was plainly insinuated that the Judges suspected that the King might command them to do illegal Things. Now by the means of that Letter, the King, being led to imagine that the Judges harbor'd a suspicion so unworthy of him, might be justly incensed against them. Therefore the Record truly says that the Letter was utterly false, and that there was couched under it an insinuation (certainly MALICIOUS) that might raise an indignation in his Majesty against the Court.—*qua litera continet in se NULLAM VERITATEM, praetexture cujus Dominus Rex erga curiam et justiciarios suos habere posset indignationem, etc.* Hence it evidently appears that not only the *falsehood* but also the *malice* was the Ground of the Judgment.

I agree with the Remarker that *Noy,* citing this case, says *that the letter contained no ill, yet the writer was punished.* But these words are absolutely absurd as they stand in the Remarks, detached from the context. *Noy* adduces *Northampton's* case to prove that a man is punishable for complaining without a cause, though the words of the complaint (simply considered) should contain no ill in them. It is not material to enquire whether the application is just: It is only an expression of a Counsel at the Bar. The case was adjourned and we hear no more of it. Yet these words of *Noy*, the Remarker would pass on to the Reader as a good authority. *This book therefore,* quoth he referring to *Godbolt's reports, follows the record of* Northampton's *case, and says that because it might incense the King against the judges he was punished, which is almost a translation of* praetextu cujus, etc. I could readily pardon our author's gibberish and want of apprehension, but cannot so easily digest his insincerity.

The Remarker in the next place proceeds to the Trial of the seven Bishops. I shall quote his own words, tho' I know they are so senseless and insipid that I run the risk of trespassing on the reader's patience. However, here they be.

Mr. Justice Powell also does say *that to make it a libel, it must be false, it must be malicious and it must tend to sedition.* Upon which words of this learned and worthy Judge, I would not presume to offer any comment, except that which other words of his own afford, that plainly show in what sense he then spoke. His subsequent words are these, *the Bishops tell His Majesty it is not out of averseness, etc.* So that the Judge put the whole upon that single point, whether it be true, that the King had a dispensing power or not; which is a question of Law and not of Fact, and accordingly the Judge appeals to his own reading in the law, not to witnesses or other Testimonies for a decision of it.

Now the Bishops had asserted, in the libel they were charged with, that the dispensing power, claimed by the King in his declaration, was illegal. The Remarker by granting that the Prelates might prove part of their assertion, viz., that the dispensing power was illegal, which is a question of law, necessarily allows them to prove the other part of their assertion, viz., that his Majesty had claimed such a power, which is a question of fact; for the former could not be decided without proving or admitting the latter. And so in all other cases where a man publishes of a Magistrate that he has acted or commanded an illegal thing; if the Defendant shall be admitted to prove the *mode* or illegality of the thing, it is evidently implied that he may prove the thing itself. So that on the Gentleman's own Premises, it is a clear consequence that a man, prosecuted for a Libel shall be admitted to give the Truth in evidence. The Remarker has a method of reasoning peculiar to himself: He frequently advances arguments, which directly prove the very point he is laboring to confute.

But in truth Judge *Powel's* words would not have given the least colour to such a ridiculous distinction, if they had been fairly quoted. He affirms with the strongest emphasis *that to make it a libel it MUST be false, it MUST be malicious and it MUST tend to sedition.* (Let it be observed that these three qualities of a Libel against the Government, are in the conjunctive.) His subsequent words are these, *as to the falsehood, I see nothing that is offered by the King's Counsel, nor any thing as to the malice.* Here the Judge puts the proof both of the falsehood and malice on the prosecutor; and though the falsehood in this case was a question of Law, it will not be denied but that the malice was a question of Fact. Now shall we attribute this omission to the inadvertency of the Remarker? No, that cannot be supposed, for the sentence immediately followed. But they were nailing, decisive words, which, if they were fairly quoted, had put an end to the dispute, and left the Remarker without the least room for an evasion; and therefore he very honestly dropt them.

Our Author says it is necessary to consult *Bracton* in order to fix our idea of a libel. Now *Bracton* throughout his five books *de legibus et consuetudinibus angliae* only once happens to mention libels, very perfunctorily. He says no more than that a man may receive an Injury by a Lampoon and things of that nature. *Fit injuria cum de eo factum carmen famosum et hujusmodi.* Pray how is any person's idea of a libel the better fixed by this description of it? Our author very sagaciously observes on these words of *Bracton* that the falsity of a libel is neither expressed nor implied by them. That it is not expressed is self-evident, but that it is not implied we have only the Re-marker's *ipse dixit* for it. But it was really idle and impertinent to draw this ancient Lawyer into the Dispute, as nothing could be learned from him, only that a libel is an injury, which every-body will readily grant. . . .

. . . Besides, the Liberty of the Press would be wholly abolished if the Remarker could have propagated the doctrine of punishing Truth. Yet he declares he would not be thought to derogate from that noble Privilege of a free people. How does he reconcile these contradictions? Why truly, thus. He says that the Liberty of the Press is a bulwark and two-edged weapon capable of cutting two ways, and is only to be trusted in the hands of men of wit and address, and not with such Fools as rail without art. I pass over the blunder of his calling a bulwark a two-edged weapon, for a Lawyer is not supposed to be acquainted with military Terms; but is it not highly ridiculous that the gentleman will not allow a squib to be fired from the Bulwark of Liberty, yet freely gives permission to erect on it a Battery of Cannon.

Again. *Satire* is painted smiling with a dagger under her gown; the more concealed, the surer and deeper it wounds. Barefaced Scurrilities founded on falsehood (such as the Re-marks are stuffed with) are the most silly harmless things imaginable, that do just as much mischief as the coarse ribaldry of a foul-mouthed waterman, or the gross raillery of a *Billings-gate* wench. Our author would encourage the former but pun-ish the latter. Mr. *Hamilton* seems to be of a contrary opinion by the contempt he shows for the Remarker's Performance.

I would not, however, by anything I have offered, be under-stood to draw into question the abilities of our author, con-sidered in his oratorial capacity; for it often happens that the Gentlemen, *qui jurgia vendunt,* appear with a *grand éclat* at the Bar, tho' they make but lamentable figures in Print.

I pursue him no further. Much less shall I take any notice of his admirer *Indus Britanicus.* This fellow is wretchedly ignorant; His little sense, if possible, sinks below contempt. His ignorance is only equalled by his malice. Yet methinks, They ought to have been contented in lashing Mr. *Hamilton* with their dull strokes of no-wit, and not have libelled the Chief Justice by declaring he knew not his Duty; and publishing it thro' the continent.

Upon the whole. To suppress enquiries into the administration is good policy in an arbitrary Government: But a Free Constitution and Freedom of Speech have such a reciprocal dependence on each other that they cannot subsist without consisting together.

William Livingston Presents a Libertarian View

William Livingston learned law and libertarian principles when studying in the office of James Alexander. In 1752 he and his friends, William Smith, Jr. (see the present volume, Document 16), and John Morin Scott, founded *The Independent Reflector*, a weekly magazine. Their purpose was "to oppose superstition, bigotry, priestcraft, tyranny, servitude, public mismanagement and dishonesty in office," and to advocate "the inestimable value of liberty." The following essay by Livingston reflects mid-century American libertarian theory at its best. Livingston was subsequently a spirited opponent of Parliamentary interference in provincial affairs. He served as a delegate to the First and Second Continental Congresses, became the first governor of the state of New Jersey, and was one of that state's representatives at the Philadelphia Constitutional Convention in 1787. The leading essays in *The Independent Reflector*, which lasted only a year, have recently been republished. Their editor, defending the following essay against attempts to minimize its libertarian character, argues: "The distinction he [Livingston] drew in this issue was not between a legitimate use of the press against executive prerogative and its abuse when employed against legislatures but rather between a press employed to promote liberty and one used to advance what he regarded as 'superstition and thralldom.'" Nevertheless, Livingston explicitly stated that certain political publications should be punished for "high Treason against the State."

11. *Of the Use, Abuse, and* LIBERTY OF THE PRESS

Whether the Art of PRINTING has been of greater Service or Detriment to the World, has frequently been made the Subject of fruitless Controversy. The best Things have been perverted to serve the vilest Purposes, their being therefore subject to Abuse, is an illogical Argument against their Utility. Before the Invention of the Press, the Progress of Knowledge was slow, because the Methods of diffusing it were laborious and expensive. The shortest Production was too costly to its Author; and unless the Writer had an opulent Fortune, or rich Patrons to pay off his *Amanuenses*, he was driven to the Necessity of retailing his Compositions. To arrive at Fame and literary Glory, was not in the Power of every great Genius; and doubtless Posterity has lost the Sentiments of many eminent Men, which might have been equally useful and important, with the Writings of those, who make the brightest Appearance in the Annals of Fame. It is otherwise since the Discovery of the Art of *Printing*. The most inferior Genius, however impoverished, can spread his Thoughts thro' a Kingdom. The Public has the Advantage of the Sentiments of all its Individuals. Thro' the Press, Writers of every Character and Genius, may promulge their Opinions; and all conspire to rear and support the Republic of Letters. The Patriot can by this Means, diffuse his salutary Principles thro' the Breasts of his Countrymen, interpose his friendly Advice unasked, warn

William Livingston, "Of the Use, Abuse, and LIBERTY OF THE PRESS," *The Independent Reflector or Weekly Essays on Sundry Important Subjects*, XL, August 30, 1753. See William Livingston and Others, *The Independent Reflector . . .* , ed. Milton M. Klein (Cambridge, Mass.: The Belknap Press of Harvard University Press, 1963), pp. 336–344.

them against approaching Danger, unite them against the Arm of despotic Power, and perhaps, at the Expence of but a few Sheets of Paper, save the State from impending Destruction. The Divine is not confined within the narrow Limits of his parochial Duties, but may preach in his Writings to the whole World. Like Powers in Mechanics, he does as it were, multiply himself: For at the Instant he Visits the Sick of his own Parish, he is perhaps consoling Hundreds against the Fears of Death, in foreign Nations and different Languages, and preaching to many Thousands at the same Time. And surely his Pleasure must equal his Labours, when he reflects, that his pastoral Care extends thro' the whole christianiz'd World; that however thin and secluded his particular Parish may be, yet that several Nations are within the Sphere of his Influence; that he shall even live after his Death, and Thousands whom he never saw, be his Crown of rejoicing at the great Day of Judgment. Such also are the Advantages of *Printing*, to the Philosopher, the Moralist, the Lawyer, and Men of every other Profession and Character, whose Sentiments may be diffused with the greatest Ease and Dispatch, and comparatively speaking at a trifling Expence. In short, as the glorious Luminary of the Heavens, darts its Rays with incredible Velocity, to the most distant Confines of our System, so the Press, as from one common Center, diffuses the bright Beams of Knowledge, with prodigious Dispatch, thro' the vast Extent of the civilized World.

Secrecy, is another Advantage, which an Author had not before the Art of *Printing* was discovered. As long as Power may be perverted, from the original Design of its being lodged with the Magistrate, for protecting the Innocent and punishing the Guilty, so long it will be necessary to conceal the Author who remarks it, from the Malice of the Officer guilty of so pernicious a Perversion; and by Means of this Art he may write undiscovered, as it is impossible to detect him by the Types of the Press.

It must indeed be confessed, that this useful Discovery has, like many others, been prostituted to serve the basest Ends. This great Means of Knowledge, this grand Security of civil Liberty, has been the Tool of arbitrary Power, Popery, Bigotry, Superstition, Profaneness, and even of Ignorance itself. The Press groans under the Weight of the most horrid Impieties, the most ruinous and destructive Principles in Religion and Politics, the idlest Romances, the most contemptible Fustian, Slander and Impotence. But to shut up the Press because it has been abused, would be like burning our Bibles and proscribing Religion, because its Doctrines have been disobeyed and misrepresented; or like throwing off all Law and Restraint, and sinking into a State of Nature, because the over-grown Power of the civil Ruler, abusing his Trust, has sacrificed the Lives and Properties of his Subjects, to lawless and tyrannical Sway. The horrid Practices of NERO, would by no Means have been a sufficient Reason for the Destruction of the Roman Polity. Nor had it been less than Madness in the *English* Nation, to have dissolved the Bonds of our Constitution, and sunk into Anarchy and Confusion, even tho' CHARLES I and JAMES II had provoked the just Resentment of an injured and oppressed People. Such a Condition would have been worse than that of SYRACUSE, under the most unlimited Despotism. The Truth is, the Tyrant should in such Case be deposed, but the State should survive him; and rather than live without Law, without Society, and the innumerable Blessings it includes, better would it be, to suffer with only a distant Hope of Redress, the ungoverned Sway of the most arbitrary Monarch the World ever saw.

The wide Influence of the Press is so dangerous to arbitrary Governments, that in some of them it is shut up, and in others greatly restrained. The Liberty of complaining, of carrying that Complaint to the Throne itself, and of breathing the Sighs of an afflicted, oppressed Nation, has too great a Tendency to produce a Revolution to be suffered in despotic Governments. No Press is tolerated in the *Ottoman* Empire. Power supported without Right, cannot bear, and therefore will not submit itself to a public Examination. Knowledge inspires a Love of Liberty, —and Liberty in the People, is incompatable with the Security of an arbitrary Legislator. To the same Causes are to be ascribed, the Restrictions on the Press in Roman Catholic Countries: Notwithstanding which, the Grand Segnior surpasses the Pope in Policy, which is not the only Proof of his Holiness's Fallibility. That Hierarchy which supports itself by keeping the People in Ignorance, and inhibiting its Devotees the Use of the Bible, oppugns its own Principles, by admitting the Use of the Press; which, as it affords the Opportunity of diffusing Knowledge and Truth thro' the World, must, by inevitable Consequence, equally spread abroad a Contempt of his *Holiness*, and the Worship, Discipline and Doctrines of his Church. Neither the Amours of HENRY VIII which to asperse Protestantism, the Papists ascribe as its Origin, nor any other natural Cause, had so happy Tendency to destroy the Power of the See of *Rome*, as the Liberty of the Press. Popery and Slavery could not stand before true Religion and Liberty; and as the Press was the Instrument of both, the Rights of St. PETER's Chair were no sooner publicly contested, then despised and diminished.

No Nation in *Europe*, is more jealous of the *Liberty of the Press* than the *English*, nor is there a People, among whom it is so grossly abused. With us, the most unbounded Licentiousness prevails. We are so besotted with the Love of Liberty, that running into Extreams, we even tolerate those Things which naturally tend to its Subversion. And what is still more surprizing, an Author justly chargeable with Principles destructive of our Constitution, with Doctrines the most abject and slavish, may proceed even with inveterate Malice, to vilify, burlesque and deny our greatest Immunities and Privileges, and shall yet be suffered to justify himself under the unrestrainable Rights of the Press. An Absurdity grossly stupid and mischievous. What! sap the Constitution, disturb the public

Tranquility, and ruin the State, and yet plead a Right to such Liberty derived from the Law of that State! The *Liberty of the Press,* like Civil Liberty, is talked of by many, and understood but by few; the latter is taken by Multitudes, for an irrefrainable Licence of acting at Pleasure; an equal Unrestraint in Writing, is often argued from the former, but both are false and equally dangerous to our Constitution. Civil Liberty is built upon a Surrender of so much of our natural Liberty, as is necessary for the good Ends of Government; and the Liberty of the Press, is always to be restricted from becoming a Prejudice to the public Weal. The Design of entering into a State of Society, is to promote and secure the Happiness of its Individuals. Whatever tends to this End, is politically lawful, and no State can permit any Practice detrimental to the public Tranquility, but in direct Opposition to its fundamental Principles. Agreeable to this Doctrine I lay it down as a Rule, that when the Press is prejudicial to the public Weal, it is abused: and that the Prohibition of printing any Thing, not repugnant to the Prosperity of the State, is an unjustifiable and tyrannical Usurpation.

If, on the one Hand, we suppose any broader Foundation for the *Liberty of the Press,* it will become more destructive of public Peace, than if it were wholly shut up: And a Freedom of publishing what is not prejudicial to the general Good, must be allowed; because, what can do no Harm can be no Evil, and there can be no Punishment without a Transgression. Besides, a Promotion of the public Welfare, of which the Press is often an Instrument, should be so far from suffering Discouragements, that as it is a political Virtue, it merits rather the Rewards than the Frowns of the Magistrate. Thus the Press will have all that Liberty which is due to it, and never be checked, but where its being unrestricted will prove an Evil, and therefore only where it ought to be checked. Liberty and Science may then spread their Wings, and take the most unbounded Flights. But should Tyranny erect its formidable Head, and extend its Iron Scepter, the Nation may publish, and any Private Person represent the general Calamity with Impunity. Does Corruption or Venality prevail, the Patriot is at Liberty to inveigh and suppress it. The boldest Criminal lies open to Censure and Satire, and any Man may expose and detect him. The Divine may put Vice at a Stand; every Attack upon the publick Welfare may be reprehended, and every destructive Scheme baffled and exposed; for all Men are free in that Way, to defeat every Project that is detrimental to the Public. This Privilege is a great One, and we should all conspire to maintain it. This is the true LIBERTY OF THE PRESS, for which Englishmen ought to contend. Such a Liberty can never be dangerous, either to the Public, or their Ruler; but on the contrary may often be necessary. What a certain great Politician said of the Freedom of Speech, is so applicable to that of the Press, that I cannot omit its Insertion. "The more," says he, "Men express of their Hate and Resentment, perhaps the less they retain, and sometimes they vent the Whole that Way; But these Passions, where they are smothered, will be apt to fester, to grow venemous, and to discharge themselves by a more dangerous Organ than the Mouth, even by an armed and vindictive Hand. Less dangerous is a railing Mouth, than a Heart filled and inflamed with Bitterness and Curses; and more terrible to a Prince, ought to be the secret Execrations of his People, than their open Revilings, or, than even the Assaults of his Enemies."

All those who oppose the Freedom I have contended for, —a Liberty of promoting the common Good of Society, and of publishing any Thing else not repugnant thereto, —are Enemies to the Common Wealth; and many will fall under this Character, who are as ready to cry out for the *Liberty of the Press* as the warmest Patriot. Of this the various Orders that obtain amongst Men, furnish sufficient Examples: I shall instance but in two.

Never does a Writer of Genius and Spirit appear, unshackled

with blind Prejudices and little Attachments to Party. A Writer who exposes the Roguery of Ecclesiastics, and displays the Beauty of genuine unadulterated Christianity, but he gives as it were Birth to a swarm of impotent Scribblers, who arrogate to themselves an Authority from God, to anathemize and deliver him over to the Devil; and the sooner to compleat his Doom, will invoke the secular Arm for Assistance. Strange that they should have a Power from God, to consign a Man over to eternal Torments, and yet be restrained by that very God, from illuminating his Understanding by Fire and Faggot, unless at the good Pleasure of the Magistrate! Such as these I call Enemies, both to the Press and the Public, tho' the former groans under the Burden of their Nonsense, Superstition and Bigotry,

The Press is for ever in the Mouths of Printers, and one would imagine, that as they live by its Liberty, they would understand its true Limits, and endeavour to preserve its rightful Extent. But the Truth is, there is scarce one in Twenty of them; that knows the one or aims at the other.

A Printer ought not to publish every Thing that is offered him; but what is conducive of general Utility, he should not refuse, be the Author a Christian, Jew, Turk or Infidel. Such Refusal is an immediate Abridgement of the Freedom of the Press. When on the other Hand, he prostitutes his Art by the Publication of any Thing injurious to his Country, it is criminal, —It is high Treason against the State. The usual Alarm rung in such Cases, the common Cry of an Attack upon the LIBERTY OF THE PRESS, is groundless and trifling. The Press neither has, nor can have such a Liberty, and whenever it is assumed, the Printer should be punished. Private Interest indeed has, with many of them, such irresistible Charms, and the general Good is so feeble a Motive, that the only Liberty they know and wish for, is of publishing every Thing with Impunity for which they are paid. I could name a Printer, so attached to his private Interest, that for the sake of advancing it, set up a Press, deserted his Religion, made himself the Tool of a Party he despised, privately contemned and vilified his own Correspondents, published the most infamous Falsehoods against others, slandered half the People of his Country, promised afterwards to desist, broke that Promise, continued the Publication of his Lies, Forgeries and Misrepresentations; and to compleat his Malignity, obstinately refused to print the Answers or Vindications of the Persons he had abused; and yet even this Wretch, had the Impudence to talk of the *Liberty of the Press*. God forbid! that every Printer should deserve so infamous a Character. There are among them, Men of Sense, Ingenuity, and rational Lovers of Liberty, for which the greater Part are less solicitous than the Generality of other Men, as a Confinement of the Press to its true Limits, is more frequently opposed to their private Advantage. It would be easy to enumerate a Variety of others, equally Pretenders to a Regard for the *Liberty of the Press,* and as evidently Enemies to the *Press* and the *Public:* But I shall reserve the farther Consideration of this Subject for a following Year, when the Conduct of Bigots and their Adherents, will, probably, supply me with some necessary Remarks.

PART TWO

The Revolutionary Period:
Patriots and Blackstonians

William Bollan Writes a Book

William Bollan, a distinguished Massachusetts lawyer who served the colony as its advocate general and then as its agent in England, earned John Adams' praise as "a faithful friend of America." In addition to several tracts in defense of the colonial cause against Great Britain, Bollan wrote what was surely the eighteenth century's most learned work in English on the liberty of the press. *The Freedom of Speech and Writing upon Public Affairs* was an elaborately detailed legal history of its subject from the time of the ancients. Its scholarship was impeccable, but its style was incredibly prolix and tedious and its recommendations were lacking in originality. The book was essentially a restatement of Zengerian principles. Its theme was that the accused in a criminal-libel case should have the right to plead truth as a defense, while the jury should have the power to decide questions of falsity and malice. It is astonishing, nevertheless, how few publications expressed this line of argument.

Bollan explained the rationale for a policy of broad freedom to criticize the government, but never assaulted the concept of seditious libel. Indeed, he thought the power of the press was so great that its abuses could be dangerous; the wrong people might use the press to "divide and destroy us." He cautioned that railing was not reasoning, and that crimination might injure and inflame but could never inform or reform. Nevertheless, the thrust of the book was libertarian. It presented an interminable rehearsal of tyranny under the Stuarts, with the Court of Star Chamber cast as the villainous body responsible for having introduced unconstitutional doctrines of criminal libel. An Anglican himself, Bollan movingly related the stories of Puritans who had been persecuted in England for their political and religious opinions. In the course of his narrative he sought to demonstrate how the repression of "free inquiry" led to arbitrary searches and seizures, cruel punishments, compulsory self-incrimination, and trial by judge instead of jury. The patriot printer Isaiah Thomas, of the *Massachusetts Spy,* quoted Bollan on the values of free discussion when the Governor's Council ordered prosecutions for seditious libel. The patriot leader Josiah Quincy, Jr., cited Bollan as an authority for challenging Chief Justice Hutchinson's exposition of the law of libels (see Document 14). In 1772 Bollan published an *Essay on the Right of Every Man in a free State to Speak and Write Freely,* which was substantially an abridgment of his book of 1766.

12. ON LIBERTY OF THE PRESS

. . . Truth being in its nature so noble, excellent, and useful, its enemies so formidable, and its acquest so difficult, the free use of the means of discovering it merits, I apprehend, our special regard. Of these, it is evident, the chief are speech and writing, or printing, a species of writing invented for the more expeditious multiplication of copies, both being modes of presenting to the eye what speech conveys to the ear; yet the right, propriety, utility, and limits of their use touching politi-

---

William Bollan, *The Freedom of Speech and Writing upon Public Affairs, Considered, with an Historical View* (London: S. Baker, 1766), pp. 3–4, 128–138.

cal subjects, have occasioned much consideration, debate and difficulty in the world. Despotism cuts this matter short, and having swept away all the rights and liberties of the people, prohibits and punishes of course the use of the means of knowing the truth, which by setting before them in full light their natural, just, and immutable rights, together with the horrid state of their slavery, would consequently make them free, or at least indanger the quiet of that tyranny whose existence so much injures, dishonours, and debases human nature. Under other forms of government this matter has received different treatment in different countries, and in them at different periods. I shall not attempt to state these differences, but observe that freedom or restraint of speech and writing upon public affairs have generally been concomitant; and power being in its nature progressive, they who are sollicitous to augment the restraints of writing would, upon their success, in all probability, proceed in like manner to restrain liberty of speech; and the more injurious the designs and actions of men are, the greater their solicitude will ever be to prevent the free examination of them; wherefore those who desire to preserve the latter ought by all means to take due care of the former.

After giving this matter the best consideration in my power, it appears to me that the free examination of public measures, with a proper representation by speech or writing of the sense resulting from that examination, is the right of the members of a free state, and requisite for the preservation of their other rights; and that all things published by persons for the sake of giving due information to their fellow subjects, in points mediately or immediately affecting the public welfare, are worthy of commendation. And it being certain, that even the proper remonstrance of the most worthy persons, made to their prince in consequence of their resolution not to become parties to his open violation of the laws of the kingdom, hath in time past been deemed libellous, I shall endeavour, notwithstanding, so many excellent things said by others upon this important subject, a little farther to illustrate it. . . .

. . . I presume that knowledge of the truth, to which a free enquiry is requisite, is as necessary to the enjoyment of civil as religious rights. With respect to the passages cited from the Holy Scriptures, they will not support the star-chamber resolution for rejecting the truth, of which they make no mention; but, instead of a tedious and unnecessary discussion of these several passages, after observing that the inhibition to curse the ruler of the people contained in the law of *Moses,* appears to me to be of universal and perpetual obligation, the common good of every state requiring that, instead of cursing, the subjects should revere and honour their chief ruler as far as may be, whose title to this desirable reverence and honour will at all times, I conceive, be best secured by his paternal conduct, I shall in defence of truth adduce the following passages. "Thou camest down also upon mount *Sinai,* and spakest with them from heaven; and gavest them right judgments, and *true* laws, good statutes and commandments." *Nehem:* ix: 13. "By mercy and truth iniquity is purged." *Prov.* xvi:6. "Wo unto them that call evil good, and good evil; that put darkness for light, and light for darkness; that put bitter for sweet, and sweet for bitter:" *Isaiah* v: 20. "they are not valiant for the truth upon the earth; for they proceed from evil to evil, and they know not me, saith the Lord." *Jerem.* ix: 3. "We are sure that the judgment of God is according to truth." *Rom.* ii: 2. For we can do nothing against the truth, but for the truth." 2 *Cor.* xiii: 8. All free and lawful governments are founded in trust, and frame your government as you please, after completing your politic with the aid of the wisdom and experience of all ages and nations, for its execution it will finally rest in trust. *Donec homines erunt vitia;* and notwithstanding the sacred nature of this trust the histories of all countries too clearly prove that authority is apt to run into power, and power into tyranny; wherefore the use of every mean of preventing this malady is desirable: and one of the chief points of excellence of the *British* constitution consisting in the frequent opportunities which it gives to the people to chuse new trustees, a faithful representation of the conduct of the former, and of the state of the times, which may loudly call for the choice of men of the greatest honour, sense and experience, with such diligence as to delight in examining to the bottom every point of public welfare, without confiding in the representation of others, which may be imperfect, erroneous, or illusory, may excite their serious consideration, with such choice as may suit the occasion, and the noble privilege they enjoy.

From what has been said, with the readers farther reflections, it will, I apprehend, plainly appear that in many cases of great importance the liberty of the press may well be employed in promoting the interests, preventing the impending mischiefs, or redressing the grievances of public societies, wherein no other means can be pursued to any effect, and in many other cases an assistant to proper measures prosecuted for the advancement of the public welfare; and it is needless to say that these advantages are to be derived from the illustration and maintenance of truth against all opponents; nevertheless, with respect to the star-chamber doctrine, that the truth of a writing prosecuted as a libel is not material, I shall farther observe, 1, that the author of "The Doctrine of Libels discussed", who seems to have searched into all *English* antiquity for precedents of judgments given in violent times, to be produced *in terrorem;* for he adduces several which, by his own confession, are not law at this day, among other things, writes thus in his introduction; "but undoubtedly slanders which might do mischief, [words of great latitude] whether true or false, were punishable by the old common law," without shewing one precedent or authority for this purpose; and lord *Coke*, or the star-chamber judges, having produced none to this effect, it may be concluded, I conceive, that there are none to be found. 2, that during the existence of the star-chamber court, as well as since, it seems to have been a point fully settled that in actions of slander the defendant might well justify his speaking of the slanderous words charged upon him, by an averment that they were true. 3, that speech and writing are not of contrary natures, but differ only in degree of certainty and permanence, and in the mode of conveying to the intellect the same object of consideration; wherefore I confess it has ever appeared strange to me that the same truth should be lawful when orally delivered, and criminal when reduced into writing. 4. Lord *Coke*, in his 2d. Institute, calls truth the mother of justice; and afterwards he cites, with approbation, this old and excellent rule, *veritas, à quocunque dicitur, a Deo est.* "Truth, by whomsoever spoken, is from God." 5. that on the tryal of the seven bishops for a libel, in presenting their petition to the king, Mr. justice *Powell*, who by his conduct acquired perpetual honour; after hearing this star-chamber case *de libellis famosis* cited and relied on, and every thing that was possible said for the rejection of truth, as immaterial, spoke thus to the jury. "Gentlemen, to make it a libel it must be false; it must be malicious; and it must tend to sedition."

The star chamber resolution touching the indifference of truth was suitable to their other conduct, being in effect a law made in their own defence. On the 17th. of October, when sitting at the council-table, they had concurred with the king in that severe and indignant order which he published respecting the merchants importing tobacco; and in Easter term following, when sitting in the court of star-chamber, they made this resolution, whereby they subjected such suffering merchants as should in writing complain of any part of their conduct relative to this illegal proceeding to such farther fines and punishments as they should think fit to impose.

The definition given of a libel in this star-chamber case, so far as relates to the present purpose, without considering the point of falsity, seems rather imperfect, to wit, A scandalous libel *in scriptis* is when a writing is composed or published to the scandal or contumely of another, which words do not necessarily include the evil intent of the writer; but may relate to the casual or undesigned effect of the writing. . . .

. . . With respect to the trial by jury of the party accused of writing a libel, the jurors, I presume, are competent judges of the falsity, malice, and the fact of writing, of the book, pamphlet or paper in question, with its contents. This, I apprehend, corresponds with their original institution. . . .

. . . Every crime is the transgression of some law, the judgment whereof necessarily comprizes the law, with the fact; and as all persons are presumed to know the laws, and are therefore punishable for the breach of them, so the jurors when a breach should come in question were presumed to have knowledge suitable to their institution. By the great charter it is provided that no free-man shall be condemned but by lawful judgment of his peers, whereby, in the plainest terms, effectual provision is made that every man when charged with a crime shall be tried by his peers, who have power to condemn or absolve him, this provision being apparently made as well for the commons as the peers of the realm.

The desire of king *James* to introduce and establish the papal tyranny with his own was so vehement, that he could not brook the noble check which the seven bishops gave to the progress of his superstition and ambition; whereupon the prosecution against them as libellers for having petitioned his majesty in the most decent and proper manner to excuse their non compliance with his illegal command took place; for the maintenance whereof every argument that could be devised was urged. *Wright*, chief justice, whom Dr. *Burnet* calls the proper tool of the court, after speaking to the facts relative to the making and publishing their petition, proceeding to enquire whether this petition was a libel, or not, declared to the jury that in his opinion it was a libel, adding that this being a point of law, if his brothers had any thing to say to it, he supposed they would deliver their opinions; and Mr. justice *Allybone* began his speech thus. "The single question that falls to my share is to give my sense of this petition, whether it shall be in construction of law a libel in itself, or a thing of great innocence;" and after advancing these prepositions, 1, "that no man can take upon himself to write against the actual exercise of the government, unless he has leave from the government, but he makes a libel, be what he writes true or false. 2. That no private man can take upon him to write concerning the government at all;" and giving his reasons, suitable to his positions, he clearly held this petition to be a libel; nevertheless not one judge upon the bench questioned the propriety of the juries judging of the whole matter, and giving a general verdict thereupon, though it has of late been publickly insisted that they ought to have found a special verdict, and not taken upon them to determine whether this petition was a libel or not.

In *Bushells* case, 22 *Car.* II., the nature of the trial by jury was thoroughly examined and considered by the court of common pleas, and upon conference with all the judges. Upon a writ of *habeas corpus* issued by that court, on behalf of *Edward Bushell,* and directed to the sheriffs of *London,* they returned that at the court of oyer and terminer, held for the city of *London* at justice hall in the *Old Baily,* he was committed to the gaol of *Newgate,* by virtue of an order of that court, whereby it was ordered that a fine of 40 marks should be severally imposed on him and eleven other persons, being the twelve jurors sworn and charged to try several issues joined between the king and *William Penn* and *William Mead,* for certain trespasses, contempts, unlawful assemblies and tumults made and perpetrated by them, together with divers other unknown persons, to the number of three hundred, unlawfully and tumultuously assembled in *Grace-Church-street,* to the disturbance of the peace, whereof the said *Penn* and *Mead* were then indicted, to which indictment they pleaded not guilty; for that they the said jurors the said *Penn* and *Mead* of the said trespasses &c. contrary to the law of the kingdom, to full and manifest evidence, and to the direction of the court in the matter of law, in court openly given and declared, acquited, in contempt of the king and his laws, and to the great obstruction of justice, as also to the evil example of all other jurors offending in the like case; and because the said *Edward* had not paid the fine aforesaid he had til that time been detained in the said gaol. "Upon this return all the judges resolved, That finding against the evidence in court, or direction of the court barely, was no sufficient cause to fine;" and the fine, comitment, and imprisonment in this case being declared illegal, the prisoners were discharged. . . .

. . . Lord chief justice *Vaughan,* to whom, with the other judges, in my poor opinion, the kingdom will ever be obliged, for establishing the right of juries to give general verdicts in criminal causes, as well as to the present lord chief justice of the same court, and the other judges, who have declared general warrants to be illegal, in *Bushells* case, observes that, "Upon all general issues; as upon not culpable pleaded in trespass, *nil debet* in debt, *nul tort, nul disseisin* in assize, *ne disturba pas* in *Quare impedit,* and the like; though it be matter of law whether the defendant be a trespassor, a debtor, disseisor, or disturber in the particular cases in issue; yet the jury find not (as in a special verdict) the fact of every case by itself, leaving the law to the court, but find for the plaintiff or defendant upon the issue to be tryed, wherein they resolve both law and fact complicately, and not the fact by itself; so as though they answer not singly to the question what is law, yet they determine the law in all matters where issue is joined, and tryed in the principal case, but where the verdict is special."

We have in part seen to what great dangers and mischiefs the subjects are exposed when trials by their peers are subverted, and other modes of trial introduced; wherefore it is extremely desirable that trials by jury should ever be equal, fair and free, influenced by truth of fact and argument only; so that, with the assistance of those excellent judges to whose opinions proper regard should be had, they may be as perfect as the nature of human affairs will permit; and to this end, among other wise provisions, to free them from all apprehensions of danger attendant on the discharge of their duty, according to serj^t. *Hawkins,* "it seemeth to be certain, That no one is liable to any prosecution whatsoever, in respect of any verdict given by him in a criminal matter, either upon a grand or petit jury; for since the safety of the innocent, and punishment of the guilty, doth so much depend upon the fair and upright proceeding of jurors, it is of the utmost consequence that they should be as little as possible under the influence of any passion whatsoever. And therefore, lest they should be biassed with the fear of being harrassed by a vexatious suit, for acting according to their consciences (the danger of which might easily be insinuated where powerful men are warmly engaged in a cause, and thoroughly prepossessed of the justice of the side which they espouse) the law will not leave any possibility for a prosecution of this kind. It is true indeed the jurors were formerly sometimes questioned in the star-chamber, for their partiality in finding a manifest offender not guilty; but this was always thought a very great grievance; and surely as the law is now settled by *Bushells* case, there is no kind of proceeding against jurors in respect of their verdicts in criminal matters allowed of at this day."

The mischiefs of slander consist in its operation on the minds of persons, with their consequent actions; and it seems to me that jurors are well qualified to judge of the whole, especially when assisted by able and impartial judges. In case a perpetual succession of judges equal to those excellent persons who now sit in the seat of judgment could be secured to the kingdom we might be less sollicitous touching this particular: but although through his majestys goodness provision has been made that his own son, or any future successor, shall not have it in his power on his accession to appoint new judges at his pleasure; yet it is possible that future times may produce such men as being devoted to the will of arbitrary princes, or dangerous

ministers, shall be ready to use every mean in their power to restrain and punish those writings which may be necessary to
expose their designs; and it being difficult in these times of
danger to stem the current of those precedents whereof an ill
use may be made, the practice of giving general verdicts, I
conceive, may contribute to the preservation of the liberty of
the press, which hath in times past been so severely restrained
by law, or lawless power. *Julius Caesar* observed that the most
dangerous precedents are made in favorable cases, and we
have lately seen even office precedents urged with vehemence
to warrant the violation of the law of liberty and safety, by
men who have since unhappily proved that their caution was
not encreased by the correction of their errors.

Notwithstanding the great utility of the liberty of the press
it is certainly liable to manifold injurious abuses, sometimes
pregnant with great mischiefs; without enumerating others, instead of being helpful to preserve, it may be employed by our
enemies to divide and destroy us; wherefore just and proper
bounds are to be observed. Every considerate and sincere
friend to the freedom of writing laments these abuses perpetrated by the various enemies of the public weal. *Libertas non
est licentia* says *Tacitus*, the great friend of liberty, railing is
not reasoning, nor are invectives arguments; vague and general
reproaches, charges and criminations may injure, provoke, and
inflame, but they neither rightly inform, nor reform. The cause
of truth and justice is not promoted by obloquy and detraction,
the *decus & tutamen* of the common-wealth is not to be as-
sailed by petulance and impertinence; yet, instead of proper
examination and representation, such a licentious use of the
press hath taken place, that neither the highest public stations,
nor the greatest public services, nor public nor private virtues,
nor the absence of the sufferers, are sufficient guards against
these abuses. All personal, provincial and national abuse is the
prostitution of the press, and may sometimes produce great
and mischievous effects. *Juncta juvant,* and in interesting cases
the errors of politicians, with the errors and incentives of

pamphleteers, encreased and diffused by that *cacoethes scribendi & male dicendi* which delights in defaming, aggravating and inflaming, instead of duly considering, informing, and composing, and, as the seeds of social as well as natural diseases generate apace, spreading far and wide a political pestilence, prejudice begeting prejudice, and error begeting error, and the whole producing violence, opposition, division and confusion, may, without the co-operation of the dangerous devices suggested by others to effectuate their deep and malignant designs, subject the most powerful state to great difficulties. Of this we have at present an instance so alarming in its nature, and uncertain in its consequences that it calls, in my poor opinion, for the closest examination, and the most calm just and equal consideration, so that being understood in its origin, progress, and present state, all future evils may as far as possible be prevented, for the accomplishment whereof every good subject, I presume, will chearfully contribute what lies in his power. I need not explain myself by naming the colonies, whose nature, rights, and interests, considered in themselves, and in their connection with their mother country, have been so egregiously misrepresented by numerous public writers in this metropolis, and in the colonies, many of whom have advanced propositions utterly incompatible with the nature of the *British* empire, and subversive of it, some oppugning the supreme authority of the state, and others the just rights of *British* subjects. . . .

A Patriot Newspaper Describes the Duties of a Free Press

The *Boston Gazette and Country Journal* was published by "those trumpeteers of sedition, the printers Edes and Gill." Lieutenant Governor Andrew Oliver complained about their "infamous paper" to the English authorities; Governor Sir Francis Bernard advised the arrest of its printers; Chief Justice Hutchinson requested a grand jury to return indictments against them for threatening "the Subversion of all Rule among us." Benjamin Edes and John Gill earned all this attention by their implacable propaganda against British measures from the early 1760's to the outbreak of the Revolution. Their paper was the spokesman for Sam Adams and the radical party. As a fiercely polemical opponent of the government, the *Boston Gazette* could be expected to possess a well-developed libertarian theory of political expression. It did not, despite the fact that it frequently quoted "Cato" and no less than four times reprinted the essay on "Freedom of Speech." The *Gazette* specialized in bombastic endorsements of freedom of speech and press, as if the terms were self-evident. That they were not is clear from the following article, signed by "Freeborn American." This sort of comparatively sustained discussion is rare in the *Gazette's* pages. The patriot position on freedom of political opinion was accurately, if acidly, summarized by Chief Justice Hutchinson when he observed that the Adamses and their supporters were "contending for an unlimited Freedom of Thought and Action, which they would confine wholly to themselves." That is the meaning of the *Gazette's* statement: "Political liberty consists in a freedom of speech and action, so far as the laws of a community will permit, and no farther: all beyond is criminal. . . ."

13. "FREEBORN AMERICAN" WRITES

Man, in a state of nature, has undoubtedly a right to speak and act without controul. In a state of civil society, that right is limited by the law—Political liberty consists in a freedom of speech and action, so far as the laws of a community will permit, and no farther: all beyond is criminal, and tends to the destruction of Liberty itself. —That society whose laws least

---

"Freeborn American," in the *Boston Gazette and Country Journal*, March 9, 1767.

restrain the words and actions of its members, is most free.
—There is no nation on the earth, where freedom of speech is
more extensive than among the English: This is what keeps the
constitution in health and vigour, and is in a great measure the
cause of our preservation as a free people: For should it ever
be dangerous to exercise this privilege, it is easy to see, without the spirit of prophecy, slavery and bondage would soon be
the portion of Britons. —Mankind never entered into society to
aggrandize rulers, but rulers were invested with power for the
good of the people; & it is to them alone they ought to be
accountable for their conduct—The rights of the subject are as
well known in the British dominions, and ought to be as sacred
as the rights of the crown; and whenever they are in danger,
or invaded, no man who is silent, will act the part of a good
subject to his King, or a friend to his country. —It is as much
the duty of a member of society to oppose every encroachment
on the subject, as it is to support the prerogative when in danger, from the licentiousness of the people. —Without this
check, we should be liable to oppression, whenever a tyrant
was in power; nay, an ambitious designing ruler, I dare to say,
fears more the correction of the Press, than any other controul
whatever; and it is to the freedom with which the conduct of
the Great is scanned in England, that we are principally indebted for our glorious constitution. —Anarchy, I grant, is as
much to be dreaded as tyranny; but surely no wise man can
say, we are in as much danger from contempt of all government, as from the corruption of it. —A wicked ruler, who, to
gratify his insatiable ambition or avarice, is trampling on the
liberties of the subject, and wading to wealth and power, thro'
the destruction of all that is dear to a free people, will always
stigmatize with the opprobrious names of licentiousness and
contempt of authority, every warrantable step taken to counterwork his destructive schemes. —He who nobly undertakes to
support an injured people, and oppose the measures of those in
power inimical to their rights, must expect to be set forth by

every court-sycophant as a licentious incendiary, a firebrand, and a disturber of public tranquility—This is a tax no friend to his country can hope to escape, while there can be found men so devoid of all benevolence and patriotism, as to worship at the shine of power, tho' at the expence of public Liberty— Unfortunate for mankind, in the present depraved state of human nature, a B——d will never meet with much difficulty to find a H———n and a O——— to support him in all his measures; but that people who have an H——y, O—s & A——s to counterwork their pernicious designs, should account themselves happy indeed. . . .

Jurists Explain the Common Law

Josiah Quincy, Jr., one of the Massachusetts radicals, described Chief Justice Thomas Hutchinson in the patriot press as "the first, the most malignant and *insatiable* enemy" of America, who had "degraded the highest station in the law to the lowest office of the inquisition. . . ." Hutchinson's dogged but futile effort to persuade grand juries to return indictments for seditious libel against Quincy and the patriot leaders accounted, in part, for Quincy's outburst. In 1767 Hutchinson defined freedom of the press in the following terms: "Pretty high Notions of the Liberty of the Press, I am sensible, have prevailed of late among us; but it is very dangerous to meddle with, and strike at this Court. The Liberty of the Press is doubtless a very great Blessing; but this liberty means no more than a Freedom for every Thing to pass from the Press without Licence.—That is, you shall not be obliged to obtain a Licence from any Authority before the Emission of Things from the Press. Unlicenced Printing was never thought to mean a Liberty of reviling and calumniating all Ranks and Degrees of Men with Impunity, all Authority with Ignominy.—To carry this absurd Notion of the Liberty of the Press to the Length some would have it—to print every Thing that is Libellous and Slan-

derous—is truly astonishing, and of the most dangerous Tendency."
This was an accurate and orthodox statement of the common law
and, indeed, differed little from the patriot view of the matter.
Hutchinson, of course, regarded defiance of crown authority as
seditious libel, but he and the patriot party were in agreement
on the fundamental principle that abuse of the press, as each respectively understood it, was punishable as a thing apart from the
true liberty of the press. Here is one of Hutchinson's lectures to a
grand jury in 1768 on the law of libels, followed, in the next
Document, by an extract on the same subject from Sir William
Blackstone's *Commentaries.* Although Blackstone was also a Tory,
Americans accorded him the utmost respect as "the oracle of the
common law." Blackstone's definition of the freedom of the press
was adopted by most American courts in the eighteenth century.
Even libertarians, who advocated constitutional guarantees for freedom of the press in the new state bills of rights, used Blackstonian
terms to describe what they meant.

14. CHIEF JUSTICE HUTCHINSON CAUTIONS

AGAINST THE DANGERS OF SEDITIOUS LIBELS

March Term
VIII Geo. 3.

The Charge given to the Grand Jury by the
Chief Justice was as follows.

Gentlemen of the Grand Jury: At the Opening of the Court
you are sensible that the Path of your Duty should be pointed

---

Chief Justice Thomas Hutchinson, Charge to the Grand Jury, 1768, in
*Reports of Cases Argued and Adjudged in the Superior Court of Judica-
ture of the Province of Massachusetts Bay, Between 1761 and 1772,* ed.
Josiah Quincy (Boston: Little Brown and Co., 1865), pp. 258–267,
passim.

out to you; and, in Order that you may have an Apprehension of what is incumbent on you, I shall endeavour to give you some Idea of those Principles, on which the Law is founded. . . .

. . . The Principle of Law which now governs us, is to punish Crimes, only as they affect Society. From hence it is, we see, many Offences in England are punished, often in no Ways proportioned to the real Heinousness of the Crime: —Thus, to counterfeit a Shilling is a higher Crime than to kill one's Father. One is High Treason—the other is only Felony. . . .

. . . There are a Multitude of other Crimes of the most dangerous Tendency, which strike the Mind of the Generality, when we hear Rumours of them, with no great Horror—yet are plainly introductive of the utmost Confusion into Society, destroy its Harmony, produce Bloodshed and Murder—in short, if allowed to increase, they must sap the Foundation of all Government. Such are Riots, Routs and unlawful Assemblies. . . .

. . . One other Offence, which tends much to disturb the Peace and destroy the Order of the Community, is that of Libelling. . . .

This Offence has increased very much, of late, and threatens the Subversion of all Rule among us. There are People who make it their Business to furnish the Press with the most scandalous and defamatory Pieces.

No Government,—in Europe, I am sure,—not one that is counted the most free, would have tolerated those libellous Pieces which we have seen in the publick Prints, within this Twelve-month past. These Publications have often brought to my Mind a Story I have heard of one Wilkes, of whom you all have heard—and whom, I am sorry to say it, some among us show too great a Desire to imitate. That Person was once asked, while he was writing, how far a Man in an English Government might go, in his Publications, and not come within the Laws of High Treason. To which he answered, he was just then trying how far he could go. These Authors among us seem to be trying the same dangerous Experiment. I will not pronounce those Authors guilty of High Treason; but I will venture to say, they come as near it as possible, and not come within it.

For these seven or eight Years, I have made it my constant Practice to read every Book upon the Crown-Law I could meet with; and I never yet read or heard, till of late, the Doctrine that some particular Person must be struck at—that Names of particular Persons were necessary—that the initial or final Letters must be inserted, in Order to make a Libel.

This Notion which has lately prevailed seems to arise from a Mistake of some of our Books, where some defamatory Pieces have been adjudged Libels, because the Authors had put down the initial or final Letters of the Names of certain Persons. But, surely, it never follows from hence, that this is the only Way of making a Libel.

The Rule of Law is, that the Person libelled must be sufficiently marked out; for, if the Person is so fully delineated, that he is well known without putting his Name, it rather adds to the Heinousness of the Offence, as it shows the deliberate Malice of the Author, and his wicked Endeavours to elude the Law.

Neither is it necessary to a Libel, that any Person at all be mentioned: As in a Libel against the Government, wrote in Queen Ann's Time, which contained a Defence of Hereditary Right, and a Denial of the Right of Parliament to fix the Crown where it then was. So there may be a Libel upon Religion,—as I remember, when I was quite young, to have heard of one Woolston who wrote several Treatises against the Miracles of Our Saviour. Thus, in publishing of a very obscene Book, as the Earl of Rochester's Works. And one Curl, I think, was condemned to the Pillory for a Libel of the same Sort. The Duke of Wharton too, who wrote a Book called Ezeriph and Sophron, in which a Parallel was run between those two Characters, making Sophron, by whom was meant the Pretender, a very wise Prince, and Ezeriph, by whom was intended the King then on the Throne, a very weak and wicked Man. In all these Writings and many more I might name, no Names were mentioned nor ever supposed necessary to make them Libels; but the Authors or Publishers were committed, and punished in the severest Manner.

And one Franklin, who wrote against Ministers, was imprisoned and punished; though it was objected, that there were Ministers of Religion, as well as State. Nothing can be clearer, than that a Libel may as well be without a Name, as with one, and without any initial or final Letters. As painting a Sign, drawing a Man's Picture with a Gallows near it, or any other Way sufficiently descriptive of the Person intended.

I remember that Lord Talbot, one of the greatest Judges that ever sat on the English Bench, lays it down as the Rule of Libels, that, if, upon the Connexion and Comparing of the several Parts, and then taking the Whole together, the Person was plainly pointed out and easily known to every Reader, it was sufficient to constitute it a Libel. —It is enough if the Thing is obvious to a common Understanding.

I expect some will cry out, our Liberties are endangered— the Liberty of the Press is struck at—but let such People consider, that, if we may write, why not speak as freely of Men? Shall a Man print that, of the first Ruler of a State, which he will not speak of any one Man in the Community? Shall our first Magistrate be thus slandered with impunity in an *infamous* Paper? —I believe I may say thus much, without incurring the Imputation of prejudging.

Formerly, no Man could print his Thoughts, ever so modestly and calmly, or with ever so much Candour and Ingenuousness, upon any Subject whatever, without a Licence. When this Restraint was taken off, then was the true Liberty of the Press. Every Man who prints, prints at his Peril; as every Man who speaks, speaks at his Peril. It was in this Manner I treated this Subject at the last Term, yet the Liberty of the Press, and the Danger of an *Imprimatur* was canted about, as if the Press was going under some new and illegal Restraint. No Gentleman of the Bar, I am sure, could have so misunderstood me. This Restraint of the Press, in the Prevention of Libels, is the only Thing which will preserve your Liberty. To suffer the licentious Abuse of Government is the most likely Way to destroy its Freedom. —But shall a Printer be punished? —why, it is said, it is his Living. —Shall a Highwayman be punished? To rob is his Living. Shall a Thief? —to steal is his Living. Whence is it, that this Difference is made between him who robs me of my Reputation, and who takes away my Property? The former is the worst of the two.

You, Gentlemen, may be at some Loss, what is Evidence of publishing a Libel. I will briefly mention what is undoubted Law in this Case. A Bookseller having a libellous Book in his Shop to sell is full Evidence enough to you, Gentlemen, of the Publisher. To send a Libel about by one's Servant to sell is Evidence also. Gentlemen, the general Rule of Law here takes Place, that who ever does a Thing by another, does it himself.

A Libel may be as well against a private Person, Gentlemen, as against one in a publick Station; and the Disturbances Things of this Sort are likely to breed, is very obvious to every Man; but the Consequences are infinitely more mischievous when the Chief Ruler is openly attacked. —There is no End to these Things.

But, it is said, if we have a bad Ruler, there is no other Means of Redress. This is a Mistake. To be sure the *Chief Ruler* of the Province *is not to be brought into this Court to answer for any Misdemeanour:* but we must seek Relief from Great Britain. If our Governour acts in an illegal Manner, we have a good King, and can *easily* have him removed. . . .

15. SIR WILLIAM BLACKSTONE CONDEMNS

PUBLICATION OF BAD SENTIMENTS

... 13. Of a nature very similar to challenges are *libels, libelli famosi,* which, taken in their largest and most extensive sense, signify any writings, pictures, or the like, of an immoral or illegal tendency; but, in the sense under which we are now to consider them, are malicious defamations of any person, and especially a magistrate, made public by either printing, writing, signs, or pictures, in order to provoke him to wrath or expose him to public hatred, contempt, and ridicule. The direct tendency of these libels is the breach of the public peace by stirring up the objects of them to revenge, and perhaps to bloodshed. The communication of a libel to any one person is a publication in the eye of the law; and therefore the sending an abusive letter to a man is as much a libel as if it were openly printed, for it equally tends to a breach of the peace. For the same reason, it is immaterial, with respect to the essence of a libel, whether the matter of it be true or false, since the provocation, and not the falsity, is the thing to be punished criminally; though, doubtless, the falsehood of it may aggravate its guilt and enhance its punishment. In a civil action, we may remember, a libel must appear to be false as well as scandalous; for, if the charge be true, the plaintiff has received no private injury, and has no ground to demand a compensation for himself, whatever offence it may be against the public peace; and therefore, upon a civil action, the truth of the accusation may be pleaded in bar of the suit. But, in a criminal prosecution, the tendency which all libels have to create animosities, and to disturb the public peace is the whole that the law considers. And, therefore, in such prosecutions the only points to be in-

---

Sir William Blackstone, *Commentaries on the Laws of England* (London: 1765–1769), Book 4 (1769), Chapter 11, pp. 151–154.

quired into are, first, the making or publishing of the book or writing; and secondly, whether the matter be criminal; and if both these points are against the defendant, the offence against the public is complete. The punishment of such libellers, for either making, repeating, printing, or publishing the libel, is fine and such corporal punishment as the court in its discretion shall inflict, regarding the quantity of the offence and the quality of the offender. By the law of the twelve tables at Rome, libels which affected the reputation of another were made a capital offence; but before the reign of Augustus the punishment became corporal only. Under the emperor Valentinian it was again made capital, not only to write, but to publish, or even to omit destroying them. Our law in this and many other respects corresponds rather with the middle age of Roman jurisprudence, when liberty, learning, and humanity were in their full vigor, than with the cruel edicts that were established in the dark and tyrannical ages of the ancient *decemvirii* or the later emperors.

In this and the other instances which we have lately considered, where blasphemous, immoral, treasonable, schismatical, seditious, or scandalous libels are punished by the English law, some with a greater, others with a less, degree of severity, the *liberty of the press,* properly understood, is by no means infringed or violated. The liberty of the press is indeed essential to the nature of a free state; but this consists in laying no *previous* restraints upon publications, and not in freedom from censure for criminal matter when published. Every freeman has an undoubted right to lay what sentiments he pleases before the public; to forbid this is to destroy the freedom of the press; but if he publishes what is improper, mischievous, or illegal, he must take the consequence of his own temerity. To subject the press to the restrictive power of a licenser, as was formerly done, both before and since the revolution, is to subject all freedom of sentiment to the prejudices of one man, and make him the arbitrary and infallible judge of all controverted points in learning, religion, and government. But to punish (as the law does at present) any dangerous or offensive writings, which, when published, shall on a fair and impartial trial be adjudged of a pernicious tendency, is necessary for the preservation of peace and good order, of government and religion, the only solid foundations of civil liberty. Thus the will of individuals is still left free; the abuse only of that free will is the object of legal punishment. Neither is any restraint hereby laid upon freedom of thought or inquiry: liberty of private sentiment is still left; the disseminating or making public of bad sentiments, destructive of the ends of society, is the crime which society corrects. A man (says a fine writer on this subject) may be allowed to keep poisons in his closet, but not publicly vend them as cordials. And to this we may add that the only plausible argument heretofore used for the restraining the just freedom of the press, "that it was necessary, to prevent the daily abuse of it," will entirely lose its force when it is shown (by a seasonable exertion of the laws) that the press cannot be abused to any bad purpose without incurring a suitable punishment; whereas it never can be used to any good one when under the control of an inspector. So true it will be found that to censure the licentiousness is to maintain the liberty of the press.

The McDougall Case as a Libertarian Cause

The next three documents are related to the McDougall case of 1770. All three originally appeared in James Parker's *New-York Gazette; or, The Weekly Post-Boy*. Parker, once an apprentice to William Bradford and a partner of Benjamin Franklin, was probably the most distinguished printer of his time. He was arrested several times for publishing material offensive to the authorities of New York. Death prevented his forced testimony as the chief prosecution witness against McDougall. Despite the ignominious role in which Parker was cast in that case, his *Post-Boy* was Mc-Dougall's stanchest defender, printing many encomiums on liberty of the press. Document 16 was written by William Smith, whose father, of the same name, was an associate of James Alexander as a contributor to Zenger's *Journal* and as his defense counsel. William Smith, Jr., a contributor to *The Independent Reflector* (which Parker printed), was the author of *The History of the Province of New-York* (1757), and at the time of this anonymous contribution was a judge of New York's highest court and a member of the Governor's Council. Document 17, whose author is unknown, is a typical blast against "Star Chamber doctrines." Document 18, McDougall's own statement written in jail, is perhaps most remarkable for its silence on the question of freedom of the press. McDougall, it should be remembered, got into his difficulties by publishing a broadside condemned as seditious by the legislature.

16. WILLIAM SMITH PERPETUATES ZENGERIAN
PRINCIPLES

Mr. Printer,

Please to insert the following Copy of a late Letter from an eminent Counsellor, and a Friend to Liberty, to his Correspondent in this City.

I rejoice at the Attack upon Capt. McDougall. Whatever was the Design of your old Lieutenant Governor and his Adherents, in stirring up a Prosecution against that gallant Son of Liberty, it will rather advance than injure the grand Cause of America. . . .

. . . I take it for granted, that he wrote or published the Paper of the 16th Dec. which all the three Branches of your

---

New-York Gazette; or, The Weekly Post-Boy, March 19, 1770.

Legislature are pleased to call a Libel. And if he is not prosecuted (as I presume he is not) for the Glances in it at Major
Pallain and Mr. Jauncey, the libellous Matter must consist in
the Charge, that your Donation of £2000, for the Use of the
Troops, and in Compliance with the Mutiny Act, was un-
friendly to the Liberties of the People; and that this was the
Effect of a late Coalition between the Lieut. Governor and a
certain Family of Influence.

The Point therefore to be tried, is, whether this is a Libel—
and can a Jury think you be found in this Day of Light and
Liberty, that will say, upon their Oaths, that it is a Crime to refuse a Submission to British Taxation; for it is this Submission
that is called a betraying the Liberties of the People. God forbid that any Province upon the Contenent should ever give
Proofs of such a profligate Apostacy from the virtuous Principles which all our Assemblies have repeatedly avowed, in their
Resolves, their Addresses, Petitions, Memorials and Representations, and in their Remonstrances to the very Commons of
Great Britain, ever since the Publication of the pestilent and
accursed Stamp Act, of 1765.

You ask my Opinion, whether Mr. Colden and his Council
have done right or wrong? If you mean, Sir, by this Question,
whether their Conduct was prudent or not; I am at a Loss,
without the Knowledge of the End they had in view, to give
you a determinate Answer. . . .

. . . But perhaps your Question is only an Enquiry about the
Law concerning Libels, and the Application of it to the Papers
abovementioned; and here too we must be careful to make
proper Distinctions. The general Course of Proceedings in England, with Respect to defamatory Publications, is conducted
according to Resolutions absurd in themselves, and subversive
of a free State; and considering the Progress of Knowledge, and
the Independency of the Judges, ever since the glorious Revolution, 'tis astonishing, that a *Holt*, a *Parker*, a *Foster*, and such
other Lights of the Age, have not established such Maxims

(extracted from the Grounds and Principles of the Law) as are compatible with common Sense, and the public Safety. Hitherto they have followed the irrational and pernicious Decisions of despotic Times; for all the State Law usually urged in Cases of this Kind, by the Informer General for the Government, has no higher Authority in its Favour than the meer *Dictum* of the judges.

Every Body will agree that private Slander ought to be punished, and few if any will deny it to be reasonable, that a Man who accuses Magistrates and Officers in high Stations, of an Abuse of their Fruits, ought to be amenable to Justice, if his Motive is a malicious Design to asperse without Cause. . . .

It seems necessary also, that the Magistrate should have the Power of committing Offenders of this King, *at Discretion,* and that while the Matter is before him upon the Question, shall I commit or not? it should be perfectly immaterial, whether the Accusation in the defamatory Writing is true or false? And upon this Principle your Governor and Chief Justice, may have a legal Apology for the Imprisonment of Capt. McDougall, if there was sufficient Proof of his Writing or Publishing the Paper laid to his Charge, whatever may be thought of the *Means* used to extract a Discovery.

But the Malignancy of the Crown Law, in the Decisions relative to Libels, respect the Mode and Power of bringing a Man to Trial, for what he writes or prints or publishes, and at the arbitrary Pleasure of an Attorney General, a dependent Will and Pleasure Officer, and the Practice of the Courts, first in over-ruling all Proof of the Truth of the Publication, then labouring to get the Jury to confine themselves merely to declare the Point of Fact by special Verdict, that the Defendant wrote or published the Paper; and last of all in pronouncing the horrid Judgment that the Truth of the Facts rather aggravates than mitigates the Offence.

This is what Englishmen call Star-Chamber Law; a Court of which no Friend to his Country can speak without Emotion;

and indeed it was such a cruel Engine of Oppression, that it deserves the sharpest Invectives.

It was a Tribunal in which our King antiently presided in Person; and his Assistants were his own Privy Counsellors. Its Name is owing to the Ceiling of the Chamber where it was held, which was garnished with golden Stars; and proceeding without a Jury, well might the *poor Subject* tremble before a Bar where every Circumstance inspired Terror and Confusion. At first it interfered only, as Lord Coke informs us, in Causes enormous and exorbitant, and sat rarely; but its Authority and Jurisdiction, was afterwards amazingly augmented by divers Acts of Parliament. In Henry 7th's Reign, the *Chancellor,* the *Treasurer* and *Keeper* of the Privy Seal, with a *Bishop,* a *Privy Councellor,* and two Judges, were authorized to proceed upon *Bill of Information,* against any Person for Maintenance, and for almost all other Crimes. In the next Reign the *President* of the Council was added to the Judges, and the Court had Power to punish *at Discretion.*

Sometimes they proceeded against a Man Ore tenus, that is in a summary Way, without any Formality, and as the Sailor says, *knocked off the Cause in a Jirk.*

Prosecutions were most commonly by Bill or Information, which the King's Attorney General brought in and managed. They heard Witnesses, examined even the accused, and pronounced Judgment both as *Judges and Jurors.*

The Inquisition of Portugal and Spain was not more inimical to the Rights of private Judgment in *Matters of Religion,* than the Star-Chamber in those, which respected the Behaviour of public Officers in *civil Concerns.* Agents themselves in the Conduct of the Affairs of the Nation, how deeply were they interested, in the Suppression of all private Complaints that might create a general Alarm! And how was it possible for any Man to lisp an Accusation with Safety, or escape with Impunity, when the Instruments of Government were to be both Parties against him and judges of his Cause.

A Court so well adapted to fan the Sparks of Ambition and Corruption, and strengthen the Arm of Oppression, exerted its formidable Power to the utmost; and then it was that those damnable Heresies (if I may so speak) crept into our Law, that a Libel is not the less so for being true, and that the accused (which by the Way seems to be its natural Consequence) shall not be permitted to say a Word in Support of the Allegations charged upon him as a Crime.

Prosecutions for Libels became a great Part of their Business, and proceeding from one Instance of Cruelty to another; the Nation at length grew impatient of this horrible Judicatory, and in the 16th Year of the Reign of Charles the First, it was totally abolished by an Act of Parliament, which records it's Enormities, and brands it with everlasting Infamy; for it expressly recites, *That the Proceedings, Answers and Decrees of that Court, have by Experience, been found to be an intollerable Burden to the Subject, and the Means to introduce an arbitrary Power and Government.*

The Precedent nevertheless survived, tho' the Court was destroyed, and a temporising Spirit in the succeeding Reigns of Charles and James, Princes not yet rid of their Fears of the Men who had cut off their Father's Head, seized, and often triumphed in the Courts of Justice, and led them to Favour as much as possible, the arbitrary Dogmas of the haughty Judges of the Star-Chamber Bench.

Upon the Demolition of that tremendous Judicature, the Business of it fell into the Court of *King's Bench,* and then no Man could be convicted without the Verdict of a Jury, according to the antient Law of the Land: But the glorious Security thereby given for Freedom in writing and speaking, was offensive to the Great, and a wicked Attempt was soon made to inslave the Jurors, and raise a new Star-Chamber, even in Westminster Hall, for to induce them to cast an obnoxious Defendant into the Hands of the Judges, it was held, that if they would not find Verdicts according to the Direction of the

Court, they were subject both to Fine and Imprisonment. An Experiment for robbing the People of this unspeakable Privilege, was made on the Trial of William Mead and the famous William Penn, the same to whom we owe one of the freest and fairest of our Colonies. Twelve undaunted Jurors at that Time resolved rather to perish than give up the Defendants to the Rage of a malicious Court, and were fined 40 Marks each, and sent to New-Gate; but to the Honour and immortal Memory of Mr. Bushel, a renowned Son of Liberty, who brought his Habeas Corpus, a Victory was soon obtained over their infamous Judges, whose Proceedings were adjudged to be illegal, nor has any Court since the Year 1670, when that memorable Trial was had, (which every Friend to Liberty, ought to read, and will find in the 2d Vol. of the State Trials at large) dared to invade this Bulwark of Safety against the Pride, Insolence and Partiality of Power.

Deprived of the Means to compell, the Judges have since laboured to persuade Juries into such Verdicts as they wished to have found, and proceeding upon the old Star-Chamber Principles, the more easily to gain Convictions, they have refused to let the Jurors hear any Proof of the Truth of the Libel, foreseeing the extreme Difficulty of persuading Twelve honest Men of common Sense, to bring in a Verdict against a Defendant, for publishing what it is proper for the Country to be informed of, and what he had clearly made out in Proof.

The Trial of Capt. McDougall, may bring the Propriety of this Practice to a solemn Decision in America; certainly it can never be discussed at a more favourable Juncture; and I hope your Judges will embrace an Opportunity of acquiring to themselves lasting and universal Applause and Renown. No Antiquity can justify what is incompatible with Reason, the public Safety and sound Principles of Law. They are bound down by no Act of Parliament. The meer Dicta of some of their Predecessors, is all the Authority they can have against an Enquiry into the Truth of the Charge; and our Books are full of Instances of a Departure from Precedent, and the Correction of *ancient grey-headed Errors*. How often have the English Judges ruled, that all Treasons out of England, may be tried there; and will an *American Judge* follow their Opinion in the Case of an *American Treason?* Undoubtedly the *English* Comment upon the Statute was erroneous—and a good Judge will depart from Error, and not only risk the Consequences of being *singularly* Right, but feel a noble Pride in his Superiority to the Influence of exceptional Examples.

The Defendant justifies in Slander, by proving the Truth of the Words spoken: On an Indictment for a Battery, on Assault Demesne, or that he gave the Blow in his own Defence, is good Evidence for an Acquittal, and daily admitted.

It is a Rule, that the *special Matter* may be proved on the Plea of Not Guilty, in criminal Prosecutions; and it is beyond the Wit of Man to reconcile the Star-Chamber Practice, with those indubitable Decisions of the Law.

It is a also a Rule not to admit explanatory Affidavits for the Mitigation of a Fine *after* a Trial had; and the very Reason assigned, why they are only read upon a Submission to the Mercy of the Court, is because on a Trial, the Judges acquire all the Information necessary for applying proper Degrees of Punishment; and how is it possible to avoid Error, unless an Opportunity is given for all the justifying, mitigating and apologetical Proof to come fairly out? Suppose a Man to be charged with robbing the Treasury of the Nation: Is it not a Virtue to make the Charge, if it is true. Admit to a Crown Hireling, that it is a Crime, is it no Mitigation that the Accusation is proved to be true? Away with all the Star-Chamber Nonsense. Nonsense do I call it! It is monstrous for a Judge to rise up and tell a Jury, that the Enquiry into the *Reality* of the Robbery is *immaterial* to the Defence; and to add, that the Libel is the greater for being true, is the Language of a Parricide, and Blasphemy, outrageous Blasphemy against the plainest Dictates of common Sense. A judge must tremble when he speaks the Words, and the People turn pale to hear them asserted for Law. Let the Arguments for the Punishment of private or public Detraction be stretched and multiplied to the Utmost, they must nevertheless be tried by the supreme Law of Safety to the Common Weal—and highly does it import Judges, Jurors, and Americans, of every Station, to eye Prosecutions for Libels at *this Juncture,* with the keenest and most suspicious Jealousy. Upon the Principles of the Mother Country, all our Vindications since the Year 1765, are seditious and libellous, if not of a Treasonable Complexion. What if a Door should be opened, to be revenged of the Patriots who have wrote and printed in our Favour? There is doubtless Malice in Store against our Delanys, and our other Advocates who founded a seasonable and courageous Alarm. The Enemy is on the Watch. Let every Impeachment for a Libel, be tried by its Tendency to subvert or promote the Liberty and Prosperity of this Country —and if a worthless, private Name happens to be drawn out of its Obscurity, or a Set of dignified Scoundrels exposed, I would never condemn as criminal, the well meant Emanations of a warm, honest Zeal for the Interest of the grand Colony Cause. The *Truth* of the Charge should be all my Enquiry as a Juror; and that known, evinced or believed, the Verdict of *Not Guilty* should ensue, in spite of a *Jefferies* on the Bench, and a Bloody *Kirk* at his Elbow.

You may depend, Sir, upon my Attendance at a Trial of such Importance to the American Cause (if my Health will permit) Dispatch me as soon as possible a Copy of the Information, for I suppose it will be no easy Matter to prevail upon a Grand Jury to proceed by Indictment. As the Prosecution is connected with the Supposition, that the Mutiny Act has the obligatory Force of a Law (a Matter well worth Consideration) I have a Curiosity to see a Composition, grounded upon a Basis which so tenderly affects the Constitution and Liberties of this Country. Besides it must of Necessity contain such an Infinity of Innuendoes, from the peculiar Frame of the Libel, as to afford no small Diversion to the Peruser, as the Reading of it doubtless, will to the Audience upon the Trial.

17. THE *New York Post-Boy* DAMNS STAR CHAMBER

DOCTRINES

MR. PRINTER,

Being desirous of some Information concerning the Law of Libels, that I might be the better able to judge for myself, at an approaching Trial of the utmost Importance to the Cause of Liberty; I borrowed the Digest of *Serjeant Hawkins,* which I am told is of the greatest Authority among the Crown Lawyers; and as his Chapter upon Libels contains, in my Opinion, Positions utterly subversive of the *Liberty of the Press,* I beg Leave to communicate an Abstract of them to the Public thro the Channel of your Paper.

Upon the Question what is a Libel, this Author is of Opinion,

1st. That in a *strict* Sense, it is a malicious Defamation in Printing or Writing, tending to blacken the *Memory of one that is dead,* or the Reputation of one that is alive, and to expose him to publick Hatred, Contempt or Ridicule.

2. That in a *large* Sense, any Defamation by Signs or Pictures, fixing a Gallows at a Man's Door, or painting him in a shameful or ignominious Manner, *is a Libel.*

3. That its Tendency to the Breach of the Peace, by provoking Parties, their Families and Friends to Revenge, is the Reason why a Libel consisting of *Signs* and *Pictures* is punishable.

4. That it will be a Libel tho' *ironically* expressed; as when

---

New-York Gazette; or, The Weekly Post-Boy, April 9, 1770.

one writing of a public Charity done by another, expresses himself thus, *You will not play the Jew or Hypocrite;* and so insinuates, that he acted from *vain-glory;* or when recommending a great Character for Imitation, instead of taking Notice of what he was famous for, such Qualities are pitched upon as he wants; as in proposing a Man to be imitated for his *Courage,* who is only a Statesman and *no Soldier;* or another for his Learning, who is a great General and no Scholar; for this, says the sagacious Sergeant, is upbraiding a Man with the Want of those Qualities.

5. That setting down only two Letters of a Name, if it is clear from the Context who is meant, will suffice in Point of Certainty, as to the Person aimed at.

6. That it is no *Justification* that the Contents of the Writing *are true,* or that the Person attacked had a *bad Character;* for adds the Sage, *the more of Truth there is in it, the more provoking it will be.*

7. That it is not the less a Libel for defaming Persons in public Office, but rather a *great Aggravation;* because it creates ill Blood, disturbs the Peace, and breeds a Dislike in the People of their Governors. But he adds,

8. That scandalous Matter in a Petition to Parliament, or in legal Proceedings in Courts of Justice, is no Libel. And,

9. That some *particular* Person must be reflected upon, to make it a Libel; after which he asserts,

10. That he, who procures another Man to compose a Libel, or he who publishes it, or procures it to be published, is punishable.

And under this Head we are told,

1. That it will not excuse the Publisher, tho he *knew nothing* of the Contents.

2. That if he who had read it, *reads* it or *repeats* it, or *lends* or *shews* it to others, he is punishable.

3. That *copying it* is conclusive Proof of a Publication of it, unless the Copier gives it to a Magistrate.

11. That writing a *provoking* Letter to another, *without publishing* it, is highly punishable; because it tends to disturb the Peace.

12. That the having a written Copy of a Libel (publickly known) in one's Custody, is Evidence of the Publication of it. And,

13. That repeating Parts of a Libel *in Merriment,* even *without* Malice, and with *no Purpose* of Defamation, is in the Serjeant's Opinion, punishable; for, says the peaceable old Gentleman, *Jests of this Kind are not to be endured, and the Injury is not lessened by the Merriment of him who makes so light of it.*

This is the Sum of the whole Doctrine of Libels, as laid down by this venerable Crown Lawyer: And if this *Star-Chamber Trumpery,* is to pass for the Law of the Land, a kind Father ought to tremble at the Thought of sending his Children to a Writing-School. What Writer does not fall under the Lash of *such Law* as this? All the Historians, all the Poets, all the Divines, all the Controversial Writers are *guilty, guilty, guilty.* Not a News Paper that is not full of Libels: The public Accounts of Thefts, Murders, Treasons, are all so many Libels. The Old-Bailey and State-Trials, and every Law Book that can be named, is more or less libellous. Nay, what can excuse the Publication of Libels even in the Journals of the Parliaments and Assemblies? According to the Star-Chamber Decisions, the Bible is a Libel, and neither Prophets nor Apostles would escape.

In a Word, this horrid Doctrine is an Enemy to Science of every King, enslaves all Men but those in Power, is destructive of human Felicity, repugnant to Reason, inconsistent with Revelation, and never was, nor can be *found Law* in any Country, possessed of the smallest Remains of common Virtue or common Sense.

Temporizing Minions of Power indeed there have been upon the Bench in the Mother Country, who have dared to vent these Blasphemies; and Hawkins refers to *these as his Vouchers*. They have had an Imitator, not but one that I have heard in America. But thanks be to God, that a Noon-Day Sun of Light and Knowledge now shines upon this Continent, —and if such Wickedness and Nonsense should ever be heard again in our Courts, I hope—but one Instance is enough to induce all the American Assemblies to bring in Bills for the Banishment of such tyrannical Tenets from the Courts of Justice, and to refuse any Support to *Government;* until *Government* will concur in a Law, *essential* to the common Weal, and *essential* to human Happiness: Under the *Starr Chamber Law,* no Country can be safe for a Month, from the wicked Arm of Oppression; a silent Press would be immediate Perdition to Liberty.

18. AMERICA'S WILKES APPEALS TO THE PUBLIC

The Public may remember, that shortly after the Paper, signed, A Son of Liberty, directed, "To the betrayed Inhabitants of the City and Colony of New York" made its Appearance, the General Assembly addressed the Lieutenant Governor, to issue his Proclamation of a Reward of One Hundred Pounds to any Person or Persons who should discover the Author or Authors, Aiders or Abettors, of the Publication of that Paper, so that he or they might be convicted, and over and above the Reward promised, his Majesty's Pardon was tendered to any of the Accomplice or Accomplices, who should discover the Author, &c. as may be seen at large in Mr. Gaine's Mercury, of the 25th of December 1769.

Early in February, an Information was lodged against Mr. Parker, as the Printer of the said Paper, and a Council called, before whom he and one of his Boys, together with Messrs. A.

Alexander McDougall's "Letter to the Freeholders," *New-York Gazette; or, The Weekly Post-Boy,* December 24, 1770.

and J. Car, were examined, touching the Author. In this Examination, 'tis said, he was threatned, if he did not discover the Author, with a Complaint against him to the Government, which might endanger his Place in the Police Office, Mr. Parker, knowing that his Journeyman and Apprentices had been examined, as he had no Opportunity to consult the Author, upon the Promise of the Lieut. Governor and Council that he should not be prosecuted as the Printer, informed them, as is said, that I had brought the Manuscript to him to be printed. 'Tis supported that it was by Order of the Council, that Mr. Chief Justice Horsmanden, on the 8th of February last, issued his Warrant to bring me before him, to be interrogated about the Charge. I was accordingly brought to his Chamber, where I declined to give any Satisfaction on that Head, and upon my refusing to give Bail, I was committed to Gaol. In April Term the Grand Jury for the Body of the City and County of New York, found a Bill of Indictment against me, charging me as the Author of a Libel against the General Assembly &c. &c. &c. &c. To which I plead, Not Guilty; and as the Indictment was brought in so late in the Term that I could not be tried, I desired to be admitted to Bail, which the Court granted, when I entered into Recognizance with two Securities, each in the Sum of £250, and myself in £500 for my Appearance at the next Term. Since that two Terms have elapsed; the Public therefore will be surprised to be informed; that on Thusday, the 13th Instant, about Noon, I was served by the Serjeant at Arms with an Order to attend the House of Assembly then sitting upon which I told him I would go with him immediately. Being brought to the Bar of the House, Mr. Speaker informed me that I was charged by a Member with being the Author or Publisher of a Paper, directed "to the betrayed Inhabitants of the City and Colony of New York," and signed, a Son of Liberty; and that I was by an Order of the House, to answer to the Question, Whether I was or was not Guilty: Upon which, I asked who were my Accusers, or what the Evidences to support the Charge. Here I was interrupted by Mr. De Noyellis who called me to Order, telling me I had no Liberty to speak; in which Declaration Mr. Speaker immediately joined, and added, that I was not to speak till I asked Liberty of the House, by the Speaker, to speak. I replied, that I understood I was ordered to proceed to answer the Question. Mr. De Noyellis again interrupted me, and declared, "that if I was not silenced he would move for a Contempt of the House, and added, that he made no Doubt from the evidence that he was furnished with, the presumptive Proofs he would make, it would appear that I was the Author or Publisher of the Paper." Upon this Mr. Clinton rose and observed, that from what had passed in the House, he did not suppose that it was the design of the House to prevent my offering any Suggestion or Arguments why I should not answer to the Question or the Charge, provided I treated the House with proper Decencey and Respect. To which the House Agreed. I then asked the Speaker if I might proceed. Leave being granted, I proceeded in the following Manner, "Mr. Speaker, as I have not had any Time or Notice to prepare for defending myself against this Charge, and being unaccustomed to speak in public Courts, especially at so respectable a Bar as that of the Representatives of the People, it cannot be expected that I can say much on the Subject, and as I have the greatest Deference for the Representatives of the People, for these Reasons I hope the Honourable House will put the most Favourable consideration on what I may say on the Occasion. Mr. Speaker, the Charge is too indefinite, but if the Honourable House means by the Paper in Question, a certain Paper signed a Son of Liberty, which this House and the Grand Jury have declared to be a Libel, I cannot answer to the Question for two Reasons." Here Mr. De Noyellis again interrupted me, by moving the House to read the Paper signed a Son of Liberty entered on their Journals of the last Sections. To which the House agreed, and the Paper was accordingly read. After which Mr. Speaker told me I might proceed: Accordingly I told Mr. Speaker, that two Reasons rendered it improper for me to answer to the Question: First, that the Paper just read to me, had been declared by the Honourable House to be a Libel; that the Grand Jury for the Body of the City and County of New York, had also declared it to be a Libel, and found a Bill of Indictment against me as the Author of it; therefore that I could not Answer a Question that would tend to impeach myself, or might otherwise be improper for me to answer. Secondly, that this Honourable House had addressed the Lieut. Governor to issue his Proclamation to offer a Reward of £100 to any Person that would discover the Author or Publisher of the Paper, signed a Son of Liberty, in order that he might be proceeded against according to Law; that in Consequence thereof Information had been made, and a Prosecution was commenced and is now depending against me in the Supreme Court, where the Matter would be tried by a Jury of my Peers; that as the Honourable House was a Party in the present Question, and the Prosecution was commenced at their Instance, I conceived they ought not to take Cognizance of the Matter; and I questioned whether any Instance could be produced on the Journals of the House of Commons, of their taking Cognizance of a supposed Libel against them, when the supposed Author or Publisher was under Prosecution in a Court of Justice; that I conceived such a Procedure would be an Infraction of the Laws of Justice, which forbid that a British Subject should be punished twice for one and the same Offence; for if he could be punished twice, he may be seven Times, and no Line could be run where the Punishment might end. These, Mr. Speaker, are my Reasons for not answering to the Question: but I desire the Honourable House would be pleased to remember, that I would not be understood to deny or affirm any Thing concerning the Paper in Question." Mr. De Noyellis then rose and said, that I might be made to Answer the Question, for the House had Power to make me Answer: That it is a Rule in the Courts below, to oblige a Person charged, to plead Guilty or Not Guilty, or be subject to the Punishment of *pain Fort et dure*. To which Mr. Clinton replied, that the House had Power to throw me over the Bar, or out of the Windows, but that the Public would judge of the Justice of it.

Upon which Mr. James De Lancey rose and said, that the House had *indulged* me to assign Reasons why I should not Answer the Question: To which I replied, I wanted no Indulgency of the House. After a short Debate, Mr. Clinton rose and said, that his Residence was so far removed from the Means of authentic Information respecting my Profession, that he could not depend on what he had heard concerning it. He confessed that the Newspaper, and sundry Persons had informed him that a prosecution had been commenced against me, in Consequence of the Address of that House to the Lieutenant Governor but he could not determine on such Evidence, he therefore moved the House to order the Clerk of the Council, and Clerk of the Supreme Court to attend the House the next morning at Ten o'Clock, to inform them whether the Order of Council to Mr. Chief Justice Horsmanden, to issue his Warrant against me, was in Consequence of the Address of the House to the Lieut. Governor, and whether I was in Consequence thereof indicted, and whether the Assembly was an Object of the Indictment.

The House, as I understood, agreed that those Gentlemen should accordingly attend. Mr. Speaker then asked the House what Entry they would have made on my Affair. Several of the Members answered, the Common Entry, with the Substance of the Reasons I assigned why I would not answer to the Question. A Draught was accordingly made, which Mr. Speaker read to the House. Upon hearing it, I apprehended that my second Reason for not answering the Question, was not fully expressed, and therefore told Mr. Speaker that I should be glad if the House would order the Substance of the Reason to be more fully entered. Mr. DeNoyellis then declared, that if I persisted in the second Reason, he would move the House against me for a Breach of Privilege. Upon this short Debate commenced, in the Course of which I conceived that my

Meaning was not clearly understood; I therefore desired Mr. Speaker to ask Leave of the Hon. House to let me say a Sentence or two by way of Explaination. Leave being granted, I told the Honourable House that I had the highest Respect and Esteem for the Representatives of the People, but that in Exoneration of myself, I must say, that the precise Idea I intended to convey in the second Reason was, that as the Prosecution had been commenced, and was then depending against me, at the Instance of the Honourable House, I conceived it would be an Infraction of the Laws of Justice, for them to take Cognizance of the Matter again. Some of the Members appearing to have some Doubt about the strict Meaning of what I had said, Mr. Speaker desired me to commit my Answers to Writing which I accordingly did in the Words following the Question put to me, which the Reader may see at large, in the Extract of the Journals of the Assembly, respecting this Transaction.

After Mr. Speaker had read my Answer to the House, he declared, that what I had committed to Writing, reflected more upon the Honour and Dignity of the House, than what I had said before; upon which Mr. James Jauncy, and Mr. James DeLancey declared it was clearly a Breach of Privilege. Mr. Clinton then rose and said That he could by no Means consider my Answer as a Breach of Privilege. For that the House had put a Question to me, and determined that I might assign Reasons why I should not answer it. That what I had wrote were only my Reasons or Opinion why I ought not to answer to the Question. —Upon this, Mr. DeNoyellis observed, That he was surprised that any Member of that House should attempt to vindicate an Insult offered to the Honour and Dignity of that House. To which Mr. Clinton replied, That he was far from vindicating an Insult offered to the Honour or Dignity of the House; but that he conceived the Honour and Dignity of it would be better supported by Justice, than by straining its authority. At length the Question was put (as I understood it) Whether I was not guilty of a Breach of Privilege and Contempt of the Authority of the house? Which was carried in the Affirmative, so Manner as appears by the Votes. It was ordered, that I should ask Pardon of the house.

Upon which Mr. Speaker looked towards me and (as I understood) put the Question. I answered, That rather than resign the Rights and Privileges of a British Subject, I would suffer my Right Hand to be cut off at the Bar of the House. Mr. Speaker then, by Order of the House, put the Question, Whether I should, Yes or Nay, ask Pardon of the House? To which I answered, That I had not committed any Crime. Some of the Members then ordered the Serjeant at Arms to take me into Custody. As no Order of the House had then been made to warrant him to do it, I told them that Mr. Serjeant knew his Duty better than to lay a finger on me, without a formal Order of the House, and charged him to do it at his Peril. Mr. Speaker was then ordered to make out his Warrant to the Gaol-Keeper of the City and County of New York, commanding him to receive me into safe and secure Custody &c. While the Clerk was making out the Warrant, as I wrote my Reasons for not answering the Question in a great Haste, I asked the Speaker for a Copy of them. Mr. James DeLancey answered, that as I had committed a Breach of Privilege, I was not intitled to it. It was accordingly refused. The Warrant to the Gaol-Keeper being finished, it was given to the Serjeant at Arms; and as I could not gather from what had past in the House, that any Order of the House had been made or entered, commanding him to take me into Custody; I told him that was no Authority for him, and therefore charged him again at his Peril, not to lay a Hand upon me without an Order of the House: He notwithstanding took hold of my Arm: Upon which I took the Spectators Witnesses. that I was deprived of my Liberty by Force, without an Order from the House. Some of the Members then cried out to him to do his Duty, that there was an Order of the House. Upon which I came with him to this place. Thus I have given the Reader a particular Account of the Cause for which I have been deprived of my

Liberty, and hope he will pardon my being so circumstantial and the Egotism in it. There have been so many Misrepresentations of this Matter artfully spread abroad, that it was judged proper to enter into the former, and the frequent Interruptions I met with, which necessarily occasioned many short Sentences unavoidably produced the latter; all which, I flatter myself, will sufficiently apologize for me to the delicate Reader. The Principal Facts are incontestibly proved by the following Extract of the Votes.

Extract from the Printed Votes of the General Assembly now sitting.

13th December 1770

A Motion was made by Mr. *De Noyellis,* in the Words following *viz.*

Mr. Speaker.
I Move, That *Alexander McDougall* may be ordered to attend forthwith at the Bar of this House, to answer to a Complaint I have to make against him, for being the supposed Author or Publisher of a certain Paper, directed "To the Betrayed Inhabitants of the City and Colony of New York;" and signed, A Son of Liberty, dated the 16th of *December,* 1769. And a Debate arising upon the said Motion, and the Question being put thereon, it was carried in the Affirmative, in Manner following, viz.

For the Affirmative		For the Negative
Mr. Boerum,	Mr. Billop,	Col. Woodhull
Mr. Rapaljie,	Capt. Seaman,	
Mr. Clinton,	Mr. Kissam,	
Mr. DeWitt,	Mr. Van Cortlandt,	
Mr. Ten Eyck,	Capt. De Lancey,	
Mr. De Noyellis,	Col. Phillips,	
Mr. Geie,	Mr. De Lancey,	
Mr. Jauncey,	Mr. Van Kleeck.	
Col. Seaman,		

Ordered therefore,
That *Alexander McDougall* attend the House forthwith.

Ordered, That the Serjeant at Arms attending this House serve him with a Copy of this Order forthwith.

The Serjeant at Arms attending at the Door, was called in; and being asked what he had done with Respect to summoning *Alexander McDougall* to attend at the Bar of this House, answered, that he was attending accordingly.

The said *Alexander McDougall* being then called in, Mr. Speaker acquainted him, that he was charged by a Member of this House, with being the Author or Publisher of a certain Paper, entered on the printed Journals of this House, on the 18th Day of *December,* 1769, Page (45) directed "To the Betrayed Inhabitants of the City and Colony of New York;" and the same being read, Mr. Speaker asked him. Whether or not he was the Author or Publisher of the same? To which said *McDougall* replied, "That as the Grand Jury and House of Assembly had declared the Paper in Question to be a Libel, he could not answer to the Question. *Secondly,* That as he was under Prosecution in the Supreme Court, he conceived it would be an Infraction of the Laws of Justice, to punish a British Subject twice for one Offence, for that no Line could be run,—that he might be punished without End: But he would not be understood to deny the Authority of the House to punish for a Breach of Privilege, when no Cognizance is taken of it in another Court."

And upon Mr. Speaker's asking, Whether the foregoing Words of said *McDougall,* were not a Contempt of the Authority of this House? A Debate arose, and the Question being put thereon, it was carried in the Affirmative, in Manner following, viz.

For the Affirmative		*For the Negative*
Mr. De Noyellis,	Mr. Boerum,	Mr. Gale,
Mr. De Lancey,	Mr. Ten Eyck,	Mr. Van Cortlandt,
Mr. Jauncey,	Mr. Van Kleeck,	Col. Woodhull,
Capt. De Lancey,	Mr. Rapaljie,	Capt. Seaman,
Mr. Billopp,	Col. Seaman,	Mr. Clinton.
Mr. Kissam,	Col. Phillips.	

Resolved therefore.

That *Alexander McDougall* in his above Reply, does deny the Authority of this House, and is therefore guilty of a high Contempt.

And the said *McDougall* refusing to ask Pardon of the House for the said Contempt.

Ordered therefore,

That the said McDougall, be taken into Custody by the Serjeant at Arms attending this House.

Ordered,

That the Speaker issue his Warrant to the Gaol Keeper of the City and County of *New York,* commanding him to receive the said *McDougall,* into safe and secure Custody, and him to keep Prisoner in the common Gaol of the said City and County, until he shall be thence discharged by due Course of Law; and that the Serjeant at Arms convey the said *McDougall,* and deliver him to the Keeper of the said Gaol.

It may not now be improper to remind the Reader, that I was, in the Law Sense, in Bonds, as the supposed Author of that Paper, when I was taken first by the Serjeant at Arms, by Order of the House to be brought to the Bar. That when I was brought there, and charged as the Author or Publisher of the Paper, signed A Son of Liberty, and the Question put to me, Whether or not I was the Author or Publisher. Not a Spark of Evidence was exhibited to the House before me to prove the Charge. That, by the Determination of the House, I was allowed to assign Reasons, if I had any, provided I offered them with Decency and Respect to the House, why I should not answer the Question. The Public then are left to judge, Whether there is any Insult or Contempt of the Authority of the House in the Reasons I assigned for not answering the question.

And whether the Liberties and Privileges of a British Subject can be secure, if an Exception to the Jurisdiction of the highest Tribunal of the Nation, is to be considered as a Contempt of its Authority. Tis the dreadful Condition of a Slave when he is injured, to be confined only to utter his Sense of it by Groans. But 'tis the peculiar Right and Privilege of Freemen, of British Freemen, not only to assert, but to complain of a Violation of their Rights. This is the very Spirit and Genius of our glorious and much envied Constitution; a Constitution, purchased at the Expence of Millions, and the Blood of Thousands. Let not my Friends then be concerned for my present Sufferings, but so far as the Cause of Liberty suffers. For myself, I feel none; and notwithstanding the Sneers of temporizing Sycophants about "my regaining Paradise." A Goal, for a noble Cause, with a self approving Conscience, is, to me, a Paradise, compared to a conscious Baseness, even with all the Smiles of the Great.

For the many Visits I have received from my Friends of all Ranks, I am affected with sincere Gratitude. They may rest assured, that none of their Rights shall be silently resigned, by the Public's most obedient humble Servant,

New Gaol, Dec.   ALEXANDER MCDOUGALL.
   22, 1770.

PART THREE

The Constitutional Period:
Neo-Blackstonians

19. JAMES WILSON UPHOLDS BLACKSTONE

Pennsylvania's constitution of 1776 provided "That the people have a right to freedom of speech, and of writing, and publishing their sentiments; therefore the freedom of the press ought not to be restrained." In the Pennsylvania convention called to ratify the federal Constitution, anti-Federalist speakers, such as John Smilie, demanded a federal bill of rights with a comparable guarantee of the press. Smilie warned, prophetically, that Congress was vested with such broad powers under the proposed Constitution that it might restrain the freedom of the press by enacting a law for the punishment of libels. Here is the reply by James Wilson, who was probably the most influential framer of the Constitution, excepting only Madison, and as great a legal expert as anyone in the new nation—which Wilson served as a member of the first Supreme Court. His reply to Smilie is notable as one of the two statements by a framer of the Constitution, during the ratification controversy, explicitly defining freedom of the press. The other, by Hugh Williamson of North Carolina, similarly endorsed the Blackstonian or common-law definition. In 1790, Wilson was the principal draftsman of the new Pennsylvania constitution, which guaranteed every citizen the liberty of the press, "being responsible for the abuse of that liberty." The same clause also provided the first guarantee in

America of the Zengerian principle that truth may be admitted in evidence in any "prosecution for the publication of papers investigating the official conduct of officers or men in a public capacity. . . ."

. . . In answer to the gentleman from Fayette (Mr. Smilie,) on the subject of the press, I beg leave to make an observation: it is very true, Sir, that this constitution says nothing with regard to that subject, nor was it necessary, because it will be found that there is given to the general government no power whatsoever concerning it; and no law in pursuance of the constitution, can possibly be enacted, to destroy that liberty.

I heard the honorable gentleman make this general assertion, that the Congress was certainly vested with power to make such a law, but I would be glad to know by what part of this constitution such a power is given? Until that is done, I shall not enter into a minute investigation of the matter, but shall at present satisfy myself with giving an answer to a question that has been put. It has been asked, if a law should be made to punish libels, and the judges should proceed under that law, what chance would the printer have of an acquittal? And it has been said he would drop into a den of devouring monsters.

I presume it was not in the view of the honorable gentleman to say there is no such thing as a libel, or that the writers of such ought not to be punished. The idea of the liberty of the press, is not carried so far as this in any country—what is meant by the liberty of the press is, that there should be no antecedent restraint upon it; but that every author is responsible when he attacks the security or welfare of the government, or the safety, character and property of the individual.

With regard to attacks upon the public, the mode of pro-

James Wilson, Speech of December 1, 1787, at the Pennsylvania Ratifying Convention, in *Pennsylvania and the Federal Constitution, 1787–1788* ed. John Bach McMaster and Frederick D. Stone (Philadelphia: Historical Society of Pennsylvania, 1888), pp. 308–309.

ceeding is by a prosecution. Now if a libel is written, it must be within some one of the United States, or the district of congress. With regard to that district, I hope it will take care to preserve this as well as the other rights of freemen; for whatever district congress may choose, the cession of it cannot be completed without the consent of its inhabitants. Now, Sir, if this libel is to be tried, it must be tried where the offence was committed; for under this constitution, as declared in the second section of the third article, the trial must be held in the State; therefore on this occasion it must be tried where it was published, if the indictment is for publishing; and it must be tried likewise by a jury of that State. Now, I would ask, is the person prosecuted in a worse situation under the general government, even if it had the power to make laws on this subject, than he is at present under the State government? It is true there is no particular regulation made, to have the jury come from the body of the county in which the offence was committed; but there are some States in which this mode of collecting juries is contrary to their established custom, and gentlemen ought to consider that this constitution was not meant merely for Pennsylvania. In some States the juries are not taken from a single county. In Virginia, the sheriff, I believe, is not confined even to the inhabitants of the State, but is at liberty to take any man he pleases, and put him on the jury. In Maryland I think a set of jurors serve for the whole Western Shore, and another for the Eastern Shore. . . .

20. CHIEF JUSTICE MCKEAN INTERPRETS THE CONSTITUTIONAL GUARANTEE OF A FREE PRESS

Thomas McKean was a signer of the Declaration of Independence, governor of Delaware, and president of the Continental Congress. Second only to James Wilson in securing Pennsylvania's ratification of the Constitution, he was chief justice of Pennsylvania for twenty-two years and finally became its Jeffersonian governor. In Oswald's case, in 1788, Chief Justice McKean ruled that freedom of the press, although constitutionally guaranteed, meant only what it had meant in England for a century. The argument to the contrary by the defendant, Eleazer Oswald, received short shrift. Oswald had been indicted for a gross libel, breaching the peace, against a private person. He defended himself in his newspaper, the *Independent Gazetteer*, alleging prejudice on the part of his judges. McKean then convicted Oswald for contempt in the form of a libel upon the court, repudiating his contention that the common law of libel was incompatible with the constitutional guarantee of a free press. After being convicted, Oswald presented a memorial to the Pennsylvania Assembly, calling upon it to determine whether the judges of the Supreme Court should not be impeached for violating the state constitution. After three days of debate, the Assembly, by a vote of 34 to 23, resolved that Oswald's charges were unsupported and, consequently, that there was no cause for impeaching the judges. William Lewis, who had been Oswald's prosecutor, in making the principal defense of the judges in the Assembly debate supported their interpretation of the free-press clause in the state constitution. Lewis' statement on this issue is reprinted here, following McKean's opinion for the court. No contrary position is presented, for the simple reason that none was argued. William Findley, one of the state's anti-Federalist leaders, who insisted that the new federal Constitution should not be ratified without a bill of rights guaranteeing freedom of the press, was Oswald's principal supporter in the Assembly. But Findley, who spoke after Lewis, barely replied on the free-press issue. He merely noted "the right of every man to publish his sentiments on public proceedings," and the danger of permitting judges to punish for written contempts against themselves. Findley's main argument was addressed to alleged procedural irregularities by the court and to the fact that Oswald had been convicted summarily by the judges, without trial by jury.

On the 12th of *July, Lewis* moved for a rule to shew cause why an attachment should not issue against *Eleazer Oswald,* the printer and publisher of the *Independent Gazetteer.*

Respublica v. *Oswald*, 1 Dallas *(United States Reports)*, 319–331 (1788).

The case was this: *Oswald* having inserted in his newspapers several anonymous pieces against the character of *Andrew Browne,* the master of a female academy, in the city of *Philadelphia, Browne* applied to him to give up the authors of those pieces; but being refused that satisfaction, he brought action for the libel against *Oswald,* returnable into the Supreme Court, *on the 2d day of July;* and therein demanded bail for £1000. Previously to the return day of the writ, the question of bail being brought by citation before Mr. *Justice* BRYAN, at his chambers, the Judge, on a full hearing of the cause of action, in the presence of both the parties, ordered the Defendant to be discharged on common bail; and the Plaintiff appealed from this order to the court. Afterwards, *on the 1st of July, Oswald* published under his own signature, an address to the public, which contained a narrative of these proceedings, and the following passages, which, I[1] conceive, to have been the material grounds of the present motion.

"When violent attacks are made upon a person under pretext of justice, and legal steps are taken on the occasion, not perhaps to redress the supposed injury, but to feed and gratify partisaning and temporising resentments, it is not unwarrantable in such person to represent the real statement of his case, and appeal to the world for their sentiments and countenance.

"Upon these considerations, principally, I am now emboldened to trespass on the public patience, and must solicit the indulgence of my friends and customers, while I present to their notice, an account of the steps lately exercised with me; from which it will appear that my situation *as a printer,* and the *rights of the press* and of *freemen,* are fundamentally struck at; and an earnest endeavour is on the carpet to involve me in difficulties to please the malicious dispositions of old and permanent enemies.

"But until the news had arrived last *Thursday,* that the *ninth* state had acceded to the new federal government, I was not

---

[1] The court reporter, Alexander Dallas. [Ed.]

called upon; and Mr. *Page* in the afternoon of that day visited me in due form of law with a writ. Had Mr. *Browne* pursued me in this line, "without loss of time," agreeably to his lawyer's letter, I should not have supposed it extraordinary—but to arrest me the moment the *federal* intelligence came to hand, indicated that the commencement to this suit was not so much the child of his own fancy, as it has been probably dictated to and urged on him by others, whose sentiments upon the new constitution have not in every respect coincided with mine. In fact, it was my idea, in the first progress of the business, that Mr. *Browne* was merely the *hand-maid* of some of my enemies among the federalists; and in this class I must rank, his great patron Doctor *Rush* (whose brother is a judge of the *Supreme Court*) I think Mr. *Brown's* conduct has since confirmed the idea beyond a doubt.

"Enemies I have had in the legal profession, and it may perhaps add to the hopes of *malignity*, that this action is instituted in the *Supreme Court* of *Pennsylvania*. However, if former prejudices should be found to operate against me on the bench, it is with a jury of my country, properly elected and empannelled, a jury of freemen and independent citizens, I must rest the suit. I have escaped the jaws of persecution through this channel on certain memorable occasions, and hope I shall never be a sufferer, let the blast of faction blow with all its furies!

"The doctrine of libels being a doctrine incompatible with law and liberty, and at once destructive of the privileges of a free country in the communication of our thoughts, has not hitherto gained any footing in *Pennsylvania:* and the vile measures formerly taken to lay me by the heels on this subject only brought down obloquy upon the conductors themselves. I may well suppose the same love of liberty yet pervades my fellow citizens, and that they will not allow the freedom of the press to be violated upon any refined pretence, which oppressive ingenuity or courtly study can invent.

"Upon trial of the cause, the public will decide for themselves, whether Mr. *Browne's* motives have been laudable and dignified; whether his conduct in declining an acquittal of his character in the paper, and suing me in the manner he did, was decent and consistent; and, in a word, whether he is not actuated by some of my inveterate foes and opponents, to lend his name in their service for the purpose of harrassing and injuring me."

A transcript from the records was read to shew that the action between *Browne* and *Oswald* was depending in the court; *James Martin* proved that the paper containing *Oswald's* address was bought at his printing office, fresh and damp from the press; and a deposition, made by *Browne,* was read to prove the preceding facts relative to the cause of action, the hearing before Mr. *Justice* BRYAN, and the appeal from his order.

Lewis then adverted to the various pieces, which were charged as libellous in the depending action; and argued, that, though the liberty of the press was invaluable in its nature, and ought not to be infringed: yet, that its value did not consist in a boundless licentiousness of slander and defamation. He contended, that the profession of *Browne,* to whom the education of more than a hundred children was sometimes entrusted, exposed him, in a peculiar manner, to be injured by wanton aspersions of his character; and he inferred the necessity of the action, which had been instituted, from this consideration, that if *Browne* were really the monster which the papers in question described him to be, he ought to be hunted from society; but, that if he had been falsely accused, if he had been maliciously traduced, it was a duty that he owed to himself and to the public to vindicate his reputation, and to call upon the justice of the laws, to punish so gross a violation of truth and decency. For this purpose, he continued, a writ had been issued, and bail was required. The defendant, if not before, was certainly, on the hearing at the Judge's chambers, apprised of the cause of action: The order of Mr. *Justice* BRYAN on that occasion, and the appeal to the court, were circumstances perfectly within his knowledge; and yet, while the whole merits of the cause were thus in suspense, he thought proper to address the public in language evidently calculated to excite the popular resentment against *Browne;* to create doubts and suspicions of the integrity and impartiality of the Judges, who must preside upon the trial; and to promote an unmerited compassion in his own favour. He has described himself as the object of former persecutions upon similar principles; he has asserted that, in this instance, an individual is made the instrument of a party to destroy him; and he artfully calls upon his fellow citizens to interest themselves to preserve the freedom of the press, which he considers as attacked in his person. . . .

. . . But, whatever the law might be in *England,* Sergeant[2] insisted, that it could not avail in *Pennsylvania.* Even in *England,* indeed, though it is said to be a contempt to report the decisions of the courts, unless under the *imprimatur* of the judges; yet, we find Burrow, and all the subsequent reporters, proceeding without that sanction. But the constitution of *Pennsylvania* authorizes many things to be done which in *England* are prohibited. Here the press is laid open to the inspection of every citizen, who wishes to examine the proceedings of the government; of which the judicial authority is certainly to be considered as a branch. *Const. Penn. sect.* 35.

MCKEAN, C. J.—Could not this be done in *England?* Certainly it could: for, in short, there is nothing in the constitution of this state, respecting the liberty of the press, that has not been authorized by the constitution of that kingdom for near a century past. . . .

THE CHIEF JUSTICE delivered the opinion of the Court to the

---

2 Oswald's counsel, John Dickinson Sergeant. [Ed.]

following effect, Judge BRYAN having shortly before taken his seat.

MCKEAN, C. J.—This is a motion for an attachment against *Eleazer Oswald,* the printer and publisher of *the Independent Gazetteer,* of the 1st of *July* last, No. 796. As a ground for granting the attachment, it is proved, that an action for a libel had been instituted in this court, in which *Andrew Browne* is the plaintiff, and *Eleazer Oswald* the defendant; that a question with respect to bail in that action, had been agitated before one of the Judges, from whose order, discharging the defendant on common bail, the plaintiff had appealed to the court; and that Mr. *Oswald's* address to the public, which is the immediate subject of complaint, relates to the action thus depending before us.

The counsel in support of their motion, have argued that this address was intended to prejudice the public mind upon the merit of the cause, by propagating an opinion that *Browne* was the instrument of a party to persecute and destroy the defendant; that he acted under the particular influence of Dr. *Rush,* whose brother is a judge of this court; and, in short, that from the ancient prejudices of all the judges, the defendant did not stand a chance of a fair trial.

Assertions and imputations of this kind are certainly calculated to defeat and discredit the administration of justice. Let us, therefore, enquire, *first,* whether they ought to be considered as a contempt of the court; and, *secondly,* whether, if so, the defendant is punishable by attachment.

And here, I must be allowed to observe, that libelling is a great crime, whatever sentiments may be entertained by those who live by it. With respect to the heart of the libeller, it is more dark and base than that of the assasin, or than his who commits a midnight arson. It is true, that I may never discover the wretch who has burned my house, or set fire to my barn; but these losses are easily repaired, and bring with them no portion of ignominy or reproach. But the attacks of the libeller admit not of this consolation: the injuries which are done to character and reputation seldom can be cured, and the most innocent man may in a moment be deprived of his good name, upon which, perhaps, he depends for all the prosperity, and all the happiness of his life. To what tribunal can he then resort? how shall he be tried, and by whom shall he be acquitted? It is in vain to object, that those who know him will disregard the slander, since the wide circulation of public prints must render it impracticable to apply the antedote as far as the poison has been extended. Nor can it be fairly said, that the same opportunity is given to *vindicate*, which has been employed to defame him; for, many will read the charge, who may never see the answer; and while the object of accusation is publicly pointed at, the malicious and malignant author, rests in the dishonorable security of an anonymous signature. Where much has been said, something will be believed; and it is one of the many artifices of the libeller, to give to his charges an aspect of general support, by changing and multiplying the style and name of his performances. But shall such things be transacted with impunity in a free country, and among an enlightened people? Let every honest man make this appeal to his heart and understanding, and the answer must be—no!

What then is the meaning of *the Bill of rights,* and *the Constitution* of *Pennsylvania,* when they declare, "That the freedom of the press shall not be restrained," and "that the printing presses shall be free to every person who undertakes to examine the proceedings of the legislature, or any part of the government?" However ingenuity may torture the expressions, there can be little doubt of the just sense of these sections: they give to every citizen a right of investigating the conduct of those who are entrusted with the public business; and they effectually preclude any attempt to fetter the press by the institution of a *licenser.* The same principles were settled in *England,* so far back as the reign of *William the Third,* and since that time, we all know, there has been the freest animadversion upon the conduct of the ministers of that nation. But is there any thing in the language of the constitution (much less in its spirit and intention) which authorizes one man to impute crimes to another, for which the law has provided the mode of trial, and the degree of punishment? Can it be presumed that the slanderous words, which, when spoken to a few individuals, would expose the speaker to punishment, become sacred, by the authority of the constitution, when delivered to the public through the more permanent and diffusive medium of the press? Or, will it be said, that the constitutional right to examine the proceedings of government, extends to warrant an anticipation of the acts of the legislature, or the judgments of the court? and not only to authorize a candid commentary upon what has been done, but to permit every endeavour to biass and intimidate with respect to matters still in suspense? The futility of any attempt to establish a construction of this sort, must be obvious to every intelligent mind. The true liberty of the press is amply secured by permitting every man to publish his opinions; but it is due to the peace and dignity of society to enquire into the motives of such publications, and to distinguish between those which are meant for use and reformation, and with an eye solely to the public good, and those which are intended merely to delude and defame. To the latter description, it is impossible that any good government should afford protection and impunity.

If, then, the liberty of the press is regulated by any just principle, there can be little doubt, that he, who attempts to raise a prejudice against his antagonist, in the minds of those that must ultimately determine the dispute between them; who, for that purpose, represents himself as a persecuted man, and asserts that his judges are influenced by passion and prejudice, —wilfully seeks to corrupt the source, and to dishonor the administration of justice.

Such is evidently the object and tendency of Mr. *Oswald's*

address to the public. Nor can that artifice prevail, which insinuates that the decision of this court will be the effect of personal resentment; for, if it could, every man might evade the punishment due to his offences, by first pouring a torrent of abuse upon his judges, and then asserting that they act from passion, because their treatment has been such as would naturally excite resentment in the human disposition. But it must be remembered, that judges discharge their functions under the solemn obligations of an oath: and, if their virtue entitles them to their station, they can neither be corrupted by favour to swerve from, nor influenced by fear to desert, their duty. That judge, indeed, who courts popularity by unworthy means while he weakens his pretensions, diminishes, likewise, the chance of attaining his object; and he will eventually find that he has sacrificed the substantial blessing of a good conscience, in an idle and visionary pursuit.

Upon the whole, we consider the publication in question, as having the tendency which has been ascribed to it, that of prejudicing the public (a part of whom must hereafter be summoned as jurors) with respect to the merits of a cause depending in this court, and of corrupting the administration of justice: We are, therefore, unanimously of opinion, on the *first* point, that it amounts to a contempt. . . .

The CHIEF JUSTICE pronounced the judgment of the court in the following words. . . .

THE COURT pronounce this sentence: —That you pay a fine of £ 10 to the *Commonwealth;* that you be imprisoned for the space of one month, that is, from the 15th day of July to the 15th day of August next; and, afterwards, till the fine and costs are paid. —Sheriff he is in your custody.

. . . Mr. Lewis . . . On the *second* point, he engaged in a long and ingenious disquisition upon the nature of what is called *the liberty of the press;* he represented the shackles which had been imposed upon it during the arbitrary periods of the *English* government; and thence deduced the wisdom and propriety of the precaution, which declares in the *bill of rights,* that the press shall not be subject to restraint. He gave an historical narrative of the *British* acts of parliament and proclamations, which debarred every man of the right of publication, without a previous licence obtained from officers, established by the government to inspect and pronounce upon every literary performance; but observed, that this oppression (which was intended to keep the people in a slavish ignorance of the conduct of their rulers) expired in the year 1694, when the dawn of true freedom rose upon that nation. 9 *vol. Stat. at large, p.* 190. Since that memorable period, the liberty of the press has stood on a firm and rational basis. On the one hand, it is not subject to the tyranny of previous restraints, and, on the other, it affords no sanction to ribaldry and slander; —so true it is, that to censure the *licentiousness,* is to maintain the *liberty* of the press. 4 *Black. Com.* 150. 151. 152. Here, then, is to be discerned the genuine meaning of this section in the *bill of rights,* which an opposite construction would prostitute to the most ignoble purposes. Every man may publish what he pleases; but, it is at his peril, if he publishes any thing which violates the rights of another, or interrupts the peace and order of society; —as every man may keep poisons in his closet, but who will assert that he may vend them to the public for cordials? If, indeed, this section of the bill of rights had not circumscribed the authority of the legislature, this house, being a single branch, might in a despotic paroxism, revive all the odious restraints, which disgraced the early annals of the *British* government. Hence, arises the great fundamental advantage of the provision, which the authors of the constitution have wisely interwoven with our political system; not, it appears, to tolerate and indulge the passions and animosities of individuals, but effectually to protect the citizens from the encroachments of men in power.

It has been asserted, however, that Mr. *Oswald's* address was of a harmless texture; that it was no abuse of the right of publication, to which, as a citizen, he was entitled; and, in short, that in considering it as a contempt of the court, the judges have acted tyrannically, illegally, and unconstitutionally. But let us divest the subject of these high-sounding epithets, and the reverse of this assertion will be evident to every candid and unprejudiced mind: For, such publications are certainly calculated to draw the administration of justice from the proper tribunals; and in their place to substitute newspaper altercations, in which the most skilful writer will generally prevail against all the merits of the case. But it is moreover the duty of the judges to protect suitors, not only from personal violence, but from insidious attempts, to undermine their claims to law and justice. . . .

21. RICHARD HENRY LEE INSISTS ON A
CONSTITUTIONAL GUARANTEE

Richard Henry Lee, one of Virginia's leading anti-Federalists, had been a signer of the Declaration of Independence and president of the Continental Congress. Within a month after the adjournment of the Constitutional Convention, he published what quickly became the most popular and influential anti-ratificationist tract, *Letters from the Federal Farmer*. Its sale prompted Lee to publish *An Additional Number of Letters*, from which the following extract is taken. It is the most extended discussion of freedom of the press to be found in any anti-Federalist statement. Freedom of the press was everywhere a grand topic for declamation, but the insistent demand for its protection on parchment was not accompanied by a reasoned analysis of what it meant, how far it extended, and under what circumstances it might be limited. Alarming the people was easier than informing them; the provocation of an emotional climate of fear made the definition or analysis of freedom of the press unnecessary. Denouncing the omission of freedom of the press was an effective and common device. This statement by Lee, who was not above demagoguery, is restrained and reasonable.

All parties apparently agree, that the freedom of the press is a fundamental right, and ought not to be restrained by any taxes, duties, or in any manner whatever. Why should not the people, in adopting a federal constitution, declare this, even if there are only doubts about it. But, say the advocates, all powers not given are reserved:—true; but the great question is, are not powers given, in the exercise of which this right may be destroyed? The people's or the printers claim to a free press, is founded on the fundamental laws, that is, compacts, and state constitutions, made by the people. The people, who can annihilate or alter those constitutions, can annihilate or limit this right. This may be done by giving general powers, as well as by using particular words. No right claimed under a state constitution, will avail against a law of the union, made in pursuance of the federal constitution: therefore the question is, what laws will congress have a right to make by the constitution of the union, and particularly touching the press? By art. 1. sect. 8. congress will have power to lay and collect taxes, duties, imports and excise. By this congress will clearly have power to lay and collect all kind of taxes whatever—taxes on houses, lands, polls, industry, merchandize, &c.—taxes on deeds, bonds, and all written instruments—on writs, pleas, and all judicial proceedings, on licences, naval officers papers, &c. on newspapers, advertisements, &c. and to require bonds of the naval officers, clerks, printers, &c. to account for the taxes that may become due on papers that go through their hands. Printing, like all other business, must cease when taxed beyond its profits; and it appears to me, that a power to tax the press

---

Richard Henry Lee, "Letter XVI, January 20, 1788," in *An Additional Number of Letters from the Federal Farmer to the Republican* (Chicago: Quadrangle Books, 1962), pp. 151–153. A reprint of the original (New York: 1788) edition.

at discretion, is a power to destroy or restrain the freedom of it. There may be other powers given, in the exercise of which this freedom may be effected; and certainly it is of too much importance to be left thus liable to be taxed, and constantly to constructions and inferences. A free press is the channel of communication as to mercantile and public affairs; by means of it the people in large countries ascertain each others sentiments; are enabled to unite, and become formidable to those rulers who adopt improper measures. Newspapers may sometimes be the vehicles of abuse, and of many things not true; but these are but small inconveniencies, in my mind, among many advantages. A celebrated writer, I have several times quoted, speaking in high terms of the English liberties, says, "lastly the key stone was put to the arch, by the final establishment of the freedom of the press." I shall not dwell longer upon the fundamental rights, to some of which I have attended in this letter, for the same reasons that these I have mentioned, ought to be expressly secured, lest in the exercise of general powers given they may be invaded: it is pretty clear, that some other of less importance, or less in danger, might with propriety also be secured. . . .

22. ALEXANDER HAMILTON DECLARES THAT A CONSTITUTIONAL GUARANTEE "AMOUNTS TO NOTHING"

The Federalist, Number 84, by Alexander Hamilton, first published May 28, 1788, was the best known explanation for the omission of a bill of rights in the new Constitution. Here is an extract from that essay, signed "Publius," on the question of the liberty of the press. The essay, especially the footnote, seems to be a response to Richard Henry Lee. Hamilton's statement that the press was as free in England as anywhere is wholly unconvincing, and implies an acceptance of the Blackstonian position. Nevertheless, there is a good deal to be said in favor of his statement that general declarations respecting the liberty of the press give it no greater security than it would have without them. *Respublica* v. *Oswald* and the Sedition Act prosecutions are cases in point. In New York the Federalists hammered away at the argument here by Hamilton that the state constitution did not contain a clause guaranteeing freedom of the press, proving that none was needed in the federal Constitution. Melancthon Smith, one of the anti-Federalist leaders of the state, replied: ". . . it is perhaps an imperfection in our constitution that the liberty of the press is not expressly reserved; but still there was not an equal necessity of making that reservation in our State as in the general Constitution, for the common and statute law of England, and the laws of the colony are established, in which this privilege is fully defined and secured."

. . . I go further, and affirm that bills of rights, in the sense and in the extent in which they are contended for, are not only unnecessary in the proposed constitution, but would even be dangerous. They would contain various exceptions to powers which are not granted; and on this very account, would afford a colourable pretext to claim more than were granted. For why declare that things shall not be done which there is no power to do? Why for instance, should it be said, that the liberty of the press shall not be restrained, when no power is given by which restrictions may be imposed? I will not contend that such a provision would confer a regulating power; but it is evident that it would furnish, to men disposed to usurp, a plausible pretence for claiming that power. They might urge with a semblance of reason, that the constitution ought not to be charged with the absurdity of providing against the abuse of an authority, which was not given, and that the provision against restraining the liberty of the press afforded a clear implication, that a power to prescribe proper regulations concerning it, was intended to be vested in the national government.

The Federalist: A Collection of Essays, Written in Favour of the New Constitution, As Agreed Upon by the Federal Convention, September 17, 1787 (New York: J. and A. McLean, 1788), Number 84.

This may serve as a specimen of the numerous handles which would be given to the doctrine of constructive powers, by the indulgence of an injudicious zeal for bills of rights.

On the subject of the liberty of the press, as much has been said, I cannot forbear adding a remark or two: In the first place, I observe that there is not a syllable concerning it in the constitution of this state, and in the next, I contend that whatever has been said about it in that of any other state, amounts to nothing. What signifies a declaration that "the liberty of the press shall be inviolably preserved?" What is the liberty of the press? Who can give it any definition which would not leave the utmost latitude for evasion? I hold it to be impracticable; and from this, I infer, that its security, whatever fine declarations may be inserted in any constitution respecting it, must altogether depend on public opinion, and on the general spirit of the people and of the government.[1] And here, after all, as intimated upon another occasion, must we seek for the only solid basis of all our rights.

---

[1] To show there is a power in the constitution by which the liberty of the press may be affected, recourse has been had to the power of taxation. It is said that duties may be laid upon publications so high as to amount to a prohibition. I know not by what logic it could be maintained that the declarations in the state constitutions, in favour of the freedom of the press, would be a constitutional impediment to the imposition of duties upon publications by the state legislatures. It cannot certainly be pretended that any degree of duties, however low, would be an abridgement of the liberty of the press. We know that newspapers are taxed in Great-Britain, and yet it is notorious that the press no where enjoys greater liberty than in that country. And if duties of any kind may be laid without a violation of that liberty, it is evident that the extent must depend on legislative discretion, regulated by public opinion; so that after all, general declarations respecting the liberty of the press will give it no greater security than it will have without them. The same invasions of it may be effected under the state constitutions which contain those declarations through the means of taxation, as under the proposed constitution which has nothing of the kind. It would be quite as significant to declare that government ought to be free, that taxes ought not to be excessive, &c., as that the liberty of the press ought not to be restrained. (Publius)

23. WILLIAM CUSHING AND JOHN ADAMS

SUPPORT TRUTH AS A DEFENSE

The following exchange of letters between Chief Justice Cushing of Massachusetts and John Adams is an almost pathetic reflection on the stunted character of American libertarian thought. Cushing, it is true, partly repudiated Blackstone in arguing that a guarantee of freedom of the press meant an exclusion of subsequent as well as previous restraints, but only if the words being prosecuted could be supported "by the truth of fact." As late as 1789, in other words, Cushing and Adams worried whether the common law should not be modified by adoption of Zengerian principles. As a matter of fact, as late as 1826 the Supreme Judicial Court of Massachusetts held, in the most explicit terms, that the state constitutional guarantee embodied Blackstone's definition of a free press. Nothing in the following letters is incompatible with the support that both Adams and Cushing gave to Sedition Act prosecutions a decade later, for they believed, as Cushing said, that falsehoods and scandals against the government should be punished "with becoming rigour." Their libertarianism was founded upon a brave acceptance of truth as they understood it. It is noteworthy that neither took the view that a good government or an honest administration could not be injured by error of opinion or even by falsehoods.

[William Cushing to John Adams]

Boston, Feby 18, 1789.

Dear Sir,

I know you will forgive me if I draw your attention, a moment, from the weighty matters that employ it, to the subject of

---

"Hitherto Unpublished Correspondence Between Chief Justice Cushing and John Adams in 1789," ed. Frank W. Grinnell, *Massachusetts Law Quarterly*, XXVII (October 1942), 12–16. The original manuscripts are in the Cushing Papers, Massachusetts Historical Society.

libels and liberty of the press, on which I had the pleasure of a word with you lately. Our 16th Article of declaration of rights, holds forth—that *"The liberty of the press is essential to the security of freedom in a State" and that it ought not, therefore, to be restrained* within this Commonwealth." I confess I have had a difficulty about the construction of it; which no gentleman, better than yourself, can, in a word, clear up.

My question is this—whether it is consistent with this article to deem and adjudge any publications of the press punishable as libels, that may arraign the conduct of persons in office, charging them with instances of malconduct, repugnant to the duty of their offices and to the public good and safety, *when* such charges are supportable by the truth of fact?

By the law of England it seems clear that, in a civil action for damages, a *libel* must appear *false* as well as scandalous; and the truth of an accusation may be pleaded in bar of a suit, whether brought for words or for a *libel,* 4 Black. 150 and elsewhere.

But on an indictment for a libel, it is held to be immaterial, whether the matter of it be true or false. And this law, Judge Blackstone says, is founded solely on the tendency of libels to create animosities and to disturb the public peace, and that the provocation, and not the falsity, is the thing to be punished criminally. And some books say, the provocation is the *greater* —if true. [Coke's Rep. and others.][1] The consequence of all which is—that a man ought to be punished more for declaring truth than for telling lies, in case the truth imports a charge of criminality against any one.

In the case of the Seven Bishops, Mr. Just. Powall (who, Lord Camden said, was the only honest man on the bench, at that time) held that to make the petition a libel, it must be *false* &c., and that the case turned upon the truth of the asser-

---

[1] Brackets are in the original letter [Ed.].

tion, *that the dispensing powers claimed by the King, was illegal.* And *he* held the position of the bishops true and right, as to ecclesiastical laws and all other laws whatsoever. He was overruled, indeed, by the other judges, especially Ch. Just. Wright and Just. Allybone; the former laying it down, that whatever disturbed the government or made mischief or a stir among the people, was within the case of libellis famosis and whether true or false, was a libel.

Allybone asserted, that a private man taking upon him to write any thing concerning government, was an intruder into other men's matters, and was a libeller; But the dernier resort, the Jury, overruled all and set them right. The indictments, in that case, charged the petition to be a *false* writing; and I believe no indictment for a libel was ever framed without an allegation of falsity, which, with the reason of the thing may be some apology for Justice Powell's mistaking the law.

It must be confessed, that as the law of England now stands, truth cannot be pleaded in bar of an indictment, though it may of a civil action, for a libel.

The question is—whether it is law now *here.*

The 6th Article of the last chapter of the Constitution is, *that all laws heretofore adopted and usually practiced on in the Courts here, shall remain excepting only such parts as are repugnant to the rights and liberties of this constitution.*

By the spirit and implication of this article, laws of England, not usually practiced on here, are not to have force with us, and laws actually practiced on, but repugnant to the Constitution, are set aside.

If therefore that point has never been adjudged here (and I don't know that it has been), perhaps we are at liberty to judge upon it *de novo* upon the reason of the thing and from what may appear most beneficial to society. And in that case it strikes me as it did honest Powell, that falsity must be a necessary ingredient in a libel.

But to come to our article respecting liberty of the press: the words of it being very general and unlimited, what guard or limitation can be put upon it? Doubtless it may and ought to be restrainable from injuring *characters;* which is one principal object and end of other articles and of government. But charging a man by word, writing or printing, with a crime, of which he is really guilty, is damnum absque Injuria, as Judge Blackstone and others justly observe. And in general no doubt it may be restrained from *injuring* the public or individuals by propagating falsehoods.

But when the article says *"The liberty of the press is essential to the security of freedom"* and that *"it ought not, therefore, to be restrained"* &c., does it not comprehend a liberty to treat all subjects and characters freely, within the bounds of truth?

Judge Blackstone says (4 V. 451) the liberty of the press consists in laying no *previous* restraints upon publications, and not in freedom from censure for criminal matter, when published. Wherein he refers to a public licenser, inspector or controller of the press. That is, no doubt, the liberty of the press as allowed by the law of England.

But the words of our article understood according to plain English, make no such distinction, and must exclude *subsequent* restraints, as much as *previous restraints.* In other words, if all men are restrained by the fear of jails, scourges and loss of ears from examining the conduct of persons in administration and where their conduct is illegal, tyrannical and tending to overthrow the Constitution and introduce slavery, are so restrained from declaring it to the public *that* will be as effectual a restraint as any *previous* restraint whatever.

The question upon the article is this—What is that liberty of the press, which is essential to the security of freedom? The propagating literature and knowledge by printing or otherwise tends to illuminate men's minds and to establish them in principles of freedom. But it cannot be denied also, that a free scanning of the conduct of administration and shewing the tendency of it, and where truth will warrant, making it manifest that it is subversive of all law, liberty and the Constitution; it can't be denied. I think that the liberty tends to the *security of freedom in a State;* even more directly and essentially than the liberty of printing upon literary and speculative subjects in general. Without this liberty of the press could we have supported our liberties against british administration? or could our revolution have taken place? Pretty certainly it could not, at the time it did. Under a sense and impression of this sort, I conceive, this article was adopted. This liberty of publishing truth can never effectually injure a good government, or honest administrators; but it may save a state from the necessity of a revolution, as well as bring one about, when it is necessary. It may be objected that a public prosecution is the safe and regular course, in case of malefeasance. But what single person would venture himself upon so invidious and dangerous a task against a man high in interest, influence and power?

But this liberty of the press having truth for its basis who can stand before it? Besides it may facilitate a legal prosecution, which might not, otherwise, have been dared to be attempted. When the press is made the vehicle of falsehood and scandal, let the authors be punished with becoming rigour.

But why need any honest man be afraid of truth? The guilty only fear it; and I am inclined to think with Gordon (Vol. 3 No. 20 of Cato's Letters) that truth sacredly adhered to, can never upon the whole prejudice, right religion, equal government or a government founded upon proper balances and checks, or the happiness of society in any respect, but must be favorable to them all.

Suppressing this liberty by penal laws will it not more endanger freedom than do good to government? The weight of government is sufficient to prevent any very dangerous consequences occasioned by *provocations* resulting from charges founded in truth; whether such charges are made in *a legal course or otherwise.* In either case, the *provocation* (which Judge Blackstone says is the sole foundation of the law against libels) being much the same.

But not to trouble you with a multipliing of words; If I am wrong I should be glad to be set right, &c., &c.

I would not wish, however, to intrude upon your busy hours, devoted to more important matters, and especially, as you are to be speedily called to the weighty concerns of a high office in the federal government, not, indeed, as head;—but to be a pillar to support the head and the whole fabrick; an office to which no man can dispute the ground of your title, as on other accounts so particularly for the share you have had (greater I suppose, in many respects than any other) at home and abroad, from the beginning to the conclusion, in the late revolution. The point now is a stable government, which it [is] to be put in motion soon, and I heartily wish you success. I am &c.

WILLIAM CUSHING.

[John Adams to William Cushing]

Braintree, March 7, 1789

DEAR SIR

I am greatly obliged by the letter you did me the Honour to write me on the 18th of February; and regret very much the want of Leisure to examine the subject of it, with that attention which its great importance requires.

That the Truth may be pleaded in Bar of a civil action for damages for actionable words, spoken or written I remembered very well; but it lay in my mind that some just cause for publishing it, must be added. You may easily conceive a case, where a Scandalous Truth may be told of a man, without any honest motive, and merely from malice. In such a case morality and religion would forbid a man from doing mischief merely from malevolence and I thought would give damages. The case in 11 Mod. cited by Blackstone I have not an opportunity to examine. But this is a point of no great consequence at present.

The difficult and important question is whether the Truth of words can be admitted by the court to be given in evidence to the jury, upon a plea of not guilty? In England I suppose it is settled. But it is a serious Question whether our Constitution is not at present so different as to render the innovation necessary? Our chief magistrates and Senators &c are annually eligible by the people. How are their characters and conduct to be known to their constituents but by the press? If the press is to be stopped and the people kept in Ignorance we had much better have the first magistrate and Senators hereditary. I therefore, am very clear that under the Articles of our Constitution which you have quoted, it would be safest to admit evidence to the jury of the Truth of accusations, and if the jury found them true and that they were published for the Public good, they would readily acquit.

In answer to the concluding part of your letter, I beg leave to say that I am indebted to your Friendship, in part at least for a destination to another office much too high, difficult and important for my Forces. But having been forced by the course of things, heretofore, so often to undertake Trusts out of all proportion to my Talents and having been supported through them by good Fortune and the favour of the world, I must again rely upon the same assistance,—one comfort has always attended me,—I have been always best supported by those whom I love and esteem the most.

With the highest respect and esteem I have the Honour to be, dear sir, your affectionate Friend and most humble sert.

JOHN ADAMS.

Chief Justice Cushing.

24. BEN FRANKLIN CENSURES ABUSES OF THE PRESS

The following article by Ben Franklin has nasty overtones. Its satirically bitter tone and its stress on the licentiousness of the press make difficult any attempt to dismiss the tar-and-feathers remark as literary horseplay. Advocates of the Sedition Act quoted this article to give the impression that Franklin would have agreed with their position. But a careful reading of the piece indicates that Franklin neither advocated nor endorsed laws against seditious libel—nor did he condemn them in a lifetime of writing. He believed that verbal criticism of the government should be guided by moderation, truth, and good motives; that no one should publish anything that hurt his country; and that scurrilous reflections on the government were an infamous disgrace. But Franklin did not have the prosecutor's spirit. The significance of the article, however, lies in its negative tone. Instead of composing a vigorous defense of freedom of the press, despite its abuses, Franklin chose to focus on the latter. As he stated, few persons had "distinct Ideas" of the "Nature and Extent" of freedom of the press; but he made no contribution to an understanding of that nature and extent.

An Account of the Supremest Court of Judicature of the State of Pennsylvania, Viz. The Court of the Press

Power of this Court.

It may receive and promulgate accusations of all kinds, against all persons and characters among the citizens of the State, and even against all inferior courts; and may judge, sentence, and condemn to infamy, not only private individuals, but public

---

Benjamin Franklin, "An Account of the Supreme Court of Judicature of the State of Pennsylvania, Viz. the Court of the Press," *The Pennsylvania Gazette* (Philadelphia), September 12, 1789, in *The Writings of Benjamin Franklin,* ed. Albert Henry Smyth (New York: The Macmillan Company, 1905–1907), X, 36–40.

bodies, &c., with or without inquiry or hearing, *at the court's discretion.*

In whose Favour and for whose Emolument this Court is established.

In favour of about one citizen in five hundred, who, by education or practice in scribbling, has acquired a tolerable style as to grammar and construction, so as to bear printing; or who is possessed of a press and a few types. This five hundredth part of the citizens have the privilege of accusing and abusing the other four hundred and ninety-nine parts at their pleasure; or they may hire out their pens and press to others for that purpose.

Practice of the Court.

It is not governed by any of the rules of common courts of law. The accused is allowed no grand jury to judge of the truth of the accusation before it is publicly made, nor is the Name of the Accuser made known to him, nor has he an Opportunity of confronting the Witnesses against him; for they are kept in the dark, as in the Spanish Court of Inquisition. Nor is there any petty Jury of his Peers, sworn to try the Truth of the Charges. The Proceedings are also sometimes so rapid, that an honest, good Citizen may find himself suddenly and unexpectedly accus'd, and in the same Morning judg'd and condemn'd, and sentence pronounc'd against him, that he is a *Rogue* and a *Villain.* Yet, if an officer of this court receives the slightest check for misconduct in this his office, he claims immediately the rights of a free citizen by the constitution, and demands to know his accuser, to confront the witnesses, and to have a fair trial by a jury of his peers.

The Foundation of its Authority.

It is said to be founded on an Article of the Constitution of the State, which establishes *the Liberty of the Press;* a Liberty which every Pennsylvanian would fight and die for; tho' few of us, I believe, have distinct Ideas of its Nature and Extent. It seems indeed somewhat like the *Liberty of the Press* that Felons have, by the Common Law of England, before Conviction, that is, to be *press'd* to death or hanged. If by the *Liberty of the Press* were understood merely the Liberty of discussing the Propriety of Public Measures and political opinions, let us have as much of it as you please: But if it means the Liberty of affronting, calumniating, and defaming one another, I, for my part, own myself willing to part with my Share of it when our Legislators shall please so to alter the Law, and shall cheerfully consent to exchange my *Liberty* of Abusing others for the *Privilege* of not being abus'd myself.

By whom this Court is commissioned or constituted.

It is not by any Commission from the Supreme Executive Council, who might previously judge of the Abilities, Integrity, Knowledge, &c. of the Persons to be appointed to this great Trust, of deciding upon the Characters and good Fame of the Citizens; for this Court is above that Council, and may *accuse, judge,* and *condemn* it, at pleasure. Nor is it hereditary, as in the Court of *dernier Resort,* in the Peerage of England. But any Man who can procure Pen, Ink, and Paper, with a Press, and a huge pair of BLACKING Balls, may commissionate himself; and his court is immediately established in the plenary Possession and exercise of its rights. For, if you make the least complaint of the *judge's* conduct, he daubs his blacking balls in your face wherever he meets you; and, besides tearing your private character to flitters, marks you out for the odium of the public, as an *enemy to the liberty of the press.*

Of the natural Support of these Courts.

Their support is founded in the depravity of such minds, as have not been mended by religion, nor improved by good education;

> "There is a Lust in Man no Charm can tame,
>   Of loudly publishing his Neighbour's Shame."

Hence;

> "On Eagle's Wings immortal Scandals fly,
>   While virtuous Actions are but born and die."
>
>   DRYDEN.

Whoever feels pain in hearing a good character of his neighbour, will feel a pleasure in the reverse. And of those who,
despairing to rise into distinction by their virtues, are happy if
others can be depressed to a level with themselves, there are a
number sufficient in every great town to maintain one of
these courts by their subscriptions. A shrewd observer once
said, that, in walking the streets in a slippery morning, one
might see where the good-natured people lived by the ashes
thrown on the ice before their doors; probably he would have
formed a different conjecture of the temper of those whom he
might find engaged in such a subscription.

Of the Checks proper to be established against the Abuse of Power in these Courts.

Hitherto there are none. But since so much has been written
and published on the federal Constitution, and the necessity of
checks in all other parts of good government has been so
clearly and learnedly explained, I find myself so far enlightened
as to suspect some check may be proper in this part also; but
I have been at a loss to imagine any that may not be construed an infringement of the sacred *liberty of the press*. At
length, however, I think I have found one that, instead of
diminishing general liberty, shall augment it; which is, by restoring to the people a species of liberty, of which they have
been deprived by our laws, I mean the *liberty of the cudgel*.
In the rude state of society prior to the existence of laws, if one
man gave another ill language, the affronted person would return it by a box on the ear, and, if repeated, by a good drubbing; and this without offending against any law. But now the

right of making such returns is denied, and they are punished as breaches of the peace; while the right of abusing seems to remain in full force, the laws made against it being rendered ineffectual by the *liberty of the press.*

My proposal then is, to leave the liberty of the press untouched, to be exercised in its full extent, force, and vigor; but to permit the *liberty of the cudgel* to go with it *pari passu*. Thus, my fellow-citizens, if an impudent writer attacks your reputation, dearer to you perhaps than your life, and puts his name to the charge, you may go to him as openly and break his head. If he conceals himself behind the printer, and you can nevertheless discover who he is, you may in like manner way-lay him in the night, attack him behind, and give him a good drubbing. Thus far goes my project as to *private* resentment and retribution. But if the public should ever happen to be affronted, *as it ought to be*, with the conduct of such writers, I would not advise proceeding immediately to these extremities; but that we should in moderation content ourselves with tarring and feathering, and tossing them in a blanket.

If, however, it should be thought that this proposal of mine may disturb the public peace, I would then humbly recommend to our legislators to take up the consideration of both liberties, that of the *press*, and that of the *cudgel*, and by an explicit law mark their extent and limits; and, at the same time that they secure the person of a citizen from *assaults*, they would likewise provide for the security of his *reputation*.

25. THE REPUBLICANS ASSAULT THE POWER TO PUNISH BREACHES OF PRIVILEGE

The New York Assembly's prosecution of William Keteltas, for aspersive publications breaching the privileges of the house, touched off a discussion that contributed a new dimension to libertarian theory. The discussion did not center on liberty of the press as such, and added nothing to an understanding of its meaning or scope. The libertarians focused, instead, on the most suppressive power of all, the power of the legislature to punish seditious contempts of its authority or reputation. There had been occasional instances during the colonial period when victims of a provincial assembly challenged its practice of punishing breaches of parliamentary privilege. But the challenge had been grounded on the contention that the provincial assemblies could not exercise the powers of Parliament. The Keteltas case, in 1796, marked the first major criticism of the use of "privilege" to muzzle offensive publications. In the following articles, "Camillus Junius," although "no friend" to libel prosecutions, thought them to be a "perfect" safeguard against abuses by the press, because the defendant's rights were protected in a trial. The thrust of the argument, however, is that trial and punishment by the Assembly was illegal and tyrannical. The claim that the Senate of the United States did not possess the power asserted by the New York Assembly was belied four years later. The Senate, over the vehement objections of the Republican minority, found William Duane, publisher of the Philadelphia *Aurora,* to be guilty of a "high breach of privileges" because of his allegedly seditious publications. On that occasion, Republican Senators repeated the arguments made here by "Camillus Junius."

I

The imprisonment of Mr. Keteltas by the house of Assembly, has excited the public opinion. . . . I presume I have an indubitable right to examine the subject for myself; of this priviledge indeed I cannot be divested, because I can enjoy it in my closet, and, as a *citizen of America.* I trust I may, without danger of imprisonment, lay the result of my researches before the public. I shall do it without dread, but not without respect.

The resolution of Mr. T. Morris (as stated in the public

"Camillus Junius," untitled articles in *The Argus, or Greenleaf's New Daily Advertiser* (New York), March 15 and April 6, 1796.

prints) after reciting that the publication of Mr. Keteltas, tended to "create distrust, and destroy that confidence, which the good people of this state have, and of right ought to have in their representatives," was as follows: "Resolved, that the said publications are a breach of the privileges of this house, and that the said William Keteltas be forthwith taken into custody by the sergeant at arms, and brought to the bar of this house, to answer to the premises."

In opposition to that resolution, and to the opinion of the majority of that house, I affirm, that the house of assembly *have not any* privileges which can be enfringed by those, or similar publications.

In order to test the above position, it will be necessary to ascertain with precision, what privileges the house of assembly really possess. To declare that there has been a violation of priviledge, before we know what priviledge means, is absurd in any man; and in a member of the house would be *criminal*—for although he might chance to punish rightly, it would be by *chance only*.

By the constitution of our state, it is declared, "that the assembly shall enjoy the same privileges, and procede in doing business, in like manner as the assemblies of the colony of New-York of *right* formerly did." Under these general words, the legislature have passed two laws, in one of which they recognize and establish freedom of speech in debate in the members of each house; and in the other, the priviledge from arrest during the session, and for fourteen days preceding its meeting, and succeeding its adjournment. These are privileges which each branch of the legislature necessarily possess—which every good man will support—and which are warranted by the nature and principles of our government. Here then the constitution has received a legislative interpretation. Any act done with a view to deter a representative in his official conduct, or to prevent his appearance in the house, by arresting him, would be an evident breach of priviledge, which ought to be severely punished; but upon what ground is it to be extended farther. It will readily be conceded, I believe, even by the warmest advocates of undefined priviledge, that there is none other than the two I have mentioned, which are recognized, either by the constitution, or any statute. If there are, let them be produced; if not, whence then do they derive it? It must be from the nature and objects of its institution, or it exists not at all. The duties of a house of assembly are plain; they are expressed in the constitution, and therefore admit of no uncertainty.

I premise then, as a maxim, that no other power has been vested in any part of our political system, than was necessary for the due execution of its duties. To have given more, would have vested energy that could never act, or if it did, must act mischievously; this would have been weakness. Hence, to establish in the house of assembly the priviledge now contended for, to prove it a *right,* and not a *usurpation,* it must be clearly demonstrated, "that it is *indispensibly necessary* for the performance of their duty." Will it be said that either of Mr. Keteltas' publications interrupted the proceedings of the house, or disturbed its deliberations? Can it be said that the suppression of them was "indispensably necessary for the performance of their constitutional duties?" If not, and if my reasoning is just, it follows clearly, that the imprisonment being unnecessary for the performance of their *duty,* was an exercise of power in a case in which it did not exist, and consequently *is illegal.* But it may be asked, if an individual declares, or publishes *falshoods* which have an evident tendency to destroy that confidence, which is reposed by the constituent in his representative, ought not the house possess a right to punish the offence? I answer *no.* First, because the exercise of such a power by no means removes the inconvenience created, it being abundantly clear that such a measure would of itself excite suspicion, and encreate distrust. Secondly, If we could believe the members perfectly free from private resentment, and that the personal satire which they may have felt, will have no influence on their conduct, still if they have lost the confidence of the people, no act of theirs will regain it; for it would be too absurd for them to confess that it was justly forfeited. Thirdly, If there is any remedy for such an offence, other than the interference of the house itself, that ought to be preferred; or else the first principles of natural justice must be violated, which forbids us to be judges when we are parties to the cause. And, fourthly, that no such power as is contended for, and was exercised in the case of Mr. Keteltas, does or ought to exist. A little reflection on the consequences that must result, and the danger to freedom that must naturally follow the reposal of such extraordinary prerogatives, in any one branch of the legislature, will carry conviction, that if we are free, they do not possess them.

To the citizen, it must be totally indifferent, whether he is deprived of his liberty by the *edict* of a despot, or the resolution of a house of assembly, provided it is not conformable to the *known* and *established* laws of the land. It is clearly deduceable from the nature and objects of a house of assembly, that they must be invested with such *rights* as are necessary for the performance of its duties—but the only *privileges* recognized by the known and established laws of the land, are the two which have been cited—freedom from arrest—and in debate. Sure neither of those have been infringed by Mr. Keteltas's publications what then are those privileges, which the resolution of the house announces to have been violated? Where are they to be found? Should it be said we have the same privileges which the House of Commons in England possess? I reply—that the House of Commons possess no privileges, except such as have been created or confirmed by statute, which can be defined, explained, or understood; even the judges of the courts in Westminster Hall declare themselves (except in those cases) ignorant of them.

Will our Assembly then claim privileges of which even the most enlightened Judges are ignorant; which cannot be defined or explained? Will they punish an individual for violating a right, the existence of which is inexplicable, and of which he is inevitably ignorant? But if we recur to the celebrated commentator[1] on that subject, we shall find—"That priviledge of Parliament was principally established in order to protect its members, not only from being molested by their fellow-subjects, but also *more especially* from being oppressed by the power of the crown" —This is, in my opinion, a very just description of privileges; thus far it is reasonable, it is right; but it is a curious privilege which gives to one branch of the legislature a power to deprive me of that liberty, which is guaranteed by *law*. Indeed the word "privilege" means no more than immunity, or a safeguard to the party who possesses it, and can never be construed into an *active* power of invading the rights of others.

Should there be any, however, that still contend for these indefinite, inexplicable privileges, let them reflect to what a miserable dilemma [dilemma] they reduce us. If we relate any circumstance which passed in the house, it may be resolved a breach of privilege, and we called to the bar. If a Printer happens to misrepresent any act of the house, he is ordered into the custody of the Serjeant at Arms—He will be allowed simply to answer whether he printed it or not. If he denies it, it can always be proved. If he confesses it, he is already convicted, and nothing remains but to punish. If, in truth, a law ever so prejudicial should pass the house, we would not dare to declare it a bad one, because this would be declaring the representatives either unwise or corrupt—would have a tendency to "destroy that confidence which the good people of this State have, and of right [*ought*] to have of their representatives," and

---

[1] Blackstone. [Ed.]

consequently be a breach of privileges but the danger, with respect to the House of Assembly, exercising *such privileges,* is not very glaring, because the people *annually* have the means of redress in their own hands, they consider their representatives as tenants, who *forfeit* their estate if they commit waste. But in another house far removed from the people, and who are, if experience is to be our guide, much more under the influence of the executive than of any other power, such prerogatives as are now contended for, and for which our immediate representatives have given a precedent, become truly formidable; they are worse indeed than the prerogatives of the King of Great Britain, because (in the latitude they are now admitted) they are less understood, nor is there any law by which they are regulated, nor any means by which they can be learned. Suppose then I was to declare, that the Senate of the United States had ratified our present *treaty* with England, without maturely considering the same, or that some of the members who had voted for it, were incompetent to decide thereon? Admit this to be false, still as far as my veracity and influence could extend, it would, in the same extent, create distrust, and destroy, in a degree, that confidence which ought to be reposed in that house. If, then, the Senate of the United States possess the same privileges which the Assembly of this State do (which can admit of no doubt) then such a declaration in me would be a *contempt* of the Senate of the United States, and a breach of privileges—I should be brought to their bar (perhaps in the city of Washington, where exclusive jurisdiction prevails). —It would be demanded of me, "Were you the author of such language?" —If I denied it, it would be proved against me, and increase my guilt. —If I confessed, I would (as if by magic) be *already convicted,* and even the solitary comfort of explaining my motives, would be refused. —Sure a doctrine so monstrous, so pregnant with oppression, can never be received in a free country. I do believe our representatives, were not aware, to what *dangerous extrava-gancies* their principle points.

It may now be objected to me, that my arguments prove too much, for that certainly there may be instances of contempt and insult to the House of Assembly, which do not fall within my own exceptions, yet in regard to the dignity of the house, ought not to pass unpunished. —Be it so. The Courts of criminal jurisdiction are open to prosecutions, which the Attorney General may commence by information or indictment. A libel tending to asperse or vilify the house of Assembly or any of its members, may be as severely punished in the Supreme Court, as a libel against government. This, then, for the reasons I have already given, is the remedy they should appeal to, if they either wish to regain the confidence of the people, or preserve their own dignity.

But if it could be proved, that the house of Assembly do really possess the power which they have exercised, either by the constitution, an express statute, or by the undeniable deductions of solid reason, nothing short of which can be received as evidence of such an *excess* of power. I still maintain that the manner in which the house proceeded, was unreasonable. It was unreasonable, because it being true, that he was the author, it was right in him to confess that fact, and exhonerate himself by shewing, that he wrote it *solely* with a view to justify the part he had taken; that the misrepresentations which it contained were not intentional; that they fostered not the design which had been imputed; that they had been misconstrued or misunderstood; that in short, the *intent*, the *motive*, which had been affixed to them, were not *his*. —Here, I say, is the very thing which ought to have been enquired into, the *motive* or *intention* of the publications; that is, the gist of the enquiry; for if they were written with a pure intention, no crime was committed. But how was that to be ascertained, when the writer was confined to the simple answer of yes or no, without the indulgence of explanation. I believe in future our representatives, if they ever again find it necessary to *vindicate* their mysterious prerogatives, will indulge a citizen to *vindicate* his intention, unless their late decision should be considered a precedent in point, and exclude a right never denied by the most *arbitrary judge* in the trial of a libel, to wit, "that the writing does not purport a *criminal intent.*"

I am aware it may be said, that our *immediate* representative will rarely do an act that can infringe the right of his constituent, and therefore we need not be overnice to define their powers. If this was true, it would go to the annihilation of our constitution. At any rate, however, it does not affect the force of my argument when applied to the Senate of the United States, who, so far from being the *immediate* representatives of the people, are (if a vacancy happens by resignation or *otherwise,* during the recess of the legislature of the state) appointed by the President.

I do not believe the Senate of the United States possess more virtue than our present Assembly: And still believe that the Assembly have exercised *power* without *right,* and in a manner too altogether inconsistent with the broad and eternal rules of Justice. If, however, we once concede such an undefined right, we can not admire that the exercise of it should *not* be restricted by *known* and established rules.

I am also aware that it may be asked, if you are afraid to trust your representatives, where will you vest the power? Can it be reposed in more proper or safe hands? I answer, yes. In that department of government designated as well by the policy of our constitution, as by the opinions of the most enlightened statesmen. The *Judiciary,* which ought ever to be distinct from the legislative, whose sole duty is to enact law— the Judiciary should expound and apply it. A citizen then can never suffer but by *known* and *established laws* of the *land, enforced* by *known* and *established rules.*

CAMILLUS JUNIUS.

II

Addresses to the Honorable, the Members of
The House of Assembly of the State of New York.

GENTLEMEN,

HISTORY and experience establish one truth—that power is
never without its courtiers and its slaves—Nature however
did not design me for the former, and she has given me a
temper which forbids the latter. I am one of those who consider "the laws" the best and indeed the only effectual security
against oppression. —By law I mean those rules, by which *all*
are bound—which are promulged, and which we may all read
—those rules by which our judges are controuled, by which
we are protected in our *lives* our *liberties,* and our *property,*
and by which alone we can be divested of either. —A country
thus governed must be *free.* —Hence it is that a violation of
our system of jurisprudence ought ever to meet the most determined and persevering resistance; infringements of our peculiar rights are not the less dangerous because they are minute.
—The vices of government like those of individuals advance by
degrees; unless they receive an immediate check, they soon
accumulate, and at last become incurable.

It was a sincere conviction of the truth of these impressions,
and a zealous attachment to the great interests of the people
that induced me to advance the sentiments contained in my
late letter to the Editor of this paper. —It is true you were
then, and still are our representatives; as such you were, and
are entitled to *respect* and *confidence.* They are both limited;
policy, justice, and public safety require it. Even you cannot
with safety to the citizen be implicitly trusted. . . . To prove
that you sometimes labour under the imbecility of human
nature, I must remind you, that when you called Mr. Keteltas
to the bar, constituted yourselves legislators, judges, jurors, and

executioners, you proceed in a way altogether new to the people. When they saw a man meeting, with firmness your severest frowns, willing to relinquish his family and his freedom, rather than confess himself guilty of a crime, which he was conscious of never commiting, the heated sympathy of many dissipated all distinction between you and them, and evinced how nearly respect and contempt are allied. I grant it was improper, but it was no excuse for you to run into a more dangerous error. Many of you, gentlemen, repeatedly exclaimed "*let the bar to be cleared.*" It is true, there was not a formal resolution; indeed there was much less form amongst you than could have been expected, when we recollect that you were then preserving the dignity of the House I say you ordered the bar to be cleared. In direct violation of the constitution, which declares, "that the doors of the Senate and Assembly, shall at *all times* be kept *open* to *all persons,* except when the welfare of the State shall require their debates to be kept secret." . . .

I again observe, that there was no formal resolutions of the house to that effect—It is not on your journals—you may therefore pronounce this to be false and scandalous; that it tends to lessen the confidence which the people of right ought to have in you (as I most sincerely believe it does) and a breach of your privileges—you may order the printer to the bar, and pass an arbitrary punishment—you may *suppress* the *liberty of the press,* and restore the confidence of the people by an act of your own—you may refuse to hear a man in his defence, and thus pave the way to legislative tyranny. It was thus the House of Commons in England advanced from annual to triennial—from triennial to septennial elections; but gentlemen submit it to proper tribunal, a court and a jury, and the above facts will be established. I am no friend to the doctrine of libels, but it is a perfect *guardian of the press,* compared with your late decision—But without recurring to the National Convention of France, the Legislature of Georgia, a British House of Commons, or yourselves, to demonstrate the necessity of some check over even the immediate representatives of the people, let it suffice to say—we have a constitution from which you cannot depart. Follow me a little further, and I trust I shall fully establish (if not to your *satisfaction,* at least to your *conviction*) what I before declared, "That the imprisonment of Mr. Keteltas is *illegal.*" If you do not profit by it yourselves, perhaps your constituents may. Our constitution, after reciting that man is endowed by the Creator with inalienable rights; among which are life, *liberty,* and the pursuit of happiness, that to secure those rights, governments are instituted among men, declares, "That no member of this State shall be disfranchised or deprived of any of the rights or privileges secured to the subjects of this State by this constitution, unless by the *law* of the *land,* or the judgments of his *peers.* The judgment of our peers technically imports *"the verdict of a jury."* . . .

Whence then do you derive the power of depriving a citizen of his liberty, for a publication of his opinion? Not from the parliament law, that being no part of the common law of England—Not from the statute law of England or Great Britain, that having been repealed since May 1788—Not from the laws of the State, that securing to you only privilege of speech and freedom from arrest—Not from the constitution, because that gives you only such as the House of Assembly of the late colony of *right* formerly had, which in my former letter I proved could be no other "than was indispensably necessary for the exercise of your constitutional duties." Whence then, I say, do you derive such terrifying powers? What are those *well-known* privileges which have been violated? Define them— explain them; shew the people where they are to be found, or else confess that your rule of inflicting punishment is *whim* and *caprice;* your own *arbitrary pleasure;* and that your resolutions are to have the force of laws! How safe our rights may be in your hands, I do not decide, tho' I confess you have fully convinced me, and I trust every *honest elector* in this State, of the utility of a Senate and Council of Revision.

In short, gentlemen, whoever considers the nature of your duties, and the political absurdity of vesting in you more power than is necessary for the due execution of those duties; whoever considers the manifest injustice of first making yourselves parties to a cause, and then constituting yourselves judges—the dread it must justly create, and the suspicion it deservedly excites; that law ceases to be a rule, prescribed by all the constitutional branches, ceases to be permanent, uniform, and universal, and becomes whatever your *caprice* or pleasure may *resolve it;* that it is not declared, until after the fact, by which it is supposed to be violated; that legislation and jurisdiction are united in the same persons, and exercised at the same moment; that a court from which there is no appeal, assumes an *original* jurisdiction in a criminal case—whoever, I say, considers these collected absurdities, and will then pronounce your imprisonment of Mr. Keteltas to be *legal, constitutional,* or consistent with the *genius* of our government, must possess either a *weak head* or a *bad heart.*

But gentlemen, though it is impossible for me so much to violate my own opinion, or insult your understanding, as to admit your having done right, I will still readily concede, that (in a certain extent) you have falsified one maxim of law, "that there is no wrong without a remedy." In the present case there is no relief by *ordinary* means; a judge cannot discharge by "habeas corpus," any committed by you whilst you continue in session. . . .

Indulge me now to call you to a view of your own situation. It must, I think, appear clear to you, and to the people, beyond a shadow of doubt, that you have assumed a power, that you do not, nor ought to possess; that you have exercised it in an arbitrary, unusual, and capricious manner; that you have imprisoned Mr. Keteltas contrary to the known principles of our constitution, and that he is now deprived of his liberty, without either the law of the land, or the judgment of his peers. What does *duty* and *justice* prescribe? *His immediate discharge.* . . .

CAMILLUS JUNIUS.

PART FOUR

The New Libertarianism

26. THE HOUSE DEBATES THE SEDITION ACT

The Sedition Act made criminal "any false, scandalous and malicious" writings, utterances, or publications against the government, Congress, or the President, with intent to defame them, bring them into contempt or disrepute, or excite against them the hatred of the people. The act also embodied Zengerian principles on truth as a defense and the power of juries "to determine the law and the fact." In their opposition the Republicans were driven to originate so broad a theory of freedom of expression that the concept of seditious libel was at last repudiated, common-law concepts were abandoned, and the overt-acts test was advocated in order to protect all political opinions. The Republican argument began to develop in the give-and-take of Congressional debate, especially in the speeches of Representatives Albert Gallatin, John Nicholas, Edward Livingston, and Nathaniel Macon. In 1799 the arguments on both sides were ably summarized in the House reports on the question whether the Sedition Act should be repealed. The report of the select committee to consider petitions for repeal was overwhelmingly adopted by the House; the vote was 52 to 28. Chauncey Goodrich of Connecticut, a stalwart Federalist, reported for the majority. The minority statement was presented by Nicholas of Virginia, one of the leaders of the Republican cause. Here are the two reports.

[The Majority Report]

The "Act in addition to an act entitled an act for the punishment of certain crimes against the United States," commonly called the sedition act, contains provisions of a twofold nature: first, against seditious acts, and, second, against libellous and seditious writings. The first have never been complained of, nor has any objection been made to its validity. The objection applies solely to the second; and on the ground, in the first place, that Congress have no power by the Constitution to pass any act for punishing libels, no such power being expressly given, and all powers not given to Congress, being reserved to the States respectively, or the people thereof.

To this objection it is answered, that a law to punish false, scandalous, and malicious writings against the Government, with intent to stir up sedition, is a law necessary for carrying into effect the power vested by the Constitution in the Government of the United States, and in the departments and officers thereof, and, consequently, such a law as Congress may pass; because the direct tendency of such writings is to obstruct the acts of the Government by exciting opposition to them, to endanger its existence by rendering it odious and contemptible in the eyes of the people, and to produce seditious combinations against the laws, the power to punish which has never been questioned; because it would be manifestly absurd to suppose that a Government might punish sedition, and yet be void of power to prevent it by punishing those acts which plainly and necessarily lead to it; and, because, under the general power to make all laws proper and necessary for carrying into effect the powers vested by the Constitution in the Government of the United States, Congress has passed

Majority and Minority Reports on Repeal of the Sedition Act, February 25, 1799, *Annals of Congress*, 5th Cong., 3rd Sess., pp. 2987–2990, 3003–3014.

many laws for which no express provision can be found in the Constitution, and the constitutionality of which has never been questioned, such as the first section of the act now under consideration for punishing seditious combinations; the act passed during the present session, for punishing persons who, without authority from the Government, shall carry on any correspondence relative to foreign affairs with any foreign Government; the act for the punishment of certain crimes against the United States, which defines and punishes misprision of treason: the 10th and 12th sections, which declare the punishment of accessaries to piracy, and of persons who shall confederate to become pirates themselves, or to induce others to become so; the 15th section, which inflicts a penalty on those who steal or falsify the record of any court of the United States; the 18th and 21st sections, which provide for the punishment of persons committing perjury in any court of the United States, or attempting to bribe any of their Judges; the 22d section, which punishes those who obstruct or resist the process of any court of the United States; and the 23d, against rescuing all offenders who have been convicted of any capital offence before these courts; provisions, none of which are expressly authorized, but which have been considered as Constitutional, because they are necessary and proper for carrying into effect certain powers expressly given to Congress.

It is objected to this act, in the second place, that it is expressly contrary to that part of the Constitution which declares, that "Congress shall make no law respecting an establishment of religion, or prohibiting the free exercise thereof, or abridging the liberty of the press." The act in question is said to be an "abridgment of the liberty of the press," and therefore unconstitutional.

To this it is answered, in the first place, that the liberty of the press consists not in a license for every man to publish what he pleases without being liable to punishment, if he should abuse this license to the injury of others, but in a permission to publish, without previous restraint, whatever he may think proper, being answerable to the public and individuals, for any abuse of this permission to their prejudice. In like manner, as the liberty of speech does not authorize a man to speak malicious slanders against his neighbor, nor the liberty of action justify him in going, by violence, into another man's house, or in assaulting any person whom he may meet in the streets. In the several States the liberty of the press has always been understood in this manner, and no other; and the Constitution of every State which has been framed and adopted since the Declaration of Independence, asserts "the liberty of the press;" while in several, if not all, their laws provide for the punishment of libellous publications, which would be a manifest absurdity and contradiction, if the liberty of the press meant to publish any and everything, without being amenable to the laws for the abuse of this license. According to this just, legal, and universally admitted definition of "the liberty of the press," a law to restrain its licentiousness, in publishing false, scandalous, and malicious libels against the Government, cannot be considered as "an abridgment" of its "liberty."

It is answered, in the second place, that the liberty of the press did never extend, according to the laws of any State, or of the United States, or of England, from whence our laws are derived, to the publication of false, scandalous, and malicious writings against the Government, written or published with intent to do mischief, such publications being unlawful, and punishable in every State; from whence it follows, undeniably, that a law to punish seditious and malicious publications, is not an abridgment of the liberty of the press, for it would be a manifest absurdity to say, that a man's liberty was abridged by punishing him for doing that which he never had a liberty to do.

It is answered, thirdly, that the act in question cannot be

unconstitutional, because it makes nothing penal that was not penal before, and gives no new powers to the court, but is merely declaratory of the common law, and useful for rendering that law more generally known, and more easily understood. This cannot be denied, if it be admitted, as it must be, that false, scandalous, and malicious libels against the Government of the country, published with intent to do mischief, are punishable by the common law; for, by the 2d section of the 3d article of the Constitution, the judicial power of the United States is expressly extended to all offences arising under the Constitution. By the Constitution, the Government of the United States is established, for many important objects, as the Government of the country; and libels against that Government, therefore, are offences arising under the Constitution, and, consequently, are punishable at common law by the courts of the United States. The act, indeed, is so far from having extended the law and the power of the court, that it has abridged both, and has enlarged instead of abridging the liberty of the press; for, at common law, libels against the Government might be punished with fine and imprisonment at the discretion of the court, whereas the act limits the fine to two thousand dollars, and the imprisonment to two years; and it also allows the party accused to give the truth in evidence for his justification, which, by the common law, was expressly forbidden.

And, lastly, it is answered, that had the Constitution intended to prohibit Congress from legislating at all on the subject of the press, which is the construction whereon the objections to this law are founded, it would have used the same expressions as in that part of the clause which relates to religion and religious texts; whereas, the words are wholly different: "Congress," says the Constitution, (amendment 3d.) "shall make no law respecting an establishment of religion, or prohibiting the free exercise thereof, or abridging the freedom of speech of the press." Here it is manifest that the Constitution intended to prohibit Congress from legislating at all on the subject of religious establishments, and the prohibition is made in the most express terms. Had the same intention prevailed respecting the press, the same expressions would have been used, and Congress would have been "prohibited from passing any law respecting the press." They are not, however, "prohibited" from legislating at all on the subject, but merely from abridging the liberty of the press. It is evident they may legislate respecting the press, may pass laws for its regulation, and to punish those who pervert it into an engine of mischief, provided those laws do not abridge its liberty. Its liberty, according to the well known and universally admitted definition, consists in permission to publish, without previous restraint upon the press, but subject to punishment afterwards for improper publications. A law, therefore, to impose previous restraint upon the press, and not one to inflict punishment on wicked and malicious publications, would be a law to abridge the liberty of the press, and, as such, unconstitutional. . . .

[The Minority Report]

The select committee had very truly stated, that only the second and third sections of the act, in addition to the act for the punishment of certain crimes against the United States, are complained of—that the part of the law which punishes seditious acts is acquiesced in, and that the part that goes to restrain what are called seditious writings, is alone the object of the petitions.

This part of the law is complained of as being unwarranted by the Constitution, and destructive of the first principles of Republican Government. It is always justifiable, in examining the principle of a law, to inquire what other laws can be passed with equal reason, and to impute to it all the mischiefs for which it may be used as a precedent. In this case, little inquiry is left for us to make, the arguments in favor of the law carrying us immediately, and by inevitable consequence, to absolute power over the press. The case chosen for our first legislation, that of "false, scandalous, and malicious writings," is specious, and as likely as any can be to establish an interest in its favor; but when it is fairly examined, it will be found to operate on cases, which could not, at first view, be expected to come under it; to be the instrument of most unjust oppression, and to restrain that free communication of honest opinion which is the soul of the Government. But when you come to inquire further, and learn, from the advocates of the law, the authority which they claim for passing it, you will find that the power claimed does not stop even with this law, mischievous as it may be, but that it extends to absolute and unlimited control. . . .

It cannot escape notice, however, that the doctrine contended for, that the Administration must be protected against writings which are likely to bring it into contempt, as tending to opposition, will apply with more force to truth than falsehood. It cannot be denied that the discovery of maladministration will bring more lasting discredit on the Government of a country than the same charges would if untrue.

This is not an alarm founded merely on construction; for the Governments which have exercised control over the press, have carried it the whole length. This is notoriously the law of England, from whence this system has been drawn; for there, truth and falsehood are alike subject to punishment, if the publication brings contempt on the officers of Government.

I have shown, as I promised, that the authority on which this act is supported, gives unlimited power over the press, as to its investigation of public affairs, which is its most important function; and I will now endeavor to show, that the effect of the present law is very little short of the complete restraint of all useful discussion on public men and measures.

The law has been current by the fair pretence of punishing

nothing but falsehood, and by holding out to the accused the liberty of proving the truth of the writing; but, it was from the first apprehended, and it seems now to have been adjudged (the doctrine has certainly been asserted on this floor) that matters of opinion, arising on notorious facts, come under the law. If this is the case, where is the advantage of the law requiring that the writing should be false, before a man shall be liable to punishment, or of his having the liberty of proving the truth of his writing? Of the truth of facts there is an almost certain test; the belief of honest men is certain enough to entitle it to great confidence; but their opinions have no certainty at all. The trial of the truth of opinions, in the best state of society, would be altogether precarious; and, perhaps, a jury of twelve men could never be found to agree in any one opinion. At the present moment, when, unfortunately, opinion is almost entirely governed by prejudice and passion, it may be more decided, but nobody will say it is more respectable; chance must determine whether political opinions are true or false, and it will not unfrequently happen, that a man will be punished for publishing opinions which are sincerely his, and which are of a nature to be extremely interesting to the public, merely because accident, or design, has collected a jury of different sentiments.

If the effect of the present law is to restrain the free communication of opinion, and its principle will justify any control Government chooses to exercise over the press, an inquiry may safely be entered on, whether Congress ought to possess the power, even if the clause giving necessary and proper power would extend to such remote cases? It is the more necessary to inquire into the usefulness of this power in the hands of Congress, since the opinion is becoming current, that that alone will give Congress a right to assume it, upon the principle that Government must have a right to do everything proper for its safety. This doctrine may be very fallacious, if not taken in the restricted sense to be found in the clause giving necessary powers. No Government can assume a power not delegated, on pretence of its being necessary; for none have a right to judge of what is necessary but the makers of the Constitution, otherwise all Governments would be competent to make every alteration in a Constitution, they might think proper, and the Constitution would rank with the laws, and not above them. For the execution of powers expressly given, there must have been some latitude allowed to those who were to execute them, the same in fact which is expressed in the clause respecting necessary powers.

Is the power claimed proper for Congress to possess? It is believed not, and will readily be admitted if it can be proved, as I think it can, that the persons who administer the Government have an interest in the power to be confided, opposed to that of the community. It must be agreed that the nature of our Government makes a diffusion of knowledge of public affairs necessary and proper, and that the people have no mode of obtaining it but through the press. The necessity for their having this information results from its being their duty to elect all the parts of the Government, and, in this way, to sit in judgment over the conduct of those who have been heretofore employed. The most important and necessary information for the people to receive is, of the misconduct of the Government; because their good deeds, although they will produce affection and gratitude to public officers, will only confirm the existing confidence, and will, therefore, make no change in the conduct of the people. The question, then, whether the Government ought to have control over the persons who alone can give information throughout a country, is nothing more than this, whether men interested in suppressing information necessary for the people to have, ought to be entrusted with the power, or whether they ought to have a power which their personal interest leads to the abuse of? I am sure no candid man will hesitate about the answer; and it may also safely be left with ingenuous men to say whether the misconduct which we sometimes see in the press, had not better be borne with, than to run the risk of confiding the power of correction to men who will be constantly urged by their own feelings to destroy its usefulness.

The mode of thinking which countenances this law, and the doctrines on which it is built, are derived from a country whose Government is so different from ours, that the situation of public officers ought to be very different. In Great Britain, the King is hereditary, and, according to the theory of their Government, can do no wrong. Public officers are his representatives, and derive some portion of his inviolability from theory, but more from the practice of the Government which has, for the most part, been very arbitrary. It was, therefore, of course, [intended] that they should receive a different sort of respect from that which is proper in our Government, where the officers of Government are the servants of the people, are amenable to them, and liable to be turned out of office at periodical elections. In Great Britain, writings are seditious, though they are true, if they tend to bring a public officer into contempt.

In this country, it is seen that the same principle is contended for, and that in practice, with respect to matters of opinion, we have gone the whole length of the principle. How long can we expect to maintain the other distinctive qualities of the magistracy of the two countries, when this sameness is established? How long can it be desirable to have periodical elections, for the purpose of judging of the conduct of our rulers, when the channels of information may be choked at their will?

But, sir, I have ever believed this question as settled by an amendment to the Constitution, proposed with others, for declaring and restricting its powers, as the preamble declares, at the request of several of the States, made at the adoption of the Constitution, in order to prevent this misconstruction and abuse. This amendment is in the following words: "Congress shall make no law respecting an establishment of religion, or prohibiting the free exercise thereof; or abridging the freedom of speech or of the press, or the right of the people peaceably to assemble and petition the Government for a redress of grievances." There can be no doubt about the effect of this amendment, unless the "freedom of the press" means something very different from what it seems; or unless there was some actual restraint upon it, under the Constitution of the United States, at the time of the adoption of this amendment, commensurate with that imposed by this law. Both are asserted, viz: that the "freedom of the press" has a defined, limited meaning, and that the restraints of the common law were in force under the United States, and are greater than those of the act of Congress; and that, therefore, either way the "freedom of the press" is not abridged.

It is asserted by the select committee, and by every body who has gone before them in this discussion, that the freedom of the press, according to the universally received acceptation of the expression, means only an exemption from all previous restraints on publication, but not to an exemption from any punishment Government pleases to inflict for what is published. This definition does not at all distinguish between publications of different sorts, but leaves all to the regulation of the law, only forbidding Government to interfere until the publication is really made. The definition, if true, so reduces the effect of the amendment, that the power of Congress is left unlimited over the productions of the press, and they are merely deprived of one mode of restraint.

The amendment was certainly intended to produce some limitation to Legislative discretion, and it must be construed so as to produce such an effect, if it is possible. This is required in the construction of all solemn acts, but must be more particularly due to this on account of the various examinations it underwent, previous to its adoption. It was first recommended by the conventions of several States, was adopted by two-thirds of both Houses of Congress, and finally ratified by three-fourths of the State Legislatures. To give it such a construction as will bring it to a mere nullity, would violate the strongest injunctions of common sense and decorum; and yet that appears to me to be the effect of the construction adopted by the committee. If subsequent punishments are sufficient to deter printers from publishing anything which is prohibited, there is no stint to the power of Congress; and yet, it appears to me that a limitation was clearly intended. I cannot doubt the power of Government to bend printers to their will by subsequent punishments, when all other offences are restrained only in this way. Government does not punish men for keeping instruments with which they can[1] commit murder, but contents itself with punishing murder when committed. The effect of the amendment, says the committee, is to prevent Government taking the press from its owner; but how is their power lessened by this, when they may take the printer from his press and imprison him for any length of time, for publishing what they choose to prohibit, although it may be ever so proper for public information? The result is, that Government may forbid any species of writing, true as well as false, to be published; may inflict the heaviest punishments they can devise for disobedience; and yet we are very gravely assured that this is "the freedom of the press."

But it is worth while to trace this definition to the place from whence it is taken, and inquire into the circumstances in which it is used. Blackstone, in his Commentaries on the Laws of England, after stating the law respecting libels, which is, that everything which brings a magistrate into contempt is punishable, whether true or false, goes on to say, that this law is not inconsistent with the liberty of the press; and then gives a definition of the liberty of the press in the manner it is used by the committee. The meaning of all Blackstone has said is this, that the press has the proper degree of liberty in Eng-

---

[1] Word was "cannot" in the original, presumably an error [Ed.].

land, and that libels, whether true or false, ought to be punished there. Let us apply what he has called a definition, in
the way he used it, to the legislation of the United States.
Suppose the present question was, whether we should punish
truth, as well as falsehood, in libels, would gentlemen venture
to tell us that it was consistent with the freedom of the press,
or that the degree of freedom proper for the United States,
would remain? I venture to say they would not. Ought they,
then, to support the doctrine which hereafter may be practised on to the full extent? Is there not reason to believe gentlemen hope to conceal the full extent of their principles, by
bringing them into operation only by degrees? But, sir, it is a
manifest abuse of Blackstone's authority to apply it as it has
been here applied. He had advanced into the fourth volume of
a panegyric on the laws of England, and after stating the law
on this subject, makes a theory to justify the actual state of the
law. It must be remarked, in his justification, that the nature
of their Government justifies more rigor than is consistent with
ours, and that the existing law, of which he was writing the
praise, had been greatly softened in practice, by public opinion. In this case, there was no danger of impairing the security
to liberty, intended by the Constitution; for England has no
Constitution but what may be altered by the Parliament, and
therefore no great precision was necessary with respect to general principles. Indeed, his observations on this subject ought
to be called a theory, and a theory adapted merely to his own
country, and not a definition. Very different are the circumstances in which his doctrine has been applied here. A restrictive clause of the Constitution of the United States, by its
application, is made to mean nothing, and when it is clearly
the intention of the Constitution to put, at least, some acts of
the press out of control of Congress, by the authority of this
writer all are subjected to their power.

But it is said, that the States have all adopted the same construction which is given to freedom of the press by the com-

mittee, for that all the State Constitutions provide for it, and yet the law of libels remains part of their codes. If this is fact, about which however I am uninformed, it is easily to be accounted for. At the Revolution, the State laws were either the law of England, or were built on it, and, of course, they would contain the monarchical doctrine respecting libels. When the State Constitutions were formed, the old law was continued in force indiscriminately, and only a general exception made of what should be found inconsistent with the State Constitutions. Now, to prove that the States have considered the law of libels consistent with the freedom of the press, gentlemen should show that this law has been practised on since the Revolution, and that the attention of the States had been called to it by its execution, and that it still remains in force. I believe this cannot be done. So far as I know, it has been a dead letter. I mean the law of libels against magistrates; and, if so, the argument is reversed, and is wholly on my side. . . .

A distinction is very frequently relied on, between the freedom and the licentiousness of the press, which it is proper to examine. This seems to me to refute every other argument which is used on this subject; it amounts to an admission that there are some acts of the press which Congress ought not to have power to restrain, and that by the amendment they are prohibited to restrain these acts. Now, to justify any act of Congress, they ought to show the boundary between what is prohibited and what is permitted, and that the act is not within the prohibited class. The Constitution has fixed no such boundary, therefore, they can pretend to no power over the press, without claiming the right of defining what is freedom, and what is licentiousness, and that would be to claim a right which would defeat the Constitution; for every Congress would have the same right, and the freedom of the press would fluctuate according to the will of the Legislature. This is, therefore, only a new mode of claiming absolute power over the press. . . .

But how was this law adopted? Was it by the Constitution?

If so, it is immutable and incapable of amendment. In what part of the Constitution is it declared to be adopted? Was it adopted by the courts? From whence do they derive their authority? The Constitution, in the clause first cited, relies on Congress to pass all laws necessary to enable the courts to carry their powers into execution; it cannot, therefore, have been intended to give them a power not necessary to their declared powers. There does not seem to me the smallest pretext for so monstrous an assumption; on the contrary, while the Constitution is silent about it, every fair inference is against it. It was thought necessary to adopt expressly many of the ancient and most valuable principles of the law of England, such as trial by jury, and the writ of habeas corpus; and wherever the Constitution gives cognizance of crimes, which were known in that law, it requires Congress to define them, and direct the punishment, except in the case of treason, which it defines itself. Perhaps it may be said, that the law of England with respect to libel was in force in all the States, and that therefore it is to be considered as adopted. When we recollect what that law is, that it punishes truth as well as falsehood, and that the Congress of 1798 did not think proper to enact its provisions in the full extent, it may be fairly denied that it could have accorded with the jealous republican temper of the Convention who adopted the Constitution. If the common law was adopted on this subject, it was adopted entire as it then existed, and must remain forever unchangeable as part of the Constitution. The power of juries must be the same that it was then, and no more, and the improvement which was immediately afterwards produced by public opinion in that respect, in England, will be denied to us, and we may even have to regret the want of some of the provisions of the present odious law; but there is too little reason for the suggestion of there being a common law in the United States, to need a refutation. If there was a uniformity in the law respecting libels, it is one of the strongest evidences of what was before said, that this whole doctrine of libels was obsolete; for nobody can doubt, after hearing what it is, that it must have undergone considerable changes, if it had ever been practised on. . . .

. . . Upon the whole, therefore, I am fully satisfied, that no power is given by the Constitution to control the press, and that such laws are expressly prohibited by the amendment. I think it inconsistent with the nature of our Government, that its administration should have power to restrain animadversions on public measures; and for protection from private injury from defamation, the States are fully competent. It is to them that our officers must look for protection of persons, estates, and every other personal right; and, therefore, I see no reason why it is not proper to rely upon it, for defence against private libels.

27. GEORGE HAY UPHOLDS FREEDOM OF THE

PRESS AS AN ABSOLUTE

The first publication embodying the new and original libertarian doctrines was George Hay's *Essay on the Liberty of the Press.* Hay was, at the time, a member of the Virginia House of Delegates. After Jefferson's election he became United States attorney for the District of Virginia and gained fame as the prosecutor in Aaron Burr's treason trials. He ended his career as a federal judge. His tract of 1799 was a radical statement, smashing through the encrustations of the common law and even of Zengerian principles. To Hay the concept of a verbal political crime was abhorrent. He explicitly favored complete freedom for all political expression, including licentiousness, falsehood, and error, even if maliciously motivated and harmful. In a second tract, published in 1803, when the first was also reprinted, he extended the same views to state laws. The 1799 statement was mainly a carefully wrought attack on the constitutionality of the Sedition Act, a federal law, and dealt with freedom of the press under the First Amendment. The second part of that tract, where Hay's exposition is more general and less legalistic, is reprinted here.

It is the object of the succeeding letters, to demonstrate, that so much of the Sedition Bill, as relates to *printed* libels, is expressly forbidden by the constitution of the United States.

This question, in strictness, ought not to be discussed; because, if Congress have not power, either expressly given or by necessary *implication,* to pass the law under consideration, it is totally immaterial whether they are forbidden to pass it or not. But as the "freedom of the press," has never yet been accurately defined, and as there is no subject in which the welfare of society is more essentially concerned, my original undertaking shall be fully performed.

The words of the constitution, which contain the express prohibition here relied on, are, "Congress shall make no law abridging the freedom of speech or of the press." See the third article of the amendments, &c.

Before any precise construction is put on these words, "freedom of the press," an argument in favor of the foregoing proposition presents itself, which to me seems conclusive.

The federal government had been organised, and its operation had commenced, some time before the third article of the amendment became a part of the constitution. During this period, the press *was free,* from any controul. It is a fact, that no law was passed by Congress to controul it. It is a truth already proved, that no law could be passed by Congress to controul it; and it is also a truth, already proved, that there neither was nor could be any *other* law, by which it could be controuled. Before the amendment was adopted, therefore,

---

"Hortensius" (George Hay), *An Essay on the Liberty of the Press. Respectfully Inscribed to the Republican Printers Throughout the United States* (Richmond, Va.: Samuel Pleasants, Jr., 1803), pp. 21–30. A reprint of the original (Philadelphia: 1799) edition.

the press was free. The measures of the government were subjects of general discussion, and were stated sometimes truly,
sometimes falsely, at the discretion of the writer. Nothing that
was said, however false, however scandalous, could be noticed
by the government. In this state of things, a clause is added to
the Constitution, which declares that the freedom of the press
shall not be abridged. In other words the press shall continue
to enjoy that total exemption from legislative controul, which
at this moment it possesses. The law, therefore, which abridges
this exemption, is expressly forbidden.

The subject before us, hath furnished the materials for much
discussion; and it has been so often said to be impossible to
draw the line between the freedom and licentiousness of the
press, that the attempt has never been made. The legal and
political writers in England contend, however, that this line
must be drawn; but, they admit, that the exact degree of
longitude has not yet been discovered.

This uncertainty in the law is well adapted to the situation
of the British government. It enables the minister to act and
punish as times and circumstances require; without subjecting
himself to the odium of having transgressed the law. But,
however important this uncertainty may be in a country, where
privilege and monopoly form the basis of the government, in
the United States it is disgraceful. In a republican government
the people ought to know, the people have a right to know,
the exact, the precise extent of every law, by which any individual may be called before a court of justice.

Fortunately for the people of the United States, the question
which has perplexed the politicians and lawyers of England,
does not exist here. The Constitution having declared, that
the freedom of the press shall not be abridged, has, in fact,
pronounced that no line of discrimination shall be drawn. For,
if the freedom of the press is not to be abridged, and if no man
can tell where freedom stops, and licentiousness begins, it is
obvious that no man can say, to what extent a law against

licentiousness shall be carried. It follows, then, that *no law can* be made to restrain the licentiousness of the press.

The words, "freedom of the press," like most other words, have a meaning, a clear, precise, and definite meaning, which the times require, should be unequivocally ascertained. That this has not been done before, is a wonderful and melancholy evidence of the imbecility of the human mind, and of the slow progress which it makes, in acquiring knowledge even on subjects the most useful and interesting.

It will, I presume, be admitted, that the words in question have a meaning, and that the framers of the amendment containing these words, meant something when they declared, that the freedom of the press should not be abridged.

To ascertain what the "freedom of the press" is, we have only to ascertain what freedom itself is. For, surely, it will be conceded, that freedom applied to one subject, means the same, as freedom applied to another subject.

Now freedom is of two kinds, and of two kinds only: one is, that absolute freedom which belongs to man, previous to any social institution; and the other, that qualified or abridged freedom, which he is content to enjoy, for the sake of government and society. I believe there is no other sort of freedom in which man is concerned.

The absolute freedom then, or what is the same thing, the freedom, belonging to man before any social compact, is the power uncontrouled by law, of doing what he pleases, *provided he does no injury to any other individual*. If this definition of freedom be applied to the press, as surely it ought to be, the press, if I may personify it, may do whatever it pleases to do, uncontrouled by any law, *taking care however to do no injury to any individual*. This injury can only be by slander or defamation, and reparation should be made for it in a state of nature as well as in society.

But freedom in society, or what is called civil liberty, is defined to be, natural liberty, so far, restrained by law as the public good requires, and no farther. This is the definition given by a writer, particularly distinguished for the accuracy of his definitions, and which, perhaps, cannot be mended. Now let freedom, under this definition, be applied to the press, and what will the freedom of the press amount to? It will amount precisely to the privilege of publishing, as far as the legislative power shall say, the public good requires: that is to say, the freedom of the press will be regulated by law. If the word freedom was used·in this sense, by the framers of the amendment, they meant to say, Congress shall make no law abridging the freedom of the press, which freedom, however, is to be regulated by law. Folly itself does not speak such language.

It has been admitted by the reader, who has advanced thus far, that the framers of the amendment meant something. They knew, no doubt, that the power granted to Congress, did not authorise any controul over the press, but they knew that its freedom could not be too cautiously guarded from invasion. The amendment in question was therefore introduced. Now if they used the word "freedom" under the first definition, they did mean something, and something of infinite importance in all free countries, the total exemption of the press from any kind of legislative controul. But if they used the word freedom under the second definition they meant nothing; for if they supposed that the freedom of the press, was absolute freedom, so far restrained by law as the public good required, and no farther, the amendment left the legislative power of the government on this subject, precisely where it was before. But it has been already admitted that the amendment had a meaning: the construction therefore which allows it no meaning is absurd and must be rejected.

This argument may be summed up in a few words. The word "freedom" has meaning. It is either absolute, that is exempt from all law, or it is qualified, that is, regulated by law. If it be exempt from the controul of law, the Sedition Bill which controuls the "freedom of the press" is unconstitutional. But if it is to be regulated by law, the amendment which declares that Congress shall make no law to abridge the freedom of the press, which freedom however may be regulated by law, is the grossest absurdity that ever was conceived by the human mind.

That by the words "freedom of the press," is meant a total exemption of the press from legislative controul, will further appear from the following cases, in which it is manifest, that the word freedom is used with this signification and no other.

It is obvious in itself and it is admitted by all men, that freedom of speech means the power uncontrouled by law, of speaking either truth or falsehood at the discretion of each individual, *provided no other individual be injured*. This power is, *as yet*, in its full extent in the United States. A man may say every thing which his passion can suggest; he may employ all his time, and all his talents, if he is wicked enough to do so, in *speaking* against the government matters that are false, scandalous, and malicious; but he is admitted by the majority of Congress to be sheltered by the article in question, which forbids a law abridging the freedom of speech. If then freedom of speech means, in the construction of the Constitution, the privilege of speaking *any thing* without controul, the words freedom of the press, which form a part of the same sentence, mean the privilege of printing *any thing* without controul.

Happily for mankind, the word "freedom" begins now to be applied to religion also. In the United States it is applied in its fullest force, and religious freedom is completely understood to mean the power uncontrouled by law of professing and publishing any opinion on religious topics, which any individual may choose to profess or publish, and of supporting these opinions by any statements he may think proper to make. The fool may not only say in his heart, there is no God, but he may announce if he pleases his atheism to the world. He may endeavor to corrupt mankind, not only by opinions that are erroneous, but by facts which are false. Still however he will be safe, because he lives in a country where religious freedom is established. If then freedom of religion, will not permit a man to be punished, for publishing any opinions on religious topics and supporting those opinions by false facts, surely freedom of the press, which is the medium of all publications, will not permit a man to be punished, for publishing any opinion on any subject, and supporting it by any statement whatever.

Again, the 6th Section of the 1st article of the Constitution of the United States declares, that the members of the Senate and House of Representatives, shall not be questioned, in any other place, for any speech or debate in either House. The object of this clause is, manifestly, to secure to the members, freedom of speech and debate. But how is this freedom secured? It is secured, in the only way, in which perfect security can be given, and that is by a total exemption from the controul of any law, or the jurisdiction of any court. Thus the meaning of the word freedom, is precisely and unequivocally established by the Constitution itself.

The power which each house has over its own members affords no argument against the inference deduced from the foregoing section of the Constitution. The power of punishing, and expelling a member, is only to be exercised, in case of "disorderly behaviour."

The word freedom when applied to debate is understood precisely in the same way in the British Parliament. Fox, Sheridan, and Grey, indulge themselves constantly in the House of Commons, in the use of expressions, concerning the government, much more violent than those for which private persons have been sent to Botany Bay. In fact freedom of debate in parliament, is secured by Statute 2d. William and Mary chap. 2d. in terms similar to those used in the Constitution of the United States.

I contend therefore, that if the words freedom of the press, have any meaning at all they mean a total exemption from any law making any publication whatever criminal. Whether the unequivocal avowal of this doctrine in the United States would produce mischief or not, is a question which perhaps I may have leisure to discuss. I must be content here to observe, that the mischief if any, which might arise from this doctrine could not be remedied or prevented, but by means of a power fatal to the liberty of the people.

That the real meaning of the words "freedom of the press," has been ascertained by the foregoing remarks, will appear still more clearly, if possible, from the absurdity of those constructions, which have been given by the advocates of the Sedition Bill.

The construction clearly held out in the bill itself, is, that it does not extend to the privilege of printing facts, that are false. This construction cannot be correct. It plainly supposes that "freedom," extends only as far as the power of doing what is morally right. If, then, the freedom of the press can be restrained to the publication of facts that are true, it follows inevitably, that it may also be restrained to the publication of opinions which are correct. There is truth in opinion, as well as in fact. Error in opinion may do as much harm, as falsity in fact: it may be as morally wrong, and it may be propagated from motives as malicious. It may do more harm, because the refutation of an opinion which is erroneous, is more difficult than the contradiction of a fact which is false. But the power of controuling opinions has never yet been claimed; yet it is manifest that the same construction, which warrants a controul in matters of fact, does the same as to matters of opinion. In addition to this, it ought to be remarked, that the difficulty of distinguishing in many cases between fact and opinion, is extremely great, and that no kind of criterion is furnished by the law under consideration. Of this more, perhaps will be said hereafter.

Again, if the congressional construction be right, if the freedom of the press consists in the full enjoyment of the privilege of printing facts that are true, it will be fair to read the amendment, without the words really used, after substituting those said by Congress to have the same import. The clause will then stand thus: "Congress shall make no law abridging the right of the press, to publish facts that are true!" If this was the real meaning of Congress, and the several States, when they spoke in the state constitutions, and in the amendment of the "freedom of the press," the very great solicitude on this subject displayed throughout the continent, was most irrational and absurd. If this was their meaning, the "palladium" of liberty is indeed a "wooden statue," and the bulwark of freedom is indeed a despicable fortification of paper. The officers of the government would have a right to invade this fortification, and to make prisoners of the garrison, whenever they thought there was a failure in the duty of publishing only the truth, of which failure persons chosen by the government are to judge. This is too absurd even for ridicule.

That such was not the meaning of the convention of Virginia is manifest. They solemnly protest against any kind of legislative controul, and declare, that the freedom of the press is not to be restrained or modified by any law whatever.

This venerable and enlightened assembly had too much wisdom to avow a meaning, so totally incompatible with the real object of their wishes. They knew that there never was a government in the world, however despotic, that dared to avow a design to suppress the truth: they knew that the most corrupt and profligate administrations, that ever brought wretchedness and oppression on a happy and free people, speak in their public acts the language of patriotism and virtue only, and that, although their real object is to stop enquiry, and to terrify truth into silence, the vengeance of the law *appears* to be directed against falsehood and malice only: in fact, they knew, that there are many truths, important to society, which are not susceptible of that full, direct, and positive evidence, which alone can be exhibited before a court and jury:

That men might be, and often would be deterred from speaking truths, which they could prove, unless they were absolutely protected from the trouble, disgrace, losses, and expense of a prosecution.

That in the violence of party spirit which government knows

too well how to produce, and to inflame evidence the most conclusive, might be rejected, and that juries might be packed,
"who would find Abel guilty of the murder of Cain."

That nothing tends more to irritate the minds of men, and
disturb the peace of society, than prosecutions of a political nature, which like prosecutions in religion, increase the evils, they
were, perhaps, intended to remove.

They knew that the licentiousness of the press, though an
evil, was a less evil than that resulting from any law to restrain
it, upon the same principle, that the most enlightened part of
the world is at length convinced, that the evils arising from
the toleration of heresy and atheism, are less, infinitely less,
than the evils of persecution.

That the spirit of inquiry and discussion, was of the utmost
importance in every free country, and could be preserved only
by giving it absolute protection, even in its excesses.

That truth was always equal to the task of combating falsehood without the aid of government; because in most instances
it has defeated falsehood, backed by all the power of government.

That truth cannot be impressed upon the human mind by
power, with which therefore, it disdains an alliance, but by
reason and evidence only.

They knew the sublime precept inculcated by the act establishing religious freedom, that "where discussion is free, error
ceases to be dangerous:" and, therefore, they wisely aimed at
the total exclusion of all congressional jurisdiction.

But, it has been said, that the freedom of the press, consists
not in the privilege of printing truth; but in an exemption from
previous restraint, and as the sedition bill imposes no previous
restraint, it does not abridge the freedom of the press. This
profound remark is borrowed from Blackstone and De Lolme,
and is gravely repeated, by those who are weak enough to take
opinions upon trust.

If these writers meant to state what the law was understood
to be in England, they are correct. Even if they meant to state

what the law ought to be in England, perhaps they are still correct; because it is extremely probable, that a press absolutely free, would in the short course of one year "humble in the dust and ashes" the "stupendous fabric" of the British government. But this definition does not deserve to be transplanted into America. In Britain, a legislative controul over the press, is, perhaps essential to the preservation of the "present order of things;" but it does not follow, that such controul is essential here. In Britain, a vast standing army is necessary to keep the people in peace, and the monarch on his throne; but it does not follow that the tranquillity of America, or the personal safety of the President, would be promoted by a similar institution.

A single remark will be sufficient to expose the extreme fallacy of the idea, when applied to the Constitution of the United States. If the freedom of the press consists in an exemption from previous restraint, Congress may, without injury to the freedom of the press, punish with death, any thing *actually* published, which a political inquisition may choose to condemn.

But on what ground is this British doctrine respecting the freedom of the press introduced here? In Britain, the parliament is acknowledged to be omnipotent. It has exercised this omnipotence, and converted three years into seven years. In Britain there is no constitution, no limitation of legislative power; but in America, there is a constitution, the power of the legislature is limited, and the object of one limitation is to secure the freedom of the press.

If this doctrine is avowed here, under the idea that the common law of England is in force in the United States, even this idea will be of no avail. The common law knows nothing of printing or the liberty of the press. The art of printing was not discovered, until towards the close of the 14th century. It was at first in England a subject of star-chamber jurisdiction, and afterwards put under a licencer by statute. This statute expired just before the commencement of the present century.

Before this event, the rights of the press, were at the mercy of a single individual. There can be no common law, no immemorial usage or custom concerning a thing of so modern a date.

The freedom of the press, therefore, means the total exemption of the press from any kind of legislative controul, and consequently the sedition bill, which is an act of legislative controul, is an abridgment of its liberty, and expressly forbidden by the constitution. Which was to be demonstrated.

In the foregoing pages, I have kept clear of authorities and quotations, even where expressly in point. These can be resorted to without my help. I do not contemn the opinions of others; but discussion is endless, where authorities are relied on. I have kept clear too of personal remarks. These would have been justified by the manners of the times, and to many would have been more acceptable than argument itself. But the influence of truth is not aided by invective and reproach. I have addressed myself therefore to the understanding only; . . . and I hope that the sacred cause of liberty and truth, if not promoted by the arguments, has not been disgraced by the temper or language of

HORTENSIUS.

Virginia, January 1799.

28. JAMES MADISON ARGUES FOR FREEDOM OF THE PRESS

In the famous Virginia Resolutions of 1798, the Old Dominion formally remonstrated against the Alien and Sedition Acts and called upon sister states to join her in bringing about a repeal of the detestable legislation. The Kentucky Resolutions were similar. Five New England states and Delaware censured the Virginia and Kentucky Resolutions; the other states remained silent. Kentucky issued a terse counter-reply in 1799, ambiguously referring to state "nullification" as the "rightful remedy." The Virginia counter-reply is by contrast memorable for different reasons, thanks to the chairman of the committee appointed by the state legislature to draft it. James Madison wrote a superlative document, outlining the principles of free government, defending the Bill of Rights, systematically attacking every argument that had been advanced on behalf of the wisdom or constitutionality of the Alien and Sedition Acts, and expressing the new libertarian theories on freedom of political opinion. Madison's "Report," which owed a great deal to Republican speakers in the debates in Congress and in the Virginia House of Delegates, was written in December of 1799 and approved by the state legislature on January 11, 1800. Jefferson immediately caused it to be reprinted, as a tract of over eighty pages, and circulated throughout the country. The introduction and sections on the Alien Act are omitted in the following extract.

. . . II. The *second* object against which the resolution protests, is the sedition-act.

Of this act it is affirmed, 1. That it exercises in like manner a power not delegated by the Constitution. 2. That the power, on the contrary, is expressly and positively forbidden by one of the amendments to the Constitution. 3. That this is a power, which more than any other ought to produce universal alarm; because it is levelled against that right of freely examining public characters and measures, and of free communication thereon, which has ever been justly deemed the only effectual guardian of every other right.

1. That it exercises a power not delegated by the Constitution.

Here again, it will be proper to recollect, that the Federal Government being composed of powers specifically granted,

---

The Virginia Report of 1799–1800, Touching the Alien and Sedition Laws; Together with the Virginia Resolutions of December 21, 1798, the Debate and Proceedings Thereon in the House of Delegates of Virginia, and Several Other Documents (Richmond, Va.: J. W. Randolph, 1850), pp. 210–229.

with a reservation of all others to the states or to the people, the positive authority under which the sedition-act could be passed must be produced by those who assert its constitutionality. In what part of the Constitution, then, is this authority to be found?

Several attempts have been made to answer this question, which will be examined in their order. The committee will begin with one, which has filled them with equal astonishment and apprehension; and which, they cannot but persuade themselves, must have the same effect on all, who will consider it with coolness and impartiality, and with a reverence for our Constitution, in the true character in which it issued from the sovereign authority of the people. The committee refer to the doctrine lately advanced as a sanction to the sedition-act, "that the common or unwritten law," a law of vast extent and complexity, and embracing almost every possible subject of legislation, both civil and criminal, makes a part of the law of these states, in their united and national capacity.

The novelty and, in the judgment of the committee, the extravagance of this pretension, would have consigned it to the silence in which they have passed by other arguments, which an extraordinary zeal for the act has drawn into the discussion: But the auspices under which this innovation presents itself, have constrained the committee to bestow on it an attention, which other considerations might have forbidden.

In executing the task, it may be of use to look back to the colonial state of this country, prior to the Revolution; to trace the effects of the Revolution which converted the colonies into independent states; to inquire into the import of the articles of confederation, the first instrument by which the union of the states was regularly established; and finally, to consult the Constitution of 1788, which is the oracle that must decide the important question.

In the state, prior to the Revolution, it is certain that the common law, under different limitations, made a part of the colonial codes. But whether it be understood that the original colonists brought the law with them, or made it their law by adoption; it is equally certain, that it was the separate law of each colony within its respective limits, and was unknown to them, as a law pervading and operating through the whole, as one society.

It could not possibly be otherwise. The common law was not the same in any two of the colonies; in some, the modifications were materially and extensively different. There was no common legislature, by which a common will could be expressed in the form of a law; nor any common magistracy, by which such a law could be carried into practice. The will of each colony, alone and separately, had its organs for these purposes.

This stage of our political history furnishes no foothold for the patrons of this new doctrine.

Did then the principle or operation of the great event which made the colonies independent states, imply or introduce the common law as a law of the Union?

The fundamental principle of the Revolution was, that the colonies were co-ordinate members with each other, and with Great Britain, of an empire, united by a common executive sovereign, but not united by any common legislative sovereign. The legislative power was maintained to be as complete in each American parliament, as in the British parliament. And the royal prerogative was in force in each colony, by virtue of its acknowledging the king for its executive magistrate, as it was in Great Britain, by virtue of a like acknowledgment there. A denial of these principles by Great Britain, and the assertion of them by America, produced the Revolution.

There was a time, indeed, when an exception to the the legislative separation of the several component and coequal parts of the empire obtained a degree of acquiescence. The British parliament was allowed to regulate the trade with foreign nations, and between the different parts of the empire. This was, however, mere practice without right, and contrary to the true theory of the Constitution. The conveniency of some regulations, in both those cases, was apparent; and as there was no legislature with power over the whole, nor any constitutional pre-eminence among the legislatures of the several parts, it was natural for the legislature of that particular part which was the eldest and the largest, to assume this function, and for the others to acquiesce in it. This tacit arrangement was the less criticised, as the regulations established by the British parliament operated in favour of that part of the empire which seemed to bear the principal share of the public burdens, and were regarded as an indemnification of its advances for the other parts. As long as this regulating power was confined to the two objects of conveniency and equity, it was not complained of, nor much inquired into. But, no sooner was it perverted to the selfish views of the party assuming it, than the injured parties began to feel and to reflect; and the moment the claim to a direct and indefinite power was ingrafted on the precedent of the regulating power, the whole charm was dissolved, and every eye opened to the usurpation. The assertion by Great Britain of a power to make laws for the other members of the empire *in all cases whatsoever,* ended in the discovery that she had a right to make laws for them *in no cases whatsoever.*

Such being the ground of our Revolution, no support nor colour can be drawn from it, for the doctrine that the common law is binding on these states as one society. The doctrine, on the contrary, is evidently repugnant to the fundamental principle of the Revolution.

The articles of confederation are the next source of information on this subject.

In the interval between the commencement of the Revolution and the final ratification of these articles, the nature and extent of the Union was determined by the circumstances of the crisis, rather than by any accurate delineation of the general authority. It will not be alleged, that the "common law" could have had any legitimate birth as a law of the United States during that state of things. If it came, as such, into existence at all, the charter of confederation must have been its parent.

Here again, however, its pretensions are absolutely destitute of foundation. This instrument does not contain a sentence or syllable that can be tortured into a countenance of the idea, that the parties to it were, with respect to the objects of the common law, to form one community. No such law is named or implied, or alluded to as being in force, or as brought into force by that compact. No provision is made by which such a law could be carried into operation; whilst, on the other hand, every such inference or pretext is absolutely precluded by Article 2d, which declares, "that each state retains its sovereignty, freedom, and independence, and every power, jurisdiction, and right, which is not by this confederation expressly delegated to the United States, in Congress assembled."

Thus far it appears that not a vestige of this extraordinary doctrine can be found in the origin or progress of American institutions. The evidence against it has, on the contrary, grown stronger at every step, till it has amounted to a formal and positive exclusion, by written articles of compact among the parties concerned.

Is this exclusion revoked, and the common law introduced as a national law, by the present Constitution of the United States? This is the final question to be examined.

It is readily admitted, that particular parts of the common law may have a sanction from the Constitution, so far as they are necessarily comprehended in the technical phrases which express the powers delegated to the government; and so far also, as such other parts may be adopted by Congress as necessary and proper for carrying into execution the powers expressly delegated. But, the question does not relate to either of these portions of the common law. It relates to the common law beyond these limitations.

The only part of the Constitution which seems to have been relied on in this case is the 2d Sect. of Art. III. "The judicial power shall extend to all cases *in law and equity,* arising *under this Constitution,* the laws of the United States, and treaties made or which shall be made under their authority."

It has been asked what cases, distinct from those arising under the laws and treaties of the United States, can arise under the Constitution, other than those arising under the common law; and it is inferred, that the common law is accordingly adopted or recognised by the Constitution.

Never, perhaps, was so broad a construction applied to a text so clearly unsusceptible of it. If any colour for the inference could be found, it must be in the impossibility of finding any other cases in law and equity, within the provision of the Constitution, to satisfy the expression; and rather than resort to a construction affecting so essentially the whole character of the government, it would perhaps be more rational to consider the expression as a mere pleonasm, or inadvertence. But, it is not necessary to decide on such a dilemma. The expression is fully satisfied, and its accuracy justified, by two descriptions of cases, to which the judicial authority is extended, and neither of which implies that the common law is the law of the United States. One of these descriptions comprehends the cases growing out of the restrictions on the legislative power of the states. For example, it is provided that "no state shall emit bills of credit," or "make anything but gold and silver coin a tender in payment of debts." Should this prohibition be violated, and a suit *between citizens of the same state* be the consequence, this would be a case arising under the Constitution, before the judicial power of the United States. A second description comprehends suits between citizens and foreigners, or citizens of different states, to be decided according to the state or foreign laws; but submitted by the Constitution to the judicial power of the United States; the judicial power being, in several instances, extended beyond the legislative power of the United States.

To this explanation of the text, the following observations may be added:

The expression, "cases in law and equity," is manifestly confined to cases of a civil nature; and would exclude cases of criminal jurisdiction. Criminal cases in law and equity would be a language unknown to the law.

The succeeding paragraph of the same section is in harmony with this construction. It is in these words: "In all cases affecting ambassadors, other public ministers, and consuls, and those in which a state shall be a party, the Supreme Court shall have original jurisdiction. *In all* the other cases (including cases in law and equity arising under the Constitution) the Supreme Court shall have *appellate* jurisdiction both as to law and *fact;* with such exceptions, and under such regulations, as Congress shall make."

This paragraph, by expressly giving an *appellate* jurisdiction, in cases of law and equity arising under the Constitution, to *fact,* as well as to law, clearly excludes criminal cases, where the trial by jury is secured; because the fact, in such cases, is not a subject of appeal. And, although the appeal is liable to such *exceptions* and regulations as Congress may adopt, yet it is not to be supposed that an *exception* of *all* criminal cases could be contemplated; as well because a discretion in Congress to make or omit the exception would be improper, as because it would have been unnecessary. The exception could as easily have been made by the Constitution itself, as referred to the Congress.

Once more; the amendment last added to the Constitution, deserves attention, as throwing light on this subject. "The judicial power of the United States shall not be construed to extend to any suit in *law* or *equity,* commenced or prosecuted against one of the United States, by citizens of another state, or by citizens or subjects of any foreign power." As it will not be pretended that any criminal proceeding could take place against a state, the terms *law* or *equity*, must be understood as appropriate to *civil*, in exclusion of *criminal* cases.

From these considerations, it is evident, that this part of the Constitution, even if it could be applied at all to the purpose for which it has been cited, would not include any cases whatever of a criminal nature; and consequently, would not authorize the inference from it, that the judicial authority extends to *offences* against the common law, as offences arising under the Constitution.

It is further to be considered, that even if this part of the Constitution could be strained into an application to every common law case, criminal as well as civil, it could have no effect in justifying the sedition-act, which is an exercise of legislative, and not of judicial power: and it is the judicial power only, of which the extent is defined in this part of the Constitution.

There are two passages in the Constitution, in which a description of the law of the United States is found. The first is contained in Art. III. sect. 2, in the words following: "This Constitution, the laws of the United States, and treaties made, or which shall be made under their authority." The second is contained in the second paragraph of Art. VI. as follows: "This Constitution, and the laws of the United States which shall be made in pursuance thereof, and all treaties made, or which shall be made, under the authority of the United States, shall be the supreme law of the land." The first of these descriptions was meant as a guide to the judges of the United States; the second, as a guide to the judges in the several states. Both of them consists of an enumeration, which was evidently meant to be precise and complete. If the common law had been understood to be a law of the United States, it is not possible to assign a satisfactory reason why it was not expressed in the enumeration.

In aid of these objections, the difficulties and confusion inseparable from a constructive introduction of the common law, would afford powerful reasons against it.

Is it to be the common law with or without the British statutes?

If without the statutory amendments, the vices of the code would be insupportable.

If with these amendments, what period is to be fixed for limiting the British authority over our laws?

Is it to be the date of the eldest or the youngest of the colonies?

Or are the dates to be thrown together, and a medium deduced?

Or is our independence to be taken for the date?

Is, again, regard to be had to the various changes in the common law made by the local codes of America?

Is regard to be had to such changes, subsequent, as well as prior, to the establishment of the Constitution?

Is regard to be had to future, as well as past changes?

Is the law to be different in every state, as differently modified by its code; or are the modifications of any particular state to be applied to all?

And on the latter supposition, which among the state codes would form the standard?

Questions of this sort might be multiplied with as much ease, as there would be difficulty in answering them.

The consequences flowing from the proposed construction, furnish other objections equally conclusive; unless the text were peremptory in its meaning, and consistent with other parts of the instrument.

These consequences may be in relation to the legislative authority of the United States; to the executive authority; to the judicial authority; and to the governments of the several states.

If it be understood, that the common law is established by

the Constitution, it follows that no part of the law can be altered by the legislature; such of the statutes already passed, as may be repugnant thereto would be nullified; particularly the "sedition-act" itself, which boasts of being a melioration of the common law; and the whole code, with all its incongruities, barbarisms, and bloody maxims, would be inviolably saddled on the good people of the United States.

Should this consequence be rejected, and the common law be held, like other laws, liable to revision and alteration, by the authority of Congress, it then follows, that the authority of Congress is co-extensive with the objects of common law; that is to say, with every object of legislation: for to every such object does some branch or other of the common law extend. The authority of Congress would, therefore, be no longer under the limitations marked out in the Constitution. They would be authorized to legislate in all cases whatsoever.

In the next place, as the President possesses the executive powers of the Constitution, and is to see that the laws be faithfully executed, his authority also must be coextensive with every branch of the common law. The additions which this would make to his power, though not readily to be estimated, claim the most serious attention.

This is not all; it will merit the most profound consideration, how far an indefinite admission of the common law, with a latitude in construing it, equal to the construction by which it is deduced from the Constitution, might draw after it the various prerogatives making part of the unwritten law of England. The English constitution itself is nothing more than a composition of unwritten laws and maxims.

In the third place, whether the common law be admitted as of legal or of constitutional obligation, it would confer on the judicial department a discretion little short of a legislative power.

On the supposition of its having a constitutional obligation, this power in the judges would be permanent and irremediable by the legislature. On the other supposition, the power would not expire, until the legislature should have introduced a full system of statutory provisions. Let it be observed, too, that besides all the uncertainties above enumerated, and which present an immense field for judicial discretion, it would remain with the same department to decide what parts of the common law would, and what would not, be properly applicable to the circumstances of the United States.

A discretion of this sort has always been lamented as incongruous and dangerous, even in the colonial and state courts; although so much narrowed by positive provisions in the local codes on all the principal subjects embraced by the common law. Under the United States, where so few laws exist on those subjects, and where so great a lapse of time must happen before the vast chasm could be supplied, it is manifest that the power of the judges over the law would, in fact, erect them into legislators; and that, for a long time, it would be impossible for the citizens to conjecture, either what was, or would be law.

In the last place, the consequence of admitting the common law as the law of the United States, on the authority of the individual states, is as obvious as it would be fatal. As this law relates to every subject of legislation, and would be paramount to the constitutions and laws of the states, the admission of it would overwhelm the residuary sovereignty of the states, and by one constructive operation, new-model the whole political fabric of the country.

From the review thus taken of the situation of the American colonies prior to their independence; of the effect of this event on their situation; of the nature and import of the articles of confederation; of the true meaning of the passage in the existing Constitution from which the common law has been deduced; of the difficulties and uncertainties incident to the doctrine; and of its vast consequences in extending the powers of the Federal Government, and in superseding the authorities of the state governments; the committee feel the utmost confidence in concluding, that the common law never was, nor, by any fair construction, ever can be, deemed a law for the American people as one community; and they indulge the strongest expectation that the same conclusion will finally be drawn, by all candid and accurate inquirers into the subject. It is indeed distressing to reflect, that it ever should have been made a question, whether the Constitution, on the whole face of which is seen so much labour to enumerate and define the several objects of federal power, could intend to introduce in the lump, in an indirect manner, and by a forced construction of a few phrases, the vast and multifarious jurisdiction involved in the common law; a law filling so many ample volumes; a law overspreading the entire field of legislation; and a law that would sap the foundation of the Constitution as a system of limited and specified powers. A severer reproach could not, in the opinion of the committee, be thrown on the Constitution, on those who framed, or on those who established it, than such a supposition would throw on them.

The argument, then, drawn from the common law, on the ground of its being adopted or recognised by the Constitution, being inapplicable to the sedition-act, the committee will proceed to examine the other arguments which have been founded on the Constitution.

They will waste but little time on the attempt to cover the act by the preamble to the Constitution; it being contrary to every acknowledged rule of construction, to set up this part of an instrument, in opposition to the plain meaning expressed in the body of the instrument. A preamble usually contains the general motives or reasons, for the particular regulations or measures which follow it; and is always understood to be explained and limited by them. In the present instance, a contrary interpretation would have the inadmissible effect, of rendering nugatory or improper every part of the Constitution which succeeds the preamble.

The paragraph in Art. I. sect. 8, which contains the power to lay and collect taxes, duties, imposts, and excise; to pay the debts, and provide for the common defence and general welfare, having been already examined, will also require no particular attention in this place. It will have been seen that in its fair and consistent meaning, it cannot enlarge the enumerated powers vested in Congress.

The part of the Constitution which seems most to be recurred to, in defence of the "sedition-act," is the last clause of the above section, empowering Congress "to make all laws which shall be necessary and proper for carrying into execution the foregoing powers, and all other powers vested by this Constitution in the government of the United States, or in any department or officer thereof."

The plain import of this clause is, that Congress shall have all the incidental or instrumental powers necessary and proper for carrying into execution all the express powers; whether they be vested in the government of the United States, more collectively, or in the several departments or officers thereof. It is not a grant of new powers to Congress, but merely a declaration, for the removal of all uncertainty, that the means of carrying into execution, those otherwise granted, are included in the grant.

Whenever, therefore, a question arises concerning the constitutionality of a particular power, the first question is, whether the power be expressed in the Constitution. If it be, the question is decided. If it be not expressed, the next inquiry must be, whether it is properly an incident to an express power, and necessary to its execution. If it be, it may be exercised by Congress. If it be not, Congress cannot exercise it.

Let the question be asked, then, whether the power over the press, exercised in the "sedition-act," be found among the powers expressly vested in the Congress? This is not pretended.

Is there any express power, for executing which it is a necessary and proper power?

The power which has been selected, as least remote, in

answer to this question, is that of "suppressing insurrections;" which is said to imply a power to *prevent* insurrections, by punishing whatever may *lead* or *tend* to them. But, it surely cannot, with the least plausibility, be said, that a regulation of the press, and a punishment of libels, are exercises of a power to suppress insurrections. The most that could be said, would be, that the punishment of libels, if it had the tendency ascribed to it, might prevent the occasion of passing or executing laws necessary and proper for the suppression of insurrections.

Has the Federal Government no power, then, to prevent as well as to punish resistance to the laws?

They have the power, which the Constitution deemed most proper, in their hands for the purpose. The Congress has power before it happens, to pass laws for punishing it; and the executive and judiciary have power to enforce those laws when it does happen.

It must be recollected by many, and could be shown to the satisfaction of all, that the construction here put on the terms "necessary and proper," is precisely the construction which prevailed during the discussions and ratifications of the Constitution. It may be added, and cannot too often be repeated, that it is a construction absolutely necessary to maintain their consistency with the peculiar character of the government, as possessed of particular and defined powers only; not of the general and indefinite powers vested in ordinary governments. For, if the power to *suppress insurrection,* includes a power to *punish libels;* or if the power to *punish,* includes a power to *prevent,* by all the means that may have that *tendency;* such is the relation and influence among the most remote subjects of legislation, that a power over a very few, would carry with it a power over all. And it must be wholly immaterial, whether unlimited powers be exercised under the name of unlimited powers, or be exercised under the name of unlimited means of carrying into execution limited powers.

This branch of the subject will be closed with a reflection

which must have weight with all; but more especially with those who place peculiar reliance on the judicial exposition of the Constitution, as the bulwark provided against undue extensions of the legislative power. If it be understood that the powers implied in the specified powers, have an immediate and appropriate relation to them, as means, necessary and proper for carrying them into execution, questions on the constitutionality of laws passed for this purpose, will be of a nature sufficiently precise and determinate for judicial cognizance and control! If, on the other hand, Congress are not limited in the choice of means by any such appropriate relation of them to the specified powers; but may employ all such means as they may deem fitted to *prevent*, as well as to *punish*, crimes subjected to their authority; such as may have a *tendency* only to *promote* an object for which they are authorized to provide; every one must perceive, that questions relating to means of this sort, must be questions of mere policy and expediency, on which legislative discretion alone can decide, and from which the judicial interposition and control are completely excluded.

2. The next point which the resolution requires to be proved, is, that the power over the press exercised by the sedition-act, is positively forbidden by one of the amendments to the Constitution.

The amendment stands in these words—"Congress shall make no law respecting an establishment of religion, or prohibiting the free exercise thereof, *or abridging the freedom of speech or of the press;* or the right of the people peaceably to assemble, and to petition the government for a redress of grievances."

In the attempts to vindicate the "sedition-act," it has been contended, 1. That the "freedom of the press" is to be determined by the meaning of these terms in the common law. 2. That the article supposes the power over the press to be in Congress, and prohibits them only from *abridging* the freedom allowed to it by the common law.

Although it will be shown, in examining the second of these positions, that the amendment is a denial to Congress of all power over the press, it may not be useless to make the following observations on the first of them.

It is deemed to be a sound opinion, that the sedition-act, in its definition of some of the crimes created, is an abridgment of the freedom of publication, recognised by principles of the common law in England.

The freedom of the press under the common law, is, in the defences of the sedition-act, made to consist in an exemption from all *previous* restraint on printed publications, by persons authorized to inspect and prohibit them. It appears to the committee, that this idea of the freedom of the press, can never be admitted to be the American idea of it: since a law inflicting penalties on printed publications, would have a similar effect with a law authorizing a previous restraint on them. It would seem a mockery to say, that no law should be passed, preventing publications from being made, but that laws might be passed for punishing them in case they should be made.

The essential difference between the British government, and the American constitutions, will place this subject in the clearest light.

In the British government, the danger of encroachments on the rights of the people, is understood to be confined to the executive magistrate. The representatives of the people in the legislature, are not only exempt themselves, from distrust, but are considered as sufficient guardians of the rights of their constituents against the danger from the executive. Hence it is a principle, that the parliament is unlimited in its power; or, in their own language, is omnipotent. Hence, too, all the ramparts for protecting the rights of the people, such as their magna charta, their bill of rights, &c., are not reared against the parliament, but against the royal prerogative. They are merely legislative precautions against executive usurpations. Under such a government as this, an exemption of the press from previous restraint by licensers appointed by the king, is all the freedom that can be secured to it.

In the United States, the case is altogether different. The people, not the government, possess the absolute sovereignty. The legislature, no less than the executive, is under limitations of power. Encroachments are regarded as possible from the one, as well as from the other. Hence, in the United States, the great and essential rights of the people are secured against legislative, as well as against executive ambition. They are secured, not by laws paramount to prerogative, but by constitutions paramount to laws. This security of the freedom of the press requires, that it should be exempt, not only from previous restraint by the executive, as in Great Britain, but from legislative restraint also; and this exemption, to be effectual, must be an exemption not only from the previous inspection of licensers, but from the subsequent penalty of laws.

The state of the press, therefore, under the common law, cannot, in this point of view, be the standard of its freedom in the United States.

But there is another view, under which it may be necessary to consider this subject. It may be alleged, that although the security for the freedom of the press, be different in Great Britain and in this country; being a legal security only in the former, and a constitutional security in the latter; and although there may be a further difference, in an extension of the freedom of the press here, beyond an exemption from previous restraint, to an exemption from subsequent penalties also; yet that the actual legal freedom of the press, under the common law, must determine the degree of freedom which is meant by the terms, and which is constitutionally secured against both previous and subsequent restraints.

The committee are not unaware of the difficulty of all general questions, which may turn on the proper boundary between the liberty and licentiousness of the press. They will leave it therefore for consideration only, how far the difference between the nature of the British government, and the nature of the American governments, and the practice under the latter, may show the degree of rigour in the former to be inapplicable to, and not obligatory in the latter.

The nature of governments elective, limited, and responsible, in all their branches, may well be supposed to require a greater freedom of animadversion than might be tolerated by the genius of such a government as that of Great Britain. In the latter, it is a maxim, that the king, an hereditary, not a responsible magistrate, can do no wrong; and that the legislature, which in two-thirds of its composition, is also hereditary, not responsible, can do what it pleases. In the United States, the executive magistrates are not held to be infallible, nor the legislatures to be omnipotent; and both being elective, are both responsible. Is it not natural and necessary, under such different circumstances, that a different degree of freedom, in the use of the press, should be contemplated?

Is not such an inference favoured by what is observable in Great Britain itself? Notwithstanding the general doctrine of the common law, on the subject of the press, and the occasional punishment of those who use it with a freedom offensive to the government; it is well known, that with respect to the responsible members of the government, where the reasons operating here, become applicable there, the freedom exercised by the press, and protected by the public opinion, far exceeds the limits prescribed by the ordinary rules of law. The ministry, who are responsible to impeachment, are at all times animadverted on, by the press, with peculiar freedom; and during the elections for the House of Commons, the other responsible part of the government, the press is employed with as little reserve towards the candidates.

The practice in America must be entitled to much more respect. In every state, probably, in the Union, the press has exerted a freedom in canvassing the merits and measures of public men, of every description, which has not been confined to the strict limits of the common law. On this footing, the freedom of the press has stood; on this footing it yet stands. And it will not be a breach, either of truth or of candour, to say, that no persons or presses are in the habit of more unrestrained animadversions on the proceedings and functionaries of the state governments, than the persons and presses most zealous in vindicating the act of Congress for punishing similar animadversions on the government of the United States.

The last remark will not be understood as claiming for the state governments an immunity greater than they have heretofore enjoyed. Some degree of abuse is inseparable from the proper use of everything; and in no instance is this more true, than in that of the press. It has accordingly been decided by the practice of the states, that it is better to leave a few of its noxious branches to their luxuriant growth, than by pruning them away, to injure the vigour of those yielding the proper fruits. And can the wisdom of this policy be doubted by any who reflect, that to the press alone, chequered as it is with abuses, the world is indebted for all the triumphs which have been gained by reason and humanity, over error and oppression; who reflect, that to the same beneficent source, the United States owe much of the lights which conducted them to the rank of a free and independent nation; and which have improved their political system into a shape so auspicious to their happiness. Had "sedition-acts," forbidding every publication that might bring the constituted agents into contempt or disrepute, or that might excite the hatred of the people against the authors of unjust or pernicious measures, been uniformly enforced against the press, might not the United States have been languishing at this day, under the infirmities of a sickly confederation? Might they not possibly be miserable colonies, groaning under a foreign yoke?

To these observations, one fact will be added, which demonstrates that the common law cannot be admitted as the *universal* expositor of American terms, which may be the same with those contained in that law. The freedom of conscience, and of religion, are found in the same instruments which assert the freedom of the press. It will never be admitted, that the meaning of the former, in the common law of England, is to limit their meaning in the United States.

Whatever weight may be allowed to these considerations, the committee do not, however, by any means intend to rest the question on them. They contend that the article of amendment, instead of supposing in Congress a power that might be exercised over the press, provided its freedom was not abridged, was meant as a positive denial to Congress, of any power whatever on the subject.

To demonstrate that this was the true object of the article, it will be sufficient to recall the circumstances which led to it, and to refer to the explanation accompanying the article.

When the Constitution was under the discussions which preceded its ratification, it is well known, that great apprehensions were expressed by many, lest the omission of some positive exception from the powers delegated, of certain rights, and of the freedom of the press particularly, might expose them to the danger of being drawn by construction within some of the powers vested in Congress; more especially of the power to make all laws necessary and proper for carrying their other powers into execution. In reply to this objection, it was invariably urged to be a fundamental and characteristic principle of the Constitution, that all powers not given by it, were reserved; that no powers were given beyond those enumerated in the Constitution, and such as were fairly incident to them; that the power over the rights in question, and particularly over the press, was neither among the enumerated powers, nor incident to any of them; and consequently that an exercise of any such power, would be a manifest usurpation. It is painful to remark, how much the arguments now employed in behalf of the sedition-act, are at variance with the reasoning which then justified the Constitution, and invited its ratification.

From this posture of the subject, resulted the interesting question in so many of the conventions, whether the doubts and dangers ascribed to the Constitution, should be removed by any amendments previous to the ratification, or be postponed, in confidence that as far as they might be proper, they would be introduced in the form provided by the Constitution. The latter course was adopted; and in most of the states, the ratifications were followed by propositions and instructions for rendering the Constitution more explicit, and more safe to the rights not meant to be delegated by it. Among those rights, the freedom of the press, in most instances, is particularly and emphatically mentioned. The firm and very pointed manner, in which it is asserted in the proceedings of the convention of this state, will be hereafter seen.

In pursuance of the wishes thus expressed, the first Congress that assembled under the Constitution, proposed certain amendments which have since, by the necessary ratifications, been made a part of it; among which amendments, is the article containing, among other prohibitions on the Congress, an express declaration that they should make no law abridging the freedom of the press.

Without tracing farther the evidence on this subject, it would seem scarcely possible to doubt, that no power whatever over the press was supposed to be delegated by the Constitution, as it originally stood; and that the amendment was intended as a positive and absolute reservation of it.

But the evidence is still stronger. The proposition of amendment as made by Congress, is introduced in the following terms: *"The conventions of a number of the states having at the time of their adopting the Constitution expressed a desire, in order to prevent misconstructions or abuse of its powers, that further declaratory and restrictive clauses should be added; and as extending the ground of public confidence in the government, will best ensure the beneficent ends of its institutions."*

Here is the most satisfactory and authentic proof, that the several amendments proposed, were to be considered as either declaratory or restrictive; and whether the one or the other, as corresponding with the desire expressed by a number of the states, and as extending the ground of public confidence in the government.

Under any other construction of the amendment relating to the press, than that it declared the press to be wholly exempt from the power of Congress, the amendment could neither be said to correspond with the desire expressed by a number of the states, nor be calculated to extend the ground of public confidence in the government.

Nay more; the construction employed to justify the "sedition-act," would exhibit a phenomenon, without a parallel in the political world. It would exhibit a number of respectable states, as denying first that any power over the press was delegated by the Constitution; as proposing next, that an amendment to it, should explicitly declare that no such power was delegated; and finally, as concurring in an amendment actually recognising or delegating such a power.

Is then the federal government, it will be asked, destitute of every authority for restraining the licentiousness of the press, and for shielding itself against the libellous attacks which may be made on those who administer it?

The Constitution alone can answer this question. If no such power be expressly delegated, and it be not both necessary and proper to carry into execution an express power; above all, if it be expressly forbidden by a declaratory amendment to the Constitution, the answer must be, that the federal government is destitute of all such authority.

And might it not be asked in turn, whether it is not more probable, under all the circumstances which have been reviewed, that the authority should be withheld by the Constitution, than that it should be left to a vague and violent construction; whilst so much pains were bestowed in enumerating other powers, and so many less important powers are included in the enumeration?

Might it not be likewise asked, whether the anxious circumspection which dictated so many *peculiar* limitations on the general authority, would be unlikely to exempt the press altogether from that authority? The peculiar magnitude of some of the powers necessarily committed to the federal government; the peculiar duration required for the functions of some of its departments; the peculiar distance of the seat of its proceedings from the great body of its constituents; and the peculiar difficulty of circulating an adequate knowledge of them through any other channel; will not these considerations, some or other of which produced other exceptions from the powers of ordinary governments, all together, account for the policy of binding the hand of the federal government, from touching the channel which alone can give efficacy to its responsibility to its constituents; and of leaving those who administer it, to a remedy for their injured reputations, under the same laws, and in the same tribunals, which protect their lives, their liberties, and their properties?

But the question does not turn either on the wisdom of the Constitution, or on the policy which gave rise to its particular organization. It turns on the actual meaning of the instrument; by which it has appeared, that a power over the press is clearly excluded, from the number of powers delegated to the federal government.

3. And in the opinion of the committee, well may it be said, as the resolution concludes with saying, that the unconstitutional power exercised over the press by the "sedition-act," ought "more than any other, to produce universal alarm; because it is levelled against that right of freely examining public

characters and measures, and of free communication among the people thereon, which has ever been justly deemed the only effectual guardian of every other right."

Without scrutinizing minutely into all the provisions of the "sedition-act," it will be sufficient to cite so much of section 2, as follows: "And be it further enacted, that if any person shall write, print, utter, or publish, or shall cause or procure to be written, printed, uttered or published, or shall knowingly and willingly assist or aid in writing, printing, uttering or publishing any false, scandalous and malicious writing or writings against the government of the United States, or either house of the Congress of the United States, or the President of the United States, *with an intent to defame the said government, or either house of the said Congress, or the President, or to bring them, or either of them, into contempt or disrepute; or to excite against them, or either, or any of them, the hatred of the good people of the United States, &c. Then such person being thereof convicted before any court of the United States, having jurisdiction thereof, shall be punished by a fine not exceeding two thousand dollars, and by imprisonment not exceeding two years.*"

On this part of the act, the following observations present themselves:

1. The Constitution supposes that the President, the Congress, and each of its houses may not discharge their trusts, either from defect of judgment or other causes. Hence, they are all made responsible to their constituents, at the returning periods of election; and the President, who is singly entrusted with very great powers, is, as a further guard, subjected to an intermediate impeachment.

2. Should it happen, as the Constitution supposes it may happen, that either of these branches of the government may not have duly discharged its trust, it is natural and proper that, according to the cause and degree of their faults, they should

be brought into contempt or disrepute, and incur the hatred of the people.

3. Whether it has, in any case, happened that the proceedings of either, or all of those branches, evince such a violation of duty as to justify a contempt, a disrepute or hatred among the people, can only be determined by a free examination thereof, and a free communication among the people thereon.

4. Whenever it may have actually happened, that proceedings of this sort are chargeable on all or either of the branches of the government, it is the duty as well as right of intelligent and faithful citizens, to discuss and promulge them freely, as well to control them by the censorship of the public opinion, as to promote a remedy according to the rules of the Constitution. And it cannot be avoided, that those who are to apply the remedy must feel, in some degree, a contempt or hatred against the transgressing party.

5. As the act was passed on July 14, 1798, and is to be in force until March 3, 1801, it was of course, that during its continuance, two elections of the entire House of Representatives, an election of a part of the Senate, and an election of a President, were to take place.

6. That consequently, during all these elections, intended by the Constitution to preserve the purity, or to purge the faults of the administration, the great remedial rights of the people were to be exercised, and the responsibility of their public agents to be screened, under the penalties of this act.

May it not be asked of every intelligent friend to the liberties of his country, whether the power exercised in such an act as this, ought not to produce great and universal alarm? Whether a rigid execution of such an act, in time past, would not have repressed that information and communication among the people, which is indispensable to the just exercise of their electoral rights? And whether such an act, if made perpetual, and enforced with rigour, would not, in time to come, either destroy our free system of government, or prepare a convulsion that might prove equally fatal to it?

In answer to such questions, it has been pleaded that the writings and publications forbidden by the act, are those only which are false and malicious, and intended to defame; and merit is claimed for the privilege allowed to authors to justify, by proving the truth of their publications, and for the limitations to which the sentence of fine and imprisonment is subjected.

To those who concurred in the act, under the extraordinary belief that the option lay between the passing of such an act, and leaving in force the common law of libels, which punishes truth equally with falsehood, and submits the fine and imprisonment to the indefinite discretion of the court, the merit of good intentions ought surely not to be refused. A like merit may perhaps be due for the discontinuance of the *corporal punishment,* which the common law also leaves to the discretion of the court. This merit of *intention,* however, would have been greater, if the several mitigations had not been limited to so short a period; and the apparent inconsistency would have been avoided, between justifying the act at one time, by contrasting it with the rigors of the common law, otherwise in force, and at another time by appealing to the nature of the crisis, as requiring the temporary rigour exerted by the act.

But, whatever may have been the meritorious intentions of all or any who contributed to the sedition-act, a very few reflections will prove, that its baneful tendency is little diminished by the privilege of giving in evidence the truth of the matter contained in political writings.

In the first place, where simple and naked facts alone are in question, there is sufficient difficulty in some cases, and sufficient trouble and vexation in all, of meeting a prosecution from the government, with the full and formal proof necessary in a court of law.

But in the next place, it must be obvious to the plainest minds, that opinions, and inferences, and conjectural observations, are not only in many cases inseparable from the facts, but may often be more the objects of the prosecution than the facts themselves; or may even be altogether abstracted from particular facts; and that opinions and inferences, and conjectural observations, cannot be subjects of that kind of proof which appertains to facts, before a court of law.

Again: It is no less obvious, that the *intent* to defame or bring into contempt or disrepute, or hatred, which is made a condition of the offence created by the act, cannot prevent its pernicious influence on the freedom of the press. For, omitting the inquiry, how far the malice of the intent is an inference of the law from the mere publication, it is manifestly impossible to punish the intent to bring those who administer the government into disrepute or contempt, without striking at the right of freely discussing public characters and measures: because those who engage in such discussions, must expect and *intend* to excite these unfavourable sentiments, so far as they may be thought to be deserved. To prohibit, therefore, the intent to excite those unfavourable sentiments against those who administer the government, is equivalent to a prohibition of the actual excitement of them; and to prohibit the actual excitement of them, is equivalent to a prohibition of discussions having that tendency and effect; which, again, is equivalent to a protection of those who administer the government, if they should at any time deserve the contempt or hatred of the people, against being exposed to it, by free animadversions on their characters and conduct. Nor can there be a doubt, if those in public trust be shielded by penal laws from such strictures of the press, as may expose them to contempt or disrepute, or hatred, where they may deserve it, in exact proportion as they may deserve to be exposed, will be the certainty and criminality of the intent to expose them, and the vigilance of prosecuting and punishing it; nor a doubt, that a government thus intrenched in penal statutes, against the just and natural effects of a culpable administration, will easily evade the responsibility, which is essential to a faithful discharge of its duty.

Let it be recollected, lastly, that the right of electing the members of the government, constitutes more particularly the essence of a free and responsible government. The value and efficacy of this right, depends on the knowledge of the comparative merits and demerits of the candidates for public trust; and on the equal freedom, consequently, of examining and discussing these merits and demerits of the candidates respectively. It has been seen, that a number of important elections will take place whilst the act is in force, although it should not be continued beyond the term to which it is limited. Should there happen, then, as is extremely probable in relation to some or other of the branches of the government, to be competitions between those who are, and those who are not, members of the government, what will be the situations of the competitors? Not equal; because the characters of the former will be covered by the "sedition-act" from animadversions exposing them to disrepute among the people; whilst the latter may be exposed to the contempt and hatred of the people, without a violation of the act. What will be the situation of the people? Not free; because they will be compelled to make their election between competitors, whose pretensions they are not permitted, by the act, equally to examine, to discuss, and to ascertain. And from both these situations, will not those in power derive an undue advantage for continuing themselves in it; which by impairing the right of election, endangers the blessings of the government founded on it?

It is with justice, therefore, that the General Assembly have affirmed in the resolution, as well that the right of freely examining public characters and measures, and free communication thereon, is the only effectual guardian of every other right, as that this particular right is levelled at, by the power exercised in the "sedition-act."

The resolution next in order is as follows:

That this state having by its convention, which ratified the federal Constitution, expressly declared, that among other essential rights, "the liberty of conscience and of the press cannot be cancelled, abridged, restrained or modified by any authority of the United States," and from its extreme anxiety to guard these rights from every possible attack of sophistry and ambition, having, with other states, recommended an amendment for that purpose, which amendment was, in due time, annexed to the Constitution, it would mark a reproachful inconsistency, and criminal degeneracy, if an indifference were now shown to the most palpable violation of one of the rights thus declared and secured; and the establishment of a precedent, which may be fatal to the other.

To place this resolution in its just light, it will be necessary to recur to the act of ratification by Virginia, which stands in the ensuing form:

We, the delegates of the people of Virginia, duly elected in pursuance of a recommendation from the General Assembly, and now met in convention, having fully and freely investigated and discussed the proceedings of the federal convention, and being prepared as well as the most mature deliberation hath enabled us to decide thereon, do, in the name and in behalf of the people of Virginia, declare and make known, that the powers granted under the Constitution, being derived from the people of the United States, may be resumed by them, whensoever the same shall be perverted to their injury or oppression; and that every power not granted thereby, remains with them, and at their will. That, therefore, no right of any denomination can be cancelled, abridged, restrained, or modified, by the Congress, by the Senate, or House of Representatives, acting in any capacity, by the President, or any depart-

*ment or officer of the United States, except in those instances
in which power is given by the Constitution for those purposes;
and that, among other essential rights, the liberty of conscience
and of the press, cannot be cancelled, abridged, restrained,
or modified, by any authority of the United States.*

Here is an express and solemn declaration by the convention
of the state, that they ratified the Constitution in the sense,
that no right of any denomination can be cancelled, abridged,
restrained, or modified by the government of the United States
or any part of it; except in those instances in which power is
given by the Constitution; and in the sense particularly, "that
among other essential rights, the liberty of conscience and freedom of the press cannot be cancelled, abridged, restrained, or
modified, by any authority of the United States."

Words could not well express, in a fuller or more forcible
manner, the understanding of the convention, that the liberty
of conscience and the freedom of the press, were *equally* and
completely exempted from all authority whatever of the United
States.

Under an anxiety to guard more effectually these rights
against every possible danger, the convention, after ratifying
the Constitution, proceeded to prefix to certain amendments
proposed by them, a declaration of rights, in which are two
articles providing, the one for the liberty of conscience, the
other for the freedom of speech and of the press.

Similar recommendations having proceeded from a number
of other states, and Congress, as has been seen, having in consequence thereof, and with a view to extend the ground of
public confidence, proposed, among other declaratory and restrictive clauses, a clause expressly securing the liberty of conscience and of the press; and Virginia having concurred in the
ratifications which made them a part of the Constitution, it will
remain with a candid public to decide, whether it would not
mark an inconsistency and degeneracy, if an indifference were
now shown to a palpable violation of one of those rights, the

freedom of the press; and to a precedent therein, which may be fatal to the other, the free exercise of religion.

That the precedent established by the violation of the former of these rights, may, as is affirmed by the resolution, be fatal to the latter, appears to be demonstrable, by a comparison of the grounds on which they respectively rest; and from the scope of reasoning, by which the power over the former has been vindicated.

First. Both of these rights, the liberty of conscience and of the press, rest equally on the original ground of not being delegated by the Constitution, and consequently withheld from the government. Any construction, therefore, that would attack this original security for the one, must have the like effect on the other.

Secondly. They are both equally secured by the supplement to the Constitution; being both included in the same amendment, made at the same time, and by the same authority. Any construction or argument, then, which would turn the amendment into a grant or acknowledgment of power with respect to the press, might be equally applied to the freedom of religion.

Thirdly. If it be admitted that the extent of the freedom of the press, secured by the amendment, is to be measured by the common law on this subject, the same authority may be resorted to, for the standard which is to fix the extent of the "free exercise of religion." It cannot be necessary to say what this standard would be; whether the common law be taken solely as the unwritten, or as varied by the written law of England.

Fourthly. If the words and phrases in the amendment, are to be considered as chosen with a studied discrimination, which yields an argument for a power over the press, under the limitation that its freedom be not abridged, the same argument results from the same consideration, for a power over the exercise of religion, under the limitation that its freedom be not prohibited.

For, if Congress may regulate the freedom of the press, provided they do not abridge it, because it is said only "they shall not abridge it," and is not said, "they shall make no law respecting it," the analogy of reasoning is conclusive, that Congress may *regulate* and even *abridge* the free exercise of religion, provided they do not *prohibit* it, because it is said only "they shall not prohibit it," and is *not* said, "they shall make no law *respecting,* or no law *abridging* it."

The General Assembly were governed by the clearest reason, then, in considering the "sedition-act," which legislates on the freedom of the press, as establishing a precedent that may be fatal to the liberty of conscience; and it will be the duty of all, in proportion as they value the security of the latter, to take the alarm at every encroachment on the former. . . .

29. THE NEW LIBERTARIANISM PRODUCES A POLITICAL THEORIST

Tunis Wortman, by his book, *A Treatise Concerning Political Enquiry, and the Liberty of the Press,* contributed pre-eminently to the new libertarian theory that emerged in the wake of the Sedition Act. A New York lawyer prominent in Tammany politics, he was both a faithful party hack and an outstanding democratic theorist of his time. A political enemy described him as "an execrable compound of every excess of vice. . . . Those who wish to view human nature in its most degenerate state will in this man find a fit object of contemplation." From 1801 to 1807 Wortman served as clerk of the city and county of New York, a position in which he distinguished himself every Election Day by certifying scores of Irish immigrants as naturalized citizens and marching them off to the polls to vote the straight ticket. But Wortman was also the author of several important tracts, one of which (*An Oration on the Influence of Social Institutions upon Human Morals and*

Happiness [New York: 1796]) outlined a democratic philosophy of social reform, and another of which (*A Solemn Address, to Christians and Patriots* [New York: 1800]) was a leading defense of Jefferson against charges of atheism in the election of 1800. Albert Gallatin supported the publication of Wortman's great book of the same year, by undertaking to place subscriptions for it among Republican members of Congress. In 1813 and 1814 Wortman published a newspaper in New York, the *Standard of Union,* to which Jefferson subscribed in the hope that it would counteract the "abandoned spirit of falsehood" of the newspapers of the country. Wortman's book is in a sense the one that Jefferson should have written but did not; no book better expresses the Jeffersonian spirit. Devoid of party polemics and of the usual legalistic character of much of the new libertarian writings, the book is a work of political philosophy that systematically presents the case for freedom of expression. "The freedom of speech and opinion," wrote Wortman in his preface, "is not only necessary to the happiness of Man, considered as a Moral and Intellectual Being, but indispensably requisite to the perpetuation of Civil Liberty. To enforce and advocate that inestimable right, is the principal object of the present Treatise." Here is an extended extract.

CHAPTER III.

On the General Rights to Investigate Political Topics (The Subject Continued)

The perfect right of society to investigate political subjects, becomes farther enforced from a consideration of the theory of mind. By the very constitution of his nature, man is an intelligent Being: every object by which he is surrounded, every principle which is presented to his understanding, necessarily become the subjects of his contemplation. When once reflection commences its career, who can determine the future extent of

---

Tunis Wortman, *A Treatise Concerning Political Enquiry, and the Liberty of the Press* (New York: George Forman, 1800), pp. 31–34, 44–46, 115–123, 128–136, 139–182 *passim*, 189–205, and 241–262.

its researches? Who can prescribe the topics it may venture to investigate, and those it shall be prohibited from examining?

Mind is the common property of man, and the capacity of knowledge is the inseparable attribute of mind. It is the constant prerogative of intellect to extend its researches into every subject. Thought springs spontaneously from the situation in which we are placed, the events by which we are affected, and the objects that are presented to our view. The succession of ideas is governed by the laws of necessary and irresistible causation. When once the intellectual train commences, its direction is not to be diverted, its force is not to be subdued; we are led from subject to subject, and reflection pursues reflection, with a rapidity and subtlety too astonishingly great to be grasped by the utmost vigilance of observation.

To prescribe bounds to the empire of thought, would of all tasks be the most herculean. He who is aware of the intimate connection existing between ideas, and has perceived the astonishing subtlety of intellect: He who has investigated the doctrine of association, and been taught

> "How thoughts to thoughts are link'd with viewless
>   chains,
> Tribes leading tribes, and trains pursuing trains;"

will never cease to wonder at the stupid perversity of that despotism which would attempt to direct the operations of the mind.

Why was man constituted an intellectual being? Why was he furnished with the sublime attribute of reason? Was it intended that his most exalted and distinguished powers, should be chained into a state of dormant quiescence and inactivity? Shall it be contended, that his mental endowments are an useless abortion of heaven? If the capacity of knowledge is our pre-eminent characteristic, why should we be debarred from investigating those topics which are most immediately connected with our interest and happiness?

Most undoubtedly, the percipient as well as the physical

faculties of every being, were bestowed for the benevolent purposes of preservation and felicity. There is no natural right more perfect or more absolute, than that of investigating every subject which concerns us. The influence of government and laws is omnipresent, and continually pursues us through every walk of life. It is not the blind impetuosity of chance; it is not the atmosphere or climate, the direction of the winds, or the rising and sinking of the mercury in the thermometer, that renders us precisely what we are. It is the force of social institution that forms our manners, and consequently shapes our disposition, and governs our conduct. Is it not, therefore, of the greatest importance, that a cause so powerful, incessant, and universal in its operation, should be thoroughly investigated and understood? The exercise of our faculties with respect to such interesting concern, is a right inseparably attached to our nature, and which cannot be subverted without destroying the fundamental laws of our moral and intellectual constitution. . . .

. . . From the reasonings contained in the preceding and present chapters, it must be evident, that as man is the constant object of moral and social duties, and the perpetual subject of political discipline; it is necessary that he should possess and exercise, the means of investigating the nature and extent of such obligation and discipline. From a just and accurate review of the theory of civil society and government, it is apparent, that political institution is but the instrument of society; intended to promote its prosperity and happiness—that the laws of morality are possessed of universal jurisdiction, and are obligatory upon the prince and the magistrate, as well as upon the obscure and private individual—that governments partake of human fallibility and imperfection, and that they are responsible to the people, for the faithful performance of their important trusts—that intelligence is the common property of human beings, and that the progress of knowledge is the only practicable method of diminishing the ascendency of vice, and destroying the dominion of the passions. From all these considerations it has been maintained, that a liberty of investigation into every subject of thought, is not only the perfect and absolute right of civil society; but that the unrestricted exercise of that right, is indispensable to the progression and happiness of mankind. It follows, therefore, that the government which attempts to impede the universal dissemination of science, or to restrain the unlimited career of intellect, may be classed among the most inveterate enemies of the human species.

Previous to dismissing the present branch of our enquiry, let it be remarked, that the cultivation of intellect, and the progress of literature, may be ranked among the foremost benefits derived from society: for, independent of the social state, what would have been the boasted faculties, and where the astonishing inventions of mankind? Where should we have sought for the arts, or how discovered the numerous truths of science? Refinement and knowledge, have been the offspring of civilized life; the solitary man would scarcely be recognized as a moral or intellectual Being: deprived of the advantages of intercourse, he would be unpossessed of language, that happy instrument so necessary in the operations of the mind, and so essential to the communication of our thoughts. It is society that has laid the foundation of knowledge; it has furnished all the means of improving the human faculties, and of perpetuating those improvements; it has recorded the discoveries of former ages for the lasting benefit of succeeding generations; it has taught us the use of language and of letters; it has united the powers of individual intellect into a common bank, and multiplied the *peculium* of each by a general combination of the whole. The government that interferes with the progress of opinion, subverts the essential order of the social state.

Let political institution be confined to its genuine objects of superintendance; let its powers be exclusively directed to the suppression of crime; let us say to government, "You have no legitimate empire over opinion. You have no equitable jurisdiction over the operations of the mind: let science explore the unlimited regions of contemplation. Truth and virtue are the only objects of her pursuit. If your dominion is established in justice, you have nothing to apprehend. Tyranny alone should tremble at the sternly inquisitive glance of enlightened investigation. Improvement is an universal law of human nature. Legislation in common with every other subject of meditation, must finally submit to its ameliorating influence." . . .

CHAPTER VIII.
On the perfect Right of Individuals to communicate their Sentiments upon Political Topics.

Thus far it has been attempted to establish the perfect right and ability of society to enter into the discussion of political topics. It will be perceived that the subject has hitherto been considered upon general grounds, and entirely independent of any particular system of social institution. We will next proceed to examine how far the reciprocal intercourse and communication of opinion upon those topics is a right attached to individuals; and whether any, and what, restrictions should be imposed upon the exercise and enjoyment of such right. We shall afterwards, in some measure, retrace the subject of the present treatise; and consider it, in the first place, with relation to representative governments in general—and, secondly, as it particularly respects the Constitution of the United States.

The right of individuals to discuss political questions, is a corollary necessarily derived from the doctrines which have been established in the preceding chapters: for as individuals are the elements which enter into the composition of society, the general rights of a community must be considered as a common bank or aggregate, of which each of its members is entitled to his *peculium*. When we assert that Society is possessed of the absolute right to investigate every subject which relates to its interests, it would be palpably contradictory to deny that every individual possesses the same right in the most perfect and extensive acceptation. The position which maintains the general right of a commonwealth to exercise the freedom of political discussion, intends that such is a common privilege appurtenant to each of its members.

Government itself must evidently have been derived from the pre-existing *rights* of Society. It is, accurately speaking, an organ of the general will, intending to answer particular and appropriate purposes. It is clearly the right of Society to institute such regulations as may best promote its own particular interests, prevent the perpetration of offences, and designate the laws by which its members shall be governed. The exercise of this right is indispensably requisite to the preservation of its existence: but as Society is incapable of exercising that right in its collective or corporate capacity, it was necessary to designate and select the particular persons who should represent and exercise its powers for those purposes. It has already been sufficiently established, that general delegation is the only legitimate basis of Government. Social Institution is the organ which represents the rights of a community in a limited degree. It is only possessed of those rights which are either expressly conferred, or those which are necessarily presumed to have been delegated: those which are retained by Society are open to the exercise of each of its individual members.

It has already been perceived that however extensive may be the powers of government, its existence must essentially depend upon the determination of the general will. Whatever may be the particular form which it has assumed, it is equally the organ of Society, instituted for the promotion of the public welfare. In every case it is responsible to the people for the faithful performance of the trust committed to its charge. It is perpetually liable to dissolution by the same power from which its origin is derived. Society, therefore, in its original capacity, possesses a revisionary right: as such right is altogether independent of positive institution, and incapable of delegation, it must ever remain the subject of individual exercise.

The general will, which is the necessary result of Public Opinion, being superior to Political Institution, must of consequence remain independent of its controul. Governments are entrusted with the exercise of the ordinary powers of sovereignty: but Society is, nevertheless, the real and substantial sovereign.

It becomes an enquiry of the most extensive importance, to discover the precise meaning to be affixed to the extremely complicated term *Public Opinion. . . .*

Society does not constitute an intellectual unity; it cannot resolve itself into one single organized percipient, in which the rays of Intelligence are concentrated and personified: each of its members necessarily retains his personal identity and his individual understanding. By Public Opinion we are, therefore, to imply an aggregation of individual sentiment.

It is the individual who is to reflect and decide. By Public Opinion we are to understand that general determination of private understandings which is most extensively predominant. When a sufficient number of the members of a community have established a coincidence of sentiment upon any particular subject, such agreement of their personal judgments may be correctly termed the general or Public Opinion. When they have concurred in volition upon any given point, that concurrent volition may be denominated the public or general will. Unless such prevalent opinion or volition of individuals constitutes the public opinion or will, the conclusion would be inevitable that it is impossible public will or opinion could exist. . . .

. . . But in a true practical sense the opinion of the majority is to be deemed the general opinion.

It is equally true that the current of public opinion must always be presumed to pursue a direction in favor of established institutions. The general acquiescence which is paid to the laws, and the uniform submission and obedience observed towards the government, must be received as conclusive testimony that they are supported by public opinion.

We are not, however, to imagine that any thing which deserves the name of Public Opinion exists with respect to every subject of research. There are some topics upon which an uniformity in sentiment is pretty generally established: there are others which may be considered as being in the infancy of discussion. The formation of general opinion upon correct and salutary principles, requires the unbiassed exercise of individual intellect; neither prejudice, authority, or terror, should be suffered to impede the liberty of discussion; no undue influence should tyrannize over mind; every man should be left to the independent exercise of his reflection; all should be permitted to communicate their ideas with the energy and ingenuousness of truth. In such a state of intellectual freedom and activity, the progress of mind would infallibly become accelerated; we would all derive improvement from the knowledge and experience of our neighbour; and the wisdom of society would be rendered a general capital, in which all must participate. Exposed to the incessant attack of Argument, the existence of Error would be fleeting and transitory; while Truth would be seated upon a basis of adamant, and receive a perpetual accession to the number of her votaries.

But here it may be affirmed, "that diversity of sentiment is the constant lot of imbecile and erring mortals:" how, then, shall such consideration become reconciled with the existence of what is denominated Public Opinion? If contrariety of judgment is perpetually the condition of society, to what party shall we attribute the intellectual, and with it the political ascendency? It is in the first place to be observed, that the tendency of such objection will be rather to abridge the extent than to annihilate the existence of Public Opinion. The idea conveyed by such compounded expression, is peculiarly abstruse and complicated; it combines the perception of all the infinite variety of knowledge, together with the separate decisions of a multitude of independent understandings. If there are many subjects of disquisition in which the determinations of human intelligences are dissonant and diversified, numberless are the truths which have established an undisputed and universal empire. In proportion as investigation continues free and unrestricted, the mass of error will be subject to continual diminution, and the determinations of distinct understandings will gradually harmonize. Upon every subject that can become presented to our attention, it is the province of Reason to deliberate and determine. The uninterrupted progression of Truth demands that the intellectual intercourse between men, should remain entirely unshackled. No ideas of terror or restraint should be associated into the discussion; no foreign consideration should enfeeble or perplex the judgment; mind should be compared with mind, and principle weighed with principle. Introduce the incessant habit of independent reflection, and the establishment of Public Opinion upon a rational and salutary basis will follow as the necessary consequence.

It is likewise to be remarked, that diversity of sentiment in the earlier stages of enquiry, is far from being unfavorable to the eventual reception of Truth. It produces Collision, engenders Argument, and affords exercise and energy to the intellectual powers; it corrects our errors, removes our prejudices, and strengthens our perceptions; it compels us to seek for the evidences of our knowledge, and habituates us to a frequent revisal of our sentiments. In the conflict between opinions we are enured to correctness of reflection, and become taught in the school of Experience to reason and expatiate. It cannot surely be visionary to predict the ultimate triumph of Truth. . . .

. . . It is evident, then, that no other salutary method can be adopted, to enable Society to investigate the measures and correct the abuses of Government, than to enlighten and increase the perceptions of individual Mind. Knowledge is capable of being communicated: every mean should, therefore, be embraced to render its illumination of extensive utility. There is no species of tyranny more pernicious in its consequences than that which is exerted to impede the progress of Intellect. Society has no other resource for the melioration of its condition, and the improvement of its political institutions, except what is derived from the reciprocal communication of Thought, and the increasing energy and correctness of individual Understanding.

All our prospects of improvement must therefore depend upon the industry and exertion of individuals. It is almost impossible to conceive the extensive effects which may be produced by the agency of a single person. One enlightened and active mind may create a light which by a series of fortunate incidents may irradiate the globe. Instead of palsying the efforts of individuals, it should rather be our study to enlarge their powers. Instead of checking the ardour of Enquiry, we should endeavour to stimulate and encourage the activity of Mind. In an exanimate or depressed state of society, there is but little chance of meeting with exalted intellectual powers; and, even if they should exist, they would seldom be furnished with the opportunity of rendering extensive benefit to the community.

Slavery will inevitably produce mental debility and degradation. Unless the mind is conscious of liberty to reflect and expatiate, it will be wholly incapable of sublime and energetic exertion: but if it can freely exercise its faculties and impart its thoughts, it will be warmed and animated; inspired by the sublimity of its emotions, it will perpetually increase in vigour and information.

Wherever Freedom of Enquiry is established, Improvement is inevitable: the smallest spark of Knowledge will be cherished and kindled into flame. If only a single individual shall have acquired superior attainments, he will speedily impart them to his companions, and exalt their minds to the elevated standard of his own. There is something peculiarly captivating in the acquisition of knowledge. The communication of learning affords perhaps equal pleasure to the preceptor and the scholar. Emulation is natural to man: it will always prompt to study. Competition will ever lead to unremitted industry; Science will increase the number of her votaries; and rising students will continually improve upon the knowledge of those by whom they are preceded. . . .

. . . In an imperfect and uncivilized state of society, two principal objects will engage our solicitude—the prevention of violence and offences, and the improvement of the people. The first of these objects must be particularly submitted to Government; but the other must be entrusted to Society itself.

To promote the improvement of Society it is essential that Mind should be free. Unless individuals are permitted to reflect and communicate their sentiments upon every topic, it is impossible that they should progress in knowledge. If we are not suffered to impart our information to others, it is evident that such information must remain useless and inactive. Without establishing the liberty of enquiry, and the right of disseminating our opinions, it must always be our portion to remain in a state of barbarism, wretchedness, and degradation.

It has sometimes been maintained, that in an unenlightened state of Society the toleration of enquiry is dangerous to the existence of Government: but the reverse of this proposition is in reality true. Ignorant nations are most prone to faction and intestine commotions. It is the want of Information which renders them liable to seduction. They feel the smart of Despotism, and blindly rush to the banners of Violence at the call of any intemperate and popular leader. Every established Government will necessarily possess the power of contributing to the public welfare. If we experience the evils arising from the imperfections of Society, Freedom of Enquiry will prompt us to submit with gratitude to the benevolent hand which administers the remedy: it will teach us to consider Government as our powerful protector. Investigation, so far from paralysing its efforts, will perceive the salutary tendency and absolute necessity of its operations. It will contribute to the security of its power; and, by gradually enlightening the public mind, diminish the difficulty of its task. . . .

CHAPTER X.
The Same Subject Considered from the Revisionary Powers of Society
(The Subject Continued)

So far we have viewed the Intercourse of Sentiment upon political subjects as it principally relates to the general interests of Society. We are now to examine the question with more immediate relation to the personal rights and duties of Individuals.

1. Man is a moral and intelligent Being, is inseparably possessed of certain absolute and perfect rights. One of the most important and essential of those rights is the liberty of exercising his faculties agreeably to his own perceptions of what is proper and desirable, provided such exercise of his faculties does not tend to the injury of others.

Our Natural Liberty terminates at the precise point at which our conduct becomes injurious. Independent of the sanctions of Civil Institution, we never could claim the right of inflicting evil upon others. It is the principal end of Society to prevent and redress our wrongs, to protect us in the enjoyment of our natural rights, and not to abolish or destroy them.

Truth may be considered as the property of every Intellectual Being: it is the vital principle of Mind, and the only element in which our percipient powers can maintain a healthful existence. We have all a common interest in its illuminations; we are all entitled to pursue it in every shape, and upon every subject in which it becomes presented.

The exercise of our mental faculties is as necessary to our existence and happiness as the employment of our corporeal powers. When we cease to reflect and speak, it may emphatically be affirmed that we cease to live.

2. Improvement is a constant law of our intellectual nature. Knowledge is a general fund, of which all have a right to participate: it is a capital which has the peculiar property of increasing its stores in proportion as they are used. We are entitled to pursue every justifiable method of increasing our perceptions and invigorating our faculties. We are equally entitled to communicate our information to others. . . .

. . . There is no subject more interesting than Politics; there is none in which every individual is more extensively concerned, or which may with greater correctness be considered as a common property. We are perpetually subject to the influence of its institutions. It is a matter of pre-eminent importance that we should be acquainted with the nature of the regulations by which we are perpetually governed. It is a right of the most perfect and positive kind, that we should possess and exercise the means of discerning whatever contributes to our benefit or may destroy our happiness.

If the acquisition of Knowledge is meritorious, it is virtuous to direct the strength of our understanding to the investigation of questions most extensively connected with the prosperity of Society. Politics is a subject of universal concern: it relates to objects of public utility. We are equally interested in supporting the genuine principles of Social Security and Happiness. We are entitled to investigate every question which concerns the Public Prosperity. We are equally entitled to communicate the result of our enquiry and deliberation. He who conceals a treason against Society, is scarcely less culpable than the traitor who mediates its ruin.

Of all the rights which can be attributed to man, that of communicating his sentiments is the most sacred and inestimable. It is impossible that the imagination should conceive a more horrible and pernicious tyranny than that which would restrain the Intercourse of Thought. Who is not aware that much of the happiness of intelligent and social Beings consists in the pleasures of unrestrained conversation, the charms of security, and the sublime delight of communicating their ideas with a confidence unmingled with terror? Deprived of this invaluable privilege, Society loses all its charms, and abdicates its most exquisite enjoyments: it no longer possesses the genial power of unfolding the buds of Science, and awakening the choicest energies of Mind.

It was an observation truly worthy of the greatest of poets, that "The moment which makes Man a Slave takes half his worth away." Liberty is the only vivifying principle that can animate his intellectual faculties, expand his mind, and invigorate his virtues. The atmosphere of Tyranny is stagnant, gloomy, and condensed: it chills the embryo Thought, and blasts the young Perception. By shackling the circulation of Sentiment, O Legislators! ye close the avenues to Knowledge and Improvement, destroy the blessings and the virtues of Social Life, and reduce the human species to a condition but little more elevated than the ferocity and barbarism of brutal nature.

CHAPTER XI.
On Restrictions upon the Intercourse of Opinion

It is an important object of our enquiry to discover whether the interests of Society require that any restraints should be imposed upon the freedom of political discussion; and to ascertain whether any judicious method can be adopted to guard against the evils of licentiousness on the one hand, and those of Despotism on the other.

In the first place it is to be observed, that the communication of Truth, so far from being criminal, should ever be viewed as eminently meritorious. He who combats a pernicious error, or destroys a dangerous Falsehood, may challenge a seat among the principal benefactors of mankind. The law which coerces the circulation of Truth cannot be vindicated upon any principle of justice, or reconciled to any rational theory of government.

Falsehood is constantly pernicious: wilful Defamation is invariably criminal. No man can have a right to utter an untruth concerning another: he is as little entitled to misrepresent the public measures of a government.

In the present state of society it would be fruitless to expect perfection. We are often reduced to the necessity of choosing between opposite evils. Whatever determination is most nearly allied to the general good, should constantly be preferred. It cannot be denied that Licentiousness is injurious: but it is extremely to be questioned whether the severity of criminal coercion is the most salutary and judicious corrective.

The reasoning of the present work will be exclusively confined to a consideration of the effects of Misrepresentation in public or political transactions. The Defamation of private character stands upon a separate and distinct foundation. Personal transactions are not the subject of general concern or notoriety: the individual whose reputation is aspersed sustains a personal injury. Attacks upon private character in general proceed from malignant or vindictive motives: they are calculated to affect our private avocations and property. The prosecution which is commenced to redress the injury entirely assumes a civil complexion: the object it embraces is Reparation rather than Punishment.

What are the evils to be apprehended from the aspersion of public characters, and from the misrepresentation of political transactions? It is usually observed, with considerable vehemence, "that the person of the civil magistrate should be regarded with reverence, and his reputation approached with deferential awe. How is it possible to separate the person of the Public Officer from that respect which is ever due to Government? The consequence of attacking his reputation will be to render him odious and suspected. Remove that esteem which is challenged by his personal virtues, and that confidence which should constantly reward his integrity, and you will infallibly lessen or destroy his means of usefulness; his authority, instead of meeting with obedience, will become openly controverted and contemned, or perhaps expose him to insult and derision. The true foundation of the power of Civil Government is the respect and reverence with which it is generally contemplated: to strike at that foundation is to aim at the dissolution of Order and Peace in Society."

Such is an epitome of the arguments generally advanced in support of the interposition of Restriction, and such the alarming picture which they usually represent. Whatever speciousness may be attached to this reasoning, it exhibits a perpetual libel against the character and discernment of Society. It argues a want of confidence in the energies of Truth, and supposes that its evidences are less powerful and captivating than the dominion of Prejudice and Error. He who contends that Misrepresentation will not invariably yield to the artless, simple, and unvarnished Tale of Truth, is egregiously ignorant of the nature of Understanding, and the genuine principles of the human heart.

The government which is actuated by corrupt and ambitious views, it will be readily admitted, has every thing to apprehend from the progress of Investigation. The authority of such government is entirely founded in Imposture, and supported by Public Ignorance and Credulity. It is, therefore, the interest of Tyranny, as it values its existence, to deceive and hoodwink the multitude. The empire of Despotism is founded upon Delusion, and is wholly irreconcilable with the liberty of political discussion. Corruption considers Truth as her inveterate enemy; Talents and Virtues are regarded as her most formidable antagonists: but shall it be contended that the perpetuation of Imposture is to become the object of our anxious solicitude? or that the interests of Society will suffer by our ceasing to respect those fatal institutions to which Probity and Integrity are the devoted victims—those pernicious systems upon whose altars the Liberties and Happiness of the people are incessantly sacrificed?

Public Good must constitute the exclusive object to the attainment of which our enquiries should ultimately be directed. To reverence Oppression and Imposture is wholly incompatible with considerations of general prosperity. The interests of Society require that the dominion of Despotism and Error should become subverted. To sympathize with Tyranny is a refinement in cruelty: it is to abandon every exalted feeling of our nature, and every noble attribute of humanity. If it is the province of Investigation to enlighten the public mind, and destroy the abuses of Political Institution, it should be assiduously cherished, and esteemed as the most powerful benefactor of mankind.

In examining the true merits of this subject, we should therefore confine our attention to a Government which is uniformly actuated by the love of justice, and impressed with a constant solicitude to promote the general happiness. Wherever such a Government exists, it is plain that every proceeding which can embarrass its operations, and diminish the respect to which it is justly entitled, will lessen its authority and usefulness, and materially injure the interests of Society. It remains to be enquired whether a Government of that description can entertain any serious apprehensions of the effects of misrepresentation; and whether a more judicious remedy than the coercion of a criminal code cannot with confidence become applied?

It is an incontrovertible position that a Government which is steadily actuated by an earnest and sincere desire of promoting the public good must infallibly possess the confidence of the people. It has been already maintained to be impossible that Society should ever become its own enemy. The will of a community must always be directed to the general benefit. If Truth is sufficiently powerful to combat Falsehood and Error, it should become a principal task of the honest and enlightened statesman to present its evidences to public view.

Is it to be imagined that where an administration is possessed of the qualifications which must necessarily secure its popularity, any misrepresentation of its measures should obtain an extensive reception, or become attended with mischievous consequences? Such supposition would inevitably imply either a want of integrity or remissness in duty. The idea of a Government uniformly actuated by laudable and patriotic sentiments, is diametrically opposed to Mystery and Concealment. Publicity is one of the principal characteristics of its proceedings; Truth, Sincerity, and Justice are the pillars upon which it is supported. A stranger to Artifice and Dissimulation, it feels no apprehension from popular emotions; it shrinks not from the eye of general observation; it acknowledges Responsibility to be an active, efficient, and substantial principle, and continually presents to public view a perspicuous and circumstantial history of its conduct. Fortified and emboldened by the consciousness of upright intention, it considers itself invulnerable and secure. Confidence is mutually reciprocated between the Government and the People. In proportion as the public mind becomes habituated to discussion, it is rendered more enlightened and informed. In proportion as political measures are accompanied with the evidences of rectitude, and enforced by the energy of reasoning, the general mind becomes invigorated and corrected; and misrepresentation has little prospect of obtaining an extensive circulation or reception. There can be no room for jealousy and suspicion where nothing is mysterious and concealed. Faction is confounded and appalled by the powerful lustre which surrounds a system of Virtue. In vain shall Malevolence direct its shafts at the venerable guardians of Liberty and Justice: those shafts will become enfeebled and shivered by the contact, or recoil with a redoubled momentum upon the hand by which they were propelled. Wherever Sincerity is an acknowledged attribute of the Government, and the civil magistrate becomes accustomed to exhibit an undisguised and faithful account of his measures; wherever a community is accustomed to the uncontrouled exercise of political discussion, its confidence in the wisdom and integrity of its public officers will become strengthened and increased; and it will be impossible to stimulate the people to intemperate opposition, or to render them the dupes and the victims of designing conspirators.

It is true that every individual possesses an appropriate sphere of influence and activity; and that his sentiments, and even his errors, will possess a certain quantity of weight upon those with whom he is ordinarily conversant. But will it be maintained that the prejudices of a few individuals are sufficiently powerful to infect the general mass of opinion? Shall it be admitted that the erroneous sentiments of a limited circle can ever be dangerous to a Government erected upon the solid adamant of Political Truth? Whatever might be the malevolent views of a few ambitious and interested conspirators, it is impossible that any respectable proportion of the community should become corrupted with hostile and treasonable designs. Nation's can never become benefited by deception. It is their eternal interest to pursue the direction of Truth and Virtue: their errors, therefore, must continually appertain to the understanding, and not belong to the heart.

What, then, are the most judicious means of preserving the Government from the wanton attacks of Licentiousness; and what the best security of Public Liberty against the hostile encroachments of Ambition? It will be found, upon an accurate examination, that the same remedy is equally adapted to the removal of each of those evils.

Such remedy is to be found in the extensive dissemination of Truth. But what is the most efficacious method of obtaining the universal reception of Truth? It has hitherto been the practice of short-sighted Policy to combat Falsehood with Force. Coercion may, indeed, be adequate to the purposes of punishment: but it never can be rendered the instructor of mankind. If you entertain the beneficent intention of removing my errors, and correcting my mistakes; if you wish to banish my vices and purify my heart, assume the salutary office of the preceptor; speak to me with kindness and clemency; tell me in what I am wrong, and point to the path of rectitude. Under such circumstances, can it be possible that I should refuse to listen with complacency? If you are sufficiently impressed with the importance of your subject, the generous glow of enthusiasm will animate your mind; and you will infallibly become imbued with captivating eloquence. There is a chord in every breast attuned to rectitude. Reason and Argument, whenever they are properly applied, possess the power of penetrating into every understanding: but nothing can be more injudicious or more at war with its own purposes than the application of Force. Instead of attracting, it perpetually repels; it engenders Animosity and Opposition, and naturally inspires distrust. The penalties of positive Law may awe me into silence; they may perpetually bear down the energies of Mind: but they are better adapted to become an engine of Oppression, than a happy instrument for the promotion of Political Virtue.

Considered as the means of counteracting the injurious effects of Falsehood, the interposition of a penal code is altogether unnecessary. On the other hand, it is invariably attended with the most pernicious and dangerous consequences to Society: for most assuredly it is of equal importance that we should guard against the encroachments and abuses of Government, as that we should endeavour to prevent the evils of licentious Misrepresentation. Criminal law is invariably liable to be exerted as an engine of Power: it may be used as the instrument of an administration for the purpose of crushing those individuals whose sentiments are viewed as obnoxious. Can we always be secure in the independence and impartiality of the tribunal by whom it is administered? Will judges never lean in favor of those constituted authorities which are the fountains of patronage and preferment? Will they never be inclined to sacrifice a victim upon the altars of Power? Will they carefully abstain from vindictive incentives, and from the infliction of aggravated and exorbitant penalties? In fine, are not more complicated and tremendous calamities to be apprehended from the introduction of coercive restriction than from the most unbounded licentiousness?

How, then, shall erroneous opinions or wilful misrepresentations be combated by the wise and provident legislator? The proper answer to this enquiry is, That Government should by no means interfere, unless by affording such information to the public as may enable them to form a correct estimate of things. Let us suppose an idea is circulated, that a certain measure of administration is likely to produce calamitous effects, or that it has originated from flagitious and dishonorable designs. It will be contended that such an idea will be injurious in proportion to the extent of its circulation. Admitted. But how shall such opinion be destroyed, or its farther propagation prevented? By fair and argumentative refutation, or by the terrible dissuasive of a statute of sedition? By the convincing and circumstantial narrative of Truth, or by the terrors of Imprisonment and the singular logic of the Pillory?

It is the constant tendency of Licentiousness to defeat its own purposes. In a state of Society, which admits of continual and unrestrained discussion, the triumph of Falsehood can never be of permanent duration. There is no character which excites general obloquy and detestation more readily than that of the malignant Slanderer. In proportion as the public mind becomes inured to the exercise of Investigation, its discriminating powers will be rendered discerning and correct; it will become enabled instantly to distinguish between Truth and Error; every man will be taught to reverence and fear the enlightened judgment of the community; Detection will closely pursue the footsteps of Misrepresentation; and none will dare to fabricate or utter the tale of Falsehood with impunity.

The nature as well as the policy of Civil Government requires that confidence should be reposed in the wisdom and virtues of the people. Prudence, as well as Magnanimity, will dictate that it should uniformly rely upon the established sanctity of its character. An extreme pertinacity in analysing syllables, and a jealous sensibility at the approach of Censure, naturally creates the suspicion that there is something vulnerable in its constitution, "*something rotten in the state of Denmark.*" If it is in reality traduced, it will invariably possess the means of vindicating its honor without resorting to the ambiguous infliction of punishment. Any erroneous sentiment that may prevail with regard to its administration can readily be removed by the salutary application of Argument. Error in the public sentiment respecting the affairs of Government arises in every instance from the want of information in the community: it is, therefore, in a great measure, attributable to the mistaken policy of administration itself, in concealing the necessary means of knowledge. Let a Government accustom itself to the publication of a succinct and accurate detail of its measures, with their operation and inducements; no room will then remain for misrepresentation; demagogues, who calumniate from criminal incentives, will become instantly silenced and confounded; and the honest but misguided victims of their artifice will relinquish their prejudices upon the first approach of the superior evidence of Truth.

Besides, as far as we suppose that men are actuated by views of personal interest, Government will never want its champions and vindicators: a croud of panegyrists, like the army of Pompey, will be readily collected by a stamp of the foot: for "wheresoever the carcase is, there will the eagles be gathered together." Patronage and Office, that "hope of reward" which "sweetens labour," will always multiply the advocates of authority. Government will ever possess an imperious advantage in the argument, without resorting to the auxiliary power of criminal jurisprudence. There are more that will always be ready to vindicate than to censure its measures from selfish or sinister considerations.

The restrictions which are enforced by the authority of a penal code will always possess an ambiguous character. In their nature they are liable to perpetual abuse: they can only be necessary to support a Government whose measures cannot survive the contact of Investigation. It is sufficiently apparent that the Government whose established reputation of virtue has secured the veneration of the people, is invulnerable to the shafts of Calumny: it cannot, consequently, be driven to the expedient of obtaining security through the severity of its criminal system. Restrictions upon the Freedom of Investigation must, therefore, be repugnant to every rational theory of Political Institution, and pregnant with the most unsalutary consequences.

We would deceive ourselves by imagining that a system of Restriction is possessed of a negative character; that if it cannot produce much benefit, at least it will not be attended with any considerable evils. On the contrary, it ever will be accompanied by the most positive and formidable mischiefs.

It will be the continual tendency of such system to damp the ardour of Political Enquiry, and to inspire the mind with terror. The investigation of public measures will incessantly be associated with the dread of prosecutions and penalties; and the apprehensions of fines and imprisonment will every where pursue us. In vain shall we attempt to estimate the precise extent of prohibition, or ascertain what we are permitted to speak, and at what point we are compelled to silence: the expressions of an unguarded moment, the innocent communication of what we have learned from another, the confidence we repose in the information of a friend, may be tortured into guilt, and subject us to the evils of oppressive and unmerited punishment. The censorial jurisdiction of Society, which can only be rendered useful so long as it continues independent and unrestricted, instead of being a powerful guardian and preventative against abuses, will only serve to amuse the people with the semblance and unsubstantial shadow of liberty; while in reality it will constantly expose the zealous and upright advocate of popular justice to the vindictive and acrimonious persecution of authority.

The system of Restriction is an awkward expedient of securing the confidence of the People, or promoting the popularity of the Government. A statute of sedition may stifle the open declarations of dissatisfaction, but it will ever be liable to strike the disorder into the internal and vital parts of the social frame. It is but illy calculated for the permanent establishment of tranquility, or for effecting a radical cure of the complaint. In a community accustomed to the enjoyment of any considerable proportion of Freedom, that which cannot be ingenuously spoken will be secretly and bitterly murmured. Government will constantly participate in the terrors it has inspired. The moment the first sensations of surprize become extinguished, Discontent will acquire the redoubled energy of an ANTAEUS, and exert the many hands of a BRIAREUS. The latent fire may cease to flame, but it will not cease to exist. Feeding upon suppressed and hidden, yet powerful combustibles, it will again burst forth, extend, and consume, with all the irresistible and convulsive fury of a volcano.

CHAPTER XII.
The Subject Continued

A position of the most serious magnitude is, that Political Institution should exhibit unity and harmony of design. It is impossible to engraft the regulations of Slavery upon the trunk of Liberty, without altering the nature and properties of the tree. One system or the other must inevitably acquire the ascendency. If the frequent prosecution of libels should excite discontent, Government will finally become compelled either to relax from its severity; or, what is more to be apprehended, will be driven to fortify its powers by the introduction of a Military Despotism.

We have already seen that the Restriction of Political Opinion, by the powerful arm of Government, is susceptible of the most dangerous abuses, and incessantly liable to be prostituted to the most invidious and oppressive purposes. Shall we, then, to prevent an inferior and almost imaginary evil (an evil which is constantly pursued by a salutary and efficacious remedy) resort to the introduction of a system which may be accompanied with such formidable calamities? While we extend our solicitude to the suppression of Licentiousness, shall we cease to remember that the Freedom of Investigation is preeminently requisite to guard against the abuses of Authority? In the exuberance of our zeal against malignant Calumny and Misrepresentation, shall we consent to paralize and cripple the most beneficial powers of Society? While we are contemplating the vices and the frailties of mankind, shall we totally forget that Governments are abundant partakers of the passions, temptations, and infirmities of our nature?

It is generally imagined that political expediency requires the libeller to be punished. "Shall the slanderer of Government be suffered to triumph with impunity? Shall he not meet with the severity due to his misdeeds?" There are a variety of considerations which may be offered as conclusive answers to such interrogations.

We must carefully distinguish between the defamation which relates to Private Individuals and that which concerns Government. In the first case a personal injury is sustained. — Private Character being tender, and not an object of notoriety, is susceptible of suffering from Misrepresentation. The erroneous impressions of a single man may be extremely pernicious to another. The prosecutions commenced for Personal Slander are founded in real damage: they aim at redress; they are entirely the objects of civil jurisdiction, and are not liable to become converted into instruments of oppression.

Our attention must therefore be confined to the Defamation of Government. Misrepresentation of the character or transactions of administration is viewed as a public offence: it is, therefore, contended that it should be punishable, as well as every other crime of a public nature.

In reply to such doctrine, it is to be observed, that the advancement of public good is the true principle upon which all crimes ought to be punished. Coercion should not be exercised for any other reason than because the conduct which is to be restrained is injurious to the community. He who perpetrates a robbery, or is guilty of fraud, commits a real injury, which will not admit of apology. The punishment of such offences is always necessary, and is never subject to abuse: but the interference of Government, to punish men for their assertions respecting itself, ever has been, and ever will be, subject to the most odious oppression.

Public prosecutions for libels are, therefore, more dangerous to Society than the misrepresentation which they are intended to punish. We should be cautious of entrusting Government with a weapon which may render it invulnerable. It has already been contended, that Punishment, abstractly considered, is a multiplication of human calamity. It should never, therefore, be resorted to, unless from momentous considerations of general utility. Few doctrines are more pernicious than that which contemplates the infliction of injury as the only effectual reformer, and pains and mutilation of the body as the best expedient to purify the mind. The inhuman error has originated in palaces, and has insinuated itself into families and schools. If the same ingenuity and fervour had been employed to enlighten the intellectual faculties, as has been exerted for the refinement of cruelty and vengeance, the world would have been advanced much nearer to maturity; and Virtue, instead of Terror, would govern our conduct.

It has been rendered sufficiently plain, that a virtuous Government cannot become materially injured by Misrepresentation: for the most acrimonious and violent invectives will be the most open to detection. Why, then, should punishment be inflicted? Will the confinement of my body within a prison, or the removal of my property to the public treasury, render me a better man? Will such severity be calculated to conciliate my affections towards the Government? or will it be likely to inspire me with lasting resentment? If I have been guilty of malicious detraction, let corroding Envy, sickening Jealousy, and vulture Passions torture and prey upon my heart. Believe me, I should be punished by misery more aggravated than the horrors of an inquisition. He who attacks Truth will be sure of disappointment: he will be shunned, detested, and, like CAIN, will be sentenced to wear a mark of infamy upon his brow. If I have mistaken the character of an influential personage, or misconceived a particular transaction of Government, my mistake should be corrected by Reason, and not by the laceration of my body. If I have wilfully misstated the measures of administration, or uttered malevolent invectives against a public officer, Coercion cannot be necessary to vindicate the character of the one, or to remove an erroneous impression with regard to the other. If punishment is intended for the gratification of personal revenge, it is evidently immoral: if founded in considerations of general utility, it is the offspring of mistaken theory. To remove an erroneous impression, nothing more is necessary than the unequivocal representation of Truth.

Government should only inflict punishment with reference to public views. As our actions respect ourselves, we should be left to our consciences and our GOD. No position can be more true, than the popular maxim, that "it is better ninety-nine guilty individuals should go unpunished, than one innocent victim be sacrificed upon the shrine of criminal law." There is no subject so delicate as the declaration of our opinions. Nothing can be more difficult than to pronounce with certainty upon the sincerity of the man who may have misstated the transactions of Government. How can it be ascertained what portion of actual Malevolence and how much of mistaken Zeal, existed within his mind? Shall I be imprisoned for credulity, or fined upon account of my imbecility of understanding? Shall we punish mankind for their prejudices and mistakes? Shall the enthusiasm of honest Opinion be scourged and fettered, because it squares not with the political standard of the cabinet? In the midst of my errors upon topics of general concern, it is more probable that I am actuated by upright design, than governed by the settled incentive of premeditated guilt. How, then, shall we discriminate between undesigned Mistake and wilful Misrepresentation? Shall a Court of Star-chamber be erected in the bosom of Society, to decide upon the import of particular phraseology, and determine what given proportion of acrimony pervaded the bosom of the speaker? In whatever point of view we consider the infliction of penalty as a mean of restricting the intercourse of Sentiment, or of preventing the progress of Falsehood, we shall find it diametrically repugnant to just and rational principles.[1]

We have not yet sufficiently considered the subject upon

---

[1] The Act of the State of Virginia for establishing Religious Freedom, passed in 1786, though confined to Theological subjects, is equally applicable to Political. It contains a summary of incontrovertible reasoning in favor of the Liberty of Enquiry, from which the following remarks are extracted:—"To suffer the Civil Magistrate to intrude his powers into the field of Opinion, and to restrain the profession or propagation of principles on supposition of their ill tendency, is a dangerous fallacy, which at once destroys all (religious) liberty: because he being, of course, judge of that tendency, will make his opinions the rule of judgment; and approve or condemn the sentiments of others, only as they shall square with or differ from his own. It is time enough for the rightful purposes of Civil Government for its officers to interfere when principles break out into overt acts against Peace and Good Order. And, finally, that Truth is great, and will prevail, if left to herself; that she is the proper and sufficient antagonist to Error; and has nothing to fear from the conflict, unless by human interposition disarmed of her natural weapons, Free Argument and Debate: errors ceasing to be dangerous when it is permitted freely to contradict them."

one of its most important and interesting grounds. An unrestricted investigation of the conduct of Magistrates, is not only a necessary preventative of the encroachments of Ambition, but it is also the only preservative of Public Liberty which can be resorted to without endangering the tranquility of a State. It will ever be found impossible in practice to admit the interference of Government for the restriction of Public Opinion, without destroying the efficiency, or enfeebling the operation of the censorial powers of Society. . . .

Public Opinion should not only remain unconnected with Civil Authority, but be rendered superior to its controul. As the guardian of Public Liberty it will lose its powers and its usefulness the moment it is rendered dependent upon the Government. The stream must flow in the direction to which it naturally inclines, and not be diverted by subtlety or force. No superintendance should be introduced, except what is exercised by the percipient faculties of Society. Coercion will stamp an awe upon the mind which will infallibly destroy the freedom of Public Opinion. However innocent or correct may be our sentiments, we shall always remain uncertain with respect to the verdict to be pronounced upon them; we shall perpetually distrust the impartiality or discernment of the tribunal before which we are liable to be summoned. The consequences of mistake will be so fatal and destructive, that we shall be driven to the pernicious alternative of silence and inexertion. The history of prosecutions for libel will constantly furnish us with the lesson, That Governments are impatient of contradiction; that they are not so zealous to punish Falsehood from an enlightened and disinterested attachment to Justice, as they are ready to smother opinions that are unfavorable to their designs. The infliction of Penalty, instead of being a wholesome corrective of Falsehood, will be perpetually abused to answer the purposes of Animosity, Oppression, and Ambition. It will infallibly destroy that censorial jurisdiction of Society which is the only salutary preservative of Public Liberty and Justice. . . .

. . . There is no view in which we can contemplate the system of Restriction, without perceiving its injustice and deformity. It can never be necessary to preserve the order and tranquility of Society, but is perpetually liable to the most pernicious prostitution. It can never be essential to the security of beneficial institutions, but may be rendered an engine of the most atrocious oppression when guided by the hand of Despotism. Public Opinion is the vital principle of Civil Society: the healthful existence of a state requires that it should always possess a considerable latitude and extensive sphere of operation, and that it should never be approached without the utmost deference and circumspection. To invest the public magistrate with the power of restricting Opinion, would be to trust the progress of Information to the mercy and pleasure of a Government! More formidable dangers are justly to be apprehended from arming the constituted organs of Authority with a power to arrest the career of Human Intellect, than from all the evils attributable to Licentiousness. Shall a vicious administration be permitted to shelter itself by the tyrannical severity of its edicts, or fortify its authority by the inhuman cruelty of its penal code? Shall it erect the pallisades of Criminal Jurisprudence to prevent the rude approach of independent Investigation? Shall statutes be enacted to render Enquiry criminal, and laws be enforced to metamorphose Reflection into Treason or Sedition? What reasoner will pretend to assert the absolute infallibility of Government, or maintain that every act of administration must necessarily be stamped with the features of Perfection? If a community may sometimes err in the formation of their sentiments, Governments will not less frequently oppress the people from premeditated design. The censorial jurisdiction of Society is the only safe and wholesome guardian of Public Liberty. It can exercise its beneficial province no longer than while it retains an absolute independence. As far as considerations of danger are implicated in the discussion, the argument unequivocally terminates in favor of the most unbounded latitude of Investigation. . . .

CHAPTER XIII.
The Freedom of Investigation Considered as a Preventative of Revolution

. . . It is impossible that Society should remain forever stationary. Perhaps its constant progression in improvement has now become inevitable. From the experience of former ages in affairs of Government, it would be hazardous exclusively to reason. The state of mankind in the ages that have passed was different from that in which they are placed at present. Greece and Rome are usually denominated enlightened countries: but in those celebrated communities Knowledge was monopolized, and confined to the possession of a few. The means of its acquisition were trivial; those of its preservation slender. If books were written, they could not be generally circulated: the multiplication of copies was scantily effected by the tedious and laborious industry of manual penmanship; and they were exclusively devoted to the perusal of the wealthy and the scientific. The unenlightened multitude were more easily deluded and governed, because it was their perpetual destiny to remain uninstructed. No periodical publications, no friendly volumes of Truth, were dedicated to their instruction, or ushered into the world for general benefit. Who cannot perceive that the invention of Printing has fixed the date of a most remarkable aera in the general history of Mankind?

These considerations cannot be pronounced a digression from the subject principally in view: for, by appreciating the horrors of a state of Revolution, the mind becomes more fervently attached to that excellent mean of prevention which supercedes its necessity, and points to the progressive melioraion of Society, by a hand unstained with blood. The influence of the press upon opinions, manners, and government, is a subject which will presently be submitted to attention. In proportion as our topic is extensive, it demands the invigorated energy of Investigation: but previous to the termination of the present Chapter, let us endeavour to rescue the advocates of Political Reformation from an imputation with which they have been unjustly stigmatized.

It is a prejudice not unfrequently entertained, that the advocates of Public Liberty are restless, turbulent, and seditious; perpetually addicted to the pursuit of novelty, and ever watchful for the opportunity of Revolution. To remove a prejudice, at once so fatal and delusive, is a duty equally owing to the safety of the Government, and the permanent welfare of the People. Such an opinion may excite the apprehensions of administration, and lead them to the adoption of measures creative of discontent, and liable to terminate in the very evils they are studious to avoid; it may influence the weak, the timid, and the affluent, and induce them to oppose the benevolent efforts of Melioration directed to the general benefit. Philosophical Reformation is not a crude and visionary projector: Rashness is not her attribute, nor physical Force her weapon. Her province is to enlighten Society by candid and argumentative addresses to the understanding. She is the benefactor of the human race, imbued with wisdom, moderation, and clemency; and not "the destroying Angel," who would sacrifice one generation from uncertain prospects of benefit to the next. Her genuine task is to preserve the lives of millions, to respect the private possessions of the people, and forbid the sanguinary streams to flow. Her constant solicitude is not to invite mankind to assemble amid the ferocious din of arms, but in the peaceful temple of Reason and Reflection.

We have already seen that the security of Government and the conservation of Public Liberty rest upon the same common basis, Public Opinion. Those very sentiments of political rectitude, which render a community solicitous for the preservation of every essential right, will infallibly deter them from resorting to revolutionary measures for the redress of public grievances. It is, therefore, more dangerous for Government to risque the destruction of that general mass of information which sustains the morals of Society, than to permit the most industrious activity and unbounded latitude of Investigation. If any case can possibly occur, which can render the violence of Revolution expedient, it must be when all hope of redress from any other remedy has completely vanished; it must be when the authority of Government debars that mutual intercourse and communication of Opinion which is essential to general knowledge and improvement. Of every possible mode of Despotism, there is none so pernicious, none from which the mind of man shrinks back with greater horror, than that which brutalizes his moral and percipient faculties, and deprives him of the inestimable property of an Intelligent Being, Freedom of Speech and Opinion. The habitude of reasoning, and the liberty of communicating our sentiments, are friendly alike to the rights of Society and to the wholesome authority of Government. Licentiousness is an evil infinitely less formidable than Restriction.

CHAPTER XIV.
The Preceding Subjects Considered with Relation to Representative Governments

Thus far the subject has been examined upon general and independent grounds. The doctrine of the preceding chapters is unconnected with any particular form of civil institution. We become furnished with an additional field of argument when it is considered with relation to the theory of Representative Systems.

The Society which is wholly erected upon the basis of Representation is undoubtedly most congenial to the nature and moral constitution of man. It embraces the sound position, That the exclusive object of Civil Government is to promote the general benefit; and it constantly exhibits the perfect equality of political rights. No hereditary aristocracy usurps the powers of the state; no privileged orders are supported at the expence of the people; and no exclusive immunities are monopolized by the partially distinguished few. Our understanding is not insulted by the insignificant parade of empty and unmeaning titles: but (except what is descriptive of substantial office) the general name of *Citizen,* which expresses our relation to the community, is the only appellation of the social state.

It has, however, been the policy of most Governments, which have either wholly or in part been founded upon the representative system, in some measure to limit the operation of the principle of Representation, by requiring certain qualifications to be possessed, not only by the candidate of office, but also by those who claim a voice in his election. Those qualifications most usually consist in the possession of property. It may be a matter of useful speculation to examine the reasoning in favor of such limitation, and the arguments by which it may become opposed.

In support of such limitation it may be urged, with considerable force, that the interest of Society is a consideration to which every other principle must bend; and that the public good requires that no man should possess a voice in the general councils unless his situation is independent. It is true, indeed, that poverty should be viewed as a misfortune, and not considered as a crime: but that he who is exposed to penury will be perpetually subjected to the influence, and implicity devoted to the views, of the rich; that the opposers of such limitation entirely mistake the means of promoting the object they profess to have in view; for that by furnishing the affluent with an opportunity to render those who are dependent upon their favor, and exposed to the temptation of their bribes, the tools and instruments of their ambition, instead of promoting, they would effectually destroy the substantial equality of political rights.

In addition to this, it is further maintained, That the welfare of Society requires every active citizen to be deeply interested in the prosperity of the state: he should feel that he has something valuable at stake; something that may operate as a perpetual pledge to ensure his political integrity. He who possesses a property in the soil may be considered as a permanent member of Society; his citizenship is established upon a solid and durable foundation: but he who has little to lose will seldom be animated by an ardent solicitude for the public prosperity. The individual who is possessed of property, will act with principle and independence: but the child of Poverty is a feather that may be wafted by the lightest breeze.

On the other hand it may be contended that it is an essential political principle, That all who are bound by the laws should possess an equal share in their formation; that the individual who is not blessed with the perishable goods of Fortune has nevertheless the more estimable treasures of Liberty and Life: shall these become subjected to the authority of institutions, in the establishment of which their possessor has no agency? Shall the individual who is poor be taught to feel that he is not a citizen? If he has no interest at stake, with what countenance can he be called upon to fight the battles of that which cannot be considered as his country? Vicissitude is an imperious law of mortals, and the clouds of Misfortune are suspended over every Son of Humanity. He who is the boasted proprietor of wealth and independence to-day, may be stripped of the fleeting gifts of PLUTUS by the unforeseen events of to-morrow.

It may further be objected, That the Aristocracy of Wealth exerts a pernicious empire over Manners and Morals; that the distinction which it creates is extremely unfavorable to the progress and the practice of Virtue; that the true use of property becomes perverted from that end for which it was originally designed; that riches are not coveted for the valuable and virtuous enjoyment which they are enabled to bestow, but for the pernicious ostentation and influence which they cherish; that Society constantly impresses the baneful lesson, "Exert all the powers you possess for the attainment of affluence, for without this you can never become respectable or happy:

> " ——— Qualrenda PECUNIA primum
> Virtus post nummos:"

That neither Talents nor Virtue enforce our esteem unless they are united with the possession of Wealth; and that accordingly Avarice has become the predominant passion of Society, and Fraud and Peculation crimes of continual recurrence: That Property will always command a sufficient degree of influence, without being rendered the subject of exclusive political privileges; and that every limitation of the representative principle is not only unjust, but highly pernicious.

Such are some of the principal considerations involved in the discussion of that interesting question. We shall not at present venture to decide to what determination the weight of argument will direct. With regard to this, as well as every other subject, the welfare of Society should constitute the exclusive standard of decision. Let it, however, be observed, that the Equalization of Property, however favorite an object it may be in Utopian theories, is perhaps altogether incapable of becoming realized in practice. If it was possible to establish the most perfect equality at one moment, it would instantly become destroyed by the avarice of one and the prodigality of another. Agrarian laws are constantly pernicious; and the interference of Government upon such occasions would amount to the most atrocious and deprecable tyranny. Let Property pursue its own level, and ebb, and flow, and fluctuate with the vicissitudes of life.

These considerations, though they belong to the Representative System, are mentioned incidentally, and do not materially affect the principal doctrines of this Chapter: for the man who is possessed of property and the elective privilege to-day, may lose them, and he who has them not may acquire them on the morrow.

Let us, then, proceed to examine the right of Political Investigation as it particularly relates to the theory of Representative Government. Whether such system of political institution is pure and unmixed, or whether it is restricted and modified, it is in either case a fundamental position, That public offices are conferred by the suffrages of Society; and that every individual either actually has, or may acquire, a right to be elected, as well as a voice in elections.

In the first place, therefore, every member of a Representative Commonwealth either is or may become eligible to be invested with public offices. It is for that reason absolutely indispensible to the existence of such system that each individual should be furnished with all the means of obtaining political information, and be permitted to exercise his faculties in the pursuit of such knowledge without interruption or restraint. The idea of Secrecy is peculiarly repugnant to the theory of Representative Institution, except in those solitary instances which render temporary concealment necessary. So far from discouraging Enquiry, it is the genuine spirit of such system to stimulate the mind to enterprize, awaken emulation, and point to the honorable rewards of superior excellence and talents. Society should constitute an University of Politics, open to the instruction of each of its members. In this extensive school each individual who will exert the powers of his mind, ought to be taught not only the general principles of political morality, but also the particular and local interests of the state.

Secondly, The liberty of investigation is equally indispensible to the judicious exercise of the elective right. It is to be presumed that the elector, who prefers between contending candidates, decides from the influence of reasons which are present to his understanding. He is supposed to assume the province of a judge with respect to their principles, talents, and political acquirements. Now, to enable one man to decide upon the qualifications of another, it is necessary that he should be conversant with that branch of knowledge which respects those qualifications. It is therefore necessary, in the discharge of such important duty, that the elector should be enabled to exercise every means of information. In proportion as a community is habituated to political discussion, its discernment will be rendered accurate and comprehensive; it will acquire the faculty of distinguishing merit; and the Representative form of Government will more nearly approach perfection than any other system, because Wisdom and Virtue will acquire the offices of state.

Thirdly, It is to be observed, That the Representative System unavoidably implies an absolute right to investigate the conduct of all public officers. And here let Attention be directed to a most important consideration, which places such system in an amiable and interesting light, and confers upon it a pre-eminent superiority over any other. While every other form of civil government is totally destitute of any regular remedy to redress the encroachments of Power, the system of Representation possesses an efficacious corrective inseparably entwined around the heart of its constitution. In monarchies and hereditary establishments a dreadful alternative is presented to our choice: we must either tamely submit to accumulated wrongs, or by resistance disorganize and convulse the social frame. But in elective governments the remedy is regular, peaceful, and of constant periodical recurrence. The magistrate whose conduct has been injurious may be displaced, and his seat bestowed upon a more upright and patriotic successor. Let, then, the advocate of Freedom be enjoined to abstain from violence; let him carefully avoid every act of disorder; let his conduct exhibit an exemplary submission to the laws; and let the public be taught to cherish and esteem the elective privilege, as the only safe and constitutional mean of redress.

But it is plain that such remedy would be feeble and inactive unless associated with its correspondent right of enquiry into the conduct of public officers. Society, as the constituent body, must determine whether they are entitled to a continuance of confidence; and whether the general welfare requires that they shall be re-elected or displaced. Every elector, therefore, must be permitted to canvass the conduct of public officers' with unshaken firmness and independence.

For this purpose it is indispensibly requisite that political measures should be published in circumstantial detail, and also that Investigation should remain entirely unrestricted. It is necessary that the public should be placed in the possession of events, and also of the reasoning and incentives with which they are connected. It is equally necessary that their decision should be rendered independent of controul. Surely it would be presumptuous in the public officer to tell his constituent, "My elevation is dependent upon the tenure of your pleasure; you possess the constitutional right to displace me: but I will not permit you to exercise that pleasure, or you shall only exercise it in such manner as I think proper to prescribe."

Fourthly, It is to be observed that the investigation of Conduct must inevitably lead to the investigation of Character. Every man who becomes a candidate for office voluntarily submits his reputation to the ordeal of Public Examination. Surely, if my suffrage is requested in favor of any individual, it is my duty to enquire what are his qualifications? What his morals? Is he entitled to public confidence? What are his pretensions to the virtue of Integrity? If PERICLES, who has already been appointed to office, should become a candidate for re-election, how is it possible that I can enter into an examination of his conduct, and yet abstain from an investigation of his character? Let me be informed of the substantial reason why I should abstain? If his conduct is too frail to admit the contact of enquiry, what are his pretensions to public promotion? If it is not feeble, why should he shrink from the touchstone of Investigation? What is Character? What are the evidences upon which it is founded? and what are the ideas associated with that term? The general tenor of our conduct has been useful and upright; we have uniformly manifested that our actions proceed from honest intentions. From such general train of procedure Character is derived. Character and general Conduct are, therefore, correlative. An examination of the one implies an examination of the other.

Lastly, the idea of Restriction is peculiarly repugnant to the theory of Representation. It is not to be expected that the investigation of public character, a right of such continual recurrence, will be altogether unaccompanied with mistake; perhaps it will be frequently attended even with intentional misrepresentation: but what tribunal shall decide upon that point? Public prosecutions in such cases will be always liable to abuse: they will infallibly be made a tremendous weapon in the hands of the officers of state to oppress and intimidate the people. Individuals concerned in administration will be influenced by a common spirit to render themselves inviolable; and, until Patriotism becomes more generally connected with Authority than it ever has been, they will gladly maintain a CERBERUS at the doors of the council chamber to prevent the rude and unbidden approach of Scrutiny.

It is better to submit to a partial evil, than by injudicious violence incur a more extensive calamity. Governments have not hitherto reposed sufficient confidence in Truth: they have too uniformly endeavoured to combat Moral Imperfection with Physical Force. If men are subject to punishment on account of their errors, they will be enfeebled with a degree of timidity and distrust which will impair the activity of the Representative System. The frequency of prosecutions in such cases will undermine the only remedy we possess against the misconduct of our representatives. It would be even better that a public officer should sustain an inconvenience, than a community be inspired with terror. But there will be ample means of redress without resorting to criminal prosecutions. The publication of Truth will be sufficient to remove any unfounded stigma; and if the representative conceives that he has sustained a personal injury, let him resort to the civil judicature. We are to consider that the elective franchise is the only constitutional corrective of abuses; and that it will be enfeebled by any power which paralizes the Liberty of Investigation. It is far better to err on the side of Latitude than on that of Restraint. Every man should be suffered to approach that inviolable palladium with a temper ardent, and a mind unterrified. Restraint is always liable to be converted into an engine of Oppression: it will constantly damp the energy of Public Spirit, and awe the timid and the irresolute into an abdication of their rights. The healthful vigour of the Representative System requires that the elective privilege, together with its correspondent rights, should be maintained in a state of incessant activity and independence. If any temporary evils do arise from Licentiousness, it is better to trust to the soundness of the political constitution than to tamper with the vital principles of the state. . . .

CHAPTER XVI.
Upon the Press, Considered as a Vehicle of Communication

Next to the invention of Language and of Letters, that of Printing may justly be considered as the most powerful benefactor of mankind. Before this important and valuable discovery, whatever may have been the attainments of a few distinguished individuals, the great majority of the human race were destined to remain unenlightened and uninformed. It is true that in the Grecian States, particularly *Athens,* where the territory was confined, and the form of Government popular, the schools of the Philosophers, and the constant habit of political discussion, diffused a considerable portion of light and knowledge among the citizens. It is nevertheless to be observed, that the information disseminated by the schools, or acquired at the public assemblies, was neither so correct nor so extensive as that which is capable of being conveyed through the medium of the Press. The Athenians were perpetually subject to be misled by the insinuating art and dangerous subtleties of their Orators, a sprightly sally of the Imagination, a brilliant stroke of Wit, or an animated address to the Passions, too often inflamed the minds and governed the measures of that ardent and lively people.

If we turn our attention to the situation of the European States previous to the introduction of Printing, we shall find ourselves surrounded by a dark and dismal gloom. The northern barbarians, who over-ran and destroyed the Empire, not content with waging war against the inhabitants and the Governments which were the unhappy victims of their fury, endeavoured to extirpate every vestige of civilization and the sciences. The establishment of the Feudal System, which followed as the consequence of their victories, produced an astonishing revolution in the manners, condition, and character of Society. After this, the annals of many centuries present a miserable spectacle of universal ignorance and oppression. If at distant intervals we behold a solitary gleam of light, we are constrained to lament that its unavailing lustre is extinguished by the impenetrable darkness with which it is surrounded. To the Clergy, and even to the regular orders, it is but candid to confess that the Republic of Letters is indebted in many obligations. Imbued with an ardent thirst of knowledge, and a vigorous curiosity, those venerable men were industrious to collect the scattered writings of the Fathers of the Church, and such remains of the ancient Poets and Philosophers as had escaped the general wreck. And if their glories were obscured by the insubstantial subtleties of metaphysical and polemic disputation, it must nevertheless be acknowledged that such disputation contributed to expand the powers of Intellect; and that to the labours of the schoolmen, we must in a great measure attribute the revival of Learning. Still the condition of society was rude and unenlightened, until the introduction of the Press afforded a new and powerful spring to human genius and activity. From this auspicious period we may date a constant succession of able writers in every department of Science, whose labours, instead of being confined to the possession of a few, have been attended with extensive circulation. The smaller periodical publications, devoted to general improvement, are entitled to particular consideration: the trifling expence at which they are procured, and the intelligible method in which they treat their subjects, render them peculiarly serviceable to those whose circumstances are limited, and whose time is chiefly occupied by necessary labour. To the Press, therefore, we are indebted for the most inestimable benefits. It will secure the Knowledge which is now extant, and perpetuate all the improvements which succeeding ages shall produce. With facility it multiplies the copies of Literary Productions, affords to Learning a more general and extensive dissemination, and becomes the useful Instructor of the people. In fine, it is a sacred pledge for the progressive improvement of the human race, and an eternal barrier against the rude attacks of future Goths and Vandals.

As a vehicle of information the Press is possessed of peculiar advantages. The rapidity of oral addresses—the declamatory stile, impassioned manner, and intemperate gesture of the Orator—may arrest the Imagination and enlist the Passions: but whatever is presented to us in Print is less alloyed with any circumstance unconnected with its merits. Reason has time to operate, and Truth an opportunity to be enforced. We have leisure to meditate and examine. If our attention has been diverted from the speaker, or we have mistaken his sentiments, our loss in the one case, and our error in the other, is not to be repaired: but the printed volume is ever open to our view; we can ponder upon its contents at leisure, and remove our hasty impressions. The latter, therefore, is more favorable to the propagation of Truth, and less liable to become converted into a pernicious engine of Design.

The Press is undeniably possessed of extensive influence upon Government, Manners, and Morals. Every exertion should, therefore, be employed to render it subservient to Liberty, Truth, and Virtue. While Society is furnished with so powerful a vehicle of Political Information, the conduct of administration will be more cautious and deliberate: it will be inspired with respect towards a Censor whose influence is universal. Ambition cannot fail to dread that vigilant guardian of Public Liberty, whose eye can penetrate, and whose voice be heard, in every quarter of the State.

It may not be considered as a whimsical speculation to remark, that the introduction of a Press particularly harmonizes with the establishment of the Representative System. That community, whose Government is administered by the wisest and most virtuous men it possesses, has certainly attained the *acme* of political perfection. When Learning was more rare and confined than it is at present, there must certainly have existed a greater aristocracy of Talents. Such, indeed, is the aristocracy which Nature and Justice will ever dictate. Eminent abilities, when united to Probity, are undoubtedly entitled to superior influence. It is the tendency of the Press to render intellectual acquirements more general. The light it diffuses will continually increase the number of accomplished individuals, and enable Society to select and distinguish Merit. The Press is, therefore, an excellent auxiliary to promote the progressive perfection of the Representative System.

It cannot be denied that the Press maintains a powerful influence over Manners and Morals. An instrument which so extensively disseminates Opinion, and which is so eminently qualified for Argument and Ridicule, cannot fail to produce a general and powerful effect. Ridicule, indeed, should never be considered as a test of Truth: but yet, it may be successfully applied in exposing Folly, and combating what may be termed the Minor Vices. Argument, however, is the most salutary and rational mean of correcting our prejudices, and establishing the empire of Truth. There is no vehicle better adapted for the circulation of reasoning, or the communication of sentiment, than the Press. There is none which is better qualified for acquiring an ascendancy over Morals and Conduct.

An instrument which is capable of becoming prostituted to so much *Mischief*, as well as rendering such important and extensive benefits (it will naturally be alledged) "should be carefully confined within the bounds of Rectitude and Virtue. While we assiduously cultivate and cherish the valuable plant, let us at the same time diligently prune its luxuriant and irregular excrescences." It would, doubtless, be desirable to controul the Licentiousness of the Press, if any means could be pursued for that purpose without endangering its Liberty.

There are two opposite extremes of Error to which the Press is liable to be perverted. The one, an interested partiality towards the Government; the other, a wanton or designing misrepresentation of its measures. In each of these cases the Press may be considered as Licentious: for the evil equally consists in a deviation from Truth. Of these evils, the former is incomparably the most formidable; because an Administration being an organized, disciplined, and powerful body, is particularly qualified to enlist in its service every Instrument that is capable of stamping a forcible impression upon the public mind. Possessed of the gifts of patronage, they have always abundant means to reward the attachment of their favorites. The candidates of preferment, that class of individuals so numerous, and so indefatigable in every community, will be constantly ready to offer the oblations of unmerited panegyric; and there will always be more to apprehend from Servility and Flattery, than from Slander or Invective.

Every departure from Truth is pernicious. Impartiality should be a perpetual attribute of the Press. Neither Fear on the one side, nor the Hope of Reward on the other, should intimidate or influence its enquiries. It should neither be bribed to lavish unmerited applause, nor menaced into silence. The usefulness of periodical publications depends upon their steady and inflexible adherence to Rectitude. The moment that corrupt or foreign considerations are suffered to bias, or to stain their pages, they become injurious to the genuine interests of Society.

Why should we examine only one side of the picture? Why this extreme solicitude to shield a Government from Licentiousness, and yet this lethargic inattention to the poison which lurks in Flattery? Is it not a real calamity when destructive Vice and Ambition become courted in the language of adulation, and their enormities varnished by the sycophantic delusions of panegyric? Is Liberty but a sounding name; and have Truth and Justice no substantial existence? Let us consider things as they are. It is proper that upon all occasions our decision should be governed by Experience. In every community in which the Press has been established, there have always been a greater number of periodical papers implicitly devoted to cabinet interests, than those which have been opposed from views extraneous to Rectitude. As far as undue influence has been engaged in the discussion of political subjects, the balance of partiality has evidently preponderated on the side of Government. If any additional check is wanting, it is for the protection of the People, and not for the preservation of Authority.

But what is the remedy proposed to correct the Licentiousness of the Press? The coercion of a Penal Code, to be applied at the discretion of the Government! Informations and criminal prosecutions, at the instance and pleasure of Public Officers! Can it be possible that there is nothing to apprehend from such vindictive and rigorous proceedings? Can the character of such restrictive system be rescued from the imputation of extreme partiality? Shall we punish for unmerited censure, and yet excuse the most false and undeserved adulation? Shall we stigmatize the man who dares to condemn, and yet protect the venal parasite who would betray his country from base and sordid views? Shall we entrench and fortify the powers of Prerogative, but remain regardless of the security of Public Liberty?

If there is any truth in the reasoning contained in the preceding Chapters, we may securely trust to the wisdom of Public Opinion for the correction of Licentiousness. It has already been maintained, that the general sentiment is the only powerful check against the encroachment of Ambition, and the only salutary guardian of the Rights of the People; that the efficacy of this sacred Preservative can only be maintained so long as its situation is independent; and that, therefore, no power whatever should be suffered to intimidate or controul it. It has also been maintained that penalties are continually liable to become an engine of oppression, and to prevent the deliberate and unembarrased formation of Public Opinion;—that a Government, founded upon the adamant of political truth, has nothing serious to apprehend from the feeble shafts of Misrepresentation;—and that the penetration of Society, continually improving in accuracy by the habit of investigation, will be a sufficient safeguard against all the evils apprehended from Licentiousness.

It is essential to examine the prominent principles of the present doctrine of Libels, in order that we may accurately appreciate the grounds upon which it is usually vindicated. Its first proposition is, that in criminal prosecutions *the tendency which all Libels have to foment animosities, and to disturb the public peace, is the sole consideration of the law;* and that it is, therefore, perfectly immaterial, with respect to the essence of a Libel, whether the matter of it be true or false—since the *provocation,* and not the *falsity,* is the thing to be punished criminally.[2]

In the first place, it is to be observed, that agreeably to such doctrine the exclusive consideration of the Law rests upon a circumstance entirely foreign to the intrinsic merits of the subject. Its sole attention is confined to the preservation of the public peace; and its principal pretext is, that the criminal coercion of Libels is indispensible to the maintainance of general tranquility. Inasmuch, therefore, as every publication which severely animadverts upon the conduct of any individual, or upon the measures of Government, whether it be founded in truth or falsehood, is presumed to have a tendency to disturb the public peace, in the eye of the Law it is equally a Libel, and its Author exposed to punishment.

Truth can never be a Libel. The system which maintains so odious a proposition, is founded in the most palpable injustice. Its obvious consequence is to render the political magistrate inviolable, and to protect him from punishment or animadversion, even for the greatest enormities. Wherever such a doctrine obtains, there is an end to Freedom and to Justice. In the most atrocious oppression that can be exercised by Government, according to such theory, there will be the greatest necessity for silence and concealment. As the most aggravated injuries to the community will be the most calculated to kindle popular resentment and indignation, a regard to public tranquility will require that every publication with respect to them should be suppressed. As the well grounded complaint will be more likely to foment disturbances than the unfolded tale of Calumny, the greater the Truth, the greater will be the Libel. If Truth is pronounced to be a Libel, can it be said that the Press possesses freedom, or that it is a check against the encroachments of Power? To maintain such doctrine, is to declare open war against Political Enquiry, entirely destroy the respon-

---

[2] Blackstone's *Commentaries.*

sibility of the Magistrate, and establish the throne of Absolute Despotism upon the ruins of Civil Liberty.

Criminal prosecutions for Libels can never be necessary to preserve the public tranquility: the coercion of Violence is abundantly sufficient for that purpose. It is requisite, indeed, that the laws should be positive and stern with regard to every act of open disorder. Nothing more can be required.—Let the punishment of every breach of the peace be severe and certain; let it be universally understood that intemperate conduct will inevitably expose the aggressor to penalty: individuals will, in such case, abstain from Violence, for the same reasons that they abstain from any other offence; and it may be pronounced, with confidence, that sufficient security is interposed for the preservation of tranquility.

Independent of its pernicious tendency in other respects, the present system of Libel is therefore unnecessary for the preservation of order in Society. It perpetually implies a want of confidence in the energy of the law, and conveys an impolitic acknowledgment of the imbecility or the insincerity of Government. It tells us that the Civil Magistrate is too impotent to suppress the ebullitions of Wrath, and must therefore act the tyrant over Truth. If a public officer has been rendered an object of sarcasm, shall it be admitted that he will be so regardless of the dignity of Character as to yield to the intemperate violence of Passion? If so, let him be punished in an exemplary manner. Suppose that a Libel has been published concerning a private individual, shall it be acknowledged that the laws are too feeble to restrain him within the bounds of moderation?

With what sentiments should we listen to a Judge, who, in a solemn and deliberate address to a Jury, should tell them, "Gentlemen, under the sacred obligation of an oath, you have pledged yourselves to try the defendant for a Libel. It is a matter of extreme indifference whether he has published Truth or Falsehood: it is enough that he has published. Although every sentence he has printed be true, still is he guilty of a crime. By your verdict you must condemn him. It is my province; and within my discretion, to fix the measure of his punishment.

"Your enquiries are altogether foreign to the jurisdiction of Justice. It is the policy of the State that even Truth herself should be punished. Her native charms; her honest simplicity, and her unspotted robes of Innocence, cannot protect her from the rigorous sentence. The public peace must be preserved. Our laws are so disgracefully imbecile and imperfect, that we cannot maintain tranquility without the sacrifice of Truth."

It would be impossible to imagine a system more hostile to morals. There is not a virtue more useful and amiable than Sincerity. It commands an incessant and inflexible adherence to Truth. It invites us to declare our opinions respecting men and manners with Candour and Fortitude. It is peculiarly favorable to the generation of excellence; because every man will be taught to feel that his character and conduct are always open to examination, and that he will not be enabled to acquire a greater degree of esteem than he in reality deserves. There will ever exist a certain proportion of Vice, which cannot be reached by the interposition of the ordinary Judicature: for the suppression of that we must exclusively depend upon the public Censorship. What then shall we say of the system which protects such Vice by the face of inviolability, or conceals it under the mask of hypocrisy? What will be the character of that Society in which the ingenuousness of Truth, and the manly openness of Sincerity, are never to be discovered, and where every man is compelled to conceal his sentiments respecting his neighbour under the most impenetrable disguise?

Another prominent principle of the present doctrine concerning Libels, is, that "the Liberty of the Press entirely consists in laying no previous restraints upon publications, and not in freedom from Censure for Criminal matter when published." This definition, of which the principal force consists in its excluding the idea of a previous *imprimatur,* is true as far as it extends; but it is extremely imperfect. Of what use is the liberty of doing that for which I am punishable afterwards? In the same sense it may be said that I have the liberty to perpetrate felony or murder, if I think proper to expose myself to the penalties annexed to those crimes. In ascertaining the rights I possess, it is not to be enquired what I may do, and be punished; but what I am entitled to perform without being subjected to punishment. The preceding explanation of the legal Liberty of the Press is fallacious in the extreme. It amounts to nothing definite. It cannot be said that any Liberty of the Press is established by law, unless the publication of Truth is expressly sanctioned, and it is particularly ascertained what species of writings shall be comprehended under the title of Libels.

It is far from being maintained that Slander should be suffered to exist with impunity. On the contrary, it is admitted, that rational and judicious measures should be taken to deprive it of its sting. But it is contended, that private prosecutions, at the suit of the injured party, are sufficient to answer every beneficial purpose, and will entirely supercede the necessity of criminal coercion.

To criminal prosecutions for Libels there will always exist the most serious objections. They are invariably more formidable than the evil they are intended to prevent. As a security to a virtuous administration, they can never be necessary. In the hands of a vicious minister, they will be prostituted to the most pernicious purposes.

In such prosecutions the defendant must seldom expect the benefit of a fair and impartial trial by Jury. In seasons which require the most unshaken constancy and fortitude, there will always be the most to apprehend from the servility or the tyranny of Judges. When Ambition and Hypocrisy become seated in the cabinet, they will generally have the address to

select a LAUD to profane the pulpit, and a JEFFERIES to prostitute the independence of the bench. If it is the wish of Government that the accused should be condemned, it is not to be
expected that such inclination should become resisted. The
Judiciary will possess a common spirit with the Executive; and
by every undue method endeavour to mislead, or to intimidate
the Jury. It is seldom, indeed, in such cases, that the real merits
of the question are determined by the latter. Notwithstanding
it is true that Juries have the constitutional right of returning a
general verdict (that is to decide as well upon the *law* as the
facts which relate to the trial) this right is generally discour-
aged by Courts, and seldom exercised by Jurors. In the prosecutions for Libels it is held to be the province of the Jury to
ascertain the fact of publication, and that of the Court to determine whether such publication is libellous or not. Now it
rarely happens that the fact of publishing will admit of dispute: the substantial enquiry is confined to the criminal contents of the writing. The consequence of such doctrine is,
therefore, in effect to deprive the defendant of a trial by Jury,
and subject him to the sole decision of the Judge: for as the
real merits of the cause, and the principal question to be determined, respects the interpretation of the publication, the
Court, and not the Jury, is in reality the Tribunal which pro-
nounces upon the subject, and decrees the punishment to be
inflicted.

Civil prosecutions, at the suit of injured individuals, are a
sufficient restraint upon the licentiousness of the Press. As in
such prosecutions it is left to the Jury to ascertain the damages
sustained, while they afford a real compensation for the injury,
they are much less likely to be rendered a dangerous weapon
in the hands of a prevailing party, or an aspiring administration. Such forum is, therefore, abundantly sufficient to answer
every valuable purpose. It is competent to inflict a sufficient
punishment upon the malignant Slanderer, and to afford an

adequate satisfaction to him who has been unjustly stigmatized. But suppose that an Officer of Government has been an object of malevolence; what difference should that circumstance occasion? Undoubtedly none. Let the Officer be placed upon the same footing with a private individual. The character of every man should be deemed equally sacred, and of consequence entitled to equal remedy. The punishment will be uniform, and the motives to abstain from aspersion will be the same in both cases. An impartial Jury of Citizens are as competent to decide upon the provocation which has been given, and the retribution it demands, as the most arbitrary tribunal; and the injured individual, whether he fills a public, or is confined to a private station, will have as little incentive to acts of turbulent aggression as if his wrongs were redressed by the terrors of a Starchamber, or the barbarity of an Inquisition.

As far as the interests of Government, in its collective capacity are concerned, it has been a principal object of this work to prove, that no necessity can exist for the criminal suppression of Libel. It is impossible that State prosecutions should not be dangerous to the Liberty of the Press; while, on the other hand, the penetration which is justly to be ascribed to Public Opinion, will always be a sufficient preservative of the powers of the Civil Magistrate.

It is forcibly observed in the works of Lord LYTTLETON, that "in a free country the Press may be very useful as long as it is under no partial restraint: for it is of great consequence that the people should be informed of every thing that concerns them; and, without printing, such knowledge could not circulate either so easily or so fast.

"To argue against any branch of Liberty from the ill use that may be made of it, is to argue against Liberty itself, since all is capable of being abused. Nor can any part of Freedom be more important, or better worth contending for, than that by which the spirit of it is *preserved, supported,* and *diffused.* By

this appeal to the judgment of the people, we lay some restraint upon those ministers who may have found means to
secure themselves from any other *less incorruptible tribunal;*
and sure they have no reason to complain if the public exercises a right which cannot be denied without avowing that
their conduct will not bear enquiry. For though the best Administration may be attached by Calumny, I can hardly believe
it would be hurt by it: because I have known a great deal of it
employed to very little purpose against gentlemen in opposition to ministers, who had nothing to defend them but the
force of Truth."

The licentiousness of the Press has of late become a theme
of fashionable invective: but those who have been most clamor-
ous in their philippics, have in general been most hostile to its
liberty. The Press is undoubtedly a powerful instrument; and,
when left to itself, its natural direction will be towards Truth
and Virtue. It is by no means surprising that Ambition should
always be jealous of so formidable and discerning an Opponent. Under Arbitrary Governments it is a practice to prohibit
every publication that has not been previously perused and
sanctioned by some of its officers. By this means every writing,
which is friendly to the spirit of freedom, is suppressed; and
nothing can appear but what is on the side of Government.
By such regulations it is obvious that the Press, instead of
being a guardian of Public Liberty, is rendered a dangerous
and servile slave to Despotism. In such case (continues Lord
LYTTELTON) there should be "An Inspector for the People as
well as one for the Court. But if nothing is to be licensed on
the one side, and everything on the other, it would be vastly
better for us to adopt the Eastern policy, and allow no printing at all, than to leave it under such a partial direction."

It should ever be remembered that the present system of
Libel, is the offspring of a Monarchy. However it may correspond with hereditary establishments, and the existence of

privileged orders, the dangerous exotic can never be reconciled to the genius and constitution of a Representative Commonwealth. . . .

30. JOHN THOMSON URGES UNFETTERED FREEDOM FOR ALL HUMAN OPINIONS

On the day that Jefferson was first inaugurated as President, a slim book of considerable originality was published in New York by John Thomson. Thomson's identity is obscure, but his book is illuminating. It represented the same viewpoint as Wortman's, had the same philosophical spirit, and inevitably duplicated Wortman's book in many respects, but it contained two added arguments that were unjaded. In the first of these, Thomson contended that the guarantee of freedom of speech and press meant that citizens should have the same unlimited expression possessed by their representatives. Others had discoursed on the relation between unfettered discussion and a representative system of government, but only Hay had drawn the conclusion that Thomson now buttressed with a reasoned argument. Thomson's second unusual thesis, no less thoroughgoing in its implications than the first, was far more subtle, and was in fact the most interesting in the entire libertarian armory. In essence, it stated that opinion should not be punished because it is involuntary. Thomson, in effect, borrowing from Locke and Jefferson, suggested a psychology of freedom, to support the overt-acts test, that would immunize opinion from prosecution. Unlike Jefferson, Thomson would have extended that test to political as well as religious opinions.

CHAPTER I.

The invention of Printing is universally allowed to have been of the first importance to the interests of mankind. All allow it to have been a blessing; but not a few have been bold enough to assert, that like many other blessings it has been abused: and the licentiousness of the Press, has, by certain descriptions of men, been loudly complained of. Mankind have, however, differed in opinion regarding the extent, as well as existance of this evil. By some it has been asserted, that if no checks were imposed upon the Press, its licentiousness would harrow up every root, and tear assunder with savage fury, every bond of human Society. Others however have denied the possibility of any such formidable evil, and treated these consequences as mere chimeras. Surely upon a subject where opinions are so diametrically opposite, a short enquiry into the merit of each cannot be deemed unimportant.

It is not a little remarkable that the opponents to the Liberty of the Press, have always been found among the members of Government interested in the duration of its abuses, or of those whose actions in private life will not bear the scrutinizing eye of moral enquiry. Knowing that free enquiry would to them be extremely fatal, they wished to oppose, if possible, an insurmountable barrier to the progress of thought, and stifle the expression of public opinion; afraid, or ashamed to have their actions canvassed by their fellow men, they dreaded appearing before the bar of public opinion.

An individual who is conscious of the rectitude of his conduct;—who is satisfied of the purity of his motives; who has no other object in view but the promotion of justice, and the consequent advantage of the human race: such a character can never be afraid of public or private animadversion. As truth is his sole aim, and as man is so liable to error, or mistake, he will rather court than shun an investigation of his motives, conduct, and opinions. The more public this investigation is,

---

John Thomson, *An Enquiry, Concerning the Liberty, and Licentiousness of the Press, and the Uncontroulable Nature of the Human Mind* (New York: Johnson and Stryker, 1801), pp. 5–22, 55–69, and 74–84.

the better, as he will either be corrected himself, or may by his reply correct those of a different opinion. If attacked in his private character, he has nothing to fear from the malignant shafts of envy or malice. In this case, let the accuser put his name to the accusation, and if *false*, it will be easily detected: if *true*, it cannot be too soon known. The reasoning between the actions of individuals and governments, hold good in a variety of instances; and in none more than in this. The actions of both ought to be just, and from investigation they have nothing to fear. The virtuous part of the community will always rally around the standard of truth; while the followers of vice will be few in number, as well as deficient in abilities. Reasoning, in this manner, I have no hesitation in asserting—that the Licentiousness of the Press, is a term destitute of any meaning; or, if it ever exists, like anarchy it carries the seeds of its immediate destruction along with it.

I have seen a variety of attempts to define wherein the Licentiousness of the Press consists. As before observed, they have uniformly proceeded from men who evidently wished nobody to enjoy the Liberty of the Press, but such as were of their opinion. Why will not these men allow the same liberty to others which they claim for themselves? Who conferred upon them the authority to say unto those who differ from them in opinion; "Hitherto shalt thou go and no farther; and here shall the progress of thy thoughts be stayed." Nature never conferred such a right; and reason, justice, and the uncontrolable freedom of thought forbid it. . . .

. . . We detest the Tyranny of the Grand Seignior and other eastern Tyrants, who prohibit printing altogether in their dominions. We pretend to view with a degree of commiseration the fate of those European countries who never enjoyed the inestimable right of speaking and publishing their opinions; or, who once having had this right, are now either totally, or almost altogether divested of it. If then, thinking and feeling in this manner, we do not guard with the most vigilant care this most important right, we shall be deficient, not only to our own interest and liberty, but also to that of our posterity; who may when it is too late, curse the memories of us their ancestors. If we allow our terrors or prejudices so far to conquer our reason as again silently to acquiesce in the renewal of the Sedition Law; or tacitly give our consent to any abridgment of the Liberty of the Press. This is the palladium of freedom, which if once destroyed, Liberty is no more.

I think I hear some worthy but mistaken individuals exclaim, "Why all this declamation? we wish not to destroy the Liberty of the Press, we only wish to correct and suppress its licentiousness. By this the barriers of liberty will be strengthened." True, they will be strengthened, but it will be a fortification from which her sons will be forever shut out; unless they storm it at the expence of oceans of human blood.

"All Nature's difference, is all Nature's peace."

And as in the natural, so in the moral world. Vain would be the task of him who should attempt to make all mankind of one opinion. Why then dare to attempt a thing which God has thought fit to render impossible? We wish no such thing, many will reply, but there are some opinions the publication of which, would be dangerous to the peace and good order of society, therefore it must be prohibited. This is the licentiousness of the Press; and this prohibition is consistent with its real liberty. Well, allow it. But where are the criterions by which you are to define this licentiousness of the Press? Produce those universal and infallible rules by which we may always know this dangerous evil, an evil fraught with such a horrid train of consequences. Let us make an appeal to the opinions of mankind in various nations. Let us see how they agree in their definitions; and we shall find them as different as their manners, customs, and languages.

Ask a native of the British dominions what is the licentiousness of the press? He will tell you (if he answers with candor) it is scrutinizing the actions of government, daring to speak differently from those in administration, presuming to say a reform in Parliament is necessary, that a republican government is preferable to a monarchical; or, having the still greater temerity to say, that the king can, may, or has done wrong.

Request a French Republican to inform you what are his ideas upon the subject? He will reply, it is advocating the cause of royalty and aristocracy; preaching up federalism; daring to call Buonaparte an usurper, or the government (what it really is) a military despotism.

Desire a Spaniard or Portuguese to answer the same question: They will tell you it is presuming to say any thing against the king, nobility, clergy, or any who are in authority; daring to express your opinions upon religious matters in public, if they differ from holy mother church!

Enquire of a Mussulman, he will tell you there is no such thing as opinion to be exercised, except by the Grand Seignior or Mufti; that all things are predestinated in the book of fate, and it is the duty of the followers of the great prophet to adore in silence, and bow down to the mortal who sends a mute with a bow string to strangle whomsoever he pleaseth.

Lastly.—Ask an Aborigine of this country to give you his opinion concerning speech and thought. If he comprehends your meaning, he will tell you to think what you please, and speak what you think.

Which of these would you choose to be regulated by in your correcting the licentiousness of the press? I believe you neither would take the Spaniard, Portuguese nor Turk. The inquisition of the *first*, and the bow string of the *last*, would soon convince you of the error of your choice. If you be a good Republican, you will hardly admire the British doctrine of royal infallibility, or the justice of about a fortieth part of the people only being represented in the Legislature; while the majority must submit to laws they never consented to: If they express their opinions of such an absurdity, and endeavour to get the evil remedied, they must run the risk of ministerial vengeance; of being hanged, drawn and quartered; or taking a voyage to Botany Bay, in company with convicts of the most abandoned characters. Will you not, if you are a man of candour, rather approve of the opinion of the "untutored Indian." Is it not founded upon justice, and the nature of man? "Yes, but we must not allow any publication to be circulated, or opinions promulgated, which may tend to alienate the affections of the people from the government of their own choice. A liberty such as this, can never be allowed in any government." Let us then investigate this opinion with that freedom with which free men should; and that temper which an enquiry after truth deserves. Open to conviction, and having no end to gain but the advancement of justice and truth, I shall not shrink from an investigation of my opinion. If instead of the weapons of reason, the force of authority be made use of against me, I must, like the Turk, submit (though not with silence) for such a mode of argumentation is not the most likely to convince.

CHAPTER II.

Seeing the task is so difficult to ascertain what the Licentiousness of the Press is, let us proceed in our enquiry concerning its liberty. I have often heard that definitions upon abstract principles were both difficult and dangerous. Difficult, because as they do not in their nature admit of occular mathematical demonstration; therefore, they never can be proved in such a manner as to acquire universal consent. Dangerous, because if not radically right, they may be apt to mislead numbers of those who are incapable of understanding abstract reasoning; and therefore, taking them upon trust, look upon them as incontrovertable. Notwithstanding these difficulties, I shall here attempt a definition of what I mean by the liberty of the press; simplified in such a manner as to be easily understood. The definition is this:

All men are endowed, by nature, with the power of thinking; yet have they no controul over their thoughts. As no individual can prevent the operation of this principle within himself, much less can he direct those of any other person. If this is the case with one individual, it must be so with all; therefore, no association of men, however numerous or respectable, can ever have a right to say you shall not think this, or you shall think that: this being a power which does not exist among mankind. Consequently it must follow, that men should be allowed to express those thoughts, with the same freedom that they arise. In other words—speak, or publish, whatever you believe to be *truth*.

Let us now examine the subject agreeable to this definition.

Man, when he comes into the world, is not conscious of his own existence. Mind he has not; or if he has, it is of no use to him. It is a total blank. Destitute of thought or ideas, he will grasp at a thing that may be hurtful to him, with the same eagerness as at that which will give him pleasure. Man then, must be the creature of education. His mind is like a sheet of blank paper, upon which you may write whatever you please. Now as *thought* is nothing more than the operations of the *mind*, it must at first be excited by outward objects. These first efforts of the mind, are, however, extremely imperfect; nor is it for a considerable time that they acquire a regular form. As the child advances, every object around him is new; and he begins to distinguish between what gives him pleasure, and that which occasions pain. The mind thus set in motion, continues its operations; and as the objects are still encreasing in number, so in proportion does his ideas expand. He begins to compare and combine, but is frequently mistaken in his conclusions, and is compelled to resort to those who are older, for assistance. He probably receives the advice and instruction of his elders at first, without examination, believing them to be true. If, however, he should find that his tutors have been mistaken, and that they told him something which he found not to be true, a more minute examination takes place, and he receives with greater caution any information in a similar manner. Hence children ought always to be told the truth; for, if they find themselves deceived, their education is injured, and their moral principles may receive a dangerous contamination.

Thus the human mind progresses; but though this be its general progress, yet there are a variety of circumstances always occur to prove, that even in this early stage of life, the mind of man is of that subtile nature, as not to be under human controul.

One child prefers a drum, his brother prefers something else. Neither of them are capable of assigning at this age any other reason, than that it pleases them. As they advance in life, they adopt different opinions; and this they can no more help, than they could preferring different play things.

Nevertheless, it is chiefly education which determines the human character; and perhaps this difference in the opinions of childhood, might be traced to this origin, were we sufficiently acquainted with all the previous circumstances thereupon attendant. In either case, it will equally serve to illustrate the subject of our present enquiry, because it shews the natural propensity of mankind to differ in opinion. So much may serve to shew the first operations of the human mind. Let us now examine the second article of the definition, viz. *That man has no controul over his own thoughts.*

From comparing this with the first part of the definition, it has a paradoxical appearance. Perhaps, however, it may upon examination be found true.

All the actions of men proceed from the operations of the mind. Pleasure and pain are the immediate determining motives. A boy is told by his father that he must not eat any unripe fruit, because it will injure his health. He has, however, frequently seen other children eat of it; and he has not been able to perceive that it hurt them; or, if he has, he has seen others that it did not hurt. In either case, if the acid taste of this fruit should be agreeable to his palate, he will in all probability eat it if he can get it. What determines him in this case? It is because the idea of *pleasure*, predominates over the idea of *pain;* and that for this reason, the pleasure is *immediate,* the pain is to *come;* and he conceives there is a chance of avoiding it. If his determination is opposite, then the idea of *pain,* predominates over that of *pleasure*. In either case, though his mind be the active agent; it is purely passive with regard to the final determination. That is, whatever for the time being is most predominant, will determine the mind for or against the action.

The case is the same throughout every stage of our existence. A proposition is proposed to two men; they view it in opposite lights; their determinations are diametrically the reverse of each other, yet each believes his own to be most agreeable to reason. This arises entirely from the different point of view in which it appears to them. And, it follows of course, that neither party has any controul over his own thought; on the contrary, it is his thought which controuls him.

Reasoning upon this theory of the human mind, a very slight examination of the subject will serve to establish my proposition.

It has been observed by some philosophers, that no two objects in nature, were ever, or can be exactly alike. Whether this be really the case or not, I shall not at this time enquire. Upon the foregoing grounds, however, I will venture to affirm —that no object whatever, whether mental, or corporeal; ever did, or can appear in the exact same point of view, to any two individuals. In a variety of cases, both may agree in their general approbation, or disapprobation; but if their motives are thoroughly examined, they will in some shape or other be found to differ, notwithstanding their final conclusion may agree. Hence arises that vast variety of opinions which exist in the world upon every art and science, as well as upon the actions of mankind, whether public or private. Were the case otherwise, we should see mankind agreeing in every opinion;

and no sooner should a new idea be started upon any subject, than its truth would be universally acknowledged, or its falsehood immediately detected. But is this the case? On the contrary, Is not the very reverse true? Men of science have differed, and still differ in many of their opinions; and it is to this very difference, that mankind are indebted for those discussions which have from time to time agitated the scientific world, and to which are justly to be ascribed, the gratitude of mankind for the superlative scientific advantages they now enjoy. No danger is ever apprehended from discussions of this kind; and if the same unrestrained freedom were permitted in political and all other investigations, the same beneficial effects would follow. If all political opinions, and discussions upon those opinions had been thus viewed, then neither sedition nor alien laws would ever have disgraced the American code.

Government then ought no more to interfere with the discussion of politics, than with that of any other art or science. Were this maxim adopted, all such discussions would be equally harmless. As man individually has no controul over his own mind, so it must follow of course, that he never could have delegated that to a government, which he did not himself possess. As well might I say to my neighbour, I will give you a million of dollars, when I have not a cent in the world. It is like the poor maniac in bedlam, who believing himself to be the Pope, granted pardons and indulgencies; and gave away empires, kingdoms and provinces every day, while he himself was confined to a cell and straw with bread and water.

But who are the government? Are they not men like ourselves, subject to the same passions, liable to the same errors, and whose minds must go through all the mechanical progress of our own? If then they are not in this respect superior to their fellow men; and if their constituents possess no power over their own individual mind; if they of course cannot give that power to the members of government; by what right moral or divine, abstract, or positive, can government exert such a power over their fellow citizens? Surely that government which imposes, or attempts to impose, restrictions upon the expression of sentiment, or interferes in the direction of opinion; such men exercise a power they never received, and which from the nature of things they never could receive. They attempt to exert an authority over the minds of the community, and yet they possess no such power over their own. . . .

CHAPTER III.

If such be the construction of the human mind; if such is its uncontroulable nature even to the individual himself, the absurdity of others directing its operations will doubtless be admitted: Governments can then have no such right, if they had it, it would be extremely injurious to their interests; for, if it be admitted that free discussion has been of advantage to other sciences; then why may it not be of equal advantage to the science of politics? The most violent advocate for the sedition law will surely acknowledge, that had it not been for *discussion,* these States had never been in a situation to have asserted and gained their independence. Had it not been for *discussion,* the Federal Government never would have existed. Certain it is, that the convention who framed this instrument, either were, or appeared to be, fully impressed with the importance of unrestrained discussion.

In the first article, and sixth section of the constitution are these words:—"And for any *speech* or *debate* in either house they shall not be questioned in *any other place.*" Thus have our Legislators secured to themselves the right of free discussion in their legislative capacities, and the people of the United States have guarantee'd this right by their acceptance of the Constitution. If then those men are at liberty to say what they please in Congress, why should they abridge this right in the people? By what principle of justice or equity is it that the people ought to submit to such restrictions as have been imposed upon them by the late Sedition law? Why should they who are the *servants* or *agents* of the people; who are paid by the people for their services, why ought they to impose restrictions upon the thoughts, words, or writings of their sovreign? That power who has created them, and can by a fiat of its will, reduce them again to the level of private citizens. If free discussion be advantageous to them, it must be equally so to the people. Without this right being exercised in the unlimitted manner secured by the Constitution, the two houses of Congress could not exercise the functions of a Legislative body; and without it is enjoyed by the people in the same way, ignorance and despotism would soon be the inevitable consequence. For, if it be necessary for the one, it is equally necessary for both. The words of the Constitution before quoted, proves this position. It is founded upon the very natural and just supposition, that among such a number of individuals, a great variety of opposite opinions must occur. It also presupposes that the *people* would pass their judgment upon the proceedings of Congress. As in passing judgment upon what they said in the course of debate, something might occur tending to displease either *states or individuals,* it was proper to guard the members of Congress against any other judgment than that of reason, and public opinion. If such be the necessity of the case to the government, (as before observed,) it is equally so to the people; and it is a fair deduction to suppose it was contemplated that the same right of free discussion should be guarantee'd to the people, in as much as it is expressly said in the twelfth article of the amendments to the Constitution, that "The powers not delegated to the United States by the Constitution, nor prohibited by it to the States, are reserved to the States respectively, or to the people." No article of the Constitution ever abridged this right in the people, and so far from being delegated, it is expressly secured to them by the third article of the amendments.

I am aware that part, if not the whole of the above reasoning may be controverted, and a conclusion directly opposite may be attempted to be drawn. It may be said, and it has been said, that this very clause in the Constitution was intended to protect members of Congress from all animadversions upon their conduct, through the medium of either speech or press. The days of terror to the honest republican it is hoped now are past; and political delusion is near its end. Such an argument will never be made use of by any, except those who may prefer sophistry to reason. It is evident both from the *words* and *spirit* of the constitution, that the members should not be prosecuted before any court or tribunal for an opinion delivered in the course of debate. It never could mean that the people in their individual capacity were not to exercise their judgment; neither could it have been intended to prevent the free operation of that judgment either by *speech* or *press.* The article in the amendments to the Constitution, which was *intended to secure* the Liberty of Speech and Press, shews it was understood in this way, by Congress themselves, as well as by the State Legislatures who ratified those articles. Even the British Parliament, who claim the proud title of omnipotence, never claimed an exemption of this kind from public censure. Pit, Dundass, and all the other members of the British administration, daily see their actions and speeches animadverted upon with great freedom, and sometimes even with severity.

Government is ostensibly for the benefit of the *governed;* not of the governors. That the reverse has often been true, does not overthrow the truth of the general position. The government of the United States is founded upon the acknowledgement of the people, being the sole, and only fountain from which all their power and authority are derived. It is the creature of the people; the people are not the creatures of its will. The Executive and Legislative, both are from the same source. If so, is it not then absurd in this government to say unto the people—"You shall not think this, or that upon certain subjects; or if you do, it is at your peril. We shall certainly punish you for such conduct. It is true, the freedom of Speech and Liberty of the Press are secured to you by the Constitution, but it is *us*, who are to determine how far this is to be exercised. If we find you too bold in your language, or too free in your enquiries concerning our conduct, we will shew you that we have *power*, and it shall be exerted."

In any government which pretends to be actuated by the principles of justice or liberty, such language would be absurd. What then shall we say of the government of the United States; that government which owes its origin and its existence to the voice of the people, if such language is made use of by them? What is the amount of the late Sedition law? It is this. "You citizens of the United States, shall believe that all we do is right; if not, you shall be fined, and imprisoned. Your understanding we despise; argument we will not bestow upon you; coercion shall convince you." This is surely the language of despotism, not of reason. . . .

CHAPTER VII.

. . . From what has been said . . . it appears, 1st. That the government of the United States being a delegation from the people; no power over the operations of the mind, or controul of public opinion could be delegated to them. Were such a thing possible, it would be a ridiculous absurdity. As well might I say unto my neighbour, "I will confer Almighty power upon you; you shall guide and direct all the operations of my mind, and every thought shall be regulated as you please."

2d. We have seen that governments are bound, or at least pretend to be regulated by *Constitutions;* and that the United States have a legitimate and authentic instrument which bears that name. The dangerous nature of precedent has been pointed out, and the encroachments upon natural rights under the British government have been traced to this source. Its violation of moral principle, has also been noticed, particularly in the British doctrine of libel; where *truth* is not only punished as a *crime*, but it is even daringly asserted that the libel is aggravated by being *true*. The violation of the Directorial Constitution of France has been exposed. It has been shewn, that these oppressions also, went upon the principle of government having a right to direct the public opinion; the absurdity and injustice of which, I hope is also evident.

3d. We have also found, that justice being universal, and immutable, must be of equal obligation upon the governors, as upon the governed. Consequently, moral evil, never can be political good.

4th. It has been shewn, that the legal governors or magistrates of a country, are the people's *servants*, and that it is only by *usurpation* they can ever become *masters*. The governments of Venice and Holland, have been cited as warning examples to the citizens of the United States, to guard with unceasing vigilance the actions of their public servants; lest as in those countries, the servants should become masters.

The first deduction which offers itself from those reasonings is, that in no case whatever, can government have a right to interfere in the direction of public opinion. The next deduction is, that if government does interfere, it saps the foundations of morality. And lastly, that it is the interest, as well as duty of the people to prevent, or check such attempts in the government; otherwise their liberty, their happiness; nay, all that they hold dear to them as rational beings, is in danger of being wrested from them.

CHAPTER VIII.

The enormities committed during the revolutionary fervour of the French, have been loudly reprobated, by the enemies of all reformation; and they have even been deplored by the friends to the liberties of mankind. Actions have certainly taken place, which cannot upon any principle of justice be defended. No doubt also, but many of those occurrences have been exaggerated. It is not a little remarkable, that all who have written concerning the massacres and executions of that nation, seem to have forgotten the cause from which they originated; or, if they did not, they have used every artifice to conceal it.

Far be it from me to take the opposite extreme; and to attempt a defence of that which is indefensible. It ought however to be remembered; that *"oppression makes a wise man mad."* If it sometimes has this effect upon an individual, it may also operate upon any given number of the human species.

At all events, violent revolutions are to be dreaded. When once the usual bonds of human society are broken, bad men are always in readiness to exercise their pernicious talents. It is true, that anarchy cannot long subsist, as it carries the seeds of its immediate destruction along with it; but the effects may long be felt, after the cause has ceased to exist. Violent revolutions are like the destructive tornado, which alike overturns the cottage and the palace; which overwhelms all within its vortex in indiscriminate dismay and destruction. If such be their nature and tendency; how ought they to be guarded against?

One of the most prominent forerunners of violent revolution, is a total suppression of the Liberty of Speech and Press; the Government usurping the sole direction of public opinion. This is dangerous in every kind of Government; but more preposterous, as well as more dangerous in a republican country, than in any other. If in a democratic republic, the people are prevented from a free investigation of the actions of their public servants, it will inevitably be productive of the following effects.

Either it will drive the people into immediate acts of violence against the Government; or, if they silently submit, it will ultimately deprive the people of that free energy of thought, word, and action, which the consciousness of liberty and independence never fail to inspire. The Government will then cease to direct the public concerns of free men; and they will rule over a nation of degraded slaves. Both of these events ought to be equally dreaded by the good politician; because both, in the end, must terminate in violent and tumultuous revolution.

Though it be true, as has been observed by Locke, that—"There remains still inherent in the people, a supreme power to remove or alter the legislature, when they find the legislative act contrary to the trust reposed in them; for, when such trust is abused, it is thereby forfeited, and devolves to those who give it:" I say, though this be true, the principle is always to be applied with caution. If this advice is due to the people; another piece of advice is also due to the Government; that is, *to avoid every thing which may occasion the necessity of its being resorted to.* The Freedom of Speech and Press ought in particular to remain inviolate and sacred. The language of Government should be, "Observe my conduct; you do well. Report it as widely as possible, provided you report it fairly; you are entitled to commendation. But the heart of man unavoidably revolts against the attempt to correct my error by the infliction of violence."

Here however I shall beg leave to differ in one point from this respectable author. He says, "Report it as widely as possible, provided *you report it fairly.*" Now a thing may be reported which is not really *true,* and yet it may be *fairly reported,* from the information the person has received; therefore report it as you believe it to be. No one can have a *right* to report a *falsehood,* but he may be himself deceived, by believing his information to be true. If he never reports this, he continues in error; but by giving it publicity, he stands the chance of being undeceived.

A free promulgation of facts and opinions, would soon be perceived to be the strongest preservative against violent revolutions. It would be doubly advantageous to the interests of a Republican Government. That Government which the people have chosen, may fairly be supposed the constant object of their solicitude and care. It can hardly be imagined, that the people will fail in a due respect for the administrators of their own Government, so long as they act with propriety, justice, and according to the Constitution. The members of such a Government are only elected for a particular period. They should then avoid all measures of a selfish or temporizing nature. If such laws be made to shield themselves from animadversion, they ought to recollect, that parties and power may change hands. In this case, they might repent the having sanctioned laws restricting the Freedom of Speech and Press. Again, do the members of a Republican Government wish to have the spontaneous approbation of their fellow citizens, or do they wish to hear the sycophantic adulation of slaves? If the *first* be their wish, they will not restrict the free expression of the public sentiment. If the *last* be what they are desirous of; it may indeed flatter the vanity of ignorant tyrants; but it ought to be remembered—that they preclude themselves from knowing their friends from their enemies. I certainly should not have told Dionysius the tyrant, that I thought him a detestable monster, because it is probable I should have lost my life. My opinion however must have been unchanged.

The disinterested legislator will always be friendly to the cause of virtue. He will know, that virtue and republicanism must rise or fall together. No people ever were ripe for despotism, until they were completely corrupted. It was the case with Greece, when the Romans overpowered it. It was the case with the Romans, when Caesar became their master. The real friends of the Government of the United States, will then do every thing in their power to promote and encourage virtue among the people. This, and this alone, will give the Government stability; and prevent the dread, or necessity of violent revolution; that is, if the Government are also virtuous.

If this principle be acknowledged, how cautious ought Governments to be in enacting laws which may in their operation tend to destroy virtue among the people? Whatever in the smallest degree, tends to the injury of morality, should both by individuals and Governments be avoided. Hence any thing which may occasion the multiplication of *fictitious signatures, oaths* or *tests, spies* or *informers,* ought to be guarded against with the most studious care.

Fictitious signatures are of no importance when attached to any other kind of publications, than those where public or private individuals are charged with improprieties. They are however totally owing to the checks which have been from time to time imposed upon the free expression of public opinion. Consequently they engender pusilanimity, insincerity and anonimous assassination of character. Sedition laws will always increase this evil. Teach men the necessity of only speaking truth. Shew them that they may do it without fear, and this evil so frequently, and sometimes justly complained of, will cease to exist. If the malicious slanderer still retreat behind this mysterious veil, let his publications be treated with that contempt they so justly deserve. Contemptuous silence will soon impress him sufficiently with an idea of his own littleness. On the contrary, the man who has nothing to relate but what he believes to be truth; why should he conceal his name? He may be mistaken, he may be misinformed, he may have drawn erronious conclusions; if he has, he may be set right; and like an honest man, let him acknowledge his error.

In order to carry sedition laws fully into effect, *spies* and *informers* must be made use of; nay, they must be encouraged. Wherever such wretches exist, and where they are employed by the hopes of pecuniary reward, liberty cannot live. The confidence of friendship, the inviolability of domestic conversation, and the unguarded effusions of the moments of hilarity; all become so many snares for the honest and unsuspecting citizen. As for the cautious villain, he is on his guard, and will always be certain to escape. That such wretches are to be found in all countries, is not more disgraceful to human nature, than it is true. The Governments who are so degraded as to employ people of this description, are sunk low indeed. They become dishonoured by a certain degree of intimacy and familiarity, with which they are obliged to treat them. Such Governments as have so far forgot their dignity as to employ spies, have always found themselves in this degraded situation; and as soon as possible have shaken them off. Instances are even upon record, where the informer and spy has paid the forfeit of his crimes, at the expence of his life; and that even by the sentence of that Government he had served. Watt, who was hanged and beheaded at Edinburgh for high treason, on the 15th October 1794, is an instance of this kind. He had been employed as a political spy, by the Lord Advocate of Scotland, at the desire of Henry Dundass secretary of state. Upon his trial, he subpoenaed the Lord Advocate as an exculpatory evidence. It then appeared upon his examination, that he had been in the habit of receiving intelligence from Watt; and that at one time he had paid him *thirty pounds sterling* for a piece of information. It also further appeared, that it was about the *price*, that they finally differed. Watt demanded a *thousand pounds sterling* for discovering that plot, of which he himself was the chief promoter. The sum was refused, his house was searched, the pretended plot was discovered, and he fell under the vengeance of Government, unpitied by all parties. May this forever be a warning to such characters, and teach them the necessity of honesty!

Such being the case, it must be evident, that laws which require such means to carry them into effect, must be extremely uncertain in their operations, as well as the punishments frequently unjust. He who can descend so low, will hardly boggle at a false oath. Few will be ambitious of such an employment, excepting such as are of the most abandoned characters; lost to every sense of honesty and honour. Perhaps a few individuals might be found in any country, who might undertake such an employment, from mistaken notions of patriotism. If such are to be found, they that moment cease to be *patriots,* and become *spies.* Wherever they are known, their company and conversation will be avoided, and they will be despised and detested. Even in *war,* where *spies* are so frequently made use of, and where the office is thought the most excusable; even there they are but *half trusted* by their employers. As for *traitors* to the cause they have espoused; the fate of an Arnold and a Dumourier are sufficient examples of the light in which such characters are beheld—of the way in which they may expect to be treated, even by those they have served. The *one* never respected, nor entrusted with any *important* command; the *other* despised and detested—driven from country to country, a wandering vagabond; refused permission to reside in the territories of those very princes whose cause he had served.

In most cases the same fate will almost inevitably follow *spies* and *informers,* when the ends for which they were employed are attained. He who to serve me, has deceived another, how am I sure but he may deceive me? If such is the fate of those characters from their employers, how must they be despised and detested by their fellow-citizens? "We disapprove of the superior, however well informed he may be, who undertakes by chastisement to induce me to alter my opinion or vary in my choice; but we disapprove still more, *and we do well,* of the man who officiates as the Argus of my tyrant, who reports my conduct, not for the purpose of encreasing my wisdom and prudence, not for the purpose of instructing others, but that he may bring down upon me the brute, the slavish and exasperating arm of power."

Oaths and *tests* are another inevitable consequence of Sedition laws. They are in all cases whatever, of the utmost injury to truth, the only foundation of all morality. To this source may be justly attributed, the prevalence of falsehood and insincerity amongst every class of society. Among the less informed part of mankind, it is most notoriously so. How often do we hear from such, when charged with having related a falsehood, —"Why sure you know I was not upon oath:" or, "I did not *swear* it was true." What sort of morality is this? How contrary to the spirit of the gospel, and the strict and positive command of Jesus Christ? "I say unto you, *swear not at all*, but let your yea be yea, and your nay, nay." He knew the pernicious tendency of oaths, and therefore prohibited his followers from making use of them. I know the generality of christians say, that this injunction is only against profane swearing in common discourse. But it ought to be recollected, that this vice was already prohibited under the law. "Thou shalt not take the name of the Lord thy God in vain." *This* prohibited vain swearing in common conversation, and one of the most respectable and virtuous denominations of christians in this country are of this opinion, viz. the Friends.

The pernicious tendency of oaths, is seen and felt in a variety of instances in private life, and these occur almost every day. The tongue of slander, the impositions of trade and traffic, are all to be attributed to this tremendous evil. Even servants are taught to deny their masters and mistresses though they are at home. Can such expect their servants will always speak the truth to themselves; from such an example taught them by those who ought to know better? It is not my business at present to enquire, whether this conduct can at any time, or under any circumstances be proper, it is sufficient to shew that it is injurious to morality. After all the sneers and satires of Dean Swift against this class of the community; the most pernicious and prominent of their vices, are to be justly attributed to the examples of their masters. With regard to *slaves*, this is peculiarly the case.

It may be asked, "how are you to obtain the truth in cases of importance, if oaths are abolished?" In the same way as it is attained from the Quakers. One of this society is hardly ever known to deceive a court or jury. If they did, their character would be lost amongst their own society; and the law would punish them for perjury, in the same way as it does those who *swear by book or hand.*

This however, I shall omit investigating any farther. If it is only acknowledged, that oaths ought not to be frequently administered; the principle for which I contend may be readily admitted. In Great-Britain the evil tendency of the multiplication of oaths has been frequently, and justly complained of, even by those who esteem them sometimes necessary. The various classes of manufacturers who are under the demon fangs of the *Excise;* are particularly exposed to temptations of *fraud upon oath,* and even to the swearing of *false* ones. One instance of this kind I shall adduce; not because it is a *solitary* one; but from its singularity. It will tend to shew, better than a folio volume upon the subject, how much a mans morals must have been injured, before he could have fallen upon so dangerous and immoral a scheme. I shall just beg to premise—that in Great Britain every retailer of foreign spirits, wines, teas and coffee, are obliged to make oath from time to time, that he has not sold more than the quantity of goods, specified by him in a certain book: that is, he must *swear that he is an honest man!*

"I recollect of hearing an anecdote of a dealer in tea, who was one of those apparently austere religious people, to be met with in every place: When the invention of shopkeepers swearing to the excise officers of the fairness of their trade, was first put in practice, this man, who had always been in the practice of smuggling a little, and was now very unwilling to forego the advantages thereof on account of an oath, set his invention to work in contriving a method of smuggling, swearing, and having a sound conscience:—the result of mature deliberation was, that on a Sacrament Sunday, he shut himself up in his room, and after a long prayer, made a solemn oath that he should never in his life speak a true sentence to a *gauger* (excise officer.) He ever afterwards considered this oath of greater weight than the other; and his conscience as very free from stain, although he perjured himself once every three months."

To this anecdote it may be perhaps, objected, that admitting this, it was an affair wherein his pecuniary interest was alone concerned; and does by no means apply to politics. This however, is a subject where party prejudice is as strong in its operations, as where self interest is concerned. It is only a few years ago, that a clergyman of the established church in Scotland; was tried for, and convicted of perjury, and stood in the pillory for the same: And this was for swearing he was qualified to give his vote for a member of Parliament, when he was not. Such are some of the consquences of the multiplication of oaths.

CHAPTER IX.

Every Government however constituted, or whatever be its form, is always possessed of an extensive influence among the people. Although it be true, that Government depends for its chief, if not its only support, upon public opinion; yet it will always have a very considerable share in the formation, and direction thereof. This arises from the unavoidable patronage which it seems necessary to confer upon it; or at least, which seems pretty generally thought so to be. It may thence be obvious, that throwing any additional weight into this already preponderating scale, must be extremely improper, and highly dangerous. To guard the Government by Sedition laws, is giving to it the power of at least attempting to direct the opinions of the people. It gives to it the authority of determining what the people shall say concerning them. It is not *falsehood* that it will guard against; otherwise *flattery* would be equally punishable; equally a libel. The flattering sycophant will always escape the censure of Government; while the honest man who boldly speaks disagreeable truths, will fall a victim to his sincerity, and patriotism. Not unfrequently, the flatterer will be rewarded for his falsehood. Like honest Mordecai, those who refuse to bow down to proud Haman, are always sure to give offence to the Satellites of power; and it is but seldom that an Ahasuerus is to be found to punish the haughty minister. The injury to the interests of morality are incalculable; because its great and only foundation, truth, is thus sapped; nay, it is overthrown. In trials for Sedition, unbiassed decisions may be given; but they are hardly to be expected. The Judges who owe their appointment to the executive branch of the Government, will generally feel influenced in such cases, even though men of the strictest honor in every other. Men during the time of public ferment, generally espouse one side or other. It is not often that characters, who differ in opinion from administration are selected upon such trials. In this case, how are impartial verdicts to be expected? They are called upon to decide, upon what? On sentiments they have already declared themselves enemies to. But supposing the truth is allowed to be given in evidence; it may only be *opinions*, how are their *truth* or *falsehood* to be determined? A decision in this case, would be as absurd as deciding which was the most palatable food, agreeable drink, or beautiful colour. A particular act of the administration appears to me unjust, and because I tell my opinion to my neighbour, write it to my friend, or communicate it to my fellow-citizens through the medium of the Press, therefore must I be punished; not because I have done evil, but because I have offended an individual high in office! Let common sense, if law does not, forbid such absurdity. However such proceedings may for a time be carried on, there is a certain point beyond which they cannot go. The sentiments of reason and truth will always ultimately prevail; those of an opposite kind, will be consigned to contempt and eternal oblivion. In vain may Government give them its support; in vain may pensioned hirelings or hungry expectants defend them with their prostituted pens; in vain may the law, armed with all its terrors of Jails, racks, gibbets or guillotines come forward to extirpate them from the face of the earth: If they be founded on Justice, if they be accordant with truth, they shall certainly triumph.

That this is the case, history sufficiently shews. A few out of innumerable instances, may not be deemed improper, to shew how illy calculated Government is to prescribe the channel in which public opinion shall flow. . . .

. . . Let it not be said, that the preceding relation of historical facts have nothing to do with the subject of this enquiry. They have much to do with it. They tend to prove, in the most incontrovertible manner, that there is always *danger* to be apprehended from Government interfering in the direction of public opinion. They also prove the omnipotence of opinion over the most energetic government that can exist. They prove that the means are insufficient to the end; when governments put in practice that authority which they so frequently wish to usurp.

The inference then is plain. No human power can prevent the progress of opinion. To the operation of this all powerful principle, in conjunction with the LIBERTY OF THE PRESS, the people of the United States are as much indebted as to their swords for their liberty and independence. Had the right of speaking, writing, and printing been prohibited, the advantages of a change of situation could never have been made sufficiently apparent. It is true, oppression speaks in the most forcible language to the feelings of mankind. But, if *feeling* instead of *reason* is to govern our actions, they will be frequently erroneous and unjust. In this particular instance, if the passions alone had been the pilot of public exertion, it is to be feared, the final result would have been very different. The opposition to British usurpation was however begun upon principles of justice and common sense; and public opinion being allowed to have free operation, the result was worthy of the cause.

CHAPTER X.

If there be anything truly valuable in the enjoyment of liberty, that unrestrained Freedom of Speech and Press contended for in the foregoing pages, must be amongst the first of its advantages. Compare the situation of mankind previous to the art of printing being discovered. Contrast the knowledge and information so generally diffused among the people now, with that almost universal ignorance which prevailed in ancient times. Contemplate the valuable discoveries in every art and science, and compare them with the crude and undigested theories of the dark ages. If after having considered these things, you can prefer ancient habits, customs or ideas; then indeed, printing has been injurious, and we ought to wish for the return of the days of ignorance and superstition. But, if we draw a different conclusion, we shall most certainly prefer the present times, with all their yet imperfections, to those when *master* and *slave,* (or what amounted to the same thing) *lord* and *vassal* were the only distinguishing appellations among the human race. Those chains of feudal tyranny have been destroyed in most European countries, and the people are gradually rising to that situation which nature seems to have designed them to occupy. That the last of these is entirely owing to the diffusion of knowledge and information, is sufficiently evident from comparing the state of society in those countries where knowledge has made little or no advances, with that of those where arts and science have been cultivated.

No people of any country have experienced the happy effects of a free discussion on political subjects, more than the people of the United States. It is their interest to guard this important privilege with the utmost vigilance and care. It will be seen from the reasonings that have been adduced; that being an inherent right, and of a nature not to be delegated; it must of course always continue with the people. It will also appear, that this right is guarantee'd to them by the Constitution of their Government, and that while their legislators are allowed a perfect freedom of debate, without being called to account; it is absurd to suppose the people divested of that which their public agents enjoy.

All the opponents of the Liberty of the Press, have sheltered themselves behind the specious veil of preserving the public peace. They say, licentiousness must be suppressed. Dangerous opinions in politics and religion must be guarded against; otherwise the social order of society will be endangered. What, it may be asked, would have been the situation of mankind at this moment, had the subjects of religion and politics never been investigated? *Orthodox* and *Hetrodox* are words of very doubtful meaning. What is orthodox at Constantinople, is hetrodox at Rome, and what is deemed sacred and indisputable by the conclave, is termed superstition at Geneva. As it is in respect to religion, so is it with politics. Those who are in the administration of Government, will always defend its principles, and its actions; whether it be that of a Turkish Bashaw, or a Prime Minister of England. Investigation is equally dreaded by both. Both are sufficiently aware that many imperfections exist in their systems of Government, and that many abuses are committed under them. It is however to be hoped, that the officers of Government on this side of the Atlantic will not again follow such pernicious examples.

The victory over British despotism by the people of the United States, was certainly a great and glorious event. At the expence of much blood and treasure they acquired the right of independent legislation; and of forming a Government of their own choice. What the people have *made*, they may surely *mend*. The State and Federal Governments of America have many excellencies. Perhaps no country can boast, with justice, of enjoying an equal degree of liberty. Does it however follow, that the Federal Constitution is the *best* that can be devised? Are there no faults in this instrument which it might be possible to remove? Is it the climax of all perfection? Its warmest supporters will not be hardy enough to answer in the affirmative. A bare *supposition* of its unalterable perfection, were it for a moment admitted, would prove too much. It would be asserting that mankind had now seen and examined the whole circle of political science. If this were the case, it ought to stop all enquiry and speculation; and the press ought no longer to investigate political subjects. If, however, it be admitted, that improvement may yet be made; why check, by restraining laws, the free operation of opinion, either with respect to principles or men?

It ought to be always remembered, that MAN is a *perfectable,* but not a *perfect* animal. He has interwoven in his nature, a principle of infinite advancement. He is capable of going on from improvement to improvement; but never destined to arrive at the end of his intellectual labours. If there was any fixed point, at which the improvement of man could stop, then indeed there would be an end to his searches; and investigation ought then to cease. That continual activity of mind which leads men on to investigate the circle of the arts and sciences with unceasing ardour, and which is communicated like our existence from one generation to another; all this would then be of no use. Could we suppose this barely possible; mankind so far from being made happy, would be deprived of the most valuable pleasures of which their nature is capable. They would be deprived of the contemplation of objects and designs conducive to the benefit of the species. If this reasoning be well founded it will naturally follow, that no limits can be assigned to our researches. Individuals die, but the species is immortal; and as the species, so are their improvements illimitable. How absurd then is it for people to talk of prescribing bounds to the progress of opinion, either in politics or religion? In the last, Jesus Christ has said—"Let the tares grow up with the wheat." Who then are they who will dare to call men to an account for particular religious tenets? It certainly belongs not to man, but to God!

Political opinions never can be destructive of social order, or public tranquility, if allowed a free operation. The law is at all times sufficiently energetic to punish disturbers of the public peace. When men are found guilty of this, let them be punished; it is well. It is not then punishing *opinion,* it is punishing actions injurious to the peace of the community.

But some have asserted, that the people may know too much. That there are certain things they ought not to be acquainted with, even though true. That in some cases our enquiries may go too far; and, that some things ought always to be concealed.

If *truth* can be in any case injurious to the interests of the community; these objections might be allowed some weight. It however yet remains to be proved, that *truth* can never be *injurious*. All enquiries are supposed to have truth for their object. Let then those noble sentiments of Dr. Conyers Middleton, in the preface to his free enquiry be adopted by every enquirer after truth.

"In enquiries, therefore, whenever I perceive any glimmering of truth before me, I readily pursue, and endeavour to trace it to its source, without any reserve or caution of pushing too far, or opening too great a glare to the public. I look upon the discovery of *any thing which is true,* as a valuable acquisition to society, which cannot hurt or obstruct the good effect of any other truth whatsoever; for they all partake of one common essence, and necessarily coincide with each other; and like the drops of rain which fall separately into the river, mix themselves at once with the stream, and strengthen the general current."

Setting aside the idea of the *perfectability* of man for a moment; still there are arguments sufficient to support the necessity and justice of an unrestrained Liberty of the Press.

It is generally allowed, that the science of Government is not as yet sufficiently understood. But will it ever be better known, if it is not allowed to be investigated? The same form of Government has existed in China for two or three thousand years.

The reason of this is the ignorance of the people. Notwithstanding the praises bestowed upon it by the Abbe Raynal and other writers; it is nothing more than a detestable system of legal tyranny. Such will all Governments become, if they are suffered to grow independent of public censure or applause. Abuses become sanctioned by time, and in proportion to their age, they acquire strength. The safest way to destroy them, is to attack them when young. It will be attended with the greatest safety both to Government, and the peace of the community. Notwithstanding all the care of the people in delegating power, still many things will afterwards be found wanting; or improvements of some kind or other necessary to be made. Let then public discussion be unrestrained. The ideas of the first proposer may be improved on by succeeding writers, and from collision of sentiment, truth will ultimately be produced.

Sedition laws are less intended for the maintenance of public tranquility; than for the defence of certain individuals. Nothing can be more pernicious, nothing more dangerous. What individual is of that vast importance to society, that he should have a particular clause in the criminal code of the country, for his particular safety. Are not the laws already sufficiently powerful to punish every offence? If they are not, let them be made so; but never let that great principle of all law be violated:—"*That of operating equally upon all, whether it protects or punishes.*" But Sedition laws violate this maxim. They prescribe certain modes of punishment, for certain supposed crimes, wherein a chief magistrate's conduct has been arraigned. Every public officer is entrusted with power for the good of the community. If so, then his actions ought to be watched; and if they over-leap the bounds of the Constitution, the public ought to know it. But how shall this be known if public opinion is fettered? Besides, it is the interest of the magistrates and public functionaries themselves, to know the state of public opinion. It will in many cases serve as a guide to their determinations. It will enable them to distinguish their friends from their enemies. But few will the enemies of that government be, whose actions are directed by the rules of justice and the Constitution; and the tenor of whose conduct has always been expressive of the sincerest wishes for the public welfare. In all investigations of a public nature, personal invective ought, in justice, to be avoided. It has, however, unfortunately happened, that for some years past, a more frequent resort has been had by writers of all parties, to personal invective and abuse, than was either necessary or just. If men differ in opinion, surely the common rules of politeness ought not therefore to be thrown aside. In all cases, where difference of opinion exists, the investigation of truth ought to be the only object. Personal dislike to the individual, will never operate upon a great mind. It ought certainly never to have a place in public discussions; neither ought extraneous circumstances with which the public have no concern, ever to be brought into view. A practice of an opposite kind, so far from convincing, will tend to irritate, and fix error deeper in the mind. In order to convince, it is necessary to make it appear that truth, and not personal revenge, is your object.

But even should this impropriety sometimes happen, it ought never to be adduced as a proof of the licentiousness of the Press; nor used as an argument for the necessity of infringing its Liberty. It arises from the remains of that terror which was inseparable from the restrictions under which the Press laboured, for a long period after the discovery of printing. It is also a consequence of that fear which too often pervades the middle and lower class of mankind; of giving offence to some rich individual, or great man in authority. Let such, if investigating public affairs, boldly speak what appears to them to be true. Let falsehood never stain the political page; and let *great* men never be offended at *little* men for freedom of political investigation. Notwithstanding all that has been said to the contrary, the poor man has as much at stake, and is as much interested in the stability of government, as the richest man in the community. And if he thinks that any observations of his may be of advantage to his fellow-citizens, he has an equal right to communicate them. It is of no consequence to enquire who writes a paper or a pamphlet, where principles and not individuals are the subjects of investigation. The only reasonable enquiry is, are the principles contended for just? If they are, let them have their due weight; if otherwise, they will meet with their merited contempt. In all cases, however, where specific or general charges are exhibited against an individual, or individuals; the persons name ought to be affixed to the publication. In this case, wilful calumny and abuse would never dare to make their appearance. He who had been once convicted of publishing a malicious falsehood, would forever after be deprived of the means of giving currency to his calumnies. Let not Government interfere. The laws of society, as before observed, are fully sufficient to the purpose.

If newspapers, and other publications, have lately teemed with misrepresentation, or with undeserved abuse of private or public character: If calumnies and invective dressed up in the language of billingsgate have been profusely dealt abroad instead of argument; what is to be done? Does it follow that we ought to be deprived of LIBERTY because it may be, or has been abused? Will justice not rather say, let misrepresentation be exposed by the force of truth. Let characters who have been unjustly accused, vindicate themselves by pointing out the falsehood of the charges; and let foul language be treated with that contempt it so justly merits. *In no case whatever use coercive measures.* Truth is at all times sufficiently powerful. Coercion may *silence,* but it never can *convince.*

It is the duty of both Government and people to act justly. Openness, sincerity, and candour, should characterise all their transactions. As men are so liable to error and mistake, they should be alike open to reason and conviction. Mankind being in a state of progressional improvement; they should avoid throwing any obstacles in its way. In a free and unrestrained Liberty of Speech and Press, many errors will undoubtedly be brought before the public eye; but, even these will not be without their use. When detected by accurate reasoning, the truth will appear with increased lustre. The only danger to be apprehended, is from *investigation being fettered*, and error allowed to become rooted in the mind.

Let the whig and tory, the royalist and aristocrat, the republican and democrat, or by whatever other name the partizans of political parties are designated; let them, I say, be allowed to express their opinions, whether by speech or press, with the same unconstrained freedom with which men of science discuss their subjects of investigation. No more danger will result from the one discussion, than arises from the other.

An unlimited freedom in the exercise of religious opinions has been recognized in the United States. The good effects of this are sufficiently visible. We here see none of that superstitious enmity; and uncharitable fanaticism of one denomination against another, which is so prevalent in all European countries where *established religions* exist. This very circumstance, which we now see realized, was at no very remote period, deemed by many well informed men to be utterly impracticable. GIVE UNTO ALL OPINIONS THE SAME FREEDOM, AND THE SAME EFFECTS WILL FOLLOW.

31. THE AMERICAN BLACKSTONE DISAVOWS BLACKSTONE

St. George Tucker, who served on the highest court of Virginia and then as a federal judge during the last twenty-five years of his life (1752–1827), succeeded the great Chancellor George Wythe in 1790 as professor of law at the College of William and Mary. Tucker used Blackstone's *Commentaries* as his text, but found that most famous of all law books inadequate for American needs. He remedied that situation by publishing, in 1803, a five-volume annotated edition of his own, adapted to American conditions, and containing almost fifteen hundred "notes," one of which was the first legal commentary on the Constitution of the United States. Another, almost thirty pages long, was a commentary on First Amendment freedoms, in which Tucker repudiated Blackstone's views on liberty of conscience and press. He habitually used the word "absolute" as a prefix to the right of speaking, writing and publishing, which he described as "unlimited as the human mind, subject to the penalties of the law only for personal defamation." There is little in Tucker's exposition that had not appeared in Madison's "Report" of 1799–1800, although Tucker significantly enlarged on Madison's comparison of political theory in England and America, to prove that British standards were inapplicable. "Tucker's Blackstone," which earned him the sobriquet of "the American Blackstone," was for many years the standard edition used by the American bench and bar and, in addition, became the textbook of American law, influencing a generation of American law students. A more strategic location for the repudiation of the Blackstonian concept of "no previous restraints" could not be imagined.

. . . The consequences of this act [the Sedition Act], as might have been foreseen, were a general astonishment, and dissatisfaction, among all those who considered the government of the United States, as a limited system of government; in it's nature altogether federal, and essentially different from all others which might lay claim to unlimited powers; or even to national, instead of federal authority. The constitutionality of the act was accordingly very generally denied, or questioned, by them. They alleged, that it is to the freedom of the press, and of speech, that the American nation is indebted for its liberty, it's happiness, it's enlightened state, nay more, for it's existence. That in these states the people are the only sov-

---

St. George Tucker, *Blackstone's Commentaries: with Notes of Reference, to the Constitution and Laws, of the Federal Government of the United States; and the Commonwealth of Virginia* (Philadelphia: William Young Birch and Abraham Small, 1803), Appendix to Volume One, Part Second of Blackstone's *Commentaries*. Note G, "Of the Right of Conscience, and of the Freedom of Speech and of the Press," pp. 15–21, 28–30.

ereign: that the government established by themselves, is for their benefit; that those who administer the government, whether it be that of the state, or of the federal union, are the agents and servants of the people, not their rulers or tyrants. That these agents must be, and are, from the nature and principles of our governments, responsible to the people, for their conduct. That to enforce this responsibility, it is indispensibly necessary that the people should inquire into the conduct of their agents; that in this inquiry, they must, or ought to scrutinize their motives, sift their intentions, and penetrate their designs; and that it was therefore, an unimpeachable right in them to censure as well as to applaud; to condemn or to acquit; and to reject, or to employ them again, as the most severe scrutiny might advise. That as no man can be forced into the service of the people against his own will and consent; so if any man employed by them in any office, should find the tenure of it too severe, because responsibility is inseparably annexed to it, he might retire: if he can not bear scrutiny, he might resign: if his motives, or designs, will not bear sifting; or if censure be too galling to his feelings, he might avoid it in the shades of domestic privacy. That if flattery be the only music to his ear, or the only balm to his heart; if he sickened when it is withheld, or turned pale when denied him; or if power, like the dagger of Macbeth, should invite his willing imagination to grasp it, the indignation of the people ought immediately to mark him, and hurl him from their councils, and their confidence forever. That if this absolute freedom of inquiry may be, in any manner, abridged, or impaired by those who administer the government, the nature of it will be instantly changed from a federal union of representative democracies, in which the people of the several states are the sovereign, and the administrators of the government their agents, to a consolidated oligarchy, aristocracy, or monarchy, according to the prevailing caprice of the constituted authorities, or of those who may usurp them. That where absolute freedom of discussion is prohibited, or restrained, responsibility vanishes. That any attempt to prohibit, or restrain that freedom, may well be construed to proceed from conscious guilt. That the people of America have always manifested a most jealous sensibility, on the subject of this inestimable right, and have ever regarded it as a fundamental principle in their government, and carefully engrafted in the constitution. That this sentiment was generated in the American mind, by an abhorrence of the maxims and principles of that government which they had shaken off, and a detestation of the abominable persecutions, and extrajudicial dogmas, of the still odious court of star-chamber; whose tyrannical proceedings and persecutions, among other motives of the like nature, prompted and impelled our ancestors to fly from the pestilential government of their native country, to seek an assylum here; where they might enjoy, and their posterity establish, and transmit to all future generations, freedom, unshackled, unlimited, undefined. That in our time we have vindicated, fought for, and established that freedom by our arms, and made it the solid, and immovable basis and foundation both of the state, and federal government. That nothing could more clearly evince the inestimable value that the American people have set upon the liberty of the press, than their uniting it in the same sentence, and even in the same member of a sentence, with the rights of conscience, and the freedom of speech. And since congress are equally prohibited from making any law abridging the freedom of speech, or of the press, they boldly challenged their adversaries to point out the constitutional distinction, between those two modes of discussion, or inquiry. If the unrestrained freedom of the press, said they, be not guaranteed, by the constitution, neither is that of speech. If on the contrary the unrestrained freedom of speech is guaranteed, so also, is that of the press. If then the genius of our federal constitution has vested the people of the United States, not only with a censorial power, but even with the sovereignty itself; if magistrates are, indeed, their agents: if they are responsible for their acts of agency; if the people may not only censure whom they disapprove, but reject whom they may find unworthy; if approbation or censure, election or rejection, ought to be the result of inquiry, scrutiny, and mature deliberation; why, said they, is the exercise of this censorial power, this sovereign right, this necessary inquiry, and scrutiny to be confined to the freedom of speech? Is it because this mode of discussion better answers the purposes of the censorial power? Surely not. The best speech can not be heard, by any great number of persons. The best speech may be misunderstood, misrepresented, and imperfectly remembered by those who are present. To all the rest of mankind, it is, as if it had never been. The best speech must also be short for the investigation of any subject of an intricate nature, or even a plain one, if it be of more than ordinary length. The best speech then must be altogether inadequate to the due exercise of the censorial power, by the people. The only adequate supplementary aid for these defects, is the absolute freedom of the press. A freedom unlimited as the human mind; viewing all things, penetrating the recesses of the human heart, unfolding the motives of human actions, and estimating all things by one invaluable standard, truth; applauding those who deserve well; censuring the undeserving; and condemning the unworthy, according to the measure of their demerits.

In vindication of the act, the promoters and supporters of it, said, that a law to punish false, scandalous, and malicious writings against the government, with intent to stir up sedition, is a law necessary for carrying into effect the power vested by the constitution in the government of the United States, and consequently such a law as congress may pass. To which it was answered, that even were the premises true, it would not authorize congress to pass an act to punish writings calculated to bring congress, or the president into contempt or disrepute. Inasmuch as such contempt or disrepute may be entertained for them, or either of them, without incurring the guilt of sedition, against the government, and without the most remote design of opposing, or resisting any law, or any act of the president done in pursuance of any law: one or the other of which would seem necessary to constitute the offence, which this argument defends the right of congress to punish, or prevent.

It was further urged in vindication of the act, that the liberty of the press consists not in a licence for every man to punish what he pleases, without being liable to punishment for any abuse of that licence; but in a permission to publish without previous restraint; and, therefore, that a law to restrain the licentiousness of the press, cannot be considered as an abridgment of its liberty.

To which it was answered that this exposition of the liberty of the press, was only to be found in the theoretical writings of the commentators on the *English* government, where the liberty of the press rests upon no other ground, than that there is now no law which imposes any actual previous restraint upon the press, as was formerly the case: which is very different from the footing upon which it stands in the United States, where it is made a fundamental article of the constitutions, both of the federal and state governments, that no such restraint shall be imposed by the authority of either. That if the sense of the state governments be wanting on the occasion, nothing can be more explicit than the meaning and intention of the state of Virginia, at the moment of adopting the constitution of the United States; by which it will clearly appear that it never was the intention of that state (and probably of no other in the union) to permit congress to distinguish between the liberty and licentiousness of the press; or, in any manner to "cancel, abridge, restrain, or "modify" that inestimable right.

Thirdly it was alleged, that the act could not be unconstitutional because it made nothing penal, which was not penal before, being merely declaratory of the common law, viz. of England.

To this it was, among other arguments, answered. That

the United States as a federal government have no common law. That although the common law of England, is, under different modifications, admitted to be the common law of the states respectively, yet the whole of the common law of England has been no where introduced: that there is a great and essential difference, in this respect, in the several states, not only in the subjects to which it is applied, but in the extent of its application. That the common law of one state, therefore, is not the common law of another. That the constitution of the United States has neither created it, nor conferred it upon the federal government. And, therefore, that government has no power or authority to assume the right of punishing any action, merely because it is punishable in England, or may be punishable in any, or all the states, by the common law.

The essential difference between the British government and the American constitutions was moreover insisted on, as placing this subject in the clearest light. In the former, the danger of encroachments on the rights of the people, was understood to be confined to the executive magistrate. The representatives of the people in the legislature are not only exempt themselves, from distrust, but are considered as sufficient guardians of the rights of their constituents against the danger from the executive. Hence it is a principle, that the parliament is unlimited in it's power, or, in their own language, is omnipotent. Hence too, all the ramparts for protecting the rights of the people, such as their *magna charta,* their bill of rights, &c. are not reared against the parliament, but against the royal prerogative. They are mere legislative precautions against executive usurpations. Under such a government as that, an exemption of the press from previous restraints, by licencers from the king, is all the freedom that can be secured to it, there: but, that in the United States the case is altogether different. The people, not the government, possess the absolute sovereignty. The legislature, no less than the executive, is under limitations of power. Encroachments are regarded as possible from the one, as well as from the other. Hence in the United States, the great and essential rights of the people, are secured against legislative, as well as against executive ambition. They are secured, not by laws paramount to prerogative; but by constitutions paramount to laws. This security of the freedom of the press requires, that it should be exempt, not only from previous restraint by the executive, as in Great-Britain; but from legislative restraint also; and this exemption, to be effectual, must be an exemption, not only from the previous inspection of licencers, but from the subsequent penalty of laws. A further difference between the two governments was also insisted on. In Great-Britain, it is a maxim, that the king, an hereditary, not a responsible magistrate, can do no wrong; and that the legislature, which in two thirds of it's composition, is also hereditary, not responsible, can do what it pleases. In the United States, the executive magistrates are not held to be infallible, nor the legislatures to be omnipotent; and both being elective, are both responsible. That the latter may well be supposed to require a greater degree of freedom of animadversion than might be tolerated by the genius of the former. That even in England, notwithstanding the general doctrine of the common law, the ministry, who are responsible to impeachment, are at all times animadverted on, by the press, with peculiar freedom. That the practice in America must be entitled to much more respect: being in most instances founded upon the express declarations contained in the respective constitutions, or bill of rights of the confederated states. That even in those states where no such guarantee could be found, the press had always exerted a freedom in canvassing the merits, and measures of public men of every description, not confined to the limits of the common law. That on this footing the press has stood even in those states, at least, from the period of the revolution. . . .

. . . It may be asked, perhaps: is there no remedy in the United States for injuries done to the good fame and reputation of a man; injuries, which to a man of sensibility, and of conscious integrity, are the most grievous that can be inflicted; injuries, which when offered through the medium of the press, may be diffused throughout the globe, and transmitted to latest posterity; may render him odious, and detestable in the eyes of the world, his country, his neighbours, his friends, and even his own family; may seclude him from society as a monster of depravity, and iniquity; and even may deprive him of sustenance, by destroying all confidence in him, and discouraging that commerce, or intercourse with him, which may be necessary to obtain the means?

Heaven forbid, that in a country which boasts of rational freedom, and of affording perfect security to the citizen for the complete enjoyment of all his rights, the most valuable of all should be exposed without remedy, or redress, to the vile arts of detraction and slander! Every individual, certainly, has a right to speak, or publish, his sentiments on the measures of government: to do this without restraint, control, or fear of punishment for so doing, is that which constitutes the genuine freedom of the press. The danger justly apprehended by those states which insisted that the federal government should possess no power, directly or indirectly, over the subject, was, that those who were entrusted with the administration might be forward in considering every thing as a crime against the government, which might operate to their own personal disadvantage; it was therefore made a fundamental article of the federal compact, that no such power should be exercised, or claimed by the federal government; leaving it to the state governments to exercise such jurisdiction and control over the subject, as their several constitutions and laws permit. In contending therefore for the absolute freedom of the press, and its total exemption from all restraint, control, or jurisdiction of the federal government, the writer of these sheets most explicitly disavows the most distant approbation of its licentiousness. A free press, conducted with ability, firmness, decorum, and impartiality, may be regarded as the chaste nurse of genuine liberty; but a press stained with falsehood, imposture, detraction, and personal slander, resembles a contaminated prostitute, whose touch is pollution, and whose offspring bears the foul marks of the parent's ignominy.

Whoever makes use of the press as the vehicle of his sentiments on any subject, ought to do it in such language as to shew he has a deference for the sentiments of others; that while he asserts the right of expressing and vindicating his own judgment, he acknowledges the obligation to submit to the judgment of those whose authority he cannot legally, or constitutionally dispute. In his statement of facts he is bound to adhere strictly to the truth; for any deviation from the truth is both an imposition upon the public, and an injury to the individual whom it may respect. In his restrictures on the conduct of men, in public stations, he is bound to do justice to their characters, and not to criminate them without substantial reason. The right of character is a sacred and invaluable right, and is not forfeited by accepting a public employment. Whoever knowingly departs from any of these maxims is guilty of a crime against the community, as well as against the person injured; and though both the letter and the spirit of our federal constitution wisely prohibit the congress of the United States from making any law, by which the freedom of speech, or of the press, may be exposed to restraint or persecution under the authority of the federal government, yet for injuries done the reputation of any person, as *an individual,* the state-courts are always open, and may afford ample, and competent redress, as the records of the courts of this commonwealth abundantly testify.

PART FIVE

The Special Case of Thomas Jefferson

An anthology on libertarian theory without Jefferson in it could be compared to Odets's play, *Waiting for Lefty*—the title character never puts in an appearance. Jefferson, of course, has been historically depicted as our foremost apostle of freedom, the noblest and most libertarian of all, caught for posterity in the mythic stance of swearing eternal hostility to every form of tyranny over the mind of man. But posterity has taken the rhetoric for the reality. Jefferson was more the democrat than the libertarian, and his libertarianism, except in the field of religious freedom, was scarcely profound, consistent, or courageous. And he had his darker side, a streak of antilibertarianism, that reflected itself in significant breaches between his principles and his practice. In the long run, happily, his pen has proved mightier than his practice, for his rhetoric helped to create an American creed that we pridefully venerate. Yet the philosopher of freedom had no philosophy of freedom, at least no theory of libertarianism like that of Wortman and Thomson or Gallatin and Madison—from whom, surprisingly, he learned little if anything. He was given to pithy, felicitous, quotable maxims, and sometimes gave imperishable expression to great principles. Style even more than substance accounts for his libertarian reputation— style as well as pre-eminence and unsurpassed contributions to religious freedom. On freedom of the press, however, his thought as well as his actions revealed ambiguity and tension, contradictions and conflict, as the following documents will show.

32. FREEDOM OF RELIGION

One of Jefferson's finest achievements, and the foremost evidence
of his libertarianism, was his Bill for Establishing Religious Freedom. The enabling clause, omitted in the following document, completely separated church and state and protected fully all "religious
opinions or belief." The philosophic preamble, reprinted below, refers, both to "religious" opinion and to opinion generally, without
the qualifying adjective, but in a context exclusively devoted to
securing religious liberty. The document has been broadly read by
distinguished Jefferson scholars to encompass intellectual liberty
and even freedom of political opinion. But we know that in 1776
and through his Presidency Jefferson believed in the power of the
state to punish seditious libel, and we know moreover that he
never applied to political opinions the overt-acts test embodied in
this bill. The bill was enacted into law in 1786 with slight deletions
from the introductory lines of the preamble.

Well aware that the opinions and belief of men depend not on
their own will but follow involuntarily the evidence proposed
to their minds; that Almighty God has created the mind free,
and manifested His supreme will that free it shall remain by
making it altogether insusceptible of restraint; that all attempts
to influence it by temporal punishments, or burdens, or by
civil incapacitations tend only to beget habits of hypocrisy and
meanness and are a departure from the plan of the holy Author
of our religion, who being Lord both of body and mind, yet
chose not to propagate it by coercions on either, as was in His
almighty power to do, but to extend it by its influence on
reason alone; that the impious presumption of legislators and
rulers, civil as well as ecclesiastical, who, being themselves but
fallible and uninspired men, have assumed dominion over the
faith of others, setting up their own opinions and modes of

A Bill for Establishing Religious Freedom, 1779, in *The Writings of
Thomas Jefferson*, ed. Paul Leicester Ford (New York: G. P. Putnam's
Sons, 1892–1899), II, 237–239.

thinking as the only true and infallible, and as such endeavoring to impose them on others, has established and maintained false religions over the greatest part of the world and through all time; that to compel a man to furnish contributions of money for the propagation of opinions which he disbelieves and abhors is sinful and tyrannical; that even the forcing him to support this or that teacher of his own religious persuasion is depriving him of the comfortable liberty of giving his contributions to the particular pastor whose morals he would make his pattern and whose powers he feels most persuasive to righteousness, and is withdrawing from the ministry those temporal rewards which, proceeding from an approbation of their personal conduct, are an additional incitement to earnest and unremitting labors for the instruction of mankind; that our civil rights have no dependence on our religious opinions any more than our opinions in physics or geometry; that therefore the proscribing any citizen as unworthy the public confidence by laying upon him an incapacity of being called to offices of trust and emolument unless he profess or renounce this or that religious opinion is depriving him injuriously of those privileges and advantages to which, in common with his fellow citizens, he has a natural right; that it tends also to corrupt the principles of that very religion it is meant to encourage, by bribing with a monopoly of worldly honors and emoluments those who will externally profess and conform to it; that though indeed these are criminal who do not withstand such temptation, yet neither are those innocent who lay the bait in their way; that the opinions of men are not the object of civil government, nor under its jurisdiction; that to suffer the civil magistrate to intrude his powers into the field of opinion and to restrain the profession or propagation of principles on supposition of their ill tendency is a dangerous fallacy which at once destroys all religious liberty, because he, being of course judge of that tendency, will make his opinions the rule of judgment and approve or condemn the sentiments of others only as they shall square with or differ from his own; that it is time enough, for the rightful purposes of civil government, for its officers to interfere when principles break out into overt acts against peace and good order; and, finally, that truth is great and will prevail if left to herself; that she is the proper and sufficient antagonist to error and has nothing to fear from the conflict unless by human interposition disarmed of her natural weapons, free argument and debate; errors ceasing to be dangerous when it is permitted freely to contradict them.

We, the General Assembly of Virginia, do enact that no man shall be compelled to frequent or support any religious worship, place, or ministry whatsoever, nor shall be enforced, restrained, molested, or burdened in his body or goods, nor shall otherwise suffer on account of his religious opinions or belief; but that all men shall be free to profess, and by argument to maintain, their opinions in matters of religion, and that the same shall in no wise diminish, enlarge, or affect their civil capacities.

And though we well know that this Assembly, elected by the people for the ordinary purposes of legislation only, have no power to restrain the acts of succeeding Assemblies constituted with powers equal to our own, and that therefore to declare this act irrevocable would be of no effect in law; yet we are free to declare, and do declare, that the rights hereby asserted are of the natural rights of mankind, and that, if any act shall be hereafter passed to repeal the present resolution or to narrow its operation, such act will be an infringement of natural right.

33. NO FREEDOM FOR FALSITY IN THE PRESS

In 1776 Jefferson drafted a proposed constitution for the state of Virginia that omitted entirely a declaration of rights. Fortunately, George Mason and the Virginia legislature were not so neglectful. In 1783 Jefferson drafted another constitution in the expectation, which proved false, that the constitution of 1776 would be superseded. There are extraordinary omissions in the 1783 draft and—

with respect to freedom of the press—a significant difference between Jefferson's proposal and the clause in the 1776 Declaration
of Rights which provided: "That the freedom of the press is one of
the great bulwarks of liberty, and can never be restrained but by
despotic governments." Jefferson, in 1783, proposed liability "to
legal prosecution for false facts printed and published"—proof that
he distinguished between religious and political opinions. The one
he exempted from prosecution except when principles broke into
overt acts of crime; the other he would have subjected to prosecution to rectify errors of fact, rather than merely expose them to
truth and reason.

. . . The General assembly shall not have power to infringe this
constitution; to abridge the civil rights of any person on account of his religious belief; to restrain him from professing
and supporting that belief, or to compel him to contributions,
other than those he shall himself have stipulated, for the support of that or any other: to ordain death for any crime but
treason or murder, or offences in the military line: to pardon or
give a power of pardoning persons duly convicted of treason
or felony, but instead thereof they may substitute one or two
new trials and no more: to pass laws for punishing actions done
before the existence of such laws: to pass any bill of attainder,
(or other law declaring any person guilty) of treason or felony:
to prescribe torture in any case: nor to permit the introduction
of any more slaves to reside in this state, or the continuance of
slavery beyond the generation which shall be living on the
31st. day of December 1800; all persons born after that day
being hereby declared free. . . .

. . . *(Every citizen)* The benefits of the writ of Habeas
corpus shall be extended by the legislature to every person
within this state and without fee, and shall be so facilitated

---

Draft Constitution for Virginia, 1783, in *The Papers of Thomas Jefferson*, ed. Julian P. Boyd (Princeton, N.J.: Princeton University Press,
1952), VI, 298, 304.

that no person may be detained in prison more than ten days after he shall have demanded and been refused such writ by the judge appointed by law, or if none be appointed, then by any judge of a superior court; nor more than ten days after such writ shall have been served on the person detaining him and no order given on due examination for his remandment or discharge.

The MILITARY shall be subordinate to the civil power.

PRINTING PRESSES shall be subject to no other restraint than liableness to legal prosecution for false*(hoods)* facts printed and published. . . .

34. ON THE IMPORTANCE OF NEWSPAPERS

In the following letter, written from Paris to a friend, Edward Carrington of Virginia, Jefferson should not be taken literally in his statement that he preferred newspapers without a government to a government without newspapers. The proposition on its face was a foolish one. The point of Jefferson's hyperbole was that a free press played an indispensable role in educating a self-governing people to govern themselves wisely. Jefferson never supported freedom of the press as an end in itself. It was always in his thinking a means to a greater end: an educated electorate.

[To Edward Carrington]

. . . The tumults in America [Shays's Rebellion] I expected would have produced in Europe an unfavorable opinion of our political state. But it has not. On the contrary, the small effect of those tumults seems to have given more confidence in the firmness of our governments. The interposition of the people themselves on the side of government has had a great effect on

---

Thomas Jefferson to Edward Carrington, January 16, 1787, in *The Papers of Thomas Jefferson*, ed. Boyd, XII, 48–49.

the opinion here. I am persuaded myself that the good sense of the people will always be found to be the best army. They may be led astray for a moment, but will soon correct themselves. The people are the only censors of their governors: and even their errors will tend to keep these to the true principles of their institution. To punish these errors too severely would be to suppress the only safeguard of the public liberty. The way to prevent these irregular interpositions of the people is to give them full information of their affairs thro' the channel of the public papers, and to contrive that those papers should penetrate the whole mass of the people. The basis of our governments being the opinion of the people, the very first object should be to keep that right; and were it left to me to decide whether we should have a government without newspapers, or newspapers without a government, I should not hesitate a moment to prefer the latter. But I should mean that every man should receive those papers and be capable of reading them. I am convinced that those societies (as the Indians) which live without government enjoy in their general mass an infinitely greater degree of happiness than those who live under European governments. Among the former, public opinion is in the place of law, and restrains morals as powerfully as laws ever did any where. Among the latter, under pretence of governing they have divided their nations into two classes, wolves and sheep. I do not exaggerate. This is a true picture of Europe. Cherish therefore the spirit of our people, and keep alive their attention. Do not be too severe upon their errors, but reclaim them by enlightening them. If once they become inattentive to the public affairs, you and I, and Congress, and Assemblies, judges and governors shall all become wolves. It seems to be the law of our general nature, in spite of individual exceptions; and experience declares that man is the only animal which devours his own kind, for I can apply no milder term to the governments of Europe, and to the general prey of the rich on the poor. . . .

35. WHAT THE PEOPLE ARE ENTITLED TO

The following letter is one of several written to Madison by Jefferson, from Paris, between the time that the work of the Philadelphia Constitutional Convention was made public and the framing of the Bill of Rights by the first Congress. As a libertarian contribution these letters (Documents 34–37), rank in importance second only to Jefferson's writings on freedom of religion. The rights he neglected to mention were numerous and vital, and he did not trouble to define those he advocated, but the principle that he supported was to his great credit—the need for a federal bill of rights. More than anything else, his letters influenced Madison to support the great libertarian amendments to the Constitution—and to support them out of conviction and conscience as well as for reasons of political expediency. Without Madison as the driving, indefatigable force, the First Congress might not have found the time or inclination to adopt those amendments which he initially framed and persistently fought for against apathy and opposition. Without these letters from Jefferson, Madison might have remained, as he was originally, cool toward amendments.

[To James Madison]

. . . I will now add what I do not like. First the omission of a bill of rights providing clearly and without the aid of sophisms for freedom of religion, freedom of the press, protection against standing armies, restriction against monopolies, the eternal and unremitting force of the habeas corpus laws, and trials by jury in all matters of fact triable by the laws of the land and not by the law of Nations. To say, as Mr. Wilson does that a bill of rights was not necessary because all is reserved in the case of the general government which is not given, while in the particular ones all is given which is not reserved might do for the

---

Thomas Jefferson to James Madison, December 20, 1787, in *The Papers of Thomas Jefferson,* ed. Boyd, XII, 440.

Audience to whom it was addressed, but is surely gratis dictum, opposed by strong inferences from the body of the instrument, as well as from the omission of the clause of our present confederation which had declared that in express terms. It was a hard conclusion to say because there has been no uniformity among the states as to the cases triable by jury, because some have been so incautious as to abandon this mode of trial, therefore the more prudent states shall be reduced to the same level of calamity. It would have been much more just and wise to have concluded the other way that as most of the states had judiciously preserved this palladium, those who had wandered should be brought back to it, and to have established general right instead of general wrong. Let me add that a bill of rights is what the people are entitled to against every government on earth, general or particular, and what no just government should refuse, or rest on inference. . . .

36. ON RIGHTS AND THE LIABILITY

OF PRINTERS

In the following letter there is an interesting distinction between freedom of the press and freedom of religion which had cropped out earlier in Jefferson's thinking (see Document 33) and would crop out again (see Documents 38 and 39). Jefferson never regarded the statement of a false fact about religion as subject to prosecution. That was an error of opinion, which should be left unfettered. By contrast, he did not advocate that false political facts should receive impunity until they dictated criminal acts.

[to James Madison]

. . . I sincerely rejoice at the acceptance of our new constitution by nine states. It is a good canvas, on which some

---

Thomas Jefferson to James Madison, July 31, 1788, in *The Papers of Thomas Jefferson*, ed. Boyd, XIII, 442–443.

strokes only want retouching. What these are, I think are sufficiently manifested by the general voice from North to South,
which calls for a bill of rights. It seems pretty generally understood that this should go to Juries, Habeas corpus, Standing
armies, Printing, Religion and Monopolies. I conceive there
may be difficulty in finding general modification of these suited
to the habits of all the states. But if such cannot be found then
it is better to establish trials by jury, the right of Habeas
corpus, freedom of the press and freedom of religion in all
cases, and to abolish standing armies in time of peace, and
Monopolies, in all cases, than not to do it in any. The few cases
wherein these things may do evil, cannot be weighed against
the multitude wherein the want of them will do evil. In dis-
putes between a foreigner and a native, a trial by jury may be
improper. But if this exception cannot be agreed to, the remedy
will be to model the jury by giving the medietas linguae in
civil as well as criminal cases. Why suspend the Hab. corp. in
insurrections and rebellions? The parties who may be arrested
may be charged instantly with a well defined crime. Of course
the judge will remand them. If the publick safety requires that
the government should have a man imprisoned on less probable testimony in those than in other emergencies; let him be
taken and tried, retaken and retried, while the necessity continues, only giving him redress against the government for
damages. Examine the history of England: see how few of the
cases of the suspension of the Habeas corpus law have been
worthy of that suspension. They have been either real treasons
wherein the parties might as well have been charged at once,
or sham-plots where it was shameful they should ever have
been suspected. Yet for the few cases wherein the suspension
of the hab. corp. has done real good, that operation is now
become habitual, and the minds of the nation almost prepared
to live under it's constant suspension. A declaration that the
federal government will never restrain the presses from printing any thing they please, will not take away the liability of the

printers for false facts printed. The declaration that religious faith shall be unpunished, does not give impunity to criminal acts dictated by religious error. . . .

37. A TEXT TO TRY ACTS OF GOVERNMENT

Madison was more tough-minded, realistic, and skeptical than Jefferson. Although Madison never opposed a bill of rights, he thought at first that its omission was not an important defect and until convinced otherwise by Jefferson was not "anxious," he said, "to supply it even by subsequent amendments." In a letter to Jefferson, dated October 17, 1788, he stated his reasons for not viewing the issue "in an important light." One of them was: "Repeated violations of these parchment barriers have been committed by overbearing majorities in every State. In Virginia I have seen the bill of rights violated in every instance where it has been opposed to a popular current." Jefferson here summarizes and persuasively answers Madison's arguments.

[To James Madison]

. . . In the arguments in favor of a declaration of rights, you omit one which has great weight with me, the legal check which it puts into the hands of the judiciary. This is a body, which if rendered independent, and kept strictly to their own department merits great confidence for their learning and integrity. In fact what degree of confidence would be too much for a body composed of such men as Wythe, Blair, and Pendleton? On characters like these the "civium ardor prava jubentium" would make no impression. I am happy to find that on the whole you are a friend to this amendment. The Declaration

---

Thomas Jefferson to James Madison, March 15, 1789, in *The Papers of Thomas Jefferson,* ed. Boyd, XIV, 659–661.

of rights is like all other human blessings alloyed with some inconveniences, and not accomplishing fully it's object. But the good in this instance vastly overweighs the evil. I cannot refrain from making short answers to the objections which your letter states to have been raised. 1. That the rights in question are reserved by the manner in which the federal powers are granted. Answer. A constitutive act may certainly be so formed as to need no declaration of rights. The act itself has the force of a declaration as far as it goes: and if it goes to all material points nothing more is wanting. In the draught of a constitution which I had once a thought of proposing in Virginia, and printed afterwards, I endeavored to reach all the great objects of public liberty, and did not mean to add a declaration of rights. Probably the object was imperfectly executed: but the deficiencies would have been supplied by others in the course of discussion. But in a constitutive act which leaves some precious articles unnoticed, and raises implications against others, a declaration of rights becomes necessary by way of supplement. This is the case of our new federal constitution. This instrument forms us into one state as to certain objects, and gives us a legislative and executive body for these objects. It should therefore guard us against their abuses of power within the field submitted to them. 2. A positive declaration of some essential rights could not be obtained in the requisite latitude. Answer. Half a loaf is better than no bread. If we cannot secure all our rights, let us secure what we can. 3. The limited powers of the federal government and jealousy of the subordinate governments afford a security which exists in no other instance. Answer. The first member of this seems resolvable into the 1st objection before stated. The jealousy of the subordinate governments is a precious reliance. But observe that those governments are only agents. They must have principles furnished them whereon to found their opposition. The declaration of rights will be the text whereby they will try all the acts of the federal government. In this view it is necessary to the federal government also: as by the same text they may try the opposition of the subordinate governments. 4. Experience proves the inefficacy of a bill of rights. True. But tho it is not absolutely efficacious under all circumstances, it is of great potency always, and rarely inefficacious. A brace the more will often keep up the building which would have fallen with that brace the less. There is a remarkeable difference between the characters of the Inconveniencies which attend a Declaration of rights, and those which attend the want of it. The inconveniences of the Declaration are that it may cramp government in it's useful exertions. But the evil of this is shortlived, moderate, and reparable. The inconveniencies of the want of a Declaration are permanent, afflicting and irreparable: they are in constant progression from bad to worse. The executive in our governments is not the sole, it is scarcely the principal object of my jealousy. The tyranny of the legislatures is the most formidable dread at present, and will be for long years. That of the executive will come in it's turn, but it will be at a remote period. I know there are some among us who would now establish a monarchy. But they are inconsiderable in number and weight of character. The rising race are all republicans. We were educated in royalism: no wonder if some of us retain that idolatry still. Our young people are educated in republicanism. An apostacy from that to royalism is unprecedented and impossible. I am much pleased with the prospect that a declaration of rights will be added: and hope it will be done in that way which will not endanger the whole frame of the government, or any essential part of it. . . .

38. IMPROVING THE BILL OF RIGHTS

The following letter to Madison was written after Jefferson received from him a copy of Madison's proposed amendments to the Constitution. One of them stated: "The people shall not be deprived or abridged of their right to speak, to write, or to publish their sentiments; and the freedom of the press, as one of the great bulwarks of liberty, shall be inviolable." Jefferson would have restricted this liberty, as the following document shows.

[To James Madison]

. . . I must now say a word on the declaration of rights you have been so good as to send me. I like it as far as it goes; but I should have been for going further. For instance the following alterations and additions would have pleased me. "Art. 4. The people shall not be deprived or abridged of their right to speak to write or *otherwise* to publish any thing but false facts affecting injuriously the life, liberty, property, or reputation of others or affecting the peace of the confederacy with foreign nations. Art. 7. All facts put in issue before any judicature shall be tried by jury except 1. in cases of admiralty jurisdiction wherein a foreigner shall be interested, 2. in cases cognisable before a court martial concerning only the regular officers and souldiers of the U.S. or members of the militia in actual service in time of war or insurrection, and 3. in impeachments allowed by the constitution. —Art. 8. No person shall be held in confinement more than —— days after they shall have demanded and been refused a writ of Hab. corp. by the judge appointed by law nor more than —— days after such writ shall have been served on the person holding him in confinement and no order given on due examination for his remandment or discharge, nor more than —— hours in any place at a greater distance than —— miles from the usual residence of some judge authorised to issue the writ of Hab. corp. nor shall that writ be suspended for any term exceeding one year nor in any place more than —— miles distant from the station or encampment of enemies or of insurgents. —Art. 9. Monopolies may be allowed to persons for their own productions in literature and their own invention in the arts for a term not exceeding —— years but for no longer term and no other purpose. —Art. 10.

Thomas Jefferson to James Madison, August 28, 1789, in *The Papers of Thomas Jefferson*, ed. Boyd, XV, 367–368.

All troops of the U.S. shall stand ipso facto disbanded at the expiration of the term for which their pay and subsistence shall have been last voted by Congress, and all officers and souldiers not natives of the U.S. shall be incapable of serving in their armies by land except during a foreign war." These restrictions I think are so guarded as to hinder evil only. However if we do not have them now, I have so much confidence in my countrymen as to be satisfied that we shall have them as soon as the degeneracy of our government shall render them necessary. . . .

39. NATURAL RIGHTS *v.* FENCES AGAINST WRONGS

Noah Webster, the great schoolmaster and Federalist publicist, believing that the Constitution was nearly perfect without amendments, criticized Jefferson for having advocated a bill of rights. In the following extract from Jefferson's reply to Webster, Jefferson's distinction between religious liberty and freedom of the press reappears. He classified the first as an "unceded" or natural right, and the second as among "fences against wrongs." The first was, in his thinking, virtually an absolute; the second he thought worthy enough but, like jury trial, a device to keep the government properly checked against injustice.

[To Noah Webster]

. . . In mentioning me in your Essays, and canvassing my opinions, you have done what every man has a right to do, and it is for the good of society that that right should be freely exercised. No republic has more zeal than that of letters, and I am the last in principles, as I am the least in pretensions, to any dictatorship in it. Had I other dispositions, the philosophi-

Thomas Jefferson to Noah Webster, December 4, 1790, in *The Writings of Thomas Jefferson,* ed. Andrew A. Lipscomb and Albert Ellery Bergh (Washington, D.C.: The Thomas Jefferson Memorial Association, 1904–1905), VIII, 112–113.

cal and dispassionate spirit with which you have expressed your own opinions in opposition to mine, would still have commanded my approbation. A desire of being set right in your opinion, which I respect too much not to entertain that desire, induces me to hazard to you the following observations. It had become an universal and almost uncontroverted position in the several States, that the purposes of society do not require a surrender of all our rights to our ordinary governors; that there are certain portions of right not necessary to enable them to carry on an effective government, and which experience has nevertheless proved they will be constantly encroaching on, if submitted to them; that there are also certain fences which experience has proved peculiarly efficacious against wrong, and rarely obstructive of right, which yet the governing powers have ever shown a disposition to weaken and remove. Of the first kind, for instance, is freedom of religion; of the second, trial by jury, habeas corpus laws, free presses. These were the settled opinions of all the States,—of that of Virginia, of which I was writing, as well as of the others. The others had, in consequence, delineated these unceded portions of right, and these fences against wrong, which they meant to exempt from the power of their governors, in instruments called declarations of rights and constitutions; and as they did this by conventions, which they appointed for the express purpose of reserving these rights, and of delegating others to their ordinary legislative, executive and judiciary bodies, none of the reserved rights can be touched without resorting to the people to appoint another convention for the express purpose of permitting it. . . .

40. NATIVISM AND THE IMPEACHMENT OF
GRAND JURORS

On May 27, 1797, a federal grand jury returned a "presentment" or formal accusation of crime against Samuel J. Cabell for disseminating "at a time of real public danger . . . unfounded calumnies against the happy government of the United States." The presentment was extraordinary. Not only was it an unprecedented first case of seditious libel against the United States; it was wholly founded on the common law, for more than a year would pass before the Sedition Act was even introduced in Congress. Moreover, the accused was a United States Congressman, from Vice President Jefferson's district no less, and his crime was committed in the form of circular letters to his constituents. Jefferson's response was as extraordinary as the presentment itself. He drafted an anonymous petition to the state legislature denouncing the presentment. The arguments in the petition merit careful scrutiny. Conspicuously absent were any attack on the concept of seditious libel and any invoking of the First Amendment. Jefferson relied, rather, on the "natural right of free correspondence." But the weight of his argument is that the principle of separation of powers had been violated by the grand jury's presentment. He defended ably the integrity of the principle of representation but claimed, too, that the grand jury breached the privileges of Congress—a sinister implication. He also advanced the principle of state's rights, and voiced (borrowing from the xenophobia that afflicted his Federalist opponents) a nativist theme. His aspersions against foreigners concluded with a recommendation that they be excluded from all jury service, and that perhaps even naturalized citizens be excluded too. Of greater import was Jefferson's main remedy for the "crime" the grand jury committed against the principle of representation when it sought to suppress the free communication of sentiment in speaking or writing: he urged the state legislature to impeach and punish the grand jurors. Punishing a jury for a disliked verdict died in England with the decision in Bushell's case in 1670. Jefferson's recommendation was as drastic a violation of the integrity of the principle of due process of law, and as great an interference with an institution of the judicial department, as the grand jury's presentment was a violation of the principle of free representation and free speech. Fortunately his suppressive recommendation was not adopted by the Virginia House of Delegates, which properly contented itself with a simple condemnation of the grand jury's action; equally happy is the fact that the presentment was never acted upon. Thus Cabell was never brought to trial. Jefferson's authorship of the petition remained unknown.

To the Speaker and House of Delegates of the Commonwealth of Virginia, being a Protest against interference of Judiciary between Representative and Constituent.

The petition of the subscribers, inhabitants of the counties of Amherst, Albemarle, Fluvanna, and Goochland, sheweth:

That by the constitution of this State, established from its earliest settlement, the people thereof have professed the right of being governed by laws to which they have consented by representatives chosen by themselves immediately: that in order to give to the will of the people the influence it ought to have, and the information which may enable them to exercise it usefully, it was a part of the common law, adopted as the law of this land, that their representatives, in the discharge of their functions, should be free from the cognizance or coercion of the co-ordinate branches, Judiciary and Executive; and that their communications with their constituents should of right, as of duty also, be free, full, and unawed by any: that so necessary has this intercourse been deemed in the country from which they derive principally their descent and laws, that the correspondence between the representative and constituent is privileged there to pass free of expense through the channel of the public post, and that the proceedings of the legislature have been known to be arrested and suspended at times until the Representatives could go home to their several counties and confer with their constituents. . . .

. . . That at the general partition of this commonwealth into districts, each of which was to choose a representative to Congress, the counties of Amherst, Albemarle, Fluvanna, and Goochland, were laid off into one district: that at the elections held for the said district, in the month of April, in the years

---

Petition to the Virginia House of Delegates, August 1797, in *The Writings of Thomas Jefferson,* ed. Ford, VII, 158–164.

1795 and 1797, the electors thereof made choice of Samuel
Jordan Cabell, of the county of Amherst, to be their representative in the legislature of the general government; that the said
Samuel Jordan Cabell accepted the office, repaired at the due
periods to the legislature of the General Government, exercised
his functions there as became a worthy member, and as a good
and dutiful representative was in the habit of corresponding
with many of his constituents, and communicating to us, by
way of letter, information of the public proceedings, of asking
and receiving our opinions and advice, and of contributing, as
far as might be with right, to preserve the transactions of the
general government in unison with the principles and sentiments of his constituents: that while the said Samuel J. Cabell
was in the exercise of his functions as a representative from
this district, and was in the course of that correspondence
which his duty and the will of his constituents imposed on him,
the right of thus communicating with them, deemed sacred
under all the forms in which our government has hitherto
existed, never questioned or infringed even by Royal judges or
governors, was openly and directly violated at a Circuit court
of the General Government, held at the city of Richmond, for
the district of Virginia, in the month of May of this present
year, 1797: that at the said court, A, B, &c., some of whom were
foreigners, having been called upon to serve in the office of
grand jurors before the said court, were sworn to the duties of
said office in the usual forms of the law, the known limits of
which duties are to make presentment of those acts of individuals which the laws have declared to be crimes or misdemeanors: that departing out of the legal limits of their said
office, and availing themselves of the sanction of its cover,
wickedly and contrary to their fidelity to destroy the rights of
the people of this commonwealth, and the fundamental principles of representative government, they made a presentment
of the act of the said Samuel J. Cabell, in writing letters to his
constituents in the following words, to wit: "We, of the grand

jury of the United States, for the district of Virginia, present as a real evil, the circular letters of several members of the late Congress, and particularly letters with the signature of Samuel J. Cabell, endeavoring, at a time of real public danger, to disseminate unfounded calumnies against the happy government of the United States, and thereby to separate the people therefrom; and to increase or produce a foreign influence, ruinous to the peace, happiness, and independence of these United States."

That the grand jury is a part of the Judiciary, not permanent indeed, but in office, *pro hac vice* and responsible as other judges are for their actings and doings while in office: that for the Judiciary to interpose in the legislative department between the constituent and his representative, to control them in the exercise of their functions or duties towards each other, to overawe the free correspondence which exists and ought to exist between them, to dictate what communications may pass between them, and to punish all others, to put the representative into jeopardy of criminal prosecution, of vexation, expense, and punishment before the Judiciary, if his communications, public or private, do not exactly square with their ideas of fact or right, or with their designs of wrong, is to put the legislative department under the feet of the Judiciary, is to leave us, indeed, the shadow, but to take away the substance of representation, which requires essentially that the representative be as free as his constituents would be, that the same interchange of sentiment be lawful between him and them as would be lawful among themselves were they in the personal transaction of their own business; is to do away the influence of the people over the proceedings of their representatives by excluding from their knowledge, by the terror of punishment, all but such information or misformation as may suit their own views; and is the more vitally dangerous when it is considered that grand jurors are selected by officers nominated and holding their places at the will of the Executive: that they are exposed to influence from the judges who are nominated immediately by the Executive, and who, although holding permanently their commissions as judges, yet from the career of additional office and emolument *actually* opened to them of late, whether *constitutionally* or not, are under all those motives which interest or ambition inspire, of courting the favor of that branch from which appointments flow: that grand juries are frequently composed in part of by-standers, often foreigners, of foreign attachments and interests, and little knowledge of the laws they are most improperly called to decide on; and finally, is to give to the Judiciary, and through them to the Executive, a complete preponderance over the legislature, rendering ineffectual that wise and cautious distribution of powers made by the constitution between the three branches, and subordinating to the other two that branch which most immediately depends on the people themselves, and is responsible to them at short periods.

That independently of these considerations of a constitutional nature, the right of free correspondence between citizen and citizen on their joint interests, public or private, and under whatsoever laws these interests arise, is a natural right of every individual citizen, not the gift of municipal law, but among the objects for the protection of which municipal laws are instituted: that so far as the attempt to take away this natural right of free correspondence is an offence against the privileges of the legislative house, of which the said Samuel J. Cabell is a member, it is left to that house, entrusted with the preservation of its own privileges, to vindicate its immunities against the encroachments and usurpations of a co-ordinate branch; but so far as it is an infraction of our individual rights as citizens by other citizens of our own State, the judicature of this commonwealth is solely competent to its cognizance, no other possessing any powers of redress: that the commonwealth retains all its judiciary cognisances not expressly alienated in the grant of powers to the United States as expressed in their constitution: that that constitution alienates only those enumerated in itself, or arising under laws or treaties of the United States made in conformity with its own tenor: but the right of free correspondence is not claimed under that constitution nor the laws or treaties derived from it, but as a natural right, placed originally under the protection of our municipal laws, and retained under the cognizance of our own courts.

Your petitioners further observe that though this crime may not be specifically defined and denominated by any particular statute, yet it is a crime, and of the highest and most alarming nature; that the constitution of this commonwealth, aware it would sometimes happen that deep and dangerous crimes, pronounced as such in the heart of every friend to his country and its free constitution, would often escape the definitions of the law, and yet ought not to escape its punishments, fearing at the same time to entrust such undescribed offences to the discretion of ordinary juries and judges, has reserved the same to the cognizance of the body of the commonwealth acting by their representatives in general assembly, for which purpose provision is made by the constitution in the following words, to wit: "The Governor, when he is out of office, and *others* offending against the State, either by mal-administration, corruption, *or other means* by which the safety of the State may be endangered, shall be impeachable by the House of Delegates. Such impeachment to be prosecuted by the Attorney General or such other person or persons as the house may appoint in the general court, according to the laws of the land. If found guilty, he or they shall be either forever disabled to hold any office under government, or removed from such offices *pro tempore*, or subjected to such pains or penalties as the law shall direct."

Considering then the House of Delegates as the standing inquest of the whole commonwealth so established by the constitution, that its jurisdiction as such extends over all persons within its limits, and that no pale, no sanctuary has been erected against their jurisdiction to protect offenders who have committed crimes against the laws of the commonwealth and rights of its citizens: that the crime committed by the said grand jurors is of that high and extraordinary character for which the constitution has provided extraordinary procedure: that though the violation of right falls in the first instance on us, your petitioners and the representative chosen immediately by us, yet in principle and consequence it extends to all our fellow-citizens, whose safety is passed away whenever their representatives are placed, in the exercise of their functions, under the direction and coercion of either of the other departments of government, and one of their most interesting rights is lost when that of a free communication of sentiment by speaking or writing is suppressed: We, your petitioners, therefore pray that you will be pleased to take your constitutional cognizance of the premises, and institute such proceedings for impeaching and punishing the said A, B, &c., as may secure to the citizens of this commonwealth their constitutional right: that their representatives shall in the exercise of their functions be free and independent of the other departments of government, may guard that full intercourse between them and their constituents which the nature of their relations and the laws of the land establish, may save to them the natural right of communicating their sentiments to one another by speaking and writing, and may serve as a terror to others attempting hereafter to subvert those rights and the fundamental principles of our constitution, to exclude the people from all direct influence over the government they have established by reducing that branch of the legislature which they choose directly, to a subordination under those over whom they have but an indirect, distant, and feeble control.

And your petitioners further submit to the wisdom of the two houses of assembly whether the safety of the citizens of this commonwealth in their persons, their property, their laws, and government, does not require that the capacity to act in the important office of a juror, grand or petty, civil or criminal, should be restrained in future to native citizens of the United States, or such as were citizens at the date of the treaty of peace which closed our revolutionary war, and whether the ignorance of our laws and natural partiality to the countries of their birth are not reasonable causes for declaring this to be one of the rights incommunicable in future to adoptive citizens.

We, therefore, your petitioners, relying with entire confidence on the wisdom and patriotism of our representatives in General assembly, clothed preëminently with all the powers of the people which have not been reserved to themselves, or enumerated in the grant to the General Government delegated to maintain all their rights and relations not expressly and exclusively transferred to other jurisdictions, and stationed as sentinels to observe with watchfulness and oppose with firmness all movements tending to destroy the equilibrium of our excellent but complicated machine of government, invoke from you that redress of our violated rights which the freedom and safety of our common country calls for. We denounce to you a great crime, wicked in its purpose, and mortal in its consequences unless prevented, committed by citizens of this commonwealth against the body of their country. If we have erred in conceiving the redress provided by the law, we commit the subject to the superior wisdom of this house to devise and pursue such proceedings as they shall think best; and we, as in duty bound, shall every pray, &c.

41. SEDITIOUS LIBEL AND STATES' RIGHTS

The Sedition Act was the occasion for the emergence of a bold new libertarianism, but Jefferson contributed to no part of it and seems not to have profited from it. Unquestionably he was convinced that the Sedition Act was mortally dangerous to freedom and was unconstitutional. Yet his principal statement, the Kentucky Resolutions of 1798, was no passionate defense of freedom of the press and of political opinion. Indeed, he did not even take the position that the Sedition Act was void and dangerous because a free, republican government could not and should not punish the press for crimes of opinion. His position, rather, was that the power to punish crimes reached by the act was exclusively reserved to the states. Here are the relevant sections of the Kentucky Resolutions. Jefferson's authorship, as in the case of his petition in the Cabell case, was kept a secret. He did not speak out in public, though the occasion called for a public defense of freedom.

... 2. *Resolved,* that the Constitution of the United States having delegated to Congress a power to punish treason, counterfeiting the securities and current coin of the United States, piracies and felonies committed on the high seas, and offenses against the laws of nations, and no other crimes whatever, and it being true as a general principle, and one of the amendments to the Constitution having also declared "that the powers not delegated to the United States by the Constitution, nor prohibited by it to the States, are reserved to the States respectively, or to the people," therefore also [the Sedition Act] passed on the 14th day of July, 1798; as also the act passed by them on the 27th day of June, 1798, entitled "An act to punish frauds committed on the Bank of the United States" (and all other their acts which assume to create, define, or punish crimes other than those enumerated in the Constitution), are altogether void and of no force, and that the power to create, define, and punish such other crimes is reserved, and of right appertains solely and exclusively to the respective States, each within its own Territory.

3. *Resolved,* that it is true as a general principle, and is also expressly declared by one of the amendments to the Constitution that "the powers not delegated to the United States by the Constitution, nor prohibited by it to the States, are reserved to the States respectively or to the people;" and that no power

---

The Kentucky Resolutions of 1798, in *The Debates in the Several State Conventions on the Adoption of the Federal Constitution,* ed. Jonathan Elliot (2nd ed.; Philadelphia: 1941), IV, 540–541.

over the freedom of religion, freedom of speech, or freedom of the press being delegated to the United States by the Constitution, nor prohibited by it to the States, all lawful powers respecting the same did of right remain, and were reserved to the States, or to the people: That thus was manifested their determination to retain to themselves the right of judging how far the licentiousness of speech and of the press may be abridged without lessening their useful freedom, and how far those abuses which cannot be separated from their use should be tolerated rather than the use be destroyed; and thus also they guarded against all abridgment by the United States of the freedom of religious opinions and exercises, and retained to themselves the right of protecting the same, as this State, by a law passed on the general demand of its citizens, had already protected them from all human restraint or interference: And that in addition to this general principle and express declaration, another and more special provision has been made by one of the amendments to the Constitution which expressly declares, that "Congress shall make no law respecting an establishment of religion, or prohibiting the free exercise thereof, or abridging the freedom of speech, or of the press," thereby guarding in the same sentence, and under the same words, the freedom of religion, of speech, and of the press, insomuch, that whatever violates either, throws down the sanctuary which covers the others, and that libels, falsehoods, defamation equally with heresy and false religion, are withheld from the cognizance of Federal tribunals. That therefore [the Sedition Act], which does abridge the freedom of the press, is not law, but is altogether void and of no effect. . . .

The Jefferson of the Jefferson Image

Documents 42–49 reflect the Jefferson who has become venerated as the apostle of liberty. The letter to Samuel Smith, Congressman from Maryland (Document 42), shows the Vice President's attitude of toleration toward the frenzied political filth being published against him by John Fenno and William Cobbett ("Porcupine"), the witch-hunting Federalist editors. Jefferson's letter to Elbridge Gerry (Document 43), who became Vice President under Madison, expresses a belief in the right of citizens to criticize, even unjustly, the conduct of public officials. The letter to the great Dr. Rush of Philadelphia (Document 44), contains the immortal line that symbolizes Jefferson for the ages; the eloquent First Inaugural Address (Document 45) contains the equally memorable passage on tolerance for subversive political opinion—the only thought of its kind to be found in the entire body of Jefferson's writings. The second letter to Gerry (Document 46) includes the new President's resolve not to invade the right of opinion, and his letter of 1802 to Attorney General Levi Lincoln (Document 47), states his policy of "getting along without public prosecutions for *libels*." His letter to a French correspondent, Monsieur Pictet (Document 48), is in the same spirit. Finally, in the letter to his old friend, John Tyler, an anti-Federalist politician and Virginia jurist (Document 49), Jefferson endorses freedom of the press, despite its abuses, and reiterates his confidence in the public judgment.

42. ENDURING NEWSPAPER CALUMNIES

[To Samuel Smith]

These observations will show you, how far the imputations in the paragraph sent me approach the truth. Yet they are not intended for a newspaper. At a very early period of my life, I determined never to put a sentence into any newspaper. I have religiously adhered to the resolution through my life, and

---

Thomas Jefferson to Samuel Smith, August 22, 1798, in *The Writings of Thomas Jefferson*, ed. Ford, VII, 279–280.

have great reason to be contented with it. Were I to undertake to answer the calumnies of the newspapers, it would be more than all my own time, & that of 20. aids could effect. For while I should be answering one, twenty new ones would be invented. I have thought it better to trust to the justice of my countrymen, that they would judge me by what they *see* of my conduct on the stage where they have placed me, & what they knew of me *before* the epoch since which a particular party has supposed it might answer some view of theirs to vilify me in the public eye. Some, I know, will not reflect how apocryphal is the testimony of enemies so palpably betraying the views with which they give it. But this is an injury to which duty requires every one to submit whom the public think proper to call into it's councils. I thank you, my dear Sir, for the interest you have taken for me on this occasion. Though I have made up my mind not to suffer calumny to disturb my tranquillity, yet I retain all my sensibilities for the approbation of the good & just. That is, indeed, the chief consolation for the hatred of so many, who, without the least personal knowledge, & on the sacred evidence of Porcupine & Fenno alone, cover me with their implacable hatred. The only return I will ever make them, will be to do them all the good I can, in spite of their teeth. . . .

43. JEFFERSON'S CREDO

[TO ELBRIDGE GERRY]

I do then, with sincere zeal, wish an inviolable preservation of our present federal constitution, according to the true sense in which it was adopted by the States, that in which it was advo-

---

Thomas Jefferson to Elbridge Gerry, January 26, 1799, in *The Writings of Thomas Jefferson,* ed. Ford, VII, 327–329.

cated by it's friends, & not that which it's enemies apprehended, who therefore became it's enemies; and I am opposed to the monarchising it's features by the forms of it's administration, with a view to conciliate a first transition to a President & Senate for life, & from that to a hereditary tenure of these offices, & thus to worm out the elective principle. I am for preserving to the States the powers not yielded by them to the Union, & to the legislature of the Union it's constitutional share in the division of powers; and I am not for transferring all the powers of the States to the general government, & all those of that government to the Executive branch. I am for a government rigorously frugal & simple, applying all the possible savings of the public revenue to the discharge of the national debt; and not for a multiplication of officers & salaries merely to make partisans, & for increasing, by every device, the public debt, on the principle of it's being a public blessing. I am for relying, for internal defence, on our militia solely, till actual invasion, and for such a naval force only as may protect our coasts and harbors from such depredations as we have experienced; and not for a standing army in time of peace, which may overawe the public sentiment; nor for a navy, which, by it's own expenses and the eternal wars in which it will implicate us, will grind us with public burthens, & sink us under them. I am for free commerce with all nations; political connection with none; & little or no diplomatic establishment. And I am not for linking ourselves by new treaties with the quarrels of Europe; entering that field of slaughter to preserve their balance, or joining in the confederacy of kings to war against the principles of liberty. I am for freedom of religion, & against all maneuvres to bring about a legal ascendancy of one sect over another: for freedom of the press, & against all violations of the constitution to silence by force & not by reason the complaints or criticisms, just or unjust, of our citizens against the conduct of their agents. And I am for encouraging the progress of science in all it's branches; and not for raising a hue and cry against the sacred name of philosophy; for awing the human mind by stories of raw-head & bloody bones to a distrust of its own vision, & to repose implicitly on that of others; to go backwards instead of forwards to look for improvement; to believe that government, religion, morality, & every other science were in the highest perfection in ages of the darkest ignorance, and that nothing can ever be devised more perfect than what was established by our forefathers. To these I will add, that I was a sincere well-wisher to the success of the French revolution, and still wish it may end in the establishment of a free & well-ordered republic; but I have not been insensible under the atrocious depredations they have committed on our commerce. The first object of my heart is my own country. In that is embarked my family, my fortune, & my own existence. I have not one farthing of interest, nor one fibre of attachment out of it, nor a single motive of preference of any one nation to another, but in proportion as they are more or less friendly to us. . . .

44. ETERNAL HOSTILITY AGAINST TYRANNY

[To Benjamin Rush]

. . . I promised you a letter on Christianity, which I have not forgotten. On the contrary, it is because I have reflected on it, that I find much more time necessary for it than I can at present dispose of. I have a view of the subject which ought to displease neither the rational Christian nor Deists, and would reconcile many to a character they have too hastily rejected. I do not know that it would reconcile the *genus irritabile vatum* who are all in arms against me. Their hostility is on too interest-

---

Thomas Jefferson to Benjamin Rush, September 23, 1800, in *The Writings of Thomas Jefferson*, ed. Ford, VII, 460–461.

ing ground to be softened. The delusion into which the X. Y. Z. plot shewed it possible to push the people; the successful experiment made under the prevalence of that delusion on the clause of the constitution, which, while it secured the freedom of the press, covered also the freedom of religion, had given to the clergy a very favorite hope of obtaining an establishment of a particular form of Christianity thro' the U. S.; and as every sect believes its own form the true one, every one perhaps hoped for his own, but especially the Episcopalians & Congregationalists. The returning good sense of our country threatens abortion to their hopes, & they believe that any portion of power confided to me, will be exerted in opposition to their schemes. And they believe rightly; for I have sworn upon the altar of god, eternal hostility against every form of tyranny over the mind of man. But this is all they have to fear from me: & enough too in their opinion, & this is the cause of their printing lying pamphlets against me, forging conversations for me with Mazzei, Bishop Madison, &c., which are absolute falsehoods without a circumstance of truth to rest on; falsehoods, too, of which I acquit Mazzei & Bishop Madison, for they are men of truth.

But enough of this: it is more than I have before committed to paper on the subject of all the lies that has been preached and printed against me. . . .

45. TOLERATING ERROR OF OPINION

. . . During the contest of opinion through which we have passed, the animation of discussions and of exertions has sometimes worn an aspect which might impose on strangers unused to think freely and to speak and to write what they think. But

---

Thomas Jefferson, First Inaugural Address, March 4, 1801, in *The Writings of Thomas Jefferson*, ed. Ford, VIII, 2–3.

this being now decided by the voice of the nation, enounced according to the rules of the Constitution, all will of course arrange themselves under the will of the law and unite in common efforts for the common good. All, too, will bear in mind this sacred principle that, though the will of the majority is in all cases to prevail, that will, to be rightful, must be reasonable; that the minority possess their equal rights, which equal laws must protect and to violate which would be oppression. Let us then, fellow citizens, unite with one heart and one mind; let us restore to social intercourse that harmony and affection without which liberty, and even life itself, are but dreary things. And let us reflect that, having banished from our land that religious intolerance under which mankind so long bled and suffered, we have yet gained little if we countenance a political intolerance as despotic, as wicked, and capable of as bitter and bloody persecutions. During the throes and convulsions of the ancient world, during the agonizing spasms of infuriated man, seeking through blood and slaughter his long-lost liberty, it was not wonderful that the agitation of the billows should reach even this distant and peaceful shore, that this should be more felt and feared by some and less by others, and should divide opinions as to measures of safety.

But every difference of opinion is not a difference of principle. We have called by different names brethren of the same principle. We are all republicans; we are all federalists. If there be any among us who would wish to dissolve this Union or to change its republican form, let them stand undisturbed as monuments of the safety with which error of opinion may be tolerated, where reason is left free to combat it. I know, indeed, that some honest men fear that a republican government cannot be strong; that this government is not strong enough. But would the honest patriot, in the full tide of successful experiment, abandon a government which has so far kept us free and firm, on the theoretic and visionary fear that this government, the world's best hope, may by possibility want energy to preserve itself? I trust not. I believe this, on the contrary, the strongest government on earth. I believe it the only one where every man, at the call of the law, would fly to the standard of the law and would meet invasions of the public order as his own personal concern. Sometimes it is said that man cannot be trusted with the government of himself. Can he then be trusted with the government of others? Or have we found angels, in the form of kings, to govern him? Let history answer this question. . . .

46. THE RIGHT OF OPINION SHALL SUFFER

NO INVASION

[To Elbridge Gerry]

. . . Mr. Adams' last appointments, when he knew he was naming counsellors & aids for me & not for himself, I set aside as far as depends on me. Officers who have been guilty of gross abuses of office, such as marshals packing juries, &c., I shall now remove, as my predecessor ought in justice to have done. The instances will be few, and governed by strict rule, & not party passion. The right of opinion shall suffer no invasion from me. Those who have acted well have nothing to fear, however they may have differed from me in opinion: those who have done ill, however, have nothing to hope; nor shall I fail to do justice lest it should be ascribed to that difference of opinion. A coalition of sentiments is not for the interest of printers. They, like the clergy, live by the zeal they can kindle, and the schisms they can create. It is contest of opinion in politics as well as religion which makes us take great interest in them, and bestow our money liberally on those who furnish aliment to our appetite. . . .

Thomas Jefferson to Elbridge Gerry, March 29, 1801, in *The Writings of Thomas Jefferson,* ed. Ford, VIII, 42.

47. PATIENCE INSTEAD OF PROSECUTIONS

[To Levi Lincoln]

I had no conception there were persons enough to support a paper whose stomachs could bear such aliment as the enclosed papers contain. They are far beyond even the Washington Federalist. To punish however is impracticable until the body of the people, from whom juries are to be taken, get their minds to rights; and even then I doubt its expediency. While a full range is proper for actions by individuals, either private or public, for slanders affecting them, I would wish much to see the experiment tried of getting along without public prosecutions for *libels*. I believe we can do it. Patience and well doing, instead of punishment, if it can be found sufficiently efficacious, would be a happy change in the instruments of government. . . .

48. THE REMEDY FOR ABUSES OF THE PRESS

[To Monsieur Pictet]

. . . I state these general outlines to you, because I believe you take some interest in our fortune, and because our newspapers, for the most part, present only the caricatures of disaffected minds. Indeed, the abuses of the freedom of the press here have been carried to a length never before known or borne by any civilized nation. But it is so difficult to draw a clear line of separation between the abuse and the wholesome use of the

---

Thomas Jefferson to Levi Lincoln, March 24, 1802, in *The Writings of Thomas Jefferson,* ed. Ford, VIII, 139.

Thomas Jefferson to Monsieur Pictet, February 5, 1803, in *The Writings of Thomas Jefferson,* ed. Lipscomb and Bergh, X, 357.

press, that as yet we have found it better to trust the public judgment, rather than the magistrate, with the discrimination between truth and falsehood. And hitherto the public judgment has performed that office with wonderful correctness. . . .

49. FREEDOM OF THE PRESS AND CONFIDENCE

IN THE PEOPLE

[To John Tyler]

DEAR SIR,—Your favor of the 10th instant has been duly received. Amidst the direct falsehoods, the misrepresentations of truth, the calumnies and the insults resorted to by a faction to mislead the public mind, and to overwhelm those entrusted with its interests, our support is to be found in the approving voice of our conscience and country, in the testimony of our fellow citizens, that their confidence is not shaken by these artifices. When to the plaudits of the honest multitude, the sober approbation of the sage in his closet is added, it becomes a gratification of an higher order. It is the sanction of wisdom superadded to the voice of affection. The terms, therefore, in which you are so good as to express your satisfaction with the course of the present administration cannot but give me great pleasure. I may err in my measures, but never shall deflect from the intention to fortify the public liberty by every possible means, and to put it out of the power of the few to riot on the labors of the many. No experiment can be more interesting than that we are now trying, and which we trust will end in establishing the fact, that man may be governed by reason and truth. Our first object should therefore be, to leave open

---

Thomas Jefferson to John Tyler, June 28, 1804, in *The Writings of Thomas Jefferson,* ed. Lipscomb and Bergh, XI, 33–34.

to him all the avenues to truth. The most effectual hitherto found, is the freedom of the press. It is, therefore, the first shut up by those who fear the investigation of their actions. The firmness with which the people have withstood the late abuses of the press, the discernment they have manifested between truth and falsehood, show that they may safely be trusted to hear everything true and false, and to form a correct judgment between them. As little is it necessary to impose on their senses, or dazzle their minds by pomp, splendor, or forms. Instead of this artificial, how much surer is that real respect, which results from the use of their reason, and the habit of bringing everything to the test of common sense.

I hold it, therefore, certain, that to open the doors of truth, and to fortify the habit of testing everything by reason, are the most effectual manacles we can rivet on the hands of our successors to prevent their manacling the people with their own consent. The panic into which they were artfully thrown in 1798, the frenzy which was excited in them by their enemies against their apparent readiness to abandon all the principles established for their own protection, seemed for awhile to countenance the opinions of those who say they cannot be trusted with their own government. But I never doubted their rallying; and they did rally much sooner than I expected. On the whole, that experiment on their credulity has confirmed my confidence in their ultimate good sense and virtue. . . .

Suppression and States' Rights

In Documents 33, 36, 38, and 41 we have seen Jefferson endorse the principle of prosecuting those who publish "false" political "facts." Indeed he even wished to exempt from the protection of the First Amendment "false facts" affecting the peace of the nation (see Document 38). Since that amendment was intended as a prohibition on the powers of Congress, Jefferson's desired exemption implied his approval of a federal power to punish the publication of false facts affecting the nation's peace. The Kentucky Resolutions, however, indicated that he believed that the states possessed exclusive power to punish "licentiousness of speech, and of the press" or "libels" and "falsehood."

His accession to power stimulated a fresh understanding of the dangers or licentiousness of an uncontrolled opposition press. He preferred a policy of sufferance or toleration, but the Federalist press, foul and vicious in its attacks, simply goaded him beyond endurance. The letter to Governor McKean of Pennsylvania (Document 50) and his not quite candid Second Inaugural Address (Document 53), indicate his reaction. He advocated selected prosecutions to avoid the appearance of a persecution and hoped, as he said to McKean and suggested to the nation in the Second Inaugural, that the states would act coercively under their laws to reform abuses of the press. His belief in the exclusive power of the states to control the press is explicitly restated in his second letter to Mrs. John Adams (Document 52). In the first (Document 51), he explains why he pardoned those convicted under the Sedition Act. The letter to Thomas Seymour, one of his Connecticut supporters (Document 54), indicates an aberrational shift in his thinking. Seymour, in a letter of December 20, 1806, informed the President that Connecticut Republicans supported "the prosecutions depending before the Circuit Court in this District (Hartford), for Libels against the President and Administration of the General Government." Seymour gave few specific facts about those prosecutions, but mentioned that the defendants, whom he did not name, included "a Judge, two political Priests, and three Federal printers." All Washington learned about those prosecutions when Connecticut Congressman Samuel W. Dana mentioned them to the House of Representatives on January 2, 1807, in order to obtain support for his abortive bill making truth a defense in federal criminal-libel trials. Jefferson, a month later in his reply to Seymour, assumed his usual Olympian pose but significantly did not denounce the prosecutions. By leaving "to others" the task of restoring the press to truth, and by failing to order his attorney general to quash the indictments, he condoned the prosecutions in a United States court.

50. JEFFERSON ADVOCATES A "FEW PROSECUTIONS"

[To Thomas McKean]

... On the subject of prosecutions, what I say must be entirely confidential, for you know the passion for torturing every sentiment & word which comes from me. The federalists having failed in destroying the freedom of the press by their gaglaw, seem to have attacked it in an opposite form, that is by pushing it's licentiousness & it's lying to such a degree of prostitution as to deprive it of all credit. And the fact is that so abandoned are the tory presses in this particular that even the least informed of the people have learnt that nothing in a newspaper is to be believed. This is a dangerous state of things, and the press ought to be restored to it's credibility if possible. The restraints provided by the laws of the states are sufficient for this if applied. And I have therefore long thought that a few prosecutions of the most prominent offenders would have a wholesome effect in restoring the integrity of the presses. Not a general prosecution, for that would look like persecution: but a selected one. The paper I now inclose appears to me to offer as good an instance in every respect to make an example of, as can be selected. However of this you are the best judge. I inclose it lest you should not have it. If the same thing be done in some other of the states it will place the whole band more on their guard. Accept my friendly salutations & assurances of my high respect & consideration.

Thomas Jefferson to Thomas McKean, February 19, 1803, in *The Writings of Thomas Jefferson*, ed. Ford, VIII, 218–219.

51. ON LIBERATING VICTIMS OF THE SEDITION ACT

[To Abigail Adams]

. . . With respect to the calumnies and falsehoods which writers and printers at large published against Mr. Adams, I was as far from stooping to any concern or approbation of them, as Mr. Adams was respecting those of Porcupine, Fenno, or Russell, who published volumes against me for every sentence vended by their opponents against Mr. Adams. But I never supposed Mr. Adams had any participation in the atrocities of these editors, or their writers. I knew myself incapable of that base warfare, & believed him to be so. On the contrary, whatever I may have thought of the acts of the administration of that day, I have ever borne testimony to Mr. Adams' personal worth; nor was it ever impeached in my presence without a just vindication of it on my part. I never supposed that any person who knew either of us, could believe that either of us meddled in that dirty work. But another fact is, that I "liberated a wretch who was suffering for a libel against Mr. Adams." I do not know who was the particular wretch alluded to; but I discharged every person under punishment or prosecution under the sedition law, because I considered, & now consider, that law to be a nullity, as absolute and as palpable as if Congress had ordered us to fall down and worship a golden image; and that it was as much my duty to arrest its execution in every stage, as it would have been to have rescued from the fiery furnace those who should have been cast into it for refusing to worship their image. It was accordingly done in every instance, without asking what the offenders had done, or against whom they had offended, but whether the pains they were suffering were inflicted under the pretended sedition law. It was cer-

---

Thomas Jefferson to Abigail Adams, July 22, 1804, in *The Writings of Thomas Jefferson,* ed. Ford, VIII, 309–310.

tainly possible that my motives for contributing to the relief of Callender, and liberating sufferers under the sedition law, might have been to protect, encourage, and reward slander; but they may also have been those which inspire ordinary charities to objects of distress, meritorious or not, or the obligations of an oath to protect the Constitution, violated by an unauthorized act of Congress. Which of these were my motives, must be decided by a regard to the general tenor of my life. On this I am not afraid to appeal to the nation at large, to posterity, and still less to that Being who sees himself our motives, who will judge us from his own knowledge of them, and not on the testimony of Porcupine or Fenno. . . .

52. THE POWER TO CONTROL FREEDOM
OF THE PRESS

[To Abigail Adams]

. . . You seem to think it devolved on the judges to decide on the validity of the sedition law. But nothing in the Constitution has given them a right to decide for the Executive, more than to the Executive to decide for them. Both magistracies are equally independent in the sphere of action assigned to them. The judges, believing the law constitutional, had a right to pass a sentence of fine and imprisonment; because that power was placed in their hands by the Constitution. But the Executive, believing the law to be unconstitutional, was bound to remit the execution of it; because that power has been confided to him by the Constitution. That instrument meant that its coordinate branches should be checks on each other. But the

---

Thomas Jefferson to Abigail Adams, September 11, 1804, in *The Writings of Thomas Jefferson*, ed. Ford, VIII, 310.

opinion which gives to the judges the right to decide what laws are constitutional, and what not, not only for themselves in their own sphere of action, but for the Legislature & Executive also, in their spheres, would make the judiciary a despotic branch. Nor does the opinion of the unconstitutionality, & consequent nullity of that law, remove all restraint from the overwhelming torrent of slander, which is confounding all vice and virtue, all truth & falsehood, in the U. S. The power to do that is fully possessed by the several State Legislatures. It was reserved to them, & was denied to the General Government, by the Constitution, according to our construction of it. While we deny that Congress have a right to control the freedom of the press, we have ever asserted the right of the States, and their exclusive right, to do so. They have accordingly, all of them, made provisions for punishing slander, which those who have time and inclination, resort to for the vindication of their characters. In general, the State laws appear to have made the presses responsible for slander as far as is consistent with its useful freedom. In those States where they do not admit even the truth of allegations to protect the printer, they have gone too far. . . .

53. "THE SALUTARY COERCIONS OF THE LAW"

. . . During this course of administration, and in order to disturb it, the artillery of the press has been levelled against us, charged with whatsoever its licentiousness could devise or dare. These abuses of an institution so important to freedom and science, are deeply to be regretted, inasmuch as they tend to lessen its usefulness, and to sap its safety; they might, in-

---

Thomas Jefferson, Second Inaugural Address, March 4, 1805, in *The Writings of Thomas Jefferson,* ed. Ford, VIII, 346–347.

deed, have been corrected by the wholesome punishments reserved and provided by the laws of the several States against falsehood and defamation; but public duties more urgent press on the time of public servants, and the offenders have therefore been left to find their punishment in the public indignation.

Nor was it uninteresting to the world, that an experiment should be fairly and fully made, whether freedom of discussion, unaided by power, is not sufficient for the propagation and protection of truth—whether a government, conducting itself in the true spirit of its constitution, with zeal and purity, and doing no act which it would be unwilling the whole world should witness, can be written down by falsehood and defamation. The experiment has been tried; you have witnessed the scene; our fellow citizens have looked on, cool and collected; they saw the latent source from which these outrages proceeded; they gathered around their public functionaries, and when the constitution called them to the decision by suffrage, they pronounced their verdict, honorable to those who had served them, and consolatory to the friend of man, who believes he may be intrusted with his own affairs.

No inference is here intended, that the laws, provided by the State against false and defamatory publications, should not be enforced; he who has time, renders a service to public morals and public tranquillity, in reforming these abuses by the salutary coercions of the law; but the experiment is noted, to prove that, since truth and reason have maintained their ground against false opinions in league with false facts, the press, confined to truth, needs no other legal restraint; the public judgment will correct false reasonings and opinions, on a full hearing of all parties; and no other definite line can be drawn between the inestimable liberty of the press and its demoralizing licentiousness. If there be still improprieties which this rule would not restrain, its supplement must be sought in the censorship of public opinion. . . .

54. CONDONING FEDERAL PROSECUTIONS FOR

SEDITIOUS LIBEL

[To Thomas Seymour]

SIR,—The mass of business which occurs during a session of the Legislature, renders me necessarily unpunctual in acknowledging the receipt of letters, and in answering those which will admit of delay. This must be my apology for being so late in noticing the receipt of the letter of December 20th, addressed to me by yourself, and several other republican characters of your State of high respectability. I have seen with deep concern the afflicting oppression under which the republican citizens of Connecticut suffer from an unjust majority. The truths expressed in your letter have been long exposed to the nation through the channel of the public papers, and are the more readily believed because most of the States during the momentary ascendancy of kindred majorities in them, have seen the same spirit of oppression prevail.

With respect to the countervailing prosecutions now instituted in the Court of the U S in Connecticut, I had heard but little, & certainly, I believe, never expressed a sentiment on them. That a spirit of indignation and retaliation should arise when an opportunity should present itself, was too much within the human constitution to excite either surprise or censure, and confined to an appeal to truth only, it cannot lessen the useful freedom of the press.

As to myself, conscious that there was not a *truth* on earth which I feared should be known, I have lent myself willingly as the subject of a great experiment, which was to prove that an administration, conducting itself with integrity and common

---

Thomas Jefferson to Thomas Seymour, February 11, 1807, in *The Writings of Thomas Jefferson*, ed. Ford, IX, 28–31.

understanding, cannot be battered down, even by the false-hoods of a licentious press, and consequently still less by the press, as restrained within the legal & wholesome limits of truth. This experiment was wanting for the world to demonstrate the falsehood of the pretext that freedom of the press is incompatible with orderly government. I have never therefore even contradicted the thousands of calumnies so industriously propagated against myself. But the fact being once established, that the press is impotent when it abandons itself to falsehood, I leave to others to restore it to it's strength, by recalling it within the pale of truth. Within that it is a noble institution, equally the friend of science & of civil liberty. If this can once be effected in your State, I trust we shall soon see it's citizens rally to the republican principles of our Constitution, which unite their sister-States into one family. It would seem impossible that an intelligent people, with the faculty of reading & right of thinking, should continue much longer to slumber under the pupilage of an interested aristocracy of priests & lawyers, persuading them to distrust themselves, & to let them think for them. I sincerely wish that your efforts may awaken them from this voluntary degradation of mind, restore them to a due estimate of themselves & their fellow-citizens, and a just abhorrence of the falsehoods & artifices which have seduced them. Experience of the use made by federalism of whatever comes from me, obliges me to suggest the caution of considering my letter as private. . . .

Jefferson in Retirement

Jefferson never lost faith in the general principle of freedom of the press, but the actual performance of the press not only disappointed him deeply but embittered him. He was convinced that

the press was hopelessly abandoned to falsehoods and licentiousness. In his letter to John Norvell, a student (Document 55), he
professed to believe that the press was doing more harm than would
result from its suppression, but he never again advocated or condoned prosecutions. In later life he read, according to his own word,
only one newspaper, the *Richmond Enquirer,* "and in that chiefly
the advertisements, for they contain the only truths to be relied on
in a newspaper." He was wrong, because there were several excellent newspapers in the country, and they were as fair and responsible as any Jefferson had ever seen. The nation's press was
strongly partisan, to be sure, and given to excesses when judging
public men and measures, but that was the price of a political
democracy and freedom of the press. The letter to a correspondent,
Dr. Walter Jones (Document 57), expresses an habitual despair
and vituperation respecting the press. Coming from one who had
backed the savage partisanship of the Republican press of the
1790's and after, this letter, like the one to Norvell, expressed a
viewpoint that would have been thrown out of a court of equity
where the doctrine of "clean hands" prevailed. The letter to Monsieur Dufief (Document 56) reveals the libertarian Jefferson protesting against censorship. His anger was provoked by the news
that a bookdealer was being prosecuted for selling a French treatise
on the creation of the world. On questions of intellectual freedom—
matters involving scholarship, philosophy, science, and of course
religion—Jefferson with very rare exceptions was a steadfast
champion of the libertarian position. It is noteworthy that he saw
this issue of censorship in terms of freedom of religion. In the final
letter in this section (Document 58), the aged Jefferson offered a
French correspondent advice on what to include in a new constitution. He had heard that a new government was being formed,
and his mind went back to the glorious, hopeful days of the 1780's.
"The American experience," he wrote pridefully, "might well be
emulated." His paragraph on freedom of the press was the finest and
most libertarian he ever composed, and it was unique in all his
thinking on the subject. He advocated that the press be liable only
for "personal injuries." By implication he rejected all criminal

prosecutions. It was his final testament on freedom of the press, and it put him, belatedly, on the side of the libertarian theorists of 1798–1803.

55. "PROSTITUTION TO FALSEHOOD"

[To John Norvell]

. . . To your request of my opinion of the manner in which a newspaper should be conducted so as to be most useful, I should answer, "by restraining it to true facts and sound principles only." Yet I fear such a paper would find few subscribers. It is a melancholy truth that a suppression of the press could not more completely deprive the nation of its benefits than is done by its abandoned prostitution to falsehood. Nothing can now be believed which is seen in a newspaper. Truth itself becomes suspicious by being put into that polluted vehicle. The real extent of this state of misinformation is known only to those who are in situations to confront facts within their knowledge with the lies of the day. I really look with commiseration over the great body of my fellow citizens who, reading newspapers, live and die in the belief that they have known something of what has been passing in the world in their time; whereas the accounts they have read in newspapers are just as true a history of any other period of the world as of the present except that the real names of the day are affixed to their fables. General facts may indeed be collected from them —such as that Europe is now at war, that Bonaparte has been a successful warrior, that he has subjected a great portion of Europe to his will, etc., etc., but no details can be relied on. I will add that the man who never looks into a newspaper is better informed than he who reads them, inasmuch as he who

---

Thomas Jefferson to John Norvell, June 11, 1807, in *The Writings of Thomas Jefferson,* ed. Lipscomb and Bergh, XI, 224.

knows nothing is nearer to truth than he whose mind is filled with falsehoods and errors. He who reads nothing will still learn the great facts, and the details are all false.

Perhaps an editor might begin a reformation in some such way as this: divide his paper into four chapters, heading the first, Truths, 2nd, Probabilities, 3rd, Possibilities, 4th, Lies. The first chapter would be very short, as it would contain little more than authentic papers and information from such sources as the editor would be willing to risk his own reputation for their truth. The second would contain what, from a mature consideration of all circumstances, his judgment should conclude to be probably true. This, however, should rather contain too little than too much. The third and fourth should be professedly for those readers who would rather have lies for their money than the blank paper they would occupy.

56. ON THE PUTRID STATE OF THE PRESS

[To Walter Jones]

. . . I deplore, with you, the putrid state into which our newspapers have passed, and the malignity, the vulgarity, and mendacious spirit of those who write for them; and I enclose you a recent sample, the production of a New England judge, as a proof of the abyss of degradation into which we are fallen. These ordures are rapidly depraving the public taste, and lessening its relish for sound food. As vehicles of information, and a curb on our functionaries, they have rendered themselves useless, by forfeiting all title to belief. That this has, in a great degree, been produced by the violence and malignity of party spirit, I agree with you; and I have read with great pleasure the paper you enclosed me on that subject, which I now return. . . .

Thomas Jefferson to Walter Jones, January 2, 1814, in *The Writings of Thomas Jefferson*, ed. Lipscomb and Bergh, XIV, 46.

57. "LET US FREELY HEAR BOTH SIDES"

[To N. G. Dufief]

DEAR SIR,—Your favor of the 6th instant is just received, and I shall with equal willingness and truth, state the degree of agency you had, respecting the copy of M. de Becourt's book, which came to my hands. That gentleman informed me, by letter, that he was about to publish a volume in French, "Sur la Création du Monde, un Système d'Organisation Primitive," which, its title promised to be, either a geological or astronomical work. I subscribed; and, when published, he sent me a copy; and as you were my correspondent in the book line in Philadelphia, I took the liberty of desiring him to call on you for the price, which, he afterwards informed me, you were so kind as to pay him for me, being, I believe, two dollars. But the sole copy which came to me was from himself directly, and, as far as I know, was never seen by you.

I am really mortified to be told that, *in the United States of America,* a fact like this can become a subject of inquiry, and of criminal inquiry too, as an offence against religion; that a question about the sale of a book can be carried before the civil magistrate. Is this then our freedom of religion? and are we to have a censor whose imprimatur shall say what books may be sold, and what we may buy? And who is thus to dogmatize religious opinions for our citizens? Whose foot is to be the measure to which ours are all to be cut or stretched? Is a priest to be our inquisitor, or shall a layman, simple as ourselves, set up his reason as the rule for what we are to read, and what we must believe? It is an insult to our citizens to question whether they are rational beings or not, and blas-

---

Thomas Jefferson to N. G. Dufief, April 19, 1814, in *The Writings of Thomas Jefferson,* ed. Lipscomb and Bergh, XIV, 126–129.

phemy against religion to suppose it cannot stand the test of truth and reason. If M. de Becourt's book be false in its facts, disprove them; if false in its reasoning, refute it. But, for God's sake, let us freely hear both sides, if we choose. I know little of its contents, having barely glanced over here and there a passage, and over the table of contents. From this, the Newtonian philosophy seemed the chief object of attack, the issue of which might be trusted to the strength of the two combatants; Newton certainly not needing the auxiliary arm of the government, and still less the holy Author of our religion, as to what in it concerns Him. I thought the work would be very innocent, and one which might be confided to the reason of any man; not likely to be much read if let alone, but, if persecuted, it will be generally read. Every man in the United States will think it a duty to buy a copy, in vindication of his right to buy, and to read what he pleases. I have been just reading the new constitution of Spain. One of its fundamental bases is expressed in these words: "The *Roman Catholic* religion, the only true one, is, and always shall be, that of the Spanish nation. The government protects it by wise and just laws, and prohibits the exercise of any other whatever." Now I wish this presented to those who question what you may sell, or we may buy, with a request to strike out the words, "Roman Catholic," and to insert the denomination of their own religion. This would ascertain the code of dogmas which each wishes should domineer over the opinions of all others, and be taken, like the Spanish religion, under the "protection of wise and just laws." It would show to what they wish to reduce the liberty for which one generation has sacrificed life and happiness. It would present our boasted freedom of religion as a thing of theory only, and not of practice, as what would be a poor exchange for the theoretic thraldom, but practical freedom of Europe. But it is impossible that the laws of Pennsylvania, which set us the first example of the wholesome and happy effects of religious freedom, can permit the inquisitorial functions to be proposed to their courts. Under them you are surely safe. . . .

58. LIABILITY FOR PERSONAL INJURIES ONLY

[To Adamantios Coray]

. . . I have stated that the constitutions of our several States vary more or less in some particulars. But there are certain principles in which all agree and which all cherish as vitally essential to the protection of the life, liberty, property, and safety of the citizen:

1. Freedom of religion, restricted only from *acts* of trespass on that of others;

2. Freedom of person, securing every one from imprisonment or other bodily restraint but by the laws of the land—this is effected by the well-known law of habeas corpus;

3. Trial by jury, the best of all safeguards for that person, the property, and the fame of every individual;

4. The exclusive right of legislation and taxation in the representatives of the people;

5. Freedom of the press, subject only to liability for personal injuries. This formidable censor of the public functionaries, by arraigning them at the tribunal of public opinion, produces reform peaceably, which must otherwise be done by revolution. It is also the best instrument for enlightening the mind of man and improving him as a rational, moral, and social being. . . .

Thomas Jefferson to Adamantios Coray, October 31, 1823, in *The Writings of Thomas Jefferson*, ed. Lipscomb and Bergh, XV, 489.

PART SIX

Epilogue: Zenger Redivivus

59. ALEXANDER HAMILTON MODERNIZES

ANDREW HAMILTON'S DEFENSE OF ZENGER

The facts of the Croswell case have been stated in the Introduction. From prosecution to appellate opinions, political expediency rather than devotion to principle governed the behavior of the participants. Vengeful New York Republicans, hoping to intimidate the Federalist press, prosecuted a small-town editor for alleged seditious libels against President Jefferson. Chief Justice Morgan Lewis, the trial judge, got a conviction by preventing the defense from proving that the libels were in fact true, and by restricting the jury to a verdict merely on the question whether the defendant published the statements charged against him—which he did not deny. Alexander Hamilton, on the appeal, argued that the jury, not the judge, should determine the libelous character of the publication, and that the defendant should have the opportunity, on retrial, to present evidence showing that Jefferson had paid to have Washington and Adams libelously denounced.

James Kent, one of the four judges of the state's high court, and a die-hard Federalist, described Hamilton's argument as "a masterpiece of pathetic, impassioned and sublime eloquence. It was probably never surpassed and made the deepest impression. I never heard him so great." The rhetoric and scholarship that so impressed Kent and others is available in the greatly abridged version of the argument published in the "Constitutional Edition" of *The Works of Alexander Hamilton*, edited by Henry Cabot Lodge (VIII, 387–

425). The Document that follows is a shorter, colder version of the speech, as reported by William Johnson, the official reporter of the court. It is this version, the one read by lawyers and judges, that has had so enduring an impact on American law. Following Hamilton's argument is a digest of Kent's opinion, probably the most cited judicial opinion on this subject in the history of American law. Kent, who became chief justice and then chancellor of New York, was the most learned judge of his time, with the exception of Joseph Story, and was one of the most influential judges in our legal history. His *Commentaries on American Law,* which went through five editions before his death in 1847, significantly affected legal developments throughout the country. His opinion in the Croswell case, giving judicial embodiment to Hamilton's argument, mustered the support of a Federalist colleague but was offset by Lewis' opinion, in which a Republican colleague joined.

Although the court was inconclusive, the prosecution against Croswell was dropped and the Hamilton-Kent position was adopted by the state legislature in the following year. That position spread rapidly throughout the nation. Today, with few exceptions, the states of the union—whether by constitutional provision, judicial decision, or statutory enactment—substantially follow the Hamilton-Kent position, which derives from Andrew Hamilton's argument in the Zenger case. In the end, then, Zengerian principles prevailed, after being abandoned by libertarian theorists like Madison and Wortman as too restrictive, and after being betrayed by such Republican jurists and politicians as Lewis, McKean, and sometimes Jefferson himself. The Hamilton-Kent definition of freedom of the press and of the restrictions on the right to criticize the government represents a position midway between the contradictory positions of the Jeffersonians.

. . . The following is a brief summary of the argument of *Hamilton,* in reply.

People v. *Croswell* (1804), in *Reports of Cases Adjudged in The Supreme Court of Judicature of the State of New York,* ed. William Johnson (7 vols.; Philadelphia: E. F. Backus 1834–1836), III, 352–367, 371–379 and 390–394.

He said, that the two great questions that arose in the cause were; 1. Can the truth be given in evidence? 2. Are the jury to judge of the intent and the law? The first point might be more embarrassing, but the second was clear.

The liberty of the press consisted in publishing with impunity, truth with good motives, and for justifiable ends, whether it related to men or to measures. To discuss measures without reference to men, was impracticable. Why examine measures, but to prove them bad, and to point out their pernicious authors, so that the people might correct the evil by removing the men? There was no other way to preserve liberty, and bring down a tyrannical faction. If this right was not permitted to exist in vigour and in exercise, good men would become silent; corruption and tyranny would go on, step by step, in usurpation, until, at last, nothing that was worth speaking, or writing, or acting for, would be left in our country.

But he did not mean to be understood as being the advocate of a press wholly without control. He reprobated the novel, the visionary, the pestilential doctrine of an unchecked press, and ill fated would be our country, if this doctrine was to prevail. It would encourage vice, compel the virtuous to retire, destroy confidence, and confound the innocent with the guilty. Single drops of water constantly falling may wear out adamant. The best character of our country, he to whom it was most indebted, and who is now removed beyond the reach of calumny, felt its corrosive effects. No, he did not contend for this terrible liberty of the press, but he contended for the right of publishing truth, with good motives, although the censure might light upon the government, magistrates, or individuals.

The check upon the press ought to be deposited, not in a permanent body of magistrates, as the court, but in an occasional and fluctuating body, the jury, who are to be selected by lot. Judges might be tempted to enter into the views of government, and to extend, by arbitrary constructions, the law of libels. In the theory of our government, the executive and legislative departments are operated upon by one influence, and act in one course, by means of popular election. How, then, are our judges to be independent? How can they withstand the combined force and spirit of the other departments? The judicial is less independent here than in *England,* and, of course, we have more reason, and stronger necessity, to cling to the trial by jury, as our greatest safety.

Men are not to be implicitly trusted, in elevated stations. The experience of mankind teaches us, that persons have often arrived at power by means of flattery and hypocrisy; but instead of continuing humble lovers of the people, have changed into their most deadly persecutors.

Lord *Camden* said, that he had not been able to find a satisfactory definition of a libel. He would venture, however, but with much diffidence, after the embarrassment which that great man had discovered, to submit to the court the following definition. *A libel is a censorious or ridiculing writing, picture or sign, made with a mischievous and malicious intent towards government, magistrates or individuals.* According to *Blackstone,* it is a malicious defamation made public, with intent to provoke or expose to public hatred and ridicule. The malice and intent enter into the essence of the crime, and must be proved, and are, accordingly, to be left to the jury, as parcel of the fact. The definition of Lord *Coke* does not oppose this result. He speaks of a libel, as having a tendency to break the peace. This, also, is a fact to be proved to the jury, for the tendency depends upon time, manner, circumstance, and must, of necessity, be a question of fact.

Texts taken from the holy scriptures, and scattered among the people, may, in certain times, and under certain circumstances, become libellous, nay, treasonable. These texts are, then, innocent, libellous, or treasonable, according to the time and intent; and surely the time, manner and intent, are matters of fact for a jury. It is the intent that constitutes the crime. This is a fundamental principle of jurisprudence. If we run through the several classes of offences, we shall perceive that in every instance, the intent constitutes and varies the crime. An instance was given in a *Star Chamber* case, of a father sending a reproachful letter to his son, and the intent was made the test whether it was to be adjudged a libel. Homicide is not, of itself, murder. Killing in battle, or in self defence, is lawful. Murder depends upon the malicious intent. Nothing is criminal, *per se,* which admits of a lawful excuse. Whether crime or not, will always depend upon intent, tendency, quality, manner, &c. and these must be matters of fact for the jury. The law cannot adjudge a paper to be a libel, until a jury have found the circumstances connected with the publication.

But it is not only the province of the jury, in all criminal cases, to judge of the intent with which the act was done, as being parcel of the fact; they are also authorized to judge of the law as connected with the fact. In civil cases, the court are the exclusive judges of the law, and this arose from the nature of pleadings in civil suits; for, anciently, matters of law arising in the defence, were required to be spread upon the record, by a special plea, and the jury were liable to an *attaint* for finding a verdict contrary to law. But in criminal cases, the law and fact are necessarily blended by the general issue, and a general verdict was always final and conclusive, both upon the law and the fact. Nor were the jury ever exposed to an *attaint* for a verdict in a criminal case; and this is decisive to prove that they had a concurrent jurisdiction with the court on questions of law; for where the law allows an act to be valid and definitive, it presupposes a legal and rightful authority to do it. This is a sure and infallible test of a legal power.

In *England,* trial by jury has always been cherished, as the great security of the subject against the oppression of government; but it never could have been a solid refuge and security, unless the jury had the right to judge of the intent and the law.

The jury ought, undoubtedly, to pay every respectful regard to the opinion of the court; but suppose a trial in a capital case, and the jury are satisfied from the arguments of counsel, the law authorities that are read, and their own judgment, upon the application of the law to the facts, (for the criminal law consists in general of plain principles,) that the law arising in the case is different from that which the court advances, are they not bound by their oaths, by their duty to their creator and themselves, to pronounce according to their own convictions? To oblige them, in such a case, to follow implicitly the direction of the court, is to make them commit perjury, and homicide, under the forms of law. Their error is fatal and cannot be corrected. The victim is sacrificed; he is executed; he perishes without redress. Was he a juror, in such a case, he would endure the rack rather than surrender his own convictions on the altar of power, rather than obey the judicial mandate.

Lord *Mansfield* showed, by his inconsistencies and embarrassment on this subject, that he was supporting a violent paradox. But he did not speak of the errors of that great man, but with the highest veneration for his memory. He would tread lightly over his ashes, and drop a tear of reverence as he passed by.

The case of the *Seven Bishops,* and *Fuller's* and *Tuchin's Cases,* are a series of precedents in favour of the right of the jury. The opposite precedents begin with Lord *Raymond,* but they have not been uniform nor undisputed. It has been constantly a floating and litigious question in *Westminster Hall.* A series of precedents only can form law. There can be no embarrassment in the court; they are at liberty to examine the question upon principles. The *English* declaratory act, recites that doubts had existed, and being declaratory, it is evidence of the sense of the nation. The Marquis of *Lansdowne* observed, in the house of lords, that the same declaratory bill had been brought in twenty years before, and was then deemed unnecessary.

The question how far the truth is to be given in evidence, depends much on the question of intent; for if the intent be a subject of inquiry for the jury, the giving the truth in evidence is requisite, as a means to determine the intent. Truth is a material ingredient in the evidence of intent. In the whole system of law there is no other case in which the truth cannot be shown; and this is sufficient to prove the proposition, which denies it in the present case, to be a paradox.

The *Roman* law permitted the truth to justify a libel. The ancient *English* statutes prove also, that in the root and origin of our law, falsity was an ingredient in the crime, and those statutes were declaratory of the common law. The ancient records and precedents prove the same thing, and they are the most authoritative evidence of the ancient law. In the celebrated case of the *Seven Bishops*, the court permitted the defendants to prove the truth of the facts stated in the petition. That case is also very important, in various views. It establishes the necessity of inquiring into the circumstances and intent of the act. It was an instance of a firm and successful effort to recall the principles of the common law, and was an important link in the chain of events that led on to the glorious era of their revolution. In *Fuller's Case*, Lord *Holt* allowed the defendant to go into proof of the truth of the charge. But while, he said, he advocated the admission of the truth, he subscribed to the doctrine of *Want's Case*, in *Moore*, that the truth ought only to be given in evidence, to determine *quo animo* the act was done. It ought not to be a justification in every case, for it may be published maliciously. It may be abused, to the gratification of the worst of passions, as in the promulgation of a man's personal defects or deformity.

The court of *Star Chamber* was the polluted source from whence the prosecutor's doctrine was derived. That is not the court from which we are to expect principles and precedents friendly to freedom. It was a most arbitrary, tyrannical and hated tribunal, under the control of a permanent body of magistrates, without the wholesome restraints of a jury. The whigs in *England,* after the revolution, in order to prop up their power, adopted, as in *Franklin's Case,* the arbitrary maxims of that court which had been reprobated at the revolution; and this ought to serve as a monitory lesson to rulers at the present day, for such is the nature, progress and effect of the human passions.

The right of giving the truth in evidence, in cases of libels, is all-important to the liberties of the people. Truth is an ingredient in the eternal order of things, in judging of the quality of acts. He hoped to see the axiom, that truth was admissible, recognised by our legislative and judicial bodies. He always had a profound reverence for this doctrine, and he felt a proud elevation of sentiment in reflecting, that the act of congress, which had been the object of so much unmerited abuse, and had been most grossly misrepresented by designing men, established this great vital principle. It was an honourable, a worthy and glorious effort in favour of public liberty. He reflected also, with much pleasure, on the fact, that so illustrious a patriot as Mr. *Jay* had laid down, correctly and broadly, the power of the jury. These acts were monuments, were consoling vestiges of the wisdom and virtue of the administration and character that produced them.

He maintained that the common law applied to the *United States.* That the common law was principally the application of natural law to the state and condition of society. That the constitution of the *United States* used terms and ideas which had a reference to the common law, and were inexplicable without its aid. That the definition of treason, of the writ of *habeas corpus,* of crimes and misdemeanors, &c. were all to be expounded by the rules of the common law. That the constitution would be frittered away or borne down by factions, (the evil *genii,* the pests of republics,) if the common law was not applicable. That without this guide, any political tenet or indiscretion might be made a crime or pretext to impeach, convict and remove from office, the judges of the federal courts. That if we departed from common law principles, we should degenerate into anarchy, and become the sport of the fury of conflicting passions. The transition from anarchy was to despotism, to an armed master.

The real danger to our liberties was not from a few provisional troops. The road to tyranny will be opened by making dependent judges, by packing juries, by stifling the press, by silencing leaders and patriots. His apprehensions were not from single acts of open violence. Murder rouses to vengeance; it awakens sympathy, and spreads alarm. But the most dangerous, the most sure, the most fatal of tyrannies, was, by selecting and sacrificing single individuals, under the mask and forms of law, by dependent and partial tribunals. Against such measures we ought to keep a vigilant eye, and take a manly stand. Whenever they arise, we ought to resist, and resist, till we have hurled the demagogues and tyrants from their imagined thrones. He concurred most readily with the learned counsel opposed to him, in the opinion that the *English* were a free, a gloriously free people. That country is free where the people have a representation in the government, so that no law can pass without their consent; and where they are secured in the administration of justice, by the trial by jury. We have gone further in this country into the popular principle, and he cordially united his prayers with the opposite counsel, that the experiment with us might be successful.

The question on the present libel ought to be again tried. It concerns the reputation of Mr. *Jefferson*. It concerned deeply the honour of our country. It concerned the fame of that bright and excellent character General *Washington*, in which he had left a national legacy of inestimable value.

He concluded, by recapitulating the substance of the doctrine for which he contended, in the following words:

"1. The liberty of the press consists in the right to publish, with impunity, truth, with good motives, for justifiable ends, though reflecting on government, magistracy, or individuals.

"2. That the allowance of this right is essential to the preservation of a free government; the disallowance of it fatal.

"3. That its abuse is to be guarded against, by subjecting the exercise of it to the animadversion and control of the tribunals of justice; but that this control cannot safely be intrusted to a permanent body of magistracy, and requires the effectual coöperation of court and jury.

"4. That to confine the jury to the mere question of publication, and the application of terms, without the right of inquiry into the intent or tendency, reserving to the court the exclusive right of pronouncing upon the construction, tendency, and intent of the alleged libel, is calculated to render nugatory the function of the jury; enabling the court to make a libel of any writing whatsoever, the most innocent or commendable.

"5. That it is the general rule of criminal law, that the intent constitutes the crime; and that it is equally a general rule, that the intent, mind, or *quo animo,* is an inference of fact to be drawn by the jury.

"6. That if there are exceptions to this rule, they are confined to cases in which not only the principal fact, but its circumstances, can be, and are, specifically defined by statute or judicial precedent.

"7. That, in respect to libel, there is no such specific and precise definition of facts and circumstances to be found; that, consequently, it is difficult, if not impossible, to pronounce that any writing is, *per se,* and exclusive of all circumstances, libellous; that its libellous character must depend on intent and tendency; the one and the other being matter of fact.

"8. That the definitions or descriptions of libels to be met with in the books, founded them upon some malicious or mischievous intent or tendency, to expose individuals to hatred or contempt, or to occasion a disturbance or a breach of the peace.

"9. That, in determining the character of a libel, the truth or falsehood is, in the nature of things, a material ingredient, though the truth may not always be decisive; but being abused may still admit of a malicious and mischievous intent, which may constitute a libel.

"10. That, in the *Roman law,* one source of the doctrine of a libel, the truth, in cases interesting to the public, was given in evidence; that the ancient statutes, probably declaratory of the common law, make the falsehood an ingredient of the crime; that the ancient precedents in the courts of justice correspond, and that the precedents to this day charge a malicious intent.

"11. That the doctrine of excluding the truth, as immaterial, originated in a tyrannical and polluted source, in the court of *Star Chamber;* and though it prevailed a considerable length of time, yet there are leading precedents down to the revolution, and ever since, in which a contrary practice prevailed.

"12. That the doctrine being against reason and natural justice, and contrary to the original principles of the common law, enforced by statutory provisions, the precedents which support it deserve to be considered in no better light than as a *malus usus,* which ought to be abolished.

"13. That, in the general distribution of power, in any system of jurisprudence, the cognisance of law belongs to the court, of fact to the jury; that as often as they are not blended, the power of the court is absolute and exclusive. That, in civil cases, it is always so, and may rightfully be so exerted. That, in criminal cases, the law and fact being always blended, the jury, for reasons of a political and peculiar nature, for the security of life and liberty, are intrusted with the power of deciding both law and fact.

"14. That this distinction results, 1. From the ancient forms of pleading, in civil cases; none but special pleas being allowed in matters of law; in criminal, none but the general issue. 2. From the liability of the jury to *attaint,* in civil cases, and the general power of the court, as its substitute, in granting new trials, and from the exemption of the jury from *attaint*, in criminal cases, and the defect of power to control their verdicts by new trials; the test of every legal power being its capacity to produce a definitive effect, liable neither to punishment nor control.

"15. That, in criminal cases, nevertheless, the court are the constitutional advisers of the jury, in matters of law, who may compromit their consciences by lightly or rashly disregarding that advice; but may still more compromit their consciences by following it, if, exercising their judgments with discretion and honesty, they have a clear conviction that the charge of the court is wrong."

On the last day of this term, the *Chief Justice* observed, that the court being equally divided in opinion, (Mr. Justice *Spencer* having, while Attorney-General, conducted the prosecution against the defendant,) the motion for a new trial was lost; that they were prepared to state their reasons at length; but that it was not thought requisite; and he took it for granted that the public prosecutor was entitled to move for judgment on the verdict. (*Cartlidge* v. *Eyles, Barnes,* 442.)

No motion, however, was made for judgment.

The following are the opinions of Kent, J. and Lewis, Ch. J. as prepared, and intended to have been delivered by them.

Kent, J. The defendant was convicted, at the last circuit court in *Columbia* county, of printing and publishing a scandalous, malicious and seditious libel upon *Thomas Jefferson,* the President of the *United States*. And a motion was made at the last term, for a new trial, on the ground of a misdirection of the judge. The motion was principally founded upon the two following objections:

1. That the *Chief Justice* charged the jury, that it was not their province to inquire or decide on the intent of the defendant, or whether the publication was libellous or not. That those were questions of law, to be decided exclusively by the

court, upon the return of the *postea;* and that the only points for their consideration were, first, whether the defendant published the paper stated in the indictment; and secondly, whether the *innuendoes* were true, and that if they were satisfied of these two points, it was their duty to find the defendant guilty.

2. That he denied to the defendant the opportunity of producing testimony to prove the truth of the libel, on the ground that the defendant could not be permitted to give in evidence to the jury, the truth of the charges contained in the libel.

I shall consider these two very important questions in the order in which they have been stated.

1. The criminality of the charge in the indictment consisted in a malicious and seditious *intention.* (*Hawk.* tit. *Libel,* s. 1. 2 *Wils.* 403. 1 *Esp. Cas.* 228.) There can be no crime without an evil mind. *Actus non facit reum, nisi mens sit rea.* The simple act of publication, which was all that was left to the jury, in the present case, was not, in itself, criminal. It is the application to times, persons and circumstances; it is the *particular* intent and tendency that constitute the libel. Opinions and acts may be innocent under one set of circumstances, and criminal under another. This application to circumstances, and this particular intent, are as much *matters of fact,* as the printing and publishing. (*Winne's Eunomus,* dial. 3. s. 53.) Where an act, innocent in itself, becomes criminal, when done with a particular intent, that intent is the material *fact* to constitute the crime. (Lord *Mansfield,* 3 *Term Rep.* 429. in the note.) And I think there cannot be a doubt, that the mere publication of a paper is not, *per se,* criminal; for otherwise, the copying of the indictment by the clerk, or writing a friendly and admonitory letter to a father, on the vices of his son, would be criminal. The intention of the publisher, and every circumstance attending the act must, therefore, be cognisable by the jury, as questions of fact. And if they are satisfied that the publication is innocent; that it has no mischievous or evil tendency; that the

mind of the writer was not in fault; that the publication was inadvertent, or from any other cause, was no libel, how can they conscientiously pronounce the defendant guilty, from the mere fact of publication? A verdict of *guilty,* embraces the whole charge upon the record, and are the jury not permitted to take into consideration the only thing that constitutes the crime, which is the malicious intent? According to the doctrine laid down at the trial, all that results from a verdict of guilty is, that the defendant has published a certain paper, and that it applies to certain persons, according to the *innuendoes;* but whether the paper be lawful or unlawful; whether it be criminal, or innocent, or meritorious; whether the intent was wicked or virtuous, are matters of law which do not belong to the jury, but are reserved for the determination of the court. The prosecutor selects and sets forth such parts only of the paper as he deems exceptionable, but the defendant is allowed (2 *Salk.* 417. 3 *Term Rep.* 429.) to read in evidence the context, in order to determine the intent, and yet how can this evidence be material or pertinent, if the jury are not to judge of that intent? Or how can it be material to the court above, on the motion in arrest of judgment, when that motion is founded entirely on the charge as it appears upon the face of the record? To bear out the doctrine, the courts have involved themselves in inconsistency and paradox; and I am induced to believe that it is a departure from the ancient, simple, and true theory of trial by jury in criminal cases. To deny to the jury the right of judging of the intent and tendency of the act, is to take away the substance, and with it the value and security of this mode of trial. It is to transfer the exclusive cognisance of crimes from the jury to the court, and to give the judges the absolute control of the press. There is nothing peculiar in the law of libels, to withdraw it from the jurisdiction of the jury. The twelve judges, in their opinion to the house of lords, (*April,* 1792,) admitted that the general criminal law of *England* was the law of libel. And by the general criminal law of *England*, the office of the jury is judicial. "They only are the judges," as Lord *Somers* observes, (*Essay on the Power and Duty of Grand Juries,* p. 7.) "from whose sentence the indicted are to expect life or death. Upon their integrity and understanding, the lives of all that are brought into judgment do ultimately depend. From their verdict there lies no appeal. They resolve both law and fact, and this has always been their custom and practice."

If the criminal intent be, in this case, an inference of law, the right of the jury is still the same. In every criminal case, upon the plea of not guilty, the jury may, and indeed they *must,* unless they choose to find a special verdict, take upon themselves the decision of the law, as well as the fact, and bring in a verdict as comprehensive as the issue; because, in every such case, they are charged with the deliverance of the defendant from the crime of which he is accused. The indictment not only sets forth the particular fact committed, but it specifies the nature of the crime. Treasons are laid to be done traitorously, felonies feloniously, and public libels to be published seditiously. The jury are called to try, in the case of a traitor, not only whether he committed the act charged, but whether he did it *traitorously;* and in the case of a felon, not only whether he killed such a one, or took such a person's property, but whether he killed with *malice prepense,* or took the property *feloniously.* So in the case of a public libeller, the jury are to try, not only whether he published such a writing, but whether he published it *seditiously.* In all these cases, from the nature of the issue, the jury are to try not only the *fact,* but the *crime,* and in doing so, they must judge of the *intent,* in order to determine whether the charge be true, as set forth in the indictment. (*Dagge on Criminal Law,* b. 1. c. 11. s. 2.) The law and fact are so involved, that the jury are under an indispensable necessity to decide both, unless they separate them by a special verdict.

This right in the jury to determine the law as well as the fact has received the sanction of some of the highest authorities in the law. . . .

. . . The weight of the decisions thus far, was clearly in favour of the right of the jury to decide generally upon the law and the fact. But, since the time of Lord *Holt,* the question before us has been an unsettled and litigious one in *Westminster Hall.* Lord *Mansfield* was of opinion (3 *Term Rep.* 429.) that the formal direction of every judge, since the revolution, had been agreeable to that given in the case of *The Dean of St. Asaph;* but the earliest case he mentions is that of *Franklin,* before Lord *Raymond,* in 1731; (9 *St. Tr.* 255.) and that has been considered as the formal introduction of the doctrine now under review. . . .

. . . To say that the jury cannot rightfully judge of the *malus animus* of the prisoner, in which his crime consists, is, in my opinion, a monstrous proposition, destructive of the essence and excellence of trial by jury, and inconsistent with the genius of the *English* judiciary, as drawn from its history and constitutional policy.

To return to the case of *Franklin;* the counsel for the defendant, who were very able lawyers, contended that the jury had a right to judge of the intent and tendency of the publication; but Lord *Raymond,* in his direction to the jury, went the whole length of the charge in the present case. He told the jury that there were two things only for their consideration; 1st. Whether the defendant was guilty of publishing; and, 2d. Whether the *innuendoes* were justly stated and applied, and that the third question, whether the publication was libellous, belonged exclusively to the court as a matter of law. . . .

The constant struggle of counsel, and of the jury, against the rule, so emphatically laid down by Lord *Raymond,* the disagreement among the judges, and the dangerous tendency of the doctrine, as it affected two very conspicuous and proud monuments of *English* liberty, trial by jury, and the freedom of the press, at length attracted and roused the attention of the nation. The question was brought before the parliament, and debated in two successive sessions. (In 1791 and 1792, see *Debates in the Senator*, vols. 3, 4, 5.) There was combined, in the discussion of this dry law question, an assemblage of talents, of constitutional knowledge, of practical wisdom, and of professional erudition, rarely, if ever before surpassed. It underwent a patient investigation and severe scrutiny, upon principle and precedent, and a bill *declaratory* of the right of the jury to give a general verdict upon the whole matter put in issue, without being required or directed to find the defendant guilty merely on the proof of publication and the truth of the *innuendoes*, was at length agreed to, and passed with uncommon unanimity. It is entitled "An act to remove doubts respecting the functions of juries in cases of libel;" and, although I admit, that a declaratory statute is not to be received as conclusive evidence of the common law, yet it must be considered as a very respectable authority in the case; and especially, as the circumstances attending the passage of this bill, reflect the highest honour on the moderation, the good sense, and the free and independent spirit of the *British* parliament.

It was, no doubt, under similar impressions of the subject, that the act of congress, for punishing certain libels against the *United States*, (*Laws U. S.* vol. 4. p. 204.) enacted and *declared*, that the jury who should try the cause, should have a right to determine the law and fact, under the direction of the court, as in other cases; and before the passing of that statute, the same doctrine was laid down in full latitude, and in explicit terms, by the supreme court of the *United States*. (3 *Dallas*, 4.)

The result, from this view, is, to my mind, a firm conviction that this court is not bound by the decisions of Lord *Raymond*, and his successors. By withdrawing from the jury the consideration of the essence of the charge, they render their function nugatory and contemptible. Those opinions are repugnant to the more ancient authorities which had given to the jury the power, and with it the right, to judge of the law and fact, when they were blended by the issue, and which rendered their decisions, in criminal cases, final and conclusive. The *English* bar steadily resisted those decisions, as usurpations on the rights of the jury. Some of the judges treated the doctrine as erroneous, and the parliament, at last, declared it an innovation, by restoring the trial by jury, in cases of libel, to that ancient vigour and independence, by which it had grown so precious to the nation, as the guardian of liberty and life, against the power of the court, the vindictive persecution of the prosecutor, and the oppression of the government. . . .

My conclusion on this first point then, is, that upon every indictment or information for a libel, where the defendant puts himself upon the country, by a plea of not guilty, the jury have a right to judge, not only of the fact of the publication, and the truth of the *innuendoes,* but of the intent and tendency of the paper, and whether it be a libel or not; and, in short, of "the whole matter put in issue upon such indictment or information." (*Stat.* 32 *Geo.* III.) That in this, as in other criminal cases, it is the duty of the court, "according to their discretion, to give their opinion and direction to the jury on the matter in issue;" and it is the duty of the jury to receive the same with respectful deference and attention, and, unless they choose to find a special verdict, they are then to exercise their own judgments on the matter in issue, with discretion and integrity.

2. The second point in the case, although a question of evidence merely, is equally important, and still more difficult. It was made a very prominent point upon the argument, and the decision of it is essential for the direction of the judge who is to preside at the new trial that may be awarded.

As a libel is a defamatory publication, made with a malicious intent, the truth or falsehood of the charge may, in many cases, be a very material and pertinent consideration with the jury, in order to ascertain that intent. There can be no doubt that it is competent for the defendant to rebut the presumption of malice, drawn from the fact of publication; and it is consonant to the general theory of evidence, and the dictates of justice, that the defendant should be allowed to avail himself of every fact and circumstance that may serve to repel that presumption. And what can be a more important circumstance than the truth of the charge, to determine the goodness of the motive in making it, if it be a charge against the competency or purity of a character in public trust, or of a candidate for public favour, or a charge of actions in which the community have an interest, and are deeply concerned? To shut out wholly the inquiry into the truth of the accusation, is to abridge essentially the means of defence. It is to weaken the arm of the defendant, and to convict him, by means of a presumption, which he might easily destroy by proof that the charge was true, and that, considering the nature of the accusation, the circumstances and time under which it was made, and the situation of the person implicated, his motive could have been no other than a pure and disinterested regard for the public welfare. At the same time, this doctrine will not go to tolerate libels upon private character, or the circulation of charges for seditious and wicked ends, or to justify exposing to the public eye one's personal defects or misfortunes. The public have no concern with, nor are they injured by, such information, and the truth of the charge would rather aggravate than lessen the baseness and evil tendency of the publication. It will, therefore, still remain, in every case, a question for the jury, what was the intent and tendency of the paper, and how far the truth, in the given case, has been used for commendable, or abused for malicious purposes.

This principle in the law of libels is considered as rational and sound, in an ethical point of view; (*Paley's Moral Philosophy*, p. 188.) and to this extent, the writers on the civil law have allowed the truth to excuse a defamatory accusation. . . .

That falsehood is a material ingredient in a public libel, is a doctrine not without precedent in former times; it has always been asserted, and occasionally admitted, by the *English* courts. In this country it has taken firmer root, and in regard to the measures of government, and the character and qualifications of candidates for public trust, it is considered as the vital support of the liberty of the press.

The *English* decisions on the subject of libels have not been consistent in principle. . . .

. . . I have thus shown, that the rule denying permission to give the truth in evidence, was not an original rule of the common law. The ancient statutes and precedents, which are the only memorials to which we can resort, all place the crime on its falsity. The court of *Star Chamber* originated the doctrine, and it was considered an innovation. When it was brought into a court of common law, it was resisted and denied; the court dared not practice upon it, and the jury gave it their negative. Lord *Holt* totally disregarded the rule, in the case of *Fuller;* and it did not become an express decision of a court of common law till *Franklin's Case,* in 1731; and there the counsel made a zealous struggle against it, as new, dangerous, and arbitrary. In the trial of *Horne,* Lord *Mansfield* laid the rule aside, and the counsel for the crown rejoiced at an opportunity to meet the defendant upon the merits of the accusation. In 1792, it was made a questionable point, in the house of lords, and one of the highest law characters in the house seems to have borne his testimony against it. I feel myself, therefore, at full liberty to examine this question upon principle, and to lay the doctrine aside, if it shall appear unjust in itself, or incompatible with public liberty, and the rights of the press.

But, whatever may be our opinion on the *English* law, there is another and a very important view of the subject to be taken, and that is with respect to the true standard of the freedom of the *American* press. In *England,* they have never taken notice of the press in any parliamentary recognition of the principles of the government, or of the rights of the subject, whereas the people of this country have always classed the freedom of the press among their fundamental rights. This I can easily illustrate by a few examples.

The first *American* congress, in 1774, in one of their public addresses, (*Journals,* vol. 1. p. 57.) enumerated five invaluable rights, without which a people cannot be free and happy, and under the protecting and encouraging influence of which these colonies had hitherto so amazingly flourished and increased. One of these rights was the *freedom of the press,* and the importance of this right consisted, as they observed, "besides the advancement of truth, science, morality, and arts in general, in its diffusion of liberal sentiments on the administration of government, its ready communication of thoughts between subjects, and its consequential promotion of union among them, whereby oppressive officers are shamed or intimidated into more honourable and just modes of conducting affairs." The next high authority I shall mention, is the *Convention* of the people of this state, which met in 1788. They declared, unanimously, (*Journals,* p. 44. 51, 52. 73, 74.) that the freedom of the press was a right which could not be abridged or violated. The same opinion is contained in the amendment to the constitution of the *United States,* and to which this state was a party. It is also made an article in most of the state constitutions, that the liberty of the press was essential to the security of freedom, and ought to be inviolably preserved; and in two of those constitutions, (*Pennsylvania* and *Ohio,*) this freedom of the press is specifically defined, by saying, that in prosecutions for any publications, respecting the official conduct of men in a public capacity, or where the matter is proper for public information, the truth may always be given in evidence. I shall mention, lastly, the act of Congress, of the 14th *July,* 1798, which prescribed penalties for certain specified libels upon the government of the *United States,* and allowed the truth to be given in evidence, on every prosecution under that act; and it is worthy of notice that the part of the act allowing the truth to be given in evidence, was *declaratory,* and thereby conveyed the sense of congress that such was the already existing law.

These multiplied acts and declarations are the highest, the most solemn, and commanding authorities, that the state or the nation can produce. They are generally the acts of the people themselves, when they came forward in their original character, to change the constitution of the country, and to assert their indubitable rights. And it seems impossible that they could have spoken with so much explicitness and energy, if they had intended nothing more than that restricted and slavish press, which may not publish any thing, true or false, that reflects on the character and administration of public men. Such is the *English* doctrine of the liberty of the press, as asserted in *Franklin's Case.* (See also *Hawk.* tit. *Libels, 7.*) A treatise on hereditary right has been held a libel, although it contained no reflections upon any part of the subsisting government. (*Queen* v. *Bedford, Str.* 189. *Gilbert's Rep.* K. B. 297.) And if the theory of the prevailing doctrine in *England,* (for even, there it is now scarcely any thing more than theory,) had been strictly put in practice with us, where would have been all those enlightened and manly discussions which prepared and matured the great events of our revolution, or which, in a more recent period, pointed out the weakness and folly of the confederation, and roused the nation to throw it aside, and to erect a better government upon its ruins? They were, no doubt, libels upon the existing establishments, because they tended to defame them, and to expose them to the contempt and hatred of the people. They were, however, libels founded in truth, and dictated by worthy motives.

I am far from intending that these authorities mean, by the freedom of the press, a press wholly beyond the reach of the law, for this would be emphatically *Pandora's box, the source of every evil.* And yet the house of delegates in *Virginia,* by their resolution of the 7th *January,* 1800, and which appears to have been intended for the benefit and instruction of the union, came forward as the advocates of a press totally unshackled, and declare, in so many words, that "the baneful tendency of the *sedition act* was but little diminished by the privilege of giving in evidence the truth of the matter contained in political writings." They seem also to consider it as the exercise of a pernicious influence, and as striking at the root of free discussion, to punish, even for a *false and malicious* writing, published *with intent* to defame those who administer the government. If this doctrine was to prevail, the press would become a pest, and destroy the public morals. Against such a commentary upon the freedom of the *American* press, I beg leave to enter my protest. The founders of our governments were too wise and too just, ever to have intended, by the freedom of the press, a right to circulate falsehood as well as truth, or that the press should be the lawful vehicle of malicious defamation, or an engine for evil and designing men, to cherish, for mischievous purposes, sedition, irreligion, and impurity. Such an abuse of the press would be incompatible with the existence and good order of civil society. The true rule of law is, that the intent and tendency of the publication is, in every instance, to be the substantial inquiry on the trial, and that the truth is admissible in evidence, to explain that intent, and not in every instance to justify it. I adopt, in this case, as perfectly correct, the comprehensive and accurate definition of one of the counsel at the bar, *that the liberty of the press consists in the right to publish, with impunity, truth, with good motives, and for justifiable ends, whether it respects government, magistracy, or individuals.*

I conclude, therefore, that a new trial ought to be awarded, for the misdirection of the judge, and that the defendant was entitled to give in evidence, upon the trial, the truth of the libel.

Index

Adams, John, vii, 83
  on truth as defense, 147, 152–153
  on falsehoods, lxviii
Adams, Sam, 95
Additional Number of Letters, An, 142
Alexander, James,
  as follower of Cato, xxvi–xxvii
  defense of Zenger, xxvii, xxx, 43–61
  on destructive criticism of government, xl, 29
  on freedom of the press, 26–32, 35–37, 62–74
  on juries in libel trials, 34
  on libel, 25, 32–35
Alien and Sedition Acts, vii, lxxii*n.*, 197
  (*See also* Sedition Act)
American Weekly Mercury, 25, 38, 38*n.*
Anglo-Americanus, 61
Anti-Federalists, lx, 129, 132, 142–144, 145
Apology for Freedom of the Press, An, lxii
Areopagitica, xxi
Assemblies, provincial
  as suppressive bodies, xxxv, xxxvi
  parliamentary privilege of, xxxv–xxxvi, xxxix–xl, lxix, xlvii, 159–166
  New York General Assembly
    charges James Parker, xlii–xliii, 117–118

Assemblies, provincial (*cont.*)
  N.Y. General Assembly (*cont.*)
    expels Samuel Mulford, xxxiii–xxxix
    Hugh Gaine summoned and released, xxxvii
    reprimands Samuel Townsend, xxxviii–xxxix
    trial of Alexander McDougall, xliii–xlvii, 117–127
    trial of William Keteltas, lxvii, 158–169
    tries John Peter Zenger, xxvii, xxx, 43–61
    versus Governor's Council, xxxvii, xxxix
  Virginia General Assembly
    power over state constitution, 331
    views on Sedition Act, 226, 229

Bernard, Francis, 95
Bills of rights
  federal, lii–liv, liii*n.*, lv, 129, 132, 141, 144–146, 334–339
  state, 138–139, 141, 330, 337, 342
Blackstone, William, 98
  Commentaries on the Laws of England, 103*n.*
  definition of freedom of the press, xlix
  on libels, 103–105, 182–183
  on previous restraints, 150
Blenman, Jonathan, 61

THE AMERICAN HERITAGE SERIES

THE COLONIAL PERIOD

Adams, John *The Political Writings of John Adams: Representative Selections* AHS 8 George A. Peek, Jr.
The English Libertarian Heritage: From the Writings of John Trenchard and Thomas Gordon in The Independent Whig *and* Cato's Letters AHS 32 David L. Jacobson
Puritan Political Thought AHS 33 Edmund S. Morgan

THE REVOLUTIONARY ERA

The Antifederalists AHS 38 Cecelia Kenyon
Early American Libertarian Thought: Freedom of the Press from Zenger to Jefferson AHS 41 Leonard W. Levy
Franklin, Benjamin *The Political Thought of Benjamin Franklin* AHS 64 Ralph Ketcham
Paine, Thomas *Common Sense and Other Political Writings* AHS 5 Nelson F. Adkins

THE YOUNG NATION

Calhoun, John C. *Disquisition on Government and Selections from the* Discourse AHS 10 C. Gordon Post
Democracy, Liberty, and Property: The State Constitutional Conventions of the 1820's AHS 43 Merrill D. Peterson
The Federal Convention and the Formation of the Union of American States AHS 19 Winton U. Solberg
From the Declaration of Independence to the Constitution: The Roots of American Constitutionalism AHS 6 Carl J. Friedrich, Robert G. McCloskey